Random Acts
of Comedy

Random Acts of Comedy

15 Hit One-Act Plays for Student Actors

Edited by
Jason Pizzarello

Playscripts
Inc.

New York, NY

Published by Playscripts, Inc.
450 Seventh Avenue, Suite 809
New York, New York, 10123
www.playscripts.com

Cover design by Another Limited Rebellion
Text design and layout by Kimberly Lew

First Edition: September 2011
10 9 8 7 6 5 4 3 2 1

ISBN-13: 978-0-9819099-7-4

Library of Congress Cataloging-in-Publication Data

Random acts of comedy : 15 hit one-act plays for student actors / edited by Jason Pizzarello. -- 1st ed.
    p. cm.
ISBN 978-0-9819099-7-4
1. Young adult drama, American. 2. One-act plays. 3. Teenagers-
-Drama. I. Pizzarello, Jason, 1980-
PS625.5.R36 2011
812'.04108--dc22
                                        2011014371

Table of Contents

Foreword

Early on in my comedy career, I had a bottle thrown at my head. I was nineteen years old and performing in a sketch group at a bar in Burlington, North Carolina. The Roadhouse was a one-room heap in the middle of a gravel parking lot where people went to drink when they were angry and alone and pregnant. It blared country music and ESPN that was so loud you couldn't hear yourself spit. It had a small stage that had been graced by some of central North Carolina's most bearded bands. That night, The Roadhouse was trying comedy for the first time because last week's Pit Bull Gladiator Wars had scared some of the bar children.

My sketch group featured five fresh-faced guys with big smiles and Chuck Taylor high tops. We should have been playing on a Disney cruise ship. Instead, we were trying to make about 30 drunks laugh who were already mad as hell because the bartender had turned off the World Series. They were loud, but we had microphones. So we decided our best strategy was to be louder. That's when the beer bottles started flying.

Ten minutes later, four of us were sitting outside in the parking lot with the car running. Inside was our fifth member who was still on stage playing acoustic Jethro Tull songs while everyone else ignored him and watched the World Series. He came out with our fee for that night: $120 split five ways, which we promptly used to buy an Egg-Bo biscuit from Bojangles and enough Milwaukee's Best to drink ourselves into oblivion. This is the kind of life-affirming, showbiz glory that I pray each of you experience some day.

Comedy is hard. Often we will leave a drama thinking, "That wasn't for me, but I certainly appreciated it." Comedy is usually put into two ruthless categories: Funny and Not Funny. And it's completely subjective as to which is which. The person who likes Woody Allen is probably not the same person who likes Martin Lawrence who is probably not the same person who likes an adorable Flash video on YouTube called "Kitty Gangstas." Trying to appeal to all of them is not going to work.

So what to do? After writing and performing comedy for the past 20 years, here's my best advice: try. Just get out there and try. Discovering what makes you consistently funny to others is a long, arduous path full of crippling silences. But you'll never make it to the other side unless you put yourself out there again and again. And if you can finally get to a place where you have your own unique, comic voice, then you won't have to worry about finding an appreciative audience. Eventually, they will find you.

One of my favorite things Lorne Michaels says about *Saturday Night Live* is, "We don't do the show because it's ready. We do it because it's Saturday at 11:30." As writers, we're still making changes to our sketches at 11:10, only a few minutes before millions of people are going to see it. And we're rarely ever sure if the sketch is going to work. Even on a legendary network television show, we're still trying.

So, take the funny plays in this collection and use them to begin your journey. They're a great start. And perhaps, if you try and try, one day you can get a beer bottle thrown at your head by a man whose hairy belly won't seem to stay in his T-shirt.

—Bryan Tucker
Staff writer, *Saturday Night Live*
2005-present

How to Get Performance Rights

If you wish to perform any of the plays in this book, you must do two things right off the bat: (1) Obtain a performance license. (2) Purchase enough acting editions for your cast and crew.

Conveniently enough, all of the plays in this book are licensed by the same company: Playscripts, Inc.

We look forward to hearing from you!

Jason Pizzarello
Publications Director

Playscripts, Inc.   Phone: 1-866-NEW-PLAY (639-7529)
450 Seventh Ave, Suite 809   Email: info@playscripts.com
New York, NY 10123   Web: www.playscripts.com

Copyright Basics

These Plays are protected by United States and international copyright law. These laws ensure that playwrights are rewarded for creating new and vital dramatic work, and protect them against theft and abuse of their work.

You'll find all of the official fine print on the next page, and these are the most important rules:

- Do *not* perform these Plays without obtaining prior permission from Playscripts, and without paying the required royalty.

- Do *not* photocopy, scan, or otherwise duplicate any part of this book.

A play is a piece of property, fully owned by the playwright, just like a house or car. You must obtain permission to use this property, and must pay a royalty fee for the privilege—*whether or not you charge an admission fee.* Playscripts collects these required payments on behalf of the author.

Anyone who violates an author's copyright is liable as a copyright infringer under United States and international law. Playscripts and the author are entitled to institute legal action for any such infringement, which can subject the infringer to actual damages, statutory damages, and attorneys' fees. A court may impose statutory damages of up to $150,000 for willful copyright infringements. U.S. copyright law also provides for possible criminal sanctions. Visit the website of the U.S. Copyright Office (www.copyright.gov) for more information.

The Bottom Line: If you break copyright law, you are robbing a playwright and opening yourself to expensive legal action. Follow the rules, and when in doubt, ask us.

The Fine Print

THE AUDITION

by Don Zolidis

For more information about rights and permissions, see page 9.

Cast of Characters

MR. TORRANCE

STAGE MANAGER

CARRIE

SOLEIL

ELIZABETH

ALISON

SARAH

TOMMY

YUMA

GINA

ELIZABETH'S MOTHER

ALISON'S FATHER

CARRIE'S MOTHER

There is also a chorus of ACTORS, who are auditioning for the play. They may be double cast in many different parts as necessary. The chorus may be expanded.

Character Notes

The roles of Stage Manager and Mr. Torrance may be cast as female if necessary.

The roles of Gina, Yuma, Elizabeth, Elizabeth's Mother, and Carrie's Mother may be cast as male if necessary.

Setting

A high school auditorium. The present.

Acknowledgments

The Audition was originally performed by North Oaks Middle School on April 12, 2008.

THE AUDITION

(A high school auditorium. A bare stage.)

(The STAGE MANAGER *runs on with a stack of sides.)*

STAGE MANAGER. Where do you want these?

MR. TORRANCE. *(Off-stage:)* Put them downstage right.

(STAGE MANAGER heads stage left.)

STAGE MANAGER. Here?

MR. TORRANCE. *(Off-stage:)* Is that stage right?

(STAGE MANAGER thinks.)

STAGE MANAGER. Whoops. I'm nervous.

(STAGE MANAGER heads stage right.)

On the edge of the stage?

MR. TORRANCE. *(Off-stage:)* Yep. All right, bring 'em in.

STAGE MANAGER. *(Shouting off:)* Okay people! Come on in!

(The ACTORS *enter from all sides of the stage.)*

MR. TORRANCE. *(Off-stage:)* All right stop right there! First off, thank you for coming out today. If you don't know me, my name is Mr. Torrance and—

(ACTOR 1 raises his hand.)

Yes?

ACTOR 1. Can I go to the bathroom?

MR. TORRANCE. *(Off:)* Just hold on.

ACTOR 2. My Mom needs to pick me up in half an hour so I need to go first—

MR. TORRANCE. *(Off:)* Okay, just—

STAGE MANAGER. Quiet please.

MR. TORRANCE. *(Off:)* I know that I'm new here but I want to talk to you a little bit about this theatre program. You might go to some other high schools around here and see some pretty good shows. They do a fine job. We don't do a fine job here. We do an amazing job. And if you're going to be in this show, you are going to be amazing. So what I am looking for today are the best of the best. Do you understand?

ACTOR 1. So I can't go to the bathroom?

STAGE MANAGER. No.

MR. TORRANCE. *(Off:)* This is Carmen. She's our stage manager. It goes from God to me to Carmen to you. You will listen to her as if she were me. If you are going to be late, you will call her, if you have a problem with scheduling you talk to her—

(ACTOR 2 *approaches* CARMEN.)

Later. This is the first audition. I'm going to call back a few of you. From those, the best will be in the show. You have three minutes to prepare yourselves.

(The ACTORS *relax and begin walking around, stretching.)*

CARRIE. *(A vocal warm-up:)* Me me me me me me me me

ALISON. *(A lip trill:)* Bbbbbbbbbbbb—

SOLEIL. To sit in solemn silence on a dull dark dock—

ELIZABETH. Guh guh guh kuk kuh kuh

ACTOR 3. Breathe in. Breathe out. Breathe in. Breathe out.

ACTOR 4. I hope I get this part. I hope I get this part.

ACTOR 5. Just a little one, I don't really need anything big—

ACTOR 6. Is anyone else here auditioning for the first time? Anyone? Anyone at all?

ACTOR 3. Breathe in. Breathe out.

ACTOR 4. I hope I get it.

ACTOR 7. I'm going to get it. I know I'm going to get something, I don't know what.

ACTOR 5. I want a line.

ACTOR 4. I want a solo.

ACTOR 5. I don't want a solo. Just a line.

ACTOR 1. I want to go to the bathroom—

ACTOR 2. Can I just go early?

ACTOR 3. Please God let me get this part.

ACTOR 4. Who's that girl?

ACTOR 5. I've never seen her before.

ACTOR 4. Is she better than me?

ACTOR 5. What is he looking for?

ACTOR 6. I've never been in a show before—

ACTOR 2. Please let me get this—

ACTOR 3. Please—

ALISON. I'm going to get the lead. No one can stop me.

SOLEIL. I need to get something, anything—

TOMMY. Is this the right place?

SARAH. Hi there I'm Sarah.

ACTOR 4. I want to get something—

SOLEIL. I need something—

ACTOR 5. I just want to be an extra. Maybe one line. I could say good morning or something, and that's it. And then I could wave at my parents in the back and then I could say that I was in the show.

ACTOR 6. *(Overlapping:)* I'll do anything—

ACTOR 7. *(Overlapping:)* I can do a Hungarian accent. Do you need anything with a Hungarian accent?

ACTOR 5. *(Overlapping:)* I just need one line—

ACTOR 1. *(Overlapping:)* Please!

ACTOR 7. *(Overlapping:)* I can burp on command—

ACTORS 1 and 2. *(Overlapping:)* Please!

ACTOR 5. *(Overlapping:)* One line is all I ask!

ACTORS 1, 2 and 3. *(Overlapping:)* Please!

ACTOR 7. I'm left-handed. Does that help?

ACTORS 1-6. *(Overlapping:)* Please!

SOLEIL. I need this—you don't understand—I need this.

ALL ACTORS. I need it—I'll be great, I'll be wonderful, I'll be the best thing you've ever seen—please please please please PLEASE!

ACTOR 1. Can I go to the bathroom now?

> *(All of the* ACTORS *exit.)*

MR. TORRANCE. *(Off:)* Who's first?

STAGE MANAGER. We have Cassie.

> *(*ACTOR 2 *enters.)*

ACTOR 2. Hi. I'm Cassie. My Mom's waiting in the parking lot.

MR. TORRANCE. *(Off:)* Great. What are you going to sing?

ACTOR 2. I have to sing?

MR. TORRANCE. *(Off:)* This is a musical.

ACTOR 2. This is a musical?

STAGE MANAGER. It said so on the posters.

ACTOR 2. There were posters?

STAGE MANAGER. Didn't you listen to the announcements?

ACTOR 2. I can't ever hear the announcements. No one ever shuts up for them.

MR. TORRANCE. *(Off:)* So you don't have a song prepared?

ACTOR 2. We're supposed to have—?

MR. TORRANCE and STAGE MANAGER. *Yes!*

ACTOR 2. Oh. Um. No. I don't have a song.

MR. TORRANCE. *(Off:)* How about Happy Birthday?

ACTOR 2. Are you sure I have to sing?

MR. TORRANCE. *(Off:)* Can you sing Happy Birthday?

ACTOR 2. Are there any non-singing parts?

MR. TORRANCE. *(Off:)* I need to hear you sing first before I can put you in a non-singing part.

ACTOR 2. That doesn't make any sense.

STAGE MANAGER. He needs to make sure that you can't sing.

ACTOR 2. Okay, um... Happy Birthday, right?

MR. TORRANCE. *(Off:)* Sure.

ACTOR 2. I forgot the words.

STAGE MANAGER. It starts with Happy Birthday.

ACTOR 2. Okay.

> *(ACTOR 2's cell phone rings. She answers it.)*

Hi. Oh. Okay. I gotta go.

> *(She runs off. She runs back on in a minute.)*

When are call-backs?

> *(She leaves.)*

> *(YUMA enters immediately.)*

YUMA. HI!!! I'm Yuma!

STAGE MANAGER. This is—

YUMA. And I just gotta dance! Kick it!

> *(Nothing happens.* YUMA *approaches the* STAGE MANAGER.*)*

When I say kick it, you hit the music okay?

> *(Without waiting for a response,* YUMA *crosses to centerstage:)*

And I just gotta *dance!* Kick it!

> *(YUMA *does one half of one dance more before realizing that no music is happening.)*

Hold on one second.

> *(She approaches the* STAGE MANAGER *again.)*

Did you understand me when I said kick it that was your cue to start the music? You got that?

STAGE MANAGER. You didn't bring any music.

YUMA. You think that's gonna stop me? I'm determined to get this role, I don't care if I didn't bring music, when I say kick it, you play it.

STAGE MANAGER. But there is no—

YUMA. Don't give me problems. Give me solutions.

STAGE MANAGER. I could hum something.

YUMA. Can you do more of a beat box thing?

> *(STAGE MANAGER *tries a beat box.)*

YUMA. I'm not feeling you. I'm really not feeling you. But it's gonna have to work.

(*YUMA approaches center again.*)

AND I JUST GOTTA *DANCE!!!* Kick it!

(*STAGE MANAGER starts a rather pathetic beat box. STAGE MAN-AGER begins to beat box more and more intensely, really getting into it. YUMA dances. She's wild, she's unpredictable and full of insane energy. She also provides her own sound effects.*)

YUMA. Uh huh. Yeah. Yeah. Y-iaao! Uh huh. Wa wa wa wa wa! Zoog! And I'm over here you can't stop me! Yeah! Uh huh. Yeah! Uh huh. Yeah! Uh huh. And stop.

(*YUMA stares forward, breathing hard.*)

What now?

MR. TORRANCE. (*Off:*) I don't know that that's really the style of dance we're looking for.

YUMA. I can do anything. Watch this. Ballet? Check it.

(*YUMA does a wild, insane ballet. Once again she provides her own sound effects to the ballet.*)

Uh huh. Yeah. Leg up in the air. Graceful. Graceful. Wa! Yeah! Uh huh! Yeah! Uh huh. And...dropping the head like a swan. Stop.

(*She stops.*)

How about that? How about *that*, son? That's how I roll in the ballet.

MR. TORRANCE. (*Off:*) Um...

(*YUMA grabs the STAGE MANAGER.*)

YUMA. You want tango?

(*She begins a tango with the STAGE MANAGER.*)

YUMA. I'm leading. Just go with me and give me a beat.

STAGE MANAGER. (*Trying to provide a tango beat:*) Dun dun dun dun da dun! Dun dun dun dun da dun! Dun dun dun dun dun da dun! Dun dun dun dun dun da dun!

YUMA. (*Simultaneously:*) Tango tango tango yeah! Uh huh! Arm up head back rose in teeth tango! Yeah! Uh huh! Zoom! Spin! Work it! And yeah. Stop.

(*YUMA stops and releases the STAGE MANAGER.*)

MR. TORRANCE. (*Off:*) Call-backs will be posted tonight.

YUMA. That's what I'm talking about!

(*She leaves, taking the STAGE MANAGER with her.*)

YUMA. You did good out there. You did good.

(*YUMA slaps the STAGE MANAGER on the butt [or hi-fives her].*)

(*GINA enters timidly.*)

GINA. What exactly are you looking for? I think I would do a better job of auditioning if I knew exactly what it was you were after, you know? Cause I can do anything. I mean, not anything. But pretty close. Like if you wanted flirty and funny, I can do that. Or if you wanted me to be like all mean and everything, I can do that too. Or if it's like a really sad role I cry just about every day. Not for any real reason, just for practice. I practice crying. In case it comes in handy sometime. You never know when you might need to cry. I'll stand in front of my mirror at home and then I'll try to imagine my Mom dying. That usually doesn't work. But then I think about all those starving kids in Africa, and that doesn't make me cry either, and then I think about puppies and they make me cry. Not like hurting the puppies or anything. Just puppies. I hate puppies. They're always looking at you like look at me I'm so cute, well you're not cute, you're just a baby dog, that doesn't automatically make you cute. And personally, I think puppies are sell-outs. I mean, try and turn on the TV and not see a puppy selling something. So I think about puppies. And then I cry. I can also burp on command.

MR. TORRANCE. *(Off:)* Next.

(Lights change. ELIZABETH *enters.)*

ELIZABETH. My life: by Elizabeth.

*(*ELIZABETH'S MOTHER *enters right behind her.)*

ELIZABETH'S MOTHER. You better hurry up.

ELIZABETH. I'm fine.

ELIZABETH'S MOTHER. You're wearing that?

ELIZABETH. No I'm changing in the car on the way there.

ELIZABETH'S MOTHER. You need to make a good impression. Holes in your jeans scream community college.

ELIZABETH. I am who I am.

ELIZABETH'S MOTHER. Well that's not good enough.

(She freezes.)

ELIZABETH. *(To the audience:)* Growing up that's all I heard.

ELIZABETH'S MOTHER. Sit up straight. Smile.

ELIZABETH. I was supposed to be—

ELIZABETH'S MOTHER. Perfect.

ELIZABETH. I was going to be—

ELIZABETH'S MOTHER. Perfect.

ELIZABETH. I was in every activity she could find: gymnastics, swimming, piano, tuba, soccer, softball, choir, debate, junior French honor society—

ELIZABETH'S MOTHER. Hurry up, we're going to be late.

ELIZABETH. I didn't even speak French and I was in junior French honor society.

ELIZABETH'S MOTHER. We can fit in girl scouts tonight after karate—

ELIZABETH. I especially hated karate.

ELIZABETH'S MOTHER. Sensei Lee was disappointed with your effort today, Elizabeth.

ELIZABETH. And what did I want to do?

ELIZABETH'S MOTHER. If you didn't have me you'd sit on your butt all day long.

ELIZABETH. That's exactly what I'd do. Nothing.

ELIZABETH'S MOTHER. How would that look on your college applications?

ELIZABETH. I don't care, Mom.

ELIZABETH'S MOTHER. You'd never get into Yale without extra-curriculars.

ELIZABETH. I don't care, Mom.

ELIZABETH'S MOTHER. And then where would you be? Without college?

ELIZABETH. I don't care, Mom.

ELIZABETH'S MOTHER. Grades aren't enough. You need to be well-rounded.

ELIZABETH. My Mom has spent so much time rounding me I feel like a circle. What part of I don't care Mom don't you understand! I don't want to be in the show, I don't want to go to Yale, I don't want to be the manager for the water polo squad! I just want to do—

ELIZABETH'S MOTHER. Nothing.

ELIZABETH. Yeah. But I never said that to her. Instead I said—okay Mom—

ELIZABETH'S MOTHER. Good.

ELIZABETH. Whatever you say. I'll go to Yale. I'll marry a doctor.

ELIZABETH'S MOTHER. Who cares about marrying a doctor? Be a doctor.

ELIZABETH. Okay I'll be a doctor.

ELIZABETH'S MOTHER. Be a dermatologist. They never get sued and they don't have to do anything disgusting.

ELIZABETH. Fine I'll go to Yale. I'll be a doctor. For you. I'll live in a great big house—

ELIZABETH'S MOTHER. Four thousand square foot minimum.

ELIZABETH. And have a great big life.

ELIZABETH'S MOTHER. Two kids or three?

ELIZABETH. For you. Because I'm—

ELIZABETH'S MOTHER. Perfect.

ELIZABETH. And when my kids are growing up you know what I'm going to make them do? Nothing.

ELIZABETH'S MOTHER. We don't have time for that. We need to go.

ELIZABETH. Yes, Mom.

ELIZABETH'S MOTHER. You're going to have a wonderful audition.

ELIZABETH. I know.

ELIZABETH'S MOTHER. You need a lead part if you're going to impress the admissions people.

ELIZABETH. I know.

ELIZABETH'S MOTHER. You know you could stand to be a little more independent. That's what they're looking for.

(They leave.)

(ALISON *enters.*)

ALISON. Hi there. I'm Alison Bass. Of course you know that. Let's see...experience...last year I was Anna in *Anna and the King.* The year before that I was Belle in *Beauty and the Beast.* The year before that I was the Crucible in *The Crucible.* Well okay I wasn't the Crucible, that's not really a role, but if there was a role for the Crucible, that would be me. And when I was a little kid I played Annie. In *Annie.*

MR. TORRANCE. *(Off:)* That's pretty impressive, Alison.

ALISON. I know, isn't it? That was a joke. Look um...do I really have to audition? I mean who are we trying to fool here, right? I know when everyone's here you can't make it look like you're going to give a part to a certain person, but...come on, we both know what's going to happen.

(Short pause.)

Does that make me sound conceited?

(She exits. SARAH *enters.)*

SARAH. Can I audition with somebody else? Is that possible?

MR. TORRANCE. *(Off:)* I'm going to need to hear you sing—

SARAH. Okay, but for the acting, can I bring in a partner?

MR. TORRANCE. *(Off:)* I guess.

SARAH. Can my partner be Tommy?

MR. TORRANCE. *(Off:)* Sure.

SARAH. You don't know how much that means to me.

MR. TORRANCE. *(Off:)* Carmen, can you get Tommy?

(The STAGE MANAGER *exits.)*

SARAH. Can I tell you something? Tommy doesn't know he's going to do a duet with me.

MR. TORRANCE. *(Off:)* Oh.

SARAH. And is it okay if we do this scene I wrote?

MR. TORRANCE. *(Off:)* Well—

(The STAGE MANAGER *brings in* TOMMY.*)*

TOMMY. I thought my audition time wasn't for another fifteen minutes.

SARAH. Hi.

TOMMY. Hey Sarah.

SARAH. Hi. What's up?

TOMMY. I'm auditioning for the show.

SARAH. I know. Me too. Isn't that awesome?

MR. TORRANCE. *(Off:)* I don't have all day people.

(SARAH pulls TOMMY aside.)

TOMMY. What's going on?

SARAH. Looks like they're pairing us up for a duet scene. Are you ready?

TOMMY. What duet scene?

SARAH. Oh here's the script.

(She hands him a copy of the script.)

TOMMY. Is this even in the play?

SARAH. They're thinking about adding it. And I overheard them talking earlier: they want passion.

TOMMY. Passion?

SARAH. Right. Passion.

TOMMY. Okay.

SARAH. You can do it. Are you ready?

TOMMY. I haven't even read the—

SARAH. Let's go.

(She pulls TOMMY back to center stage.)

SARAH. Hi my name is Sarah Arlen and this is Tommy Hartley and we're going to be auditioning for you now.

(She gets into character. TOMMY reads from the script. SARAH has it memorized.)

TOMMY. I don't know if I love Anne any more.

SARAH. How can you say that?

TOMMY. I think there's somebody else that I love more.

SARAH. Gregory, don't. Please. You can't mean me.

TOMMY. I do. You see, Anne is...fat and ugly and wears too much make-up around her eyes. It makes her look like a pig ran through a department store. Also I hate her high, whiny voice. It's like when she talks all the dogs in the neighborhood come running. And she smells like bacon all the time. I don't know why. Why did I ever start going out with her?

SARAH. You were crazy.

TOMMY. I was, but now I see you.

SARAH. You do?

TOMMY. Yes, compared to you, my current girlfriend is a bloated dead octopus washing up on the shore punctured with thirty hypodermic needles left over by the mafia. But you—

SARAH. Yes?

TOMMY. You are the most beautiful girl in the world. You are a star, a diamond, a diamond star, you are the cherry on top of my sundae, you are the whipped cream in my hot chocolate, you are the teeth in my mouth. I want to kiss you. And not just a regular kiss, a super kiss, the kind of kiss where it's like you've been hit in the head with the brick of love and you're bleeding out the side of your head where you got hit with that brick, and even the blood that's oozing down your hair is beautiful. Like that.

SARAH. Kiss me then you sad wonderful fool.

(TOMMY stops. SARAH whispers to him loudly.)

SARAH. It says you're supposed to kiss me.

TOMMY. I know, I'm just—

SARAH. You need to kiss me to get the part. He wants passion.

TOMMY. Okay, um...

MR. TORRANCE. *(Off:)* That's enough, thank you.

TOMMY. Thank you. I need to go.

(He leaves, relieved.)

SARAH. So is there like a romantic duo we could be cast as? Did you see that chemistry?

(Lights change.)

STAGE MANAGER. Break for the day!

(The ACTORS appear, each headed home in different directions. CARRIE settles downstage.)

CARRIE. My life: by Carrie.

(CARRIE'S MOTHER enters wearily and sits.)

CARRIE'S MOTHER. What are you doing this time?

CARRIE. I'm practicing.

CARRIE'S MOTHER. For what?

CARRIE. There's a musical at school.

CARRIE'S MOTHER. Oh.

CARRIE. I'm auditioning for it.

CARRIE'S MOTHER. Can you practice somewhere else? I'm trying to watch T.V.

CARRIE. Don't you want to know what the show is?

CARRIE'S MOTHER. I'm sure it's fine.

(Short pause.)

Fine. What's the show?

CARRIE. *A Chorus Line.*

CARRIE'S MOTHER. Okay.

CARRIE. It won the Pulitzer Prize.

CARRIE'S MOTHER. I'm sure it did.

(CARRIE'S MOTHER sighs heavily.)

CARRIE. Are you feeling okay?

CARRIE'S MOTHER. No I'm tired because I had a long day. I just want to sit here and relax. Is that all right with you?

CARRIE. Do you want something to eat? I could make dinner.

CARRIE'S MOTHER. No.

CARRIE. Can I make myself some dinner?

CARRIE'S MOTHER. Do whatever you want just quit bothering me.

CARRIE. Okay.

(CARRIE approaches the audience again.)

My life: by Carrie. My life is the most wonderful thing.

(She stops.)

My life is the...when I was ten years old I got cast in the school play. We were doing this play our teacher wrote about *Winnie the Pooh.* I was Tigger. Probably because I was pretty hyper. I even got to sing a song about Tiggers. I was so excited I stayed after school every day, and I learned my lines in the first week, and every night at home I'd sing my song about Tiggers and how they were made out of rubber and everything. Our school didn't have a lot of money, but my friend's Mom made me a costume and we had a lot of fun. And I felt really good about it. I mean, I felt...amazing. It was like my whole life I was looking for something I was good at, and then all of a sudden here it was, I was good at being Tigger. I couldn't run fast, I wasn't good at math, I couldn't even spell, but when I sang that Tigger song, I was proud. So the day of the show came, and I was backstage in my Tigger costume, and I was really nervous, I had to pee like every five minutes, and then I went out there on the stage, and the lights were really bright, and I could see the outline of all these heads out there, and I could hear them, and I did my song—and I just put everything I had into it, and I wasn't nervous any more, I was happy, and when I finished...the whole audience applauded for me. For me. I had never been applauded for anything my whole life. And then after the show, all the parents were coming up and hugging their kids, even the kids who played trees, I remember this Dad came up and he was like, "you were the most realistic tree of all of them" and everyone was there. And everyone was getting hugged. And there were all these flowers. And I looked around for my Mom...and I kept looking around for her...and I kept looking. And then everyone started to go home. And I was still there. And I was still in that stupid Tigger costume. I asked her later why she didn't come to my show, and she said, "what show?"

(Pause.)

I was really good, too.

(Lights change.)

(ACTOR 5 enters.)

ACTOR 5. (Extremely quiet:) Hi my name is Marissa.

MR. TORRANCE. (Off:) What?

ACTOR 5. (Just as quiet:) Marissa Leon.

MR. TORRANCE. (Off:) Can you be louder please?

ACTOR 5. What?

MR. TORRANCE. (Off:) Louder!

ACTOR 5. This is as loud as I get.

MR. TORRANCE. (Off:) I can't hear what you're saying!

(The STAGE MANAGER enters.)

STAGE MANAGER. You need to project.

ACTOR 5. (Barely audible:) I am projecting.

STAGE MANAGER. No. Out there. To the director.

ACTOR 5. What?

STAGE MANAGER. Let me help you. HELLLLOOO. Did you hear that? Did you hear how it reverberated in the theatre? You try it.

ACTOR 5. What am I supposed to say?

STAGE MANAGER. HELLLLLOOOO.

ACTOR 5. (Barely audible:) Hello.

MR. TORRANCE. (Off:) Okay, thank you.

STAGE MANAGER. All right, you're done.

(ACTOR 5 whispers in STAGE MANAGER's ear.)

STAGE MANAGER. She wants to know if there are any non-speaking roles.

(Lights change.)

(SOLEIL enters.)

STAGE MANAGER. Okay, this is so-leel.

SOLEIL. So-lay.

STAGE MANAGER. Why is it spelled so-leel then?

SOLEIL. It's French. It means the sun.

STAGE MANAGER. You were named after the French sun?

SOLEIL. Actually I was named after the girl who played Punky Brewster. Soleil Moon Frye.

STAGE MANAGER. What?

SOLEIL. Punky Brewster. You know that show?

STAGE MANAGER. No. You're weird.

SOLEIL. That's what people have been telling me.

(Various ACTORS begin to enter. These roles do not need to be played by the "auditioning" actors.)

ACTOR 1. Have you seen that girl?

ACTOR 2. What a freak.

ACTOR 3. Who wears that?

ACTOR 4. Does she do that to her clothes herself?

ACTOR 1. She's like just sitting there reading a book.

ACTOR 2. What is wrong with her?

ACTOR 3. Do you think she's on drugs?

ACTOR 4. She's totally on drugs.

ACTOR 1. You think you're special or something?

ACTOR 2. Why do you look like that?

ACTOR 3. *(Overlapping:)* Why do you talk like that?

ACTOR 4. *(Overlapping:)* Why do you think like that?

ACTOR 1. No one likes you.

(The ACTORS speak to the audience as SOLEIL sits in the middle of them.)

ACTOR 1. All the time we see these girls.

ACTOR 2. *(Overlapping on "see":)* Walking in here like they own everything.

ACTOR 3. *(Overlapping on "own":)* Like nothing applies to them.

ACTOR 4. *(Overlapping on "nothing":)* So weird.

(They surround SOLEIL and speak at her.)

ACTOR 1. Head in your book.

ACTOR 2. Eyes down.

ACTOR 3. Don't you care what people think of you?

ACTOR 4. Did you take a shower this morning?

ACTOR 1. You're nothing.

ACTOR 2. *(Overlapping:)* You're nothing.

ACTOR 3. *(Overlapping:)* You're nothing.

ACTOR 4. *(Overlapping:)* You're nothing.

SOLEIL. I can do this. I can be here.

ACTOR 1. The world takes people like you and chews them up—

ACTORS 2-4. *(Overlapping with* ACTOR 1:*)* You can't. You can't. You can't.

ACTOR 1. You're probably going to bring a gun to school.

SOLEIL. I can be in the show.

ACTOR 1. You're a shadow—

ACTOR 2. You're a nightmare—

ACTOR 3. You're the thing we left behind—

ACTOR 4. I wish I could be like you.

ACTORS 1-3. Shhhh!

ACTOR 1. Don't you know the world belongs to us?

ACTOR 2. To the pretty.

ACTOR 3. The popular.

ACTOR 4. The rich.

ACTOR 1. Don't you know we're happier than you?

ACTOR 4. I'm not happy.

ACTORS 1-3. Shhhh!

SOLEIL. I'm plenty happy.

ACTOR 1. You're a freak.

ACTOR 2. Disease—

ACTOR 3. Emo—

ACTOR 4. You're a depressed little doll in the corner.

SOLEIL. I'm not like you!

ACTORS 1-4. Of course you're not!

SOLEIL. I'm not like you!

ACTORS 1-4. You wish you were. You wish you were.

SOLEIL. No I don't!

ACTORS 1-4. You wish you were.

SOLEIL. I wish I was. Like you.

ACTORS 1-4. That's all we wanted to hear.

> *(The* ACTORS *retreat to the shadows but remain visible.)*

SOLEIL. I grew up alone. My Dad left us. My Mom didn't make it. And I was alone.

ACTORS 1-4. *(Whispering:)* Ugly.

SOLEIL. And I'd look at the girls who were pretty and the girls who were thin and the girls who seemed to know everything. They knew everything about clothes and money and music and what to say and how to laugh and they were so beautiful and I looked at myself in the mirror and I wasn't like them. I wasn't like them.

ACTORS 1-4. *(Whispering:)* No.

SOLEIL. I was something ugly, something diseased, something to be laughed at and destroyed and hated because I existed, just because I existed I was wrong and they were so easy, life was so easy for all of them as they got in their cars with their mothers on the way home and I was on the bus, I was alone on the bus and I'd always put my bag next to me on the seat and I'd sit up front next to the bus driver, and there was this boy who would sit behind me and he said I was the garbage can.

ACTORS 1-4. *(Whispering:)* Hey there garbage can.

SOLEIL. And they'd throw garbage at me and he'd flick my ears and every day at recess I didn't want to go outside, I prayed for rain every day and I never wanted to go outside because I had no one. No one at all near me.

ACTORS 1-4. *(Whispering:)* Garbage can.

SOLEIL. No one liked me. No one to talk to, and I just hoped the other kids would leave me alone and they wouldn't say anything to me and they'd just let me read a book, and most days they just ignored me, but sometimes they'd take the kickball and they'd throw it at me, and they'd back me up into the wall and I'd stand there with my head against the wall and they'd throw the ball at me again and again and every once in a while a girl would come up and shove my head against the wall or kick me in the back of the legs or put mud in my hair. The teachers watched. They thought we were playing. And I went home alone and I cried on the way home and then I cried at night for my Mom who died when I six and after that I just wanted her to come back and they stared at me all the time they stared—

ACTORS 1-4.
You're different—
You're weird
You're ugly
You're poor
Sleep on dirt
Take a shower today?
Why don't you just die?

SOLEIL. But I didn't. Sorry to disappoint you. And I stopped caring what they said. And I stopped wishing I was like them.

ACTORS 1-4. You're weird you're ugly you're poor you're stupid—

SOLEIL. No I'm not. No I'm not. No I'm not. No I'm not. I'm going to be better than all of you. And when I got here—when I got to high school—I found this. And suddenly it wasn't all that bad to be different. And suddenly it wasn't all that awful to be weird. And I'm happy. And if someone asked me tomorrow if I'd trade it all to be average, to be just like them, to be pretty and simple and not think too much and have boys fall in love me and write me notes and go to the movies with my friends on weekends—if someone offered me that trade, you know what I'd say?

(Short pause.)

Yes. In a heartbeat.

(ELIZABETH enters.)

ELIZABETH. Hi. My name is Elizabeth Walker and I'll be performing the role of Hamlet.

STAGE MANAGER. Isn't that for a guy?

ELIZABETH. I think it was meant for a woman.

MR. TORRANCE. *(Off:)* That's fine, Elizabeth.

(ELIZABETH performs the monologue. She's very good.)

ELIZABETH. I have of late—but wherefore I know not—lost all my mirth, forgone all custom of exercises; and indeed it goes so heavily with my disposition, that this goodly frame the earth seems to me a sterile promontory, this most excellent canopy the air, look you, this brave o'er-hanging firmament, this majestical roof fretted with golden fire, why it appeareth to me nothing but a foul and pestilent congregation of vapors. What a piece of work is a man, how noble in reason, how infinite in faculties, in form and moving how express and admirable, in action, how like an angel, in apprehension, how like a god: the beauty of the world, the paragon of animals. And yet to me, what is this quintessence of dust? Man delights not me.

MR. TORRANCE. Thank you Elizabeth.

(CARRIE enters as ELIZABETH exits.)

CARRIE. Hi. I'm Carrie. Do you mind if I sing a song?

MR. TORRANCE. Please do. This is a musical people! You're going to have to sing!

(ACTOR 3 enters.)

ACTOR 3. But there are non-singing roles, right?

MR. TORRANCE. A few.

ACTOR 3. Can I have one of the non-singing roles?

MR. TORRANCE. Please wait for your turn.

ACTOR 3. Oh.

(ACTOR 3 exits.)

CARRIE. Okay. Um...

(CARRIE presses an accompaniment CD in a boom box and presses play. She sings.)

[Productions may choose whichever audition song they would like. CARRIE should be an excellent singer and performer.]

(Lights down on her. The STAGE MANAGER enters.)

STAGE MANAGER. Call-backs are up. Call-backs are up.

(The ACTORS stream onto the stage. Some are delighted. Some are sad.)

YUMA. YES! YES! YES! YES!

ACTOR 1. Why don't they love me? Why don't they love me?

ACTOR 6. I made it! Oh my gosh!

ACTOR 5. My life is complete!

SARAH. Did you make it? Did you make it?

TOMMY. They want to see me again.

SARAH. They want to see us again. I have a whole new scene for us—I think you should come over to my house and rehearse it.

TOMMY. I'm sorry, I'm grounded.

SARAH. I'll come over to your house then.

ACTOR 3. How many people made it?

ACTOR 4. How many parts are there?

ELIZABETH. Oh darn it.

CARRIE. Did you make it?

ALISON. There must be some kind of mistake here.

ACTOR 6. They LOVE ME! I knew it! They LOVE ME!

ALISON. Wait a minute. Hold on.

ACTOR 3. It's only call-backs, it's only call-backs.

ACTOR 2. I'm so getting a part in this show—

ALISON. Wait! Hold on! Wait! SHUT UP EVERYONE!

(Everyone stops.)

ALISON. Um... Why isn't my name on the list?

(Everyone slinks off.)

ALISON. This is a mistake, right? Right?

(She exits. STAGE MANAGER enters.)

STAGE MANAGER. Come back tomorrow everyone.

(ALISON'S FATHER enters as the STAGE MANAGER leaves.)

ALISON'S FATHER. Is Mr. Torrance here? IS MR. TORRANCE HERE?!

MR. TORRANCE. *(Off:)* I'll be right there.

ALISON'S FATHER. What is the meaning of this?!

(MR. TORRANCE enters.)

MR. TORRANCE. I'm not sure I know what you're talking about.

ALISON'S FATHER. I'm Alison's father.

MR. TORRANCE. Oh. Nice to meet you.

ALISON'S FATHER. I realize you're new this year and you're trying to change things—

MR. TORRANCE. Well Alison didn't even really give an audition—

ALISON'S FATHER. Can I finish? That girl sings like an angel. All right? All these other kids sound like monkeys being shot. My girl is beautiful, she's talented, and she's amazing.

MR. TORRANCE. I'm sure she is, but—

ALISON'S FATHER. Can I finish? That girl has more talent in her freaking foot than you've ever seen in your life. When she did Belle, the audience was weeping for joy. Weeping. An old woman had a heart attack she was so good. And she kept watching the show, okay? This woman is dying and she's happy because she's watching my girl on stage.

MR. TORRANCE. She's welcome to audition next year—

ALISON'S FATHER. Are you not listening to me? Do you have some kind of brain problem? Put Alison in the show.

MR. TORRANCE. No.

ALISON'S FATHER. Put Alison in the show.

MR. TORRANCE. I can't do that.

ALISON'S FATHER. YOU ARE A MORON AND I WILL DESTROY YOU!!!

MR. TORRANCE. You need to calm down sir!

ALISON'S FATHER. I WILL CALM DOWN WHEN YOU ARE DEAD OR ALISON IS IN THE SHOW!!

MR. TORRANCE. I'm not putting Alison in the show!

ALISON'S FATHER. Let's go! Let's go!

(ALISON'S FATHER *raises his hands in fists.*)

MR. TORRANCE. I think you're taking this a little overboard.

ALISON'S FATHER. Come on! Let's see what you got!

MR. TORRANCE. I'm not going to fight you.

ALISON'S FATHER. THEN YOU WILL BE DESTROYED!

(ALISON'S FATHER *attacks. He does a few karate moves.* MR. TORRANCE *runs. Finally he turns around and pushes* ALISON'S FATHER, *who immediately collapses.*)

ALISON'S FATHER. Aaaarrghgghgh!

MR. TORRANCE. What? I didn't even—

ALISON'S FATHER. Ow my hip! My hip! You broke my hip!

MR. TORRANCE. I barely touched you.

ALISON'S FATHER. You assaulted me! I've been battered and assaulted! I'm barely alive! I need to go to the hospital. It's going dark. Why? Why?! What did I ever did to you?!

MR. TORRANCE. You said you were going to destroy me.

ALISON'S FATHER. I didn't mean it. Oh...this is the end... I'm dying... I'm not going to make it. Goodbye cruel world. I'm coming for ya Papa. I'm coming...

(ALISON'S FATHER passes out. MR. TORRANCE looks around.)

MR. TORRANCE. Um...help?

(ALISON'S FATHER wakes up slightly.)

ALISON'S FATHER. Please...I have to tell you...something... Come closer...

MR. TORRANCE. Um...

ALISON'S FATHER. Please...closer...

(MR. TORRANCE leans in close.)

MR. TORRANCE. What?

ALISON'S FATHER. I'm suing you.

MR. TORRANCE. I'm still not putting her in the show.

ALISON'S FATHER. Fine.

(He gets up and leaves. The STAGE MANAGER enters.)

STAGE MANAGER. Okay, everyone out here.

(The ACTORS emerge, ready for call-backs.)

STAGE MANAGER. I need you in two lines. We need to test your dancing ability—

YUMA. Yes!

(YUMA takes a center position.)

STAGE MANAGER. Here's the move: kick kick step kick shuffle spin kick. Got it? Everyone. Kick kick step kick shuffle spin kick. Again. Kick kick step kick shuffle spin kick. Again. Kick kick step kick shuffle spin kick. Rows switch!

(The first row and second row switch.)

Kick kick step kick shuffle spin kick. Moving on. Twirl twirl stomp kick step kick. Again. Twirl twirl stomp kick step kick. So the whole thing: kick kick step kick shuffle spin kick twirl twirl stomp kick step kick. Rows switch.

(The first row and second row switch.)

Kick kick step kick shuffle spin kick twirl twirl stomp kick step kick.

(YUMA steps forward.)

YUMA. Then we add: sashay sashay work it work it work it! Everybody!

STAGE MANAGER. Wait no—

YUMA. Sashay sashay work it work it work it! Then shake it shake it shake it work it shake it work it shake it! Yeah! Yeah! Everybody!

ACTORS. Sashay sashay work it work it work it! Shake it shake it shake it work it shake it work it shake it! Yeah! Yeah!

STAGE MANAGER. Stop stop stop!

YUMA. *(To* SARAH:*)* Um...are you aware that you suck?

STAGE MANAGER. Yuma! You are not the dance captain!

YUMA. Oh really? Maybe it's time for a dance-off.

STAGE MANAGER. It's not time for a dance-off.

YUMA. That's cause you can't bring it.

ACTOR 4. Aw no you di'in!

(They look at her.)

What? I'm street, I can't help it.

YUMA. Whatchu got? Come on. Bring it.

STAGE MANAGER. You want me to bring it?

YUMA. I want you to bring it like the pizza delivery man. Piping hot and fresh. In under thirty minutes. Or it's free.

STAGE MANAGER. All right. Let's go.

(The ACTORS *form a circle.)*

STAGE MANAGER. Kick kick step kick shuffle kick stomp twirl twirl hands us hands up kick step shuffle kick step!

YUMA. Oh yeah? Shake it shake it shake it thriller thriller thriller! Zombie thing zombie thing up down sprinkler sprinkler sprinkler.

STAGE MANAGER. *(Interrupting:)* Kick shuffle kick step shuffle kick—

YUMA. *(Overlapping:)* Work it work it work it thriller thriller thriller sprinkler sprinkler sprinkler yeah yeah yeah YEAH!

(They stop. Pause. Then both begin simultaneously again.)

STAGE MANAGER. *(Simultaneous:)* Kick step kick step flare flare flare spin twirl kick!

YUMA. *(Simultaneous:)* Shake it shake it shake it in your face in your face in your face!

(They stop again.)

YUMA. Aw, you been served.

*(*YUMA *walks away. The* ACTORS *begin a slow clap.)*

STAGE MANAGER. Oh stop it.

ACTOR 4. Aw no you di'in!

(The ACTORS *look at her.)*

Is that not appropriate right now? I'm not sure. Should I have said, "aw snap"? I can never figure out the difference between the two.

MR. TORRANCE. *(Off:)* The cast list is up.

(The ACTORS *surge to the side of the stage.)*

SARAH. I'm girl number seven! I'm girl number seven! I've always wanted to be girl number seven! What part are you?

TOMMY. I'm boy number seven.

SARAH. It's fate.

TOMMY. I have to go.

*(*TOMMY *escapes.)*

ACTOR 3. I'm boy number two? But I'm a girl.

ACTOR 4. I didn't get it.

ACTOR 5. I have one line! One line!

ELIZABETH. I'm in the show! Darn it.

ACTOR 7. Was there something wrong with my audition?

SOLEIL. I got a part!

(Lights change. CARRIE *is left on-stage alone.)*

CARRIE. Mom!

*(*CARRIE'S MOTHER *is sitting in the chair.)*

CARRIE'S MOTHER. What?

CARRIE. I got the lead!

CARRIE'S MOTHER. In what?

CARRIE. In the musical.

CARRIE'S MOTHER. Oh. Good.

CARRIE. It's so cool, I have two songs, and then I get to...

CARRIE'S MOTHER. Wait a minute, when are you rehearsing this thing?

CARRIE. After school.

CARRIE'S MOTHER. Which days after school?

CARRIE. Every day after school. It's only about two hours a day, though.

CARRIE'S MOTHER. You're going to be at the school an extra two hours a day?

CARRIE. Yeah, but it won't be a problem.

CARRIE'S MOTHER. When are you going to do your homework?

CARRIE. At night.

CARRIE'S MOTHER. I thought you were going to get a job.

CARRIE. I never said I was getting a job.

CARRIE'S MOTHER. You were going to apply at the grocery store.

CARRIE. When was that going to happen?

CARRIE'S MOTHER. You need to get a job.

CARRIE. Why?

CARRIE'S MOTHER. I don't know, Carrie. For fun. Why do you think people have jobs?

CARRIE. But when was—?

CARRIE'S MOTHER. You need to help out around here. I pay for your food, I pay for your insurance. It's not cheap. Where do you think the money's gonna come from for you to go to college?

CARRIE. I can work at night—

CARRIE'S MOTHER. That's not enough.

CARRIE. I'll get a job after the show's over—

CARRIE'S MOTHER. I don't think so—

CARRIE. And then I'll get a job over the summer, I can work plenty—

CARRIE'S MOTHER. And what are we going to do for money until then?

CARRIE. What have we been doing for money before now?

CARRIE'S MOTHER. You want to see my credit card bill? You want to? I need you to work. I don't need you to waste your time with this thing.

CARRIE. I'm the lead role.

CARRIE'S MOTHER. They'll find somebody else. You weren't the only one who auditioned, right?

CARRIE. No there were lots of people who auditioned and I got the part—

CARRIE'S MOTHER. Then they'll put one of them in. End of discussion. Go in tomorrow and tell your teacher.

(She goes back to watching television. CARRIE *waits there.)*

CARRIE. *(Under her breath:)* You probably wouldn't of come anyway.

CARRIE'S MOTHER. What?

CARRIE. I want to do this.

CARRIE'S MOTHER. I know you do and I'm sorry about that but there's nothing I can do.

CARRIE. What do you mean there's—

CARRIE'S MOTHER. I'm tired of talking about it.

CARRIE. I'm sorry am I taking up too much of your laying around time?

CARRIE'S MOTHER. I'm tired.

CARRIE. You're always tired!

CARRIE'S MOTHER. Cause I work twelve hours a day, that's why! And if you don't want to be like me, you better work now so you can go to college.

CARRIE. Mom. I'll make the money somehow but I'm going to do this show.

(Her MOTHER *is about to say something.)*

CARRIE. Just listen to me for a minute, okay? I'm going to go to college and I'm not going to be like you. You understand that? I'm not like you.

And you know what that means? That means when I have a child I'm going to love them and support them and I'm going to take an interest in their life. And when my kid is in a show I'm going to be there every single night cheering for them. Do you understand that? I've stopped waiting for you to appreciate me. I appreciate myself. And maybe that's not everything, but it's enough.

(Pause.)

CARRIE'S MOTHER. *(Getting up:)* Maybe you should live on your own then.

CARRIE. That's not what I want—

CARRIE'S MOTHER. Where'd you get those clothes? Where'd you get those shoes? What did you have to eat today? Do I charge you rent? I don't really have anyone helping me out here, kid. Your father isn't around to do it. And you got all that stuff from me. From me. So don't sit there and say I didn't give you anything. I gave you everything you own.

(CARRIE'S MOTHER leaves.)

CARRIE. Being a mother is about more than that.

(CARRIE sits. She sings a part of her audition song softly to herself.)

(She stops and cannot continue.)

(Lights change back to the auditorium. The STAGE MANAGER enters.)

STAGE MANAGER. All right! Let's take it from the top!

(All the ACTORS cast in the show come marching out in two lines. There is a hole in the line where CARRIE should be.)

MR. TORRANCE. *(Off:)* I want smiles! Big smiles! Keep those heads up! Soleil. Doing great. And kick! Kick! Kick! I want to see you believe it! Everybody should have a big face! Big face! Sarah big face!

(SARAH creates a "big face.")

Tommy get close to her! Act like you like her! Sarah...

(SARAH acts like she likes TOMMY.)

And the music is going, the music is going, we're singing—

(YUMA begins to break out of the line.)

Yuma stay in the line! Don't say anything just stay in the line! And big finish! Big finish! Sell it sell it Elizabeth sell it! And curtain. Everybody loves you.

STAGE MANAGER. Two minutes!

ACTORS. Thank you two.

(The ACTORS break out of character and wander off.)

MR. TORRANCE. *(Entering:)* Soleil. Hold up.

SOLEIL. Yeah?

MR. TORRANCE. If Carrie can't make it, I want you to do her part.

SOLEIL. ...Okay.

MR. TORRANCE. Good.

(Short pause.)

By the way, you're terrific.

(MR. TORRANCE walks off. SOLEIL remains for a moment, smiling. CARRIE enters in a rush.)

CARRIE. Hey. Where is everybody?

SOLEIL. On break.

CARRIE. I can do the show.

SOLEIL. Really?

CARRIE. Yeah. I just got word—I got a scholarship.

SOLEIL. That's awesome.

CARRIE. Thanks! I couldn't believe it. I was like, are you kidding me? I gotta tell Mr. Torrance—hey, do you know who they were gonna have do my part?

SOLEIL. Yeah.

CARRIE. Let me guess, Elizabeth?

SOLEIL. Me.

CARRIE. Oh. That makes sense.

SOLEIL. Why?

CARRIE. Cause you woulda been great. By the way, I'm gonna try and get some people to go out to IHOP after rehearsal tonight, you wanna come?

SOLEIL. I hate IHOP. They're disgusting. I went there one time and I wanted to get blueberry pancakes you know, and everybody knows that blueberry pancakes actually have blueberries in the batter...but you know what they do, they just dump blueberry pie filling on top. I mean, what is that? Did I order pancakes with blueberry pie filling dumped on top? No. If you're going to call yourself the International House of Pancakes, you should know how to make blueberry pancakes. That's all I'm saying.

CARRIE. Okay. Well um...maybe some other time then.

SOLEIL. No I'll still come.

CARRIE. Great.

(CARRIE runs off.)

Mr. Torrance! Mr. Torrance I can be in the show!

(The STAGE MANAGER returns.)

STAGE MANAGER. All right let's do it again people! With the singing this time!

ACTOR 5. Is it okay if I just lip synch? I'm just really not a good singer.

ACTOR 3. It's true. She's horrible.

STAGE MANAGER. Everybody sings! You just sing quietly.

MR. TORRANCE. *(Off:)* Places!

STAGE MANAGER. Places!

MR. TORRANCE. *(Off:)* And...showtime!

(Lights down.)

End of Play

LAW & ORDER: FAIRY TALE UNIT

by Jonathan Rand

For more information about rights and permissions, see page 9.

Cast of Characters

INTENSE VOICEOVER

CHUH-CHUNK

LOCATION

TIME

DETECTIVE H.D.

DETECTIVE CINDY

ZELLE

JACK

JILLIAN

HANSEL

GRETEL

UGLY D

OFFICER GOLD

PINOCCHIO

CAPT. HOOK

DOC

HAPPY

GRUMPY

BASHFUL

SLEEPY

SNEEZY

DOPEY

B.B. WOLF

EXECUTIVE A.D.A. STILTSKIN

A.D.A. MERM

PIG 1

PIG 2

PIG 3

PEEP

QUEENAN

BLIND MOUSE 1

BLIND MOUSE 2

BLIND MOUSE 3

ROBIN HOOD

SLEEPING BEAUTY

MUFFIN MAN

PETER PETER PUMPKIN EATER

CAT

FIDDLE

COW

LITTLE DOG

DISH

SPORK

JUDGE F. GODMOTHER

COURT REPORTER SPRAT

THREE BAILIFFS GRUFF

Setting

Far, far away.

40

Production Notes

Delivery: If it wasn't already immediately obvious from the title, this play is meant to be a send-up of the ever-popular *Law & Order* TV series. Intense delivery is crucial. Avoid going over the top at all costs. The more serious and intense these characters are about these ridiculous situations, the better the payoff.

Costumes: Go with whatever your budget allows, but simplicity might be funnier anyway. For instance: For the actor playing Dish, instead of going overboard with an elaborate, full-size Dish costume, maybe poke eye- and mouth-holes through a paper plate and strap it to the actor's face. Pig snouts for the Pigs should be all you need to make it clear they're pigs.

Gender: Please be as flexible as necessary with gender. There seems to be no good reason why this whole play couldn't be performed by an all-female or all-male cast. For example: Even though the Seven Dwarfs have traditionally been male, I see no reason why they can't all be female in this play. Wherever necessary, I approve the changing of pronouns to fit such casting requirements.

Pop culture references: Wherever necessary, please replace any outdated pop culture references if they will no longer resonate with audiences.

Small casts: It should be possible to produce the play with a minimum of 12 performers who play multiple roles. In order to minimize the scenes that currently call for more than 12 characters, follow these steps:

    * Cut the entire jury selection scene.

    * Make the following changes to the final courtroom scene:

      —Replace THREE BAILIFFS GRUFF with GINGERBREAD BAILIFF.

      —Change the following on pg. 68:

          STILTSKIN. Ladies and gentlemen of the jury... who are sitting way over there... As you have heard [continued]

      —Cut all lines, references, and appearances of the MUFFIN MAN and COURT REPORTER SPRAT.

For brotherman, Doug

Thanks for the push.

LAW & ORDER:
FAIRY TALE UNIT

(The title appears from darkness: Law & Order: Fairy Tale Unit.*)*
INTENSE VOICEOVER. In the fairy tale criminal justice system, the characters from fairy tales and nursery rhymes are represented by two separate yet equally ridiculous groups: the fairy tale police who investigate fairy tale crime, and the fairy tale district attorneys who prosecute the fairy tale offenders. These are their stories.

(Lights up on the part of the stage where we find CHUH-CHUNK, LOCATION, *and* TIME *throughout the play. They always face straight ahead toward the audience, without emotion. Perhaps they wear shirts with their character names on them in block letters. They are the human equivalent of the sound and the setting titles from the TV show.)*

CHUH-CHUNK. Chuh-chunk.

LOCATION. Chestnut and Hill.

TIME. 7:26 A.M.

(Lights shift.)

(A pile of rubble, entirely made of straw. CINDY *and* H.D. *arrive on the scene, each with a cheap cup of coffee.* CINDY *wears only one shoe;* H.D. *has his arm in a sling, a bandage wrapped around his head, maybe some other bandages and some bruises.)*

(ZELLE is already analyzing the crime scene.[1] Her hair is styled in a tall beehive.)

H.D. Well well well—you're up early for a Sunday, Zelle.

ZELLE. And *you're* late. But hey, I'm glad t'see both of ya got your beauty rest.

H.D. You noticed.

CINDY. All right, kids, break it up... So what're we lookin' at...

ZELLE. Well you *would* be lookin' at 328 Chestnut—if it was here anymore.

CINDY. Accident?

ZELLE. Not a chance. Perp struck the property from the rear, letting loose some form of windpower.

CINDY. Windpower...

ZELLE. *(To* CINDY:*)* Hey what's with the missing shoe?

CINDY. Eh, lost it last night at a Prince concert. Long story.

---

[1] There can be other crime scene investigators on the scene doing their work in the background.

ZELLE. *(To* H.D.*:)* What about *you?* Looks like you had a special night.

H.D. How 'bout we stick to the crime...

ZELLE. Ooh, testy.

CINDY. Any leads so far on our perp?

ZELLE. No dice. And the boys downtown got nothin' on the tenant either. But come take a look at this.

> *(She holds up some straw.)*

See this yellow-tinted, fibrous material here? We're stumped on what it might be. Tommy ran it through the Crime Scene Scanning Device and it told us diddly-squat.

H.D. Dilly-squat, huh? Sounds like my first marriage.

> *(They all laugh like tough cops and then quickly stop laughing.)*

H.D. Let's have a look. *(He does.)* The texture and appearance is almost *straw*-like in nature.

CINDY. Straw-like, huh... You may be on t'something.

ZELLE. Whatever it is, the whole building was made out of it.

CINDY. And I'm assuming no witnesses?

ZELLE. Actually, Blue questioned a husband and wife who were a block away. *(She hands* H.D. *a photo.)* Running pretty fast from the scene, these two. But they didn't see anything, so we sent 'em on their way.

H.D. Where they headed?

ZELLE. Forest Circle, why?

H.D. I've got a few questions of my own... A few questions...for them to answer...

> *(Beat.)*

H.D. *(To* CINDY*:)* Let's ride.

> *(H.D. and CINDY start to leave. H.D. turns around.)*

H.D. And Zelle...

ZELLE. Yeah.

H.D. Treat yourself to a night on the town tonight, will ya?

ZELLE. *(Dismissive:)* What're you talkin' about...

H.D. You been cooped up in that high-rise apartment for months. Get out there—let your hair down.

ZELLE. All right, maybe I will. *(Jocularly:)* For the right man, anyway.

CINDY. Ain't that the truth. You deserve a *prince.*

ZELLE. Okay, beat it. I'll be stuck here all day if I don't get busy with this straw-like material.

> *(ZELLE goes elsewhere to do more crime scene investigation. H.D. and CINDY take a moment to look at the rubble.)*

H.D. What a mess...

CINDY. My gut's tellin' me someone's got a problem with the tenant, and for some reason, destroyed the place in retaliation.

H.D. And whatever the reason— *(Beat.)* —it was the last straw...

> *(Lights shift.)*

CHUH-CHUNK. Chuh-chunk.

LOCATION. Forest Circle.

TIME. 7:54 A.M.

> *(Lights shift.)*
>
> *(CINDY and* H.D. *are waiting for* JACK *and* JILLIAN, *who jog onto the scene.* CINDY *and* H.D. *hold up their badges.)*

CINDY. FTPD. Finish line's right here, folks.

> *(JACK and* JILLIAN *stop running.[2])*

JACK. What seems to be the problem?

H.D. The problem is that you can run...but you can't hide.

CINDY. Let's hear your names.

JACK. I'm Jack.

H.D. Sprat? BeNimble? AndTheBeanstalk?

JACK. Just Jack. *(Beat.)* And this is my wife, Jillian.

JILLIAN. But my friends call me Ian.

CINDY. That's odd.

JILLIAN. I've got weird friends.

CINDY. Where were the two of you at seven this morning?

JACK. Walking up Chestnut, headed out here to do our daily morning jog.

H.D. And?

JACK. That's it. Just walking.

H.D. Word on the street is that you were walkin' pretty fast.

JILLIAN. What are you getting at...?

H.D. *(Outrageously livid, getting all up the grills of* JACK *and* JILLIAN:*)* You were *running!!* Not walking! *Running!!*

CINDY. Take it easy, man.

> *(CINDY subdues* H.D. H.D. *takes a moment to himself to cool off.)*

We've got an eyewitness who paints a somewhat different picture. Does the threat of perjury *jog* your memory?

JACK. Okay, okay. Fine. We were running. But let me explain.

---

[2]   Other runners can silently jog in the background throughout the scene. Jack and Jillian might do some stretching to keep limber.

The two of us were headed up Chestnut like usual, when Jillian suddenly got dehydrated. So I ran up Hill Street to the Quick-Stop to buy her some Propel.

CINDY. Propel?

JACK. It's fitness water.

JILLIAN. No, it's water with sugar. I wasn't dehydrated. He made that up so he could use a coupon.

JACK. That's not true!

JILLIAN. He does this all the time. Last week he pretended that both of us had broken legs 'cause Target had a Buy One Get One Free sale on wheelchairs.

H.D. *(To* CINDY:*)* I swear, if they don't get to the point right now, I will escort them to the point with my fist!

CINDY. C'mon, man. Take it easy. *(To* JACK *and* JILLIAN:*)* So then what?

JACK. She followed me into the Quick-Stop and then we left.

CINDY. That it?

JACK. Well, I doubt this is relevant, but I heard a loud noise, which caused me to trip and fall head-first on the sidewalk and crack the crown on my lateral incisor.

(He shows the tooth to the cops.)

CINDY. *(To* JACK *and* JILLIAN:*)* Okay, so let me get this straight: Jack... you and Jill—

JILLIAN. Ian.

CINDY. *(Without missing a beat:)* You and Ian went up Hill to buy a bottle of water—

JACK. Propel.

JILLIAN. *(Scoffs.)*

CINDY. Then Jack here fell down, broke the crown on his lateral incisor.

H.D. Then let me guess: *(To* JILLIAN:*)* You came tumbling after.

JILLIAN. No. Why would I tumble? That doesn't make any sense.

CINDY. Then what?

JILLIAN. We got stopped by those other cops, jogged here, then got stopped by you guys, who made us late for work.

H.D. I'll make *you* late for work! With my fist!

CINDY. *(To* H.D.:*)* Heyyy, cool it! *(To* JACK *and* JILLIAN:*)* Did you see anything out of the ordinary? Anything at all?

JILLIAN. Come to think of it, while we were buying the sugarwater we did see a couple of shady youths in the candy aisle.

CINDY. Shady youths, huh...? Catch where they were headed?

JILLIAN. Nope.

JACK. Actually, while I was eye-level with the sidewalk, I noticed something odd.

H.D. What's that?

JACK. Skittles.

CINDY. Skittles?

H.D. Skittles...

JACK. Yeah, I was surprised, too. There was a line of them trailing behind the hoodlums as they walked away. Maybe there was a hole in their bag. So I'm thinking if you follow the rainbow trail of Skittles...

H.D. ...we'll find our pot of gold...

CINDY. *(To* JACK *and* JILLIAN:*)* We'll take it from here. Enjoy your jog.

*(*JACK *and* JILLIAN *jog away.)*

H.D. We'd better move. In this business, every second counts.

CINDY. Yes. Time, it seems, is *running* out.

(Lights shift.)

CHUH-CHUNK. Chuh-chunk.

LOCATION. Center Park.

TIME. 8:20 A.M.

(Lights shift.)

*(*H.D. *and* CINDY *enter.* HANSEL *and* GRETEL *are there, scattering various types of candy to either unseen birds, or some silly representation of birds.[3] They do so throughout the scene. They are dressed like normal teenagers, except for a few German accessories—a German hat and short pants. They both speak with a stereotypical German dialect.)*

*(*H.D. *and* CINDY *flash their badges.)*

H.D. Well well well. I guess the old expression is right: Follow ten blocks of Skittles and you'll find two Germans at a pond.

HANSEL. Ve don't vant any trouble.

GRETEL. Ja. Ve are innocence.

CINDY. How about answering some questions.

HANSEL. Ve cannot talk now; ve are busy feeding ze vild birdies.

CINDY. I wasn't aware that "birdies" ate candy.

---

[3] Some ideas for representation of the birds: stuffed animal birds or cardboard cut-out birds just sitting on stage, not moving; cast members dressed as birds; cast members dressed in black holding fake birds and moving them around as if they were real.

GRETEL. Oh absolutely, policemen-man. Ze candies ist very popular mit ze birdies. Ze pigeons, zey prefer ze Junior Meentz.[4] Ze geese, zey go vild for ze Tvizzlahs.[5] Und ze duckies?—ze Goobahs.[6]

HANSEL. Vere you avare zat in some foreign lands, ze people feed ze birdies mit breadcrumb?

GRETEL. Breadcrumb! Can you believe zat? Ist nastygross! I get qveasy tummy just brainzinking[7] of it.

H.D. If you two Dum-Dums don't shut your Wax Lips, you're gonna make friends with the Jawbreakers. *(Referring to his fists.)*

HANSEL. Ve don't have to take zees vehbal abuse! Zees ist police brutalities.

CINDY. *(Asking H.D.:)* Hey—I forget... How many years of jail time for resisting arrest?

H.D. Five hundred years.

> (HANSEL *and* GRETEL *look at each other, and decide that it would be best to give in.)*

GRETEL. Okay, okay—ve will do as you vish.

HANSEL. First of all, you should know zat ve are Gehrman.

H.D. You almost threw us off with those hats. We were thinking you were from Detroit.

HANSEL. Zees are traditional Gehrman alpine hats.

GRETEL. Ja.

CINDY. And the lederhosen are a nice touch.

GRETEL. No, zees are extremely short capri pants.

HANSEL. On sale last veek at Marshalls.

H.D. Get on with it.

HANSEL. Ja, so okay. My name ist Hansel, und zees ist Gretel.

GRETEL. Hallo!!

HANSEL. Vee are brozer und seester, und yesterday morgen, our schtepmommy kicked us out of ze house.

CINDY. Why did your stepmom kick you out?

HANSEL. Schtepmommy ist evil...

GRETEL. Schtepmommies ist *alvays* evil...

HANSEL. She vas so sick of zees fake German accents.

> *(Beat.)*

---

4   Junior Mints.
5   Twizzlers.
6   Goobers.
7   Brainthinking.

CINDY. Wait, you're faking your accents? *(Without skipping a beat, they both speak without their ridiculous German accents.[8])*

HANSEL. Yeah, I mean—sure. You didn't pick up on that?

GRETEL. It sounds really annoying to us, but we just figured everyone else expects it from Germans.

HANSEL. Give the people what they want, right?

H.D. All Germans are faking it?

GRETEL. Oh sure. I thought that was common knowledge.

H.D. Wow...

CINDY. I know...

H.D. All this time...

CINDY. I know...

HANSEL. *(Back to thick, ridiculous German:)* Anyvay, vhere vere vee—

CINDY / H.D. No-no-no! / Wait!

CINDY. We prefer your natural dialect.

H.D. Please.

HANSEL. Really? All right—sweet. What a load off.

GRETEL. Yeah.

HANSEL. So as I was saying: Last night our stepmom kicked us out and left us alone and lost in the middle of town.

GRETEL. She's evil.

HANSEL. We started retracing our steps with Google Maps on Gret's cell, but the batteries died.

GRETEL. There we were—lost, tired, and über-hungry—when we run into this huge candy sale at the Quick-Stop!

HANSEL. So we bought like eight Halloweens' worth of candy and then split before the cashier noticed that we went over the per-item limit on Milk Duds.

GRETEL. Then we went home.

HANSEL. And at home we got *more* good news! Our stepmom wasn't evil after all. It was just low blood-sugar.

HANSEL. Her evil disappeared after we gave her eight boxes of Mike-n-Ikes.

H.D. That's a very fascinating story, and we're thrilled to hear it had a happy ending, and I'd very much appreciate a Tootsie Roll— *(GRETEL hands him one.)* —but we have a more pressing issue to discuss.

---

8   Now they just speak with the most common dialect of your community.

CINDY. Did either of you see anything out of the ordinary while at the Quick-Stop?

GRETEL. No. Though I did see a hairy guy walking across the street with an industrial fan.

(H.D. and CINDY *look at each other.)*

CINDY. Did you see where he was headed?

GRETEL. Hard to say. I was so hopped up on Fun Dip.

*(*CINDY's *phone rings. She takes it.)*

CINDY. Yeah. ...Thanks, Piper.

(Hangs up. She turns to H.D.*)*

Strike two.

H.D. Our furry fanman?

CINDY. Downed building out in the boonies. We gotta fly. *(To* HANSEL *and* GRETEL:*)* Thanks, kids. Stay outta trouble.

HANSEL / GRETEL. Danke schoen!!

*(*HANSEL *and* GRETEL *turn their attention to the birds.)*

CINDY. Whoever our hairy perp is, he's got a *sweet tooth* for destruction.

(Lights shift.)

CHUH-CHUNK. Chuh-chunk.

LOCATION. The Sticks.

TIME. 9:37 A.M.

(Lights shift.)

*(*UGLY D *is on the scene, investigating. She's gorgeous, but wears nerdy glasses and a ponytail.)*

(H.D. and CINDY *enter.)*

UGLY D. Took you fellas long enough.

H.D. Awww, Ugly D missed me.

UGLY D. Dream on, Prince Charming.

H.D. So tell me what you got.

UGLY D. Well I heard on the wire about the pile over on Chestnut. Based on that report and on the workmanship here, it looks like the same perp. Identical approach on the building from the backside; identical wind velocity. This time, though? Different substance.

*(*UGLY D *shows a bundle of sticks.)*

CINDY. What are those?

H.D. They're almost *stick*-like in nature.

CINDY. Yes, yes—stick-like!

UGLY D. *(Simply:)* They're sticks.

(Beat.)

CINDY. Oh.

UGLY D. And the other one was straw.

(Beat.)

H.D. Huh.

(Moving on...)

CINDY. Well I gotta question: Why would anyone build a home outta sticks?

H.D. Same reason you'd build one outta straw.

UGLY D. Why's that?

H.D. *(Intensely:)* That's what they pay us to find out...

(Beat.)

UGLY D. *(Indicating H.D.'s injuries:)* What happened t'*you?*

(Pause.)

(H.D. blatantly dodges the subject.)

H.D. *(Gesturing yonder:)* Looks like Gold's got a witness.

UGLY D. Next door neighbor. Was on his way home and was first on the scene.

H.D. *(To CINDY:)* Shall we?

CINDY. Much thanks, D. Sorry we can't *stick*...around.

UGLY D. Be careful, you two.

CINDY. Careful's my middle name.

UGLY D. I thought it was Yolanda.

CINDY. I had it changed.

UGLY D. Nice.

(CINDY and H.D. leave UGLY D.)

CINDY. Why does she go by Ugly D again?

H.D. It was a nickname I gave 'er.

CINDY. Why?

H.D. *Why?* She's got a ponytail and glasses. There's no *way* she's actually hot under all that.

CINDY. I've heard that it's what's on the *inside* that counts.

H.D. Like organs?

CINDY. Yeah, I guess that doesn't make any sense.

(They head over to GOLD, who has been questioning PINOCCHIO. GOLD has very blonde hair, and is drinking a cup of coffee. PINOCCHIO is a normal-looking guy, except for his outrageously long nose. The longer the nose, the better. On the nose is a white bandage.)

CINDY. Hey there, Goldie. How's that coffee?

GOLD. Lukewarm. *(Beat.)* I'm guessing you wanna meet our new friend.

H.D. Whatsyername, Dumbo.

PINOCCHIO. Uhh, I'm...Marcus.

> *(Suddenly* PINOCCHIO *experiences noticeable nose pain. He puts his hand to it.)*

PINOCCHIO. Ow.
Look, I told her what I know.

GOLD. Just tell them exactly what you told me.

PINOCCHIO. Okay. I was walking home from a...doctor's appointment... and I suddenly heard this noise. Like...like someone dropped a box of toothpicks. I look up and I see that mess over there. And that's it. Now can I go home? I'd rather not get wrapped up in a big investigation.

CINDY. Did you see anything besides the pile of sticks?

PINOCCHIO. No, no, that's all.

> *(Nose pain again.)*

Ow.

CINDY. Is everything all right, sir?

PINOCCHIO. Yeah, everything's fine. I feel great. *(Nose pain.)* Ow.

> *(The detectives are suspicious.* H.D. *has an idea. He leans in and says something briefly and quietly to* CINDY. H.D. *then directs his attention to* PINOCCHIIO.*)*

H.D. Marcus, let me ask you...
What's the square root of sixty-four?

PINOCCHIO. Eight.

H.D. What do you call a group of geese?

PINOCCHIO. A gaggle.

H.D. How often do you work out at the gym?

PINOCCHIO. Twice a day. *(Nose pain.)* Ow.

> *(Everyone else looks at each other.)*

CINDY. Mind telling us what's going on, "Marcus"?

H.D. Howsabout telling us who you really are, Namey McFake.

PINOCCHIO. Okay, fine. FINE. *(Beat.)* My name isn't Marcus. *(Beat.)* It's Pinocchio.

GOLD. Ohhhh. I saw a thing about this guy on Oprah.

PINOCCHIO. Well I guess there's no hiding it now.

H.D. Let's hear it, Maria Menou-nose.

PINOCCHIO. Okay. *(Pause.)* I'm what you'd call a test tube kid. There's this rebel scientist—my "dad"—who created me, and for some reason decided it would be a brilliant idea to endow me with an unbelievably enormous honker. I think he read in Maxim that women like men with "striking features." He somehow translated "striking" as "huge," and "feature" as "schnoz." So he merged the DNA of a human and an ant-eater, and tadahhhh, Abercrombie model!

Oh and as if that wasn't enough, Doctor Frankenstupid thought it might be, I don't know...fun? A challenge?...if my nose were connected to nerve endings in my brain in such a way that when I lie about anything, my trunk here grows three inches.

How 'bout you? What's your life story? Pretty much the same, right?

H.D. Listen, Rhino—you may have been through a lot, but that doesn't give you the right to disrespect the man who gave you life. After all, father *nose* best.

PINOCCHIO. All right... You know, I realize that it's part of a police detective's job to use bad puns to emphasize points? But could you do me a solid and limit the nose humor? I'm really sensitive about it.

> *(Pause. H.D. thinks it over.)*

H.D. No deal.

GOLD. I don't understand. When you lied before, it didn't look like your nose grew; it looked like you were in pain.

PINOCCHIO. Yeah, well, I can explain that. I wasn't at the doctor for a routine checkup, if ya get my meaning. Right after getting my nose "taken care of," the doctor warned me that my nerve endings would still be sensitive to lies.

H.D. I see.

CINDY. Now did you see anything suspicious at the scene of the crime?

PINOCCHIO. No. *(Nose pain.)* Ow. Fine, fine. I'll tell you what I saw, but please keep me out of the papers. I don't need this sort of press.

H.D. Out with it, Toucan Sam.

PINOCCHIO. See, that was uncalled for.

CINDY. What'd you see?

PINOCCHIO. I saw a bunch of people in basketball jerseys, poking around the rubble. Once the sirens started up, they jumped into an SUV and peeled outta there.

H.D. Any-a these guys have a fan or excessive body hair?

PINOCCHIO. I don't know.

CINDY. How many of 'em did you see?

PINOCCHIO. Hard to say.

> *(Beat.)*

> *(H.D. has an idea. He points at PINOCCHIO's bandaged nose.)*

H.D. Out of curiosity: Does that thing only give you trouble during *intentional* lies, or do you experience pain whenever you say anything inaccurate?

PINOCCHIO. Anything inaccurate—unfortunately.

H.D. I see. Do me this favor: Answer yes to everything I'm about to ask you.

PINOCCHIO. *(Suspiciously:)* Okay...

H.D. Were there more than four people digging around the rubble?

PINOCCHIO. Yes.

H.D. More than ten?

PINOCCHIO. Yes. Ow.

H.D. How about exactly five?

PINOCCHIO. Yes. Ow.

H.D. Nine?

PINOCCHIO. Yes. Ow.

H.D. Six?

PINOCCHIO. Yes. Ow.

H.D. Eight?

PINOCCHIO. Yes. Ow.

H.D. Seven?

PINOCCHIO. Yes.

> *(Pause.)*

H.D. Seven it is.

> *(PINOCCHIO is in a great deal of pain by now.)*

CINDY. *(To PINOCCHIO:)* Thanks.

PINOCCHIO. *(Sarcastically:)* Happy to help. *(Pain.)* Ow.

CINDY. *(Taking H.D. aside:)* So we got seven ballers but no way of finding them. Without the plates, we're sunk.

H.D. Jiminy Cricket...

> *(Beat.)*

PINOCCHIO. Excuse me, officers.

H.D. Keep your nose outta this, will ya?!

PINOCCHIO. SNOWMEN.

H.D. Excuse me...?

PINOCCHIO. The license plate. SNOWMEN. Kinda hard to forget something that strange.

> *(Pause.)*

H.D. Snowmen... *(To CINDY:)* Call it in.

(CINDY dials.)

PINOCCHIO. Maybe it's that Frosty guy and his posse.

H.D. How 'bout you leave the predictions to us, *Nose*-tradamus.

(PINOCCHIO looks to GOLD and points at H.D., with a blank "C'mon..." face.)

CINDY. *(On the phone:)* Hey Piper. I need a trace on plate number SNOW-MEN. ...Yeah, I'll hold.

(CAPTAIN storms in. She has a hook for a hand. She's livid. She speaks extremely quickly and to the point.)

CAPTAIN. You two better have some news.

CINDY. Captain—good morning.

CAPTAIN. It's gonna be the opposite of a good morning if I don't hear some results. We've got two downed buildings and zero arrests. When I do the math, that's two buildings too many, and zero is a darn low number of arrests.

H.D. It's the lowest number.

CINDY. What about negative numbers?

H.D. True.

CAPTAIN. I don't need a math lesson! I need a *results* lesson! I got the commissioner, the mayor, and Governor Grimm, all breathin' down my neck—

PINOCCHIO. Uh, can I go now?

CAPTAIN. You two had better track down whoever nixed the straw and the sticks and you better *book 'em.* You hear me? You *book 'em.*

CINDY. Captain, we just got a lead on seven guys who just may be our perps—

CAPTAIN. *May* be the perps?! I never wanna hear *"May"* from you, ever! Unless it's the *month* of May, but it's not. *(Looks to TIME:)* Right?

TIME. *(Thumb up.)*

CAPTAIN. Now look here—the 911 call just came in from the vics; we're bringin' 'em down to HQ for questioning.

H.D. You found 'em?!

CINDY. Who are they?

CAPTAIN. Pigs. They're pigs.

H.D. Cops?

CAPTAIN. Real pigs, you nitwit. Swine, hogs, ham.

H.D. Oh.

CAPTAIN. Now what time is it?

TIME. 9:44.

CAPTAIN. Thanks. Some slimy crock stole my watch.

CINDY. A crock?

CAPTAIN. However you pronounce it—crook, crock. It's a regional thing, like tomato/tomahto, potato/potahto, Florida/Flahrida. It's a quarter till. By eleven, I want answers, I want arrests, I want *something!* Or I will put you both on unpaid suspension faster than you can say "unpaid suspension." And that's only five syllables, so you better be done in *four.*

(CAPTAIN storms out.)

CINDY. Unpaid suspensh?

H.D. This is not good. This is not good at all. As a matter of fact, it's bad.

(CINDY's phone rings. She picks it up.)

CINDY. Talk to me. ...Got it. Thanks, Piper. *(To H.D.:)* Plates are in. Shaker Lows.

H.D. Let's move. Fast.

(H.D. and CINDY start to head out.)

(Pause. PINOCCHIO and GOLD are left alone. Eventually, PINOCCHIO breaks the ice.)

PINOCCHIO. How's it goin'.

(Pause.)

GOLD. If you got a nose job, why is it still long?

PINOCCHIO. It actually used to be ten feet longer—because of my career.

GOLD. What do you do?

PINOCCHIO. I'm running for President.

(Lights shift.)

CHUH-CHUNK. Chuh-chunk.

LOCATION. Shaker Lows.

TIME. 10:10 A.M.

(Lights shift.)

(A yard sale. Seven guys are wearing basketball jerseys. They are the SEVEN DWARFS—though they aren't necessarily shorter than anyone else. The SEVEN DWARFS are doing the selling and organizing, while various customers browse the junk and periodically interact with the DWARFS.[9] SLEEPY is asleep throughout—not snoring; just silently passed out.)

(H.D. and CINDY enter and flash their badges.)

CINDY. FTPD. Whose SUV is that parked on the curb?

HAPPY. That's mine, officer.

---

[9]   Customers are optional, if your cast can't accommodate.

H.D. What's your name.

HAPPY. I'm Happy.

H.D. I said What's your name!

HAPPY. I told you: I'm Happy.

H.D. I don't care if you're *ecstatic*— You don't tell me your name right now, I'll see to it you're never happy again for the rest of your life!

HAPPY. But I've always been Happy.

H.D. All right, punk—I'm takin' you in.

DOC. Pardon me, officers, but I believe there's been a misunderstanding. His *name* is Happy. We all have irregular names. For instance, my name's Doc. Happy, you've met.

HAPPY. Hello again!

DOC. Then there's Grumpy.

GRUMPY. *(Grunts:)* Eh.

DOC. Sleepy.

SLEEPY. *(Asleep.)*

DOC. Sneezy.

SNEEZY. *(About to sneeze:)* Sorry, hold on.

DOC. Bashful.

BASHFUL. Hi...

DOC. And last but not least, Dopey.

DOPEY. *(Tipping his head like a top hat:)* Onion rings.

DOC. And we're the Seven Dwarfs!

> *(The* DWARFS *all react in their character-specific ways.* HAPPY *cheers;* SNEEZY *blows his nose;* GRUMPY *grumbles aloud dismissively;* DOPEY *says "Onion rings" again; etc.)*

CINDY. Dwarfs?

DOC. Yes, I know what you're thinking: none of us are that dwarfish in size. You see, the Seven Dwarfs is our official team name. We belong to a 7-on-7 hoops league. The name was actually Coach White's idea. We're not short, but compared to everyone else out on the court, we're tiny. It's all relative.

SNEEZY. Like Dwyane Wade. He's six-four, but next to Shaq he looks like Justin Bieber.

DOC. Or like today, when Grumpy had to post up on that huge center.

GRUMPY. I hate that guy. All he does is complain about his yard. Wahhhh, I have trouble with weed control. Wahhhh, there's an oversized beanstalk blocking out the light in my sunroom.

HAPPY. Give him a break, you guys—he's been robbed like three times this week.

H.D. OKAY!! Enough *small*-talk.

CINDY. We need to know where you were earlier this morning.

DOPEY. Unicorn!

DOC. Dopey, please—I'll take care of this.
We were at the game, then we rushed back here to kick off our yard sale.

H.D. According to an eyewitness, it sounds like you made a pit stop on the way.

DOPEY. Unicorn!

DOC. Dopey...

DOPEY. Unicorn?

BASHFUL. No, you're right. We did stop.

HAPPY. That demolished building was a gold mine for us!

H.D. What are you talking about?

DOC. For we Dwarfs, schooling the opposition on the hardwood is just a hobby. We make a living selling antiques, rare gems, and knick-knacks at yard sales. So when we were lucky enough to come across that rubble on our way home from the game, well—off to work we went. And it was quite a successful excavation.

CINDY. You do realize that tampering with a crime scene is a federal offense.

DOC. We didn't know it was a crime scene. And besides, we've got junk-excavation permits. Boys?

(Suddenly they all simultaneously reveal their identical, official permits. DOPEY reveals a turkey hoagie.)

H.D. And let me guess. You didn't see anybody suspicious?

(They all shake their heads.)

CINDY. What about this Coach White of yours? Any chance he's hairy and owns an industrial fan?

SNEEZY. No, and he's a she.

DOC. She's coaching without pay in exchange for free housing in the room above our garage. Actually, she's been stuck in bed ever since she had some two-week-old McDonald's apple pie. Doctor Charming's stopping by later with "True Love's Kiss."

SNEEZY. Which is just a corny rebranded name for Imodium AD.

GRUMPY. Not sure why we need to waste money on a doctor, since this guy's *(Pointing to DOC:)* been out of med school for five years.

DOC. *Dental* school. You *know* that.

GRUMPY. Well then maybe you shouldn't go by Doc.

SNEEZY. Yeah, what about Dent?

DOC. I hate you all.

CINDY. *(To* H.D.*:)* Another dead-end. And that was the best lead we had. Captain's not gonna be happy.

HAPPY. That's my name, don't wear it out!

H.D. *Can* it, short-stack!

HAPPY. *(Thumbs up:)* You betcha!

H.D. *(Back to* CINDY*:)* What if during their excavation the Tiny Tims found a clue?

> *(They turn to the* DWARFS.*)*

CINDY. We're gonna need to see your loot from the crime scene.

DOC. Sure thing. Boys, let's give 'em an inventory. What'd you find?

> *(They each reveal an item.)*

SNEEZY. Lunch pail.

GRUMPY. Shovel.

HAPPY. Tool belt.

BASHFUL. Blueprints.

DOPEY. *(Presenting a hard hat:)* Turkey hoagie.

DOC. And I found this ID card for a construction site.

> (CINDY *and* H.D. *ponder this.* H.D. *takes the ID card.)*

H.D. No obvious thread that links the clues... *Unless—*

CINDY. Unless?

H.D. *Unless*...these are props and costume pieces for a music video about construction workers...!

CINDY. You may be on to something...

H.D. Which means our perp must be a hairy pop star who sings Top-40 hits about construction!

ALL. Yeah. / That must be the case. / Exactly.

> (SLEEPY *lifts his head.)*

SLEEPY. Or he's a construction worker.

> (SLEEPY *returns to slumber.)*
>
> *(Pause.)*
>
> (H.D. *looks down at the ID card.)*
>
> *(Pause.)*

H.D. It's a small world...after all.

> *(Lights shift.)*

CHUH-CHUNK. Chuh-chunk.

LOCATION. High Rise East construction site.

TIME. 10:42 A.M.

> *(Lights shift.)*

(WOLF is measuring a cinder block with measuring tape. H.D. and CINDY enter, displaying their badges.)

H.D. FTPD. We've been lookin' for you.

(WOLF looks up. Notices the cops. Bolts.)

CINDY. Hey!!

(Chase scene!! H.D. and CINDY pursue WOLF with musical accompaniment conducive to an action-packed chase. Slow-motion might work nicely.)

(The chase ends with H.D. and CINDY prevailing, pressing WOLF against a surface, cuffing him.)

WOLF. I didn't do anything!!

H.D. The innocent ones always run... *(To CINDY:)* Book 'im.

CINDY. *(As she books 'im:)* You're under arrest for the unwonted destruction of homes built out of foolish raw materials.

H.D. May I be first to welcome you to Justicetown—population: you.

WOLF. Listen, man—you got the wrong wolf.

H.D. Oh yeah? We'll see about that. 'Cause in Justicetown, I'm the mayor.

WOLF. *(Indicating CINDY:)* What about her?

CINDY. I'm on the school board.

(Lights shift.)

CHUH-CHUNK. Chuh-chunk.

LOCATION. Fairy County Courthouse, District Attorney's Office.

TIME. 12:30 P.M.

(Lights shift.)

(An office. STILTSKIN and MERM are speaking with the THREE PIGS. STILTSKIN is draped in flashy gold jewelry, including one of those enormous dollar-sign necklaces—or a similar necklace with the scales of justice. MERM has a little trouble walking around, stabilizing herself with a cane. She wears a large seashell brooch and has sunscreen on her nose.)

(PIG 1 speaks with a stereotypical Brooklyn accent; PIG 2 speaks with a stereotypical Southern accent; and PIG 3 speaks with a stereotypical highfalutin British accent, and maybe has a pipe in his mouth.)

STILTSKIN. I know you three have been through a lot today, but I promise that we'll get past this as quickly and painlessly as possible. First of all, my name is Executive Assistant District Attorney Stiltskin, and to my right is Assistant District Attorney Merm.

MERM. Afternoon.

STILTSKIN. First off, let's get your names, for the record?

PIG 1. I'm Pig #1.

PIG 2. I'm Pig #2.

STILTSKIN. *(Earnestly:)* Which makes you...

PIG 3.	**STILTSKIN.**
Pig #3.	Pig #85.

STILTSKIN. *(Discouraged:)* Ah!

MERM. So let's review your story. Pig One, you were alone in your straw house; Wolf approaches the house; knocks it down.

PIG 1. Yeah. Kept sayin' he'd blow my house in, which, sounded a little weird. I told him to hold on, that I was shavin'—y'know, the really tough part right here *(Indicates his chin area.)* —and then before I know it, bam, my house is kaput.

STILTSKIN. Then what?

PIG 1. Well, I was freakin' out, right? So I curly-tail it to my bro's.

PIG 2. He showed up all discombob-uh-lated. Pork almighty... I felt his forehead. He was bakin'. An' I mean sizzlin'.

> *(Beat.)*

MERM. Go on.

PIG 2. Same thing, basically. I'm shavin', and the hairy guy shows up with that fan-a-his, and before ya know it, my bachelor pad's yardwaste.

MERM. And that's where you come in.

PIG 3. Quite. They arrived at my doorstep, utterly frazzled, and I comforted them with tea and crumpets.

STILTSKIN. At which point, the perpetrator arrived, attempted identical fan-powered destruction, but failed.

PIG 3. That is affirmative, counselor.

MERM. Now what about this Wolf character? You know him?

PIG 3. We did. He was the highest bidder on the contract for all three of our houses. But all of us withdrew at the last minute.

MERM. Why?

PIG 2. We saw him and that poor girl in the red hoodie on *Judge Judy*.

STILTSKIN. *(To* MERM*:)* That B&E mess last month with the old lady.

MERM. The one with the schnauzer and the empty kitchen cabinet?

STILTSKIN. No.

MERM. Oh, the one who lives in the Reebok.

STILTSKIN. No, that other old lady—y'know: "the better to blank you with, my dear."

MERM. Right.

PIG 3. So we certainly didn't want any association with a convicted felon.

MERM. Was he angry about your pulling the contract?

PIG 3. Absolutely livid.

MERM. *(To* STILTSKIN:*)* Hello, motive.

STILTSKIN. Chances are we'll need you to testify in court about what you just told us.

PIG 3. We will do whatever is necessary.

STILTSKIN. One thing I'm not clear on: Why the disparity in the composition of your respective residences?

PIG 2. It's a pretty simple story, really. See, Maw and Paw passed away about ten years back.

PIG 1. Luau...

(The PIGS *pause for a somber moment of reflection.)*

PIG 3. And they left behind a sizable trust fund for each of us.

PIG 2. Problem is, me and Pig One, we got our vices. Me, I invested mosta my inheritance as the executive producer of Kim Kardashian's debut album.

STILTSKIN. *(To* PIG 1:*)* What about you?

*(*PIG 1 *points to himself.)*

PIG 1. This little piggy went to Vegas.

PIG 2. He lost everything on the roulette wheel.

PIG 1. Always bet on pink...

PIG 2. So as you can imagine, given that red and black are the only options in roulette, and given that Kim Kardashian—well, y'know... —Pig One and I didn't have much money left over to invest in real estate.

PIG 1. Hence my straw.

PIG 2. And m'sticks.

STILTSKIN. *(Indicating* PIG 3:*)* What about you?

PIG 3. I invested my inheritance in a new condominium—replete with fortified Ukrainian stainless steel, state-of-the-art motion-sensory alarm system, and most importantly: wind-proof foundation.

MERM. Sounds not cheap.

PIG 3. Indeed. I, too, no longer have money.

PIG 2. But at least we have each other!

PIG 1. Brothers in a blanket?

PIGS. AWWWwwww. *(They group hug.)*

(Lights shift.)

CHUH-CHUNK. Chuh-chunk.

LOCATION. Plea-bargain session.

TIME. 1:13 P.M.

(Lights shift.)

(STILTSKIN *and* MERM *sit across from* WOLF *and Defense Attorney* PEEP. PEEP *has a shepherd hook and wears a bonnet.*[10])

STILTSKIN. We're coming in full-steam on this one: Two counts each of malicious destruction of property and reckless endangerment—nothing less. And given your client's history, we can't go anywhere near minimum jailtime, but if you hand us a guilty plea we'll lowball at ten years with eligibility for parole.

PEEP. My client pleads not guilty to all counts.

STILTSKIN. Oh come off it, Peep. No jury out there would swallow that even if it was corn-battered and served on a stick. We've got eyewitness testimony of your client fleeing the scene with a fan, his personal effects in the rubble, we've got motive, opportunity, and let's not forget the guy's got a rap sheet longer than Lindsay Lohan's.

MERM. Picnic-basket theft, nursing home B&E, impersonation of the aged—and I'm just getting warmed up.

PEEP. For each of those crimes, my client was falsely accused.

MERM. Exactly. That's why his first and middle names are Big and Bad.

WOLF. That's not my name.

(PEEP *whispers in* WOLF's *ear.*)

WOLF. No, it's okay. I wanna talk. I gotta get it off my chest. (*To* STILT-SKIN *and* MERM:) My name is B.B. Wolf, yes, but that stands for Bernard Bartholomew Wolf. After the Riding Hood incident, the tabloids invented "Big Bad." I'm not bad, and I'm certainly not big. I'm five-seven.[11] That's not big. Biggie Smalls was big. Not me. I'm not big, I'm not bad—I'm just a smalltown wolf living in a lonely world. A wolf who always seems to end up at the wrong place at the wrong time.

STILTSKIN. Well today you ended up in the *wrong* place, at the *wrong* time.

WOLF. I just said that.

STILTSKIN. We don't care if you're big and bad, small and good, or medium and half-decent—our offer doesn't budge.

WOLF. And my innocence doesn't budge.

MERM. And budge rhymes with fudge.

(*They all look at* MERM.)

MERM. I haven't eaten today.

STILTSKIN. If you're insistent you're not guilty, why were you at the scene of each crime with a fan?

PEEP. Again, my client has already explained to the police that he received three invitations to BYOF parties on Facebook.

---

[10] This role would probably be funniest if the actor is a very large and/or masculine male who looks especially awkward in a bonnet.

[11] Or a believable height for that actor.

STILTSKIN. And again, we found no such invitation.

PEEP. Someone could have easily deleted it...

MERM. You're scrapin', Bo.

STILTSKIN. What about that slow-motion chase sequence?

WOLF. I was afraid! Okay?! I was afraid... How many times do I have to get arrested for crimes I don't commit? First the Little Red misunderstanding, then the whole mix-up with that Peter kid, and now this! I can't take it anymore!

STILTSKIN. I have some brilliant advice: Stop committing crimes.

PEEP. My client's innocent, Stilt. The plea stands.

STILTSKIN. Have it your way.

(STILTSKIN begins to pack up her papers to prepare for her exit.)

MERM. Glad to see you're still at it, Peep. As usual, doing what's expected of you. Repping a criminal. Following the herd.

PEEP. Say what you will—I'm just doing what I'm supposed to.

MERM. And what's that...?

(Beat.)

PEEP. *(Intensely:)* My job...

(Lights shift.)

CHUH-CHUNK. Chuh-chunk.

LOCATION. District Attorney's Office.

TIME. 2:20 P.M.

(Lights shift.)

(STILTSKIN and MERM are talking with District Attorney QUEENAN. She's wearing a purple outfit and is eating a caramel apple.)

QUEENAN. Two houses in the same day, both taken down by a fan-toting wolf...

MERM. I know, boss. It's crazy.

QUEENAN. Didn't this same thing happen in Eastwick a coupla months back? It was in the paper.

STILTSKIN. I forgot about that...

QUEENAN. So you might say...that this case has been ripped from the headlines.

MERM / STILTSKIN. Hmmmm. / Good point.

QUEENAN. Anyway—headline-ripping aside, we gotta talk about this B.B. Wolf character, who I don't have to remind you has been a thorn in my side for longer than I care to remember.

MERM. We remember.

QUEENAN. I get grief from Castle Hill every time Hairy Gary here walks. I need you to drop a net on this guppy.

STILTSKIN. Queenan, this case is water-tight. We'll get a conviction before gavel hits wood.

QUEENAN. You better be right. 'Cause I don't care what you have to do: Stack that jury with a coupla ringers if you have to. You didn't hear that from me, though.

MERM. Hear *what* from you?

QUEENAN. Exactly. *(Looking at her half-eaten caramel apple in disgust:)* Ugh, this is *terrible.* *(Indicating* MERM's *cane:)* So what happened to you?

STILTSKIN. Merm here just got back from vacation. Scuba diving in Maui.

MERM. I'm still not used to walking on dry land. It's weird—it's like the opposite of sea legs.

QUEENAN. I'll tell ya: Life under the sea, by and large, is far superior to anything we've got up here.

MERM. Don't I know it.

QUEENAN. Well you better recover and recover fast, 'cause I need you both on your A-game this afternoon.

STILTSKIN. We won't let you down, Queenan. Within the hour, our big and bad perp's gonna be wolfin' down prison food.

MERM. You'll hear all about his guilty verdict from Wolf Blitzer.

QUEENAN. You both are hungry like the wolf and I like that. Now I'll see you both tomorrow. I'm cutting out early.

MERM. Where to?

QUEENAN. Headed out to Queens for a Queen concert.

STILTSKIN / MERM. Hey, nice. / Great band.

QUEENAN. *(Looking in a mirror:)* How do I look?

MERM. *Wicked*-hot.

STILTSKIN. You're the hottest of 'em all.

QUEENAN. That's clearly kissing up, but you're both promoted.
(Lights shift.)

CHUH-CHUNK. Chuh-chunk.

LOCATION. Jury selection room.

TIME. 3:09 P.M.
(Lights shift.)
(We see MERM, STILTSKIN, PEEP, *and many* JUROR PROSPECTS.*)*
(MERM points to the THREE BLIND MICE, *who wear sunglasses.)*

MERM. What about these?

PEEP. Are all three of you blind for the same reason?

THREE BLIND MICE. No. / No. / Uh-unh.

BLIND MOUSE 1. I was born blind.

BLIND MOUSE 2. I'm not blind; I just wear these so I can eye the ladies unnoticed.

> *(BLIND MOUSE 2 removes his sunglasses and we see that his eyes are not looking at PEEP, but in fact looking way off to the side at a female character. He says, with sketchy seductiveness:)*

Hi there.

PEEP. *(To* BLIND MOUSE 3:) What about you?

BLIND MOUSE 3. I was blinded by a pack of stray wolves.

> *(Beat.)*

PEEP. All right, lose Mouse 3.

STILTSKIN. Fine. *(To* BLIND MOUSE 3:*)* You're free to go.

> *(BLIND MOUSE 3 chucks his sunglasses and bolts out of the room.)*

BLIND MOUSE 3. Suckerrrs!!

STILTSKIN. Okay, so we've approved two thirds of the blind-slash-fake-blind Mickeys. Also, we're good to go on the cocky archer with the ugly green hat...

> *(ROBIN HOOD points with two fingers and makes that pompous clicking noise.)*

...the narcoleptic hottie...

> *(SLEEPING BEAUTY looks up from her mocha frappuccino in drowsy confusion.)*

SLEEPING BEAUTY. Hmmm? Muh?

STILTSKIN. ...and Chef Boyardee.

> *(The* MUFFIN MAN *is there with a tray of muffins and a tall chef's hat.)*

MUFFIN MAN. I live on Drury Lane!

STILTSKIN. Good for you. *(Beat.)* Oh, and I almost forgot: we also have a guy who for some reason is eating an entire pumpkin.

> *(PETER PETER PUMPKIN EATER looks up, looks around, then casually returns to his slow chewing of the pumpkin.)*

PEEP. What about Juror Number Six?

> *(PEEP gestures to LITTLE RED RIDING HOOD, who is wearing her classic red outfit, carrying a basket, and wearing an obviously fake mustache.)*

MERM. That one? This is Carl Herbert, a retired stock broker.

PEEP. Are you sure? It looks a lot like the vic from my client's case last summer.

MERM. What, you mean—what was her name... Little Red something something?

PEEP. Yes.

MERM. I don't think so. What's your name?

LITTLE RED. Carl Herbert.

PEEP. It looks a lot like Little Red. And she would be a very biased juror.

MERM. True, but... Did Little Red have a mustache?

(Beat.)

PEEP. Touché.

STILTSKIN. Great. And to recap on the six we finalized earlier—

(STILTSKIN indicates the CAT, FIDDLE, COW—who has a huge, unchanging smile plastered on her face—and LITTLE DOG.)

—we got a cat, a fiddle; a cow, who in sort of a disturbing way appears to be over the moon about something; a small dog, and— Hold on...didn't we have two more here?

(LITTLE DOG is stifling a laugh.)

STILTSKIN. Is something funny to you?!

LITTLE DOG. They— They ran off to the john.

(DISH and SPORK enter.)

DISH / SPORK. Sorry. / My bad.

STILTSKIN. So as I was saying, we got a cat with a fiddle—

FIDDLE. A *viola*, actually.

STILTSKIN. —a viola, a dog with authority issues, a dish—

DISH. Why thank you.

STILTSKIN. —and what are you—a ladle?

SPORK. Spork.

STILTSKIN. And that makes twelve.

(She turns to PEEP.)

Which means we'll see you in court.

MERM. Sure you're ready for this, Peep?

PEEP. I was born ready...

STILTSKIN. You were born with a law degree?

PEEP. *(Seriously:)* Yes.

(Lights shift.)

CHUH-CHUNK. Chuh-chunk.

LOCATION. Courtroom.

TIME. 4:30 P.M.

(Lights shift.)

(JUDGE F. GODMOTHER is presiding with her magic wand gavel. The JURY is present. H.D. is on the stand. STILTSKIN is in the middle of questioning him. Also present are PEEP, WOLF, MERM, and THREE BAILIFFS GRUFF. There is an audience, which includes the THREE PIGS and others.)

STILTSKIN. And when you approached the defendant at the construction site, did he acquiesce?

H.D. He did not. He attempted to flee, but Detective Rella and I were able to subdue the defendant and arrest him.

STILTSKIN. Ladies and gentlemen of the jury... As you have heard, the defendant was witnessed *fleeing* the crime scene with an industrial fan, after which he blatantly resisted arrest. *(Beat.)* Nothing further.

JUDGE. Cross examine?

(PEEP rises, and paces.)

PEEP. I wonder, Detective...H.D. is it...? Given your physical...liabilities... if you're fit to give testimony...

H.D. *(Starts to charge PEEP:)* I'll show *you* physical liabilities...

(The BAILIFFS restrain H.D.)

JUDGE. Order!! Order!!

STILTSKIN. Objection, your honor. The witness's physical condition is not on trial.

PEEP. Your honor, I put forth that the cause of the witness's recently sustained injuries may very well have something to do with the apprehension of my client and would therefore render this witness unfit for testimony.

JUDGE. Proceed.

(STILTSKIN throws up her hands in disgust.)

PEEP. Now Detective... How did you sustain these injuries?

H.D. *(To the JUDGE:)* I'm not gonna answer these questions.

JUDGE. And I will hold you in contempt of court.

(Pause.)

H.D. All right... You wanna know? Fine. I'll tell you. I'll tell you right now. But don't blame me if you're plagued with nightmares for the rest of your life...

(The lights dim and focus on H.D. What follows is a highly emotional monologue, as slow and gripping as it needs to be.)

It was Thursday afternoon. I was on my lunch break. There I was, sitting, minding my own business. But I wasn't sitting just anywhere. No... No I wasn't... I was sitting on a wall. That's right, a wall. It seemed stable enough, sure. Why wouldn't a wall be stable? *(Pause.)* But then out of the blue...without warning...it gave way. Before I could get my bearings, I lost my balance, and... *(Pause.)* ...and I fell.

And it wasn't just your average fall. No it wasn't. It's not easy to describe the kind of the fall it was, but...if I had to choose a word...I'd say it was...great. A great fall. *(Quietly:)* It was great...

I regained consciousness in a gurney over at King's County. They did everything they could to fix my bone fractures, my torn joints, ...my broken soul. All the finest doctors lent a hand—human doctors, of course, but also horse doctors... After surgery...the chief resident put his hoof in my hand and told me everything was gonna be all right.

But he was *all wrong*...

No matter how hard they tried, they failed...they failed at putting me back together again.

You wanna know about my physical stability? Oh I'll be all right. Sure. I'll survive. But after a fall of such...great...magnitude...I may not ever recover...up here. *(Points to his head.)* And in here. *(Points to his heart.)* And along here. *(He indicates the side of his pinky.)*

For those of you out there—you young people, especially—listen to me and listen close... 'Cause I'll only say it once: The next time you see a wall... *respect* that wall... And don't sit on it. Sit on a chair... Or maybe a futon.

> *(Pause.)*

H.D. *(To* PEEP:*)* Happy now?

I quit.

> *(He drops his badge on the floor and exits the courtroom.)*
>
> *(If there is no real audience applause after this stirring performance, a Slow Clap from the courtroom audience may be in order.[12])*

JUDGE. Order!! I will have order!! Let's move this along, counselors. My pumpkin Hummer is double-parked. Prosecution, present your next witness.

STILTSKIN. We call Pigs 1 through 3.

> *(The* PIGS *all take the stand together.)*

BAILIFF. Do you swear to tell the truth the whole truth and nothing but the truth, so help you Goose?

PIGS. We do.

STILTSKIN. Now...the members of the jury have already heard a detailed, point-by-point analysis of today's horrifying events. But does such an analysis convey the pure emotional turmoil that you three had to endure?

PIG 1. No, it was horrible.

PIG 3. Truly frightening.

---

[12] For examples of the Slow Clap phenomenon, watch *Cool Runnings* or *Mystery, Alaska.*

PIG 2. *(Looking at the* JUDGE:*)* Your Honor, I can't even make eye-contact with the defendant without feelin' *unclean.*

PEEP. Objection! Pigs frequently root in their own filth.

JUDGE. Sustained. *(To* COURT REPORTER SPRAT:*)* Pig Two's comments will be stricken from the record.

COURT REPORTER SPRAT. Wait, I was supposed to be writing this down?

STILTSKIN. I'll rephrase. More specifically: Are you *afraid* of the Big Bad Wolf?

PIG 1. The Big Bad Wolf?

PIG 3. The Big Bad Wolf?

PEEP. Objection!

STILTSKIN. Are you *afraid* of Bernard Bartholomew Wolf?

PIG 1. Tra la la la la.[13]

PIG 3. You'll have to excuse my brother. He is speaking in an archaic version of Pig Latin. "Tra la la la la" roughly translates into English as... "Yes."

STILTSKIN. And would you describe that fear?

PIG 2. It was terrifyin'. I was just shavin' like any other day, and then outta nowhere this ferocious beast walked right up to my front door and blew my house in.

PIG 1. Can any of you in the jury imagine lookin' out the peep hole of your own front door and seeing that?

(An ominous sound effect. The lights suddenly narrow to STILTSKIN. *Echoes of the characters are in her mind. Each of them appear in their own light as this happens.)*

PIG 2. ...walked right up to my front door, front door, front door...

PIG 1. ...lookin' out the peep hole, peep hole, peep hole...

ZELLE. Perp struck the property from the rear, rear, rear...

UGLY D. ...Identical approach on the building from the backside, backside, backside.

PIG 3. I, too, no longer have money, money, money.

PIG 1. Always bet on pink, pink, pink...

PIG 2. I invested mosta my inheritance on on Kim Kardashian, Kardashian, Kardashian...

MUFFIN MAN. This is a muffin, muffin, muffin.

ALL OF THE ABOVE. *(Repeated:)* Front door... / Backside... / Peep hole... Rear... / Pink... / Kardashian... / Muffin.

(Suddenly...)

---

[13] Use a similar rhythm to the song.

STILTSKIN. Objection!

(The lights are back to normal, and the people who were echoing are no longer echoing.)

JUDGE. Mr. Stiltskin, did you just object to your own line of questioning?

STILTSKIN. Indeed I did, Your Honor. Indeed I did.

JUDGE. This is highly unorthodox.

STILTSKIN. We live in a highly unorthodox time, Your Honor. Why just yesterday I saw a man walking a cat.

JUDGE. I'll allow it.

MERM. *(Loudly whispered:)* What are you *doing?*

(STILTSKIN looks at MERM, then at PEEP.)

STILTSKIN. My job...

(Pause.)

PEEP. *(An aside:)* Technically that's my job.

(PEEP's line isn't acknowledged by anyone, as STILTSKIN turns to the PIGS.)

STILTSKIN. Pigs Number 1 and 2... In your testimony just now, you revealed to this court that the defendant approached your *front door* in order to topple your comically flimsy houses with an industrial fan.

PIG 1 / PIG 2. Yeah. / Yes sir.

STILTSKIN. But the crime scene investigators have confirmed that the point of attack took place from the *rear* of each house...

(The PIGS are frozen, unflinching.)

Therefore, it is my supposition that you three pigs *staged* the destruction of your homes, knowing you could easily frame a convicted wolfen criminal, and in the end, walk away free pigs having collected on the windfall of insurance money you so desperately desire.

(STILTSKIN gets in the PIGS' faces.)

That is my supposition!! *That* is what really happened!! *How* do you plead...?!

PIG 1.	PIG 2.	PIG 3.
Okay okay!	All right! We did it!	Guilty... Guilty...

PIG 1. We were broke! We needed the money so badly. I haven't bet on pink in almost 48 hours.

PIG 2. And KimKard lied to me! She promised that her music would bridge the generation gap and end world hunger with its hypnotic funky rhythms! And that was false! Neither of those things happened!

JUDGE. Bailiffs Gruff, take them away.

(As the BAILIFFS cart off the PIGS, PIG 3 stops and turns to STILTSKIN.)

PIG 3. Well-played, Stiltskin. Well-played...

> *(The* BAILIFFS *and* PIGS *exit.)*

PEEP. Your Honor, motion for dismissal?

JUDGE. Motion granted. This court is adjourned.

> *(She bangs her magic wand gavel.)*
>
> *(Everyone quickly files out except for* STILTSKIN, MERM, PEEP, *and* WOLF. *Either that or the lights focus in on the four.)*
>
> *(*WOLF *shakes* STILTSKIN's *hand.)*

WOLF. Thank you...for everything.

STILTSKIN. Don't thank me. Thank echo-y flashbacks.

WOLF. *(Nodding, with a twinkle in his eye:)* Will do.

> *(*PEEP *and* STILTSKIN *share a moment.)*

PEEP. Not bad, Counselor. Not bad at all...

> *(*PEEP *and* WOLF *begin to exit.* PEEP *slips back for a second and speaks quickly.)*

By the way, technically I won that case. *(Quick beat.)* All right, see ya.

> *(They quickly exit.)*
>
> *(*STILTSKIN *and* MERM *are reflecting.)*

MERM. Well that was a twist ending I had to see to believe.

> *(Beat.)*

Let's get outta here. Dinner's on me.

STILTSKIN. I won't argue with that.

MERM. What do you feel like?

STILTSKIN. Well you know what I'm always hungry for...

MERM. What's that?

> *(Beat.)*

STILTSKIN. Justice...

> *(Beat.)*

MERM. That, my friend, has already been served.

> *(Blackout.)*

End of Play

13 WAYS TO SCREW UP YOUR COLLEGE INTERVIEW

by Ian McWethy

For more information about rights and permissions, see page 9.

Cast of Characters

INTERVIEWER 1
INTERVIEWER 2
HAROLD
KIMBERLY
PRODUCER
MARIA
BRETT
LILY
MELVIN
KELLY
JEFF
EVE
ELIZABETH
BEN
JASON
EMILY

Production Notes

This play should a have a quick pace so keep the tempo up. Other than that, have fun and be as creative with the characters as you want.

If for some reason you have a bigger cast than 16 or would simply like a few more interviews, there is a sequel to this play called *14 More Ways To Screw Up Your College Interview.* You're welcome to add or swap scenes from that play or peform both plays together. For more information, please visit www.playscripts.com.

13 WAYS TO SCREW UP YOUR COLLEGE INTERVIEW

Scene 1

(Two Desks. Each desk has two seats on either side.)

(INTERVIEWER 1 sits at his desk. INTERVIEWER 2 enters, a worried look on his/her face.)

INTERVIEWER 1. So?

INTERVIEWER 2. We're short.

INTERVIEWER 1. We're short?

INTERVIEWER 2. We are...short.

INTERVIEWER 1. By how much?

INTERVIEWER 2. That's the kicker. We're short by one student.

INTERVIEWER 1. One student!

INTERVIEWER 2. One stupid...student.

INTERVIEWER 1. Are you kidding me? The dean really thinks one student is going to make a difference?

INTERVIEWER 2. You know how anal he is with budgets. He's convinced if we can get one more kid to enroll this year, all our financial problems will be solved.

INTERVIEWER 1. But we don't have any more interviews scheduled. When does he want our recommendation by?

INTERVIEWER 2. Today.

INTERVIEWER 1. Today?

INTERVIEWER 2. Or we're fired.

INTERVIEWER 1. Or we're...fired? What sense does that make?

INTERVIEWER 2. I think he still blames us for accepting that pyromaniac that burned down the science center.

INTERVIEWER 1. But he had an amazing essay! How were we to know?

(INTERVIEWER 2 shrugs. INTERVIEWER 1 shakes his head in disgust.)

INTERVIEWER 1. Well, what are we going to do? We finished our interviews last week.

INTERVIEWER 2. Look through the wait listed files and start calling. If any of them can see us today, let's give them a shot.

INTERVIEWER 1. The wait list? Oh God.

INTERVIEWER 2. Hey, our backs are against the wall here. If we don't find a diamond in the rough...we're out of here.

(INTERVIEWER 1 *nods his head.*)

INTERVIEWER 1. Alright, I'll start making calls. Good luck.

INTERVIEWER 2. Hey, keep your head up. The wait listed kids aren't as bad as you think.

(INTERVIEWER 2 *leaves.*)

Scene 2

(HAROLD, *normal, nice kid, enters* INTERVIEWER 1's *office.*)

INTERVIEWER 1. Harold, thanks for coming in.

HAROLD. Thanks for having me.

INTERVIEWER 1. Did you have any trouble finding the Barrow building?

HAROLD. Um...that's a personal matter and...I'd rather not answer it.

(*Beat. Huh?*)

INTERVIEWER 1. Well, okay, shall we get started?

HAROLD. Sometimes.

INTERVIEWER 1. I...well let me start by telling you about how this University differs from others in the state. We're a smaller school, with smaller class sizes and personal attention, but we have the resources of a big state school. These resources include amazing internships, and a faculty of practicing professionals.

HAROLD. Well I'm glad to hear that. When I applied in-state one of my big fears was being overwhelmed by huge lecture classes.

INTERVIEWER 1. Well that is exactly the atmosphere we try to avoid here. Now, have you thought about a major yet?

HAROLD. That is my MOTHER you're talking about here!

(*Beat.*)

Oh dear, you didn't just ask to see my mother in a two-piece bathing suit, did you?

INTERVIEWER 1. No, I didn't.

HAROLD. Allow me to explain. I have an extremely rare disorder known as "Chronaquestimixidous." It's a neurological condition which renders a person incapable of hearing a question...correctly.

INTERVIEWER 1. And by correctly you mean—

HAROLD. Every time you ask a question, I hear a completely different one.

INTERVIEWER 1. I see. How come I've never heard of "chronaquestimixidous" before?

HAROLD. Eleanor Roosevelt...probably.

(HAROLD *hands* INTERVIEWER 1 *a doctor's note.*)

HAROLD. I probably should've told you as soon as I came in. Sorry, I just don't like to make a big deal about it.

INTERVIEWER 1. Well...Harold, I don't know what I can do exactly. A college interview is primarily the asking of questions.

HAROLD. So...if a deaf person came into your office, you'd just refuse to do the interview?

INTERVIEWER 1. No, I would make sure a translator fluent in sign language was available to aid in the interview.

HAROLD. Well I'm sorry that the AMA hasn't recognized CQM as a legitimate medical condition, but I try to live my life in a normal and healthy way, and I would appreciate it if you treated me the same as any other prospective student.

INTERVIEWER 1. I...suppose you're right but, well...okay, shall we continue with the interview?

HAROLD. It's in Argentina, isn't it?

INTERVIEWER 1. Um, yes...sure is. So, what kind of extra-curricular activities are you interested in?

HAROLD. Seventh grade, Melissa Bloch. We both had braces, it was kind of awkward.

INTERVIEWER 1. What's your favorite subject in school?

HAROLD. I would take South Pike road, except during rush hour.

INTERVIEWER 1. What's your favorite color?

HAROLD. Every Sunday.

INTERVIEWER 1. Is it me or is this completely pointless?

HAROLD. I don't know too much about the salivary gland. Sorry.

INTERVIEWER 1. Well, that went well, thank you so much for stopping by.

HAROLD. Thank you.

(HAROLD *stands up to leave.*)

INTERVIEWER 1. Do you need directions to get back on the I-40?

HAROLD. Cookie Monster. I guess I just like googley eyes. Is that weird?

INTERVIEWER 1. A little. Yeah.

(HAROLD *leaves.*)

Scene 3

(KIMBERLY *meets with* INTERVIEWER 2.)

INTERVIEWER 2. Thank you for coming in on such short notice.

KIMBERLY. I'm glad you could fit me in. My life has just been so busy lately.

INTERVIEWER 2. Oh yeah, with what?

KIMBERLY. Oh, you know, applying to schools, end of the year club wrap-ups. Trying to get in to prestigious summer programs. On top of all that, I'm being filmed for a documentary.

INTERVIEWER 2. A documentary? Really?

KIMBERLY. Yeah, I know it's crazy. My brother knows this guy...and he's doing this thing about highschoolers, like a gritty, realistic piece about kids all over the country and...you know, they just thought I was interesting I guess.

INTERVIEWER 2. So they follow you around everywhere?

KIMBERLY. Yeah and actually...I probably should have told you this on the phone, but they're...right outside the door.

INTERVIEWER 2. Oh, well...

KIMBERLY. And I know it's weird and everything, but they're completely respectful, very quiet, you'll hardly know they're here.

INTERVIEWER 2. I'm sure they are, it's just, I have a reputation at this school and I don't—

KIMBERLY. Oh they'll blur your face, no one will even know it's you if you want. Plus it's free publicity for the school.

INTERVIEWER 2. I...suppose. But you promise you'll blur my face and disguise my voice.

KIMBERLY. Oh yeah, if you just sign this, and check this box, we'll make sure your likeness isn't used in any way.

(INTERVIEWER 2 *signs the paper.*)

INTERVIEWER 2. It's not that I don't trust you, it's just you have to be very careful these days—

KIMBERLY. HE SIGNED IT!

(A PRODUCER *comes in holding a camera.*)

PRODUCER. Great, great, great. Hey how are you? Okay, Kim. You're makin' the college rounds now, but remember what I said: We're trying to be the next Jessica Simpson, the next fat guy on biggest loser, the next Sanjaya. So let's up the awful factor. I want you to be dumb and loud and MEAN! I wanna hate you so much I can't turn away. AND ACTION!

(INTERVIEWER 2 *is frozen.* KIMBERLY *starts chewing gum and texting.*)

(Beat.)

INTERVIEWER 2. I thought you said this was for a documentary film.

PRODUCER. Cut! Come on man, can you just do your job? Can you just ask questions? We all want this to be quick. Let's do this quick.

INTERVIEWER 2. But she said this was a—

PRODUCER. YES! It's a documentary! It's a series of documentary short films, premiering on the T4 network at ten o'clock on Sundays.

INTERVIEWER 2. T4?!? The Reality Teen Music Channel? With those horrible shows about spoiled birthdays and Karaoke drama queens?

PRODUCER. Oh, good, you're a fan. Look, just ask a few questions and we're out of here.

INTERVIEWER 2. NO! I won't...I can't be on that channel.

PRODUCER. Ah, should've looked at the contract, friend. If you DON'T do this, you'll be fined twenty thousand dollars.

INTERVIEWER 2. Twenty thousand?!?

(INTERVIEWER 2 reads the contract over.)

PRODUCER. Look man, we're not asking you to do anything crazy. Just do your job, ask a few questions, and we'll be out of your hair.

INTERVIEWER 2. Fine, let's just, fine.

PRODUCER. Alright, and Kimberly, remember what we talked about. ACTION!

INTERVIEWER 2. Okay, Kim.

KIMBERLY. *(Acting like a brat:)* It's pronounced KIM-BAAARRR-El. No E. The e is silent.

INTERVIEWER 2. Okay, fine, Kim-Bar-El. Why is it you want to go to this University?

KIMBERLY. First of all, to party. Second of all, to meet some totes hot guys. Like totes 'n' totes.

INTERVIEWER 2. Totes you say, well...anything else that you would want to do here? What...major are you interested in?

KIMBERLY. What do you mean? Major?

INTERVIEWER 2. You know, a major. Your degree?

KIMBERLY. What do you mean, degree? Like, how hot it is outside?

INTERVIEWER 2. No. What...you don't know what a college degree is?

KIMBERLY. No. I'm totally dumb. But at least I'm not old, like you!

PRODUCER. Cut! PERFECT KIM! You were stupid, obnoxious...a completely terrible person. Just the kind of thing we like to see on reality TV.

(They start to leave.)

KIMBERLY. *(Acting normal:)* Oh, when we do my confessionals, I should say how creepy the interviewer was and that he was, like, hitting on me.

PRODUCER. Perfect, I got some shots of him, that if we put it in slow-motion, will make him look really creepy. Like lecherous and...

(They leave. INTERVIEWER 2 looks defeated. He picks up the phone.)

INTERVIEWER 2. Hi, is the Dean in...no, could you leave a message...ask him how he would feel if the University appeared in a...documentary? Thank you.

Scene 4

(INTERVIEWER 1 *sits with* MARIA, *who's very still.*)

INTERVIEWER 1. And our women's basketball team, while not nationally ranked, has gone to the AA tournament for the last several years. And even if you're not interested in that level of commitment, we have several clubs where you can play on a more casual level.

(MARIA *barely acknowledges.*)

INTERVIEWER 1. You know, I feel like I've been talking this entire time. You've been very quiet.

(MARIA *moves forward as if to speak...and vomits on* INTERVIEWER 1's *desk.*)

(*They sit for a moment.*)

MARIA. I don't think I feel so good.

INTERVIEWER 1. What gave you that idea?

Scene 5

(INTERVIEWER 2 *is making notes in a file when* BRETT, *dressed in a suit, talking on a blackberry, comes into the room and paces around.*)

BRETT. Okay, okay! I'm totally on it, I'm on it, trust me. I'm gonna push my five o'clock to six, my Tuesday to Friday, and flip another thing with a thing I got next month so don't worry about it.

INTERVIEWER 2. Excuse me—

BRETT. Yeah, yeah, yeah, hold on. (*To* INTERVIEWER 2:) I'll be done in a few, I'm so grateful for your patience, I can't express that enough. We're gonna have a great convo, I can feel it. (*Back to the phone:*) Okay chief, I gotta wrap this up. I'm psyched, I'm hungry, I'm pumped, we're gonna blow this out of the water and blow people's minds. Mañana.

(*He hangs up the phone.*)

BRETT. Again, appreciate your patience and your general attitude! You're an ace in the hole. Up! Una momento.

(BRETT *takes out his phone.*)

Ah, it's my broham, Marty. He's such a jerk. I just gotta (*Starts texting:*) "Put your money where your mouth is, Marty Mar. No Doubt!" Ah! Marty. Love 'em but wouldn't trust him with a pencil, know what I mean? Okay! Let's do this thing.

INTERVIEWER 2. You're Brett? You're thirty minutes late.

BRETT. I know, I know, I got caught up in conference call, a nightmare lunch meeting...and this girl I'm dating...blah blah blah...you know.

INTERVIEWER 2. Well, it's inconvenient for me. I have another prospective student...

BRETT. I know, I know, I've got a meet and greet in a fiver so let's just bulldoze through this thing, shall we?

INTERVIEWER 2. Well, alright...I guess—

BRETT. You know what? I'm gonna take the reigns here and skip the whole "you ask questions part." So here's me: I'm a self-motivator, I'm extremely competitive, and I'm the life of the party. I like your school's aggressive economic program, its ties to Harvard Business school, and its Greek social scene. Gonna pledge Alpha-Phi-Beta, or Delta-Kai-Delta...depending on the pledge class. My stats are well above your average so let's make this happen. If you're in the boat, I'm driving the ship. We good?

INTERVIEWER 2. No. Not at all.

BRETT. Cranberries, baby!

(BRETT *sticks his hand out for a fist bump.* INTERVIEWER 2 *doesn't respond. Not noticing,* BRETT *stands up and answers his phone.)*

BRETT. Whattup buttercup! Yeah, I just had to do this lame face-to-face, I'm on my way. Kidding me, nailed it! It's the Brettster you're talking about here.

(BRETT *leaves.* INTERVIEWER 2 *throws Brett's file in the trash.)*

Scene 6

(INTERVIEWER 1 *with* LILY.)

INTERVIEWER 1. Thanks again for coming in on such short notice.

LILY. Please, it was no trouble at all.

INTERVIEWER 1. So tell me about yourself. What subjects do you like in school, do you have any hobbies? You know stuff like that.

LILY. Hobbies? I have a few, I suppose. I used to be really into swimming but...I haven't...not since...that day...

(LILY *simmers with emotion.)*

INTERVIEWER 1. Are you okay? We don't have to...

LILY. No, it's okay...I want to, I...I need to talk about it. It was a blistering summer day, Bill Blakemore, Poughkeepsie's local weatherman, said it was one of the hottest days in recorded history and advised us to stay in at all costs. But I ignored his warnings. Swimming was my life and life... doesn't stop, not even for a handsome weatherman with salt and pepper hair. I went to the pool early, got on my swimming suit, and began my morning stretches. It was during my warm-ups that I saw him...a little boy, fiery red hair, freckles sprinkled across his pale white skin, teetering on the edge on the pool. Before I could even think to warn him, he tumbled into the watery abyss. His body thrashed about violently, his eyes closed shut from the sting of chlorine, his voice silenced from all the water he was swallowing. I jumped into the water and swam over as quickly as I could but...I was too late...he was...

(LILY is overcome with emotion.)

That was eight years ago and...I've never set foot in a pool since.

INTERVIEWER 1. Lily, that was very brave of you to share this with me. Witnessing a death like that...especially that of such a young child—

LILY. No, he didn't die.

INTERVIEWER 1. He didn't?

LILY. No, the lifeguard pulled him out of the water.

INTERVIEWER 1. Oh, well even seeing a near death experience—

LILY. He was only in the water a few seconds when the lifeguard pulled him out.

INTERVIEWER 1. He was?

LILY. Yes.

INTERVIEWER 1. I thought you said "it was too late"?

LILY. IT WAS TOO LATE FOR ME! I couldn't save him because...I was TOO ...late...

(LILY is overcome with emotion. INTERVIEWER 1 is confused.)

INTERVIEWER 1. So...you saw a child fall into the pool, and then a lifeguard pulled him out...and that...?

(LILY is too distraught to answer.)

INTERVIEWER 1. You know what, let's just...move on.

(LILY nods her head.)

INTERVIEWER 1. What is it about this school that interests you? Why do you want to come here?

LILY. There are many reasons I suppose but...only one that ever really mattered. It was a crisp day in March, much like today. Amanda Barker, my best friend since the third grade, and I were leaving Mrs. Fleener's excessively boring Geometry class. Amanda asked me if I had thought about applying to college. I told her, "a little." Then she told me about this university, how her sister was going here, and that I should "check it out." I said, "maybe...yeah." I was flippant, disregarding my best friend's advice with two little inarticulate words...and those words... were the last I ever said to Amanda.

(LILY is once again overcome with emotion.)

INTERVIEWER 1. I am...so sorry. Losing a best friend like that...I can't imagine how awful that must have been for you.

LILY. It was, it really was.

INTERVIEWER 1. How old was Amanda when she passed?

LILY. Passed?

INTERVIEWER 1. Died.

LILY. She didn't die.

INTERVIEWER 1. What?

LILY. No. She's going to Yale in the fall. She's very smart.

INTERVIEWER 1. I thought you said that was the last time you ever spoke to her.

LILY. It was. We had a falling out after that.

INTERVIEWER 1. A falling out, what like a big fight or...

LILY. No, we just went our separate ways. It was mutual.

INTERVIEWER 1. So...just to set the record straight. You saw a kid fall into a pool who was almost immediately picked up by a lifeguard, and you lost touch with a friend. These are the events that have shaped your life and caused you so much emotional distress?

LILY. You weren't there! You don't know what it's like to actually...be there and...see it!

(Beat. INTERVIEWER 1 *gives up.)*

INTERVIEWER 1. Well, it was great to meet you. I have a meeting in a few minutes, so...

LILY. Oh. Of course. Thank you for seeing me.

INTERVIEWER 1. And uh, I know it's not my place but...you might want to consider some kind of...therapy.

LILY. Therapy...yes, I...went to a therapist. Once. It was a chilly autumn day and I had been feeling...optimistic.

(INTERVIEWER 1 groans and slumps into his chair.)

Scene 7

(MELVIN sits across from INTERVIEWER 2, *lifting his shirt up and doing a drum solo on his stomach. It comes to a big finish.)*

MELVIN. And that was "Wipeout."

(INTERVIEWER 2 just stares.)

INTERVIEWER 2. ...Okay, well...

MELVIN. And now, the orchestral opening to *Sweeney Todd.*

(A few loud smacks on MELVIN's *tummy.* INTERVIEWER 2 *rubs his head.)*

Scene 8

(KELLY, tightly wound, a Stepford wife-ish smile, enters the room. INTERVIEWER 1 stands to greet her.)

INTERVIEWER 1. Hi, you must be Kelly.

KELLY. Yes! Hi...

INTERVIEWER 1. Great, take a seat.

KELLY. Sure!

INTERVIEWER 1. *(Opening her file:)* So, let's see here...oh! You know what, we never received your college essay.

KELLY. Is that right?!?

INTERVIEWER 1. Yeah, I'm not, uh, sure what happened. Do you have a copy of it?

KELLY. Oh absolutely. I've got it right here in my bag!

(She reaches into her bag, pulls out a single sheet of paper, and hands it to INTERVIEWER 1.)

INTERVIEWER 1. That's great, thank you...so, uh...I'm sorry, this is your college essay?

KELLY. That's right.

INTERVIEWER 1. But...it's...this is a drawing of a girl...in a pink dress... saying "oh boy!"

KELLY. Oh boy!

(A very awkward beat.)

INTERVIEWER 1. Okay, well, let's look at your transcript shall we...

(INTERVIEWER 1 opens Kelly's file and is speechless.)

INTERVIEWER 1. You have no GPA?

KELLY. That's right.

INTERVIEWER 1. And you didn't take the SATs?

KELLY. Well now, how about that!

INTERVIEWER 1. According to this, you have a perfect attendance record, but have refused do any homework or take any tests.

KELLY. That's right.

INTERVIEWER 1. But...Kelly, I'm not even sure how you got to this point. You can't go to college without a GPA.

KELLY. Perhaps you'd like to see my recommendation.

INTERVIEWER 1. No, Kelly, I'm...there is no way any University, let alone ours, is going to—

(KELLY hands INTERVIEWER 1 another piece of paper.)

INTERVIEWER 1. This is a picture of a cat...saying "meow."

KELLY. *(Correcting:)* Me-ow. Yes.

(KELLY *nods her head and gives a big "dead behind the eyes" smile.*)

INTERVIEWER 1. Well, thank you for coming, we'll be in touch.

KELLY. Alright then, you take care.

INTERVIEWER 1. Okay.

KELLY. Oh boy!

(KELLY *doesn't get up.)*

INTERVIEWER 1. Please leave, you're freaking me out.

(She doesn't.)

Scene 9

(JEFF, *slacker, is either asleep, dead, or in a coma, in his chair.* INTERVIEWER 2 *enters.)*

INTERVIEWER 2. Oh, sorry. Didn't know...uh...

(No response from JEFF.*)*

INTERVIEWER 2. Uh, hello, are you—

JEFF. What?

INTERVIEWER 2. You're awake?

JEFF. Yeah.

INTERVIEWER 2. I thought you were asleep.

JEFF. *(Annoyed:)* I'm not asleep, okay!

INTERVIEWER 2. Right. Sorry. So, should we get started?

JEFF. *(Tired:)* Whatever.

INTERVIEWER 2. Okay. So, what is it that made you interested in our university?

JEFF. I dunno.

INTERVIEWER 2. You don't know?

JEFF. *(Exasperated:)* I just...don't, okay!?! God!

INTERVIEWER 2. Okay, well...fine. So, what kind of things are you interested in? You know, school wise, or hobbies?

JEFF. Stuff.

INTERVIEWER 2. Stuff?

JEFF. And things.

INTERVIEWER 2. Stuff and things?

JEFF. Yeah! Stuff. Things! And whatever!

INTERVIEWER 2. Well you must do something?

JEFF. I eat. That usually wipes me out.

INTERVIEWER 2. But what about clubs, sports, social things?

JEFF. I tried to start a nap club once but man...it was so hard.

INTERVIEWER 2. To start a club where you...nap?

JEFF. Yeah, you have to fill out forms and stuff. And get signatures. And... get a...

(JEFF *trails off and spaces out.*)

INTERVIEWER 2. Jeff?

JEFF. What?

INTERVIEWER 2. But haven't you ever...been inspired to...do anything?

(JEFF *thinks, then sits up a little.*)

JEFF. Well there was one thing...I saw it on TV and it really got me thinking, in a motivated kinda way.

INTERVIEWER 2. Yeah? What was it?

JEFF. I was watching the news and there was this woman in the hospital and she...went into a coma from this weird stroke and...they kept trying and trying to get her out of it...like doctors spent years trying to revive her...but they never figured it out.

INTERVIEWER 2. So this made you...maybe interested in medicine? Or healthcare?

JEFF. No, it just made me jealous. This woman, she was like, having these tubes feed her and breathe for her. And they put on the TV all day. I mean you know how like sometimes, breathing is just like...so much work sometimes, ya know.

(*Beat.*)

INTERVIEWER 2. So...this inspired you...to be in a coma?

JEFF. Totally.

(INTERVIEWER 2 *slouches in his chair.*)

JEFF. What's the matter?

INTERVIEWER 2. I'm...just...tired.

JEFF. Yeah, me too.

(*They exhale.*)

Scene 10

(INTERVIEWER 1 *watches in horror as* EVE *belts out the end to* "Defying Gravity" *from* "Wicked.")

EVE. NOTHING'S GONNA BRING....ME......DOOOOOWWWWWWN!

(*Beat.*)

INTERVIEWER 1. Wow, well you are obviously very talented, but...again, and I can't stress this enough, this IS NOT the audition for the theatre program so...a monologue and two songs really aren't—

EVE. *(In full "Music Man" performance mode:)*
TROUBLE, OH WE GOT TROUBLE,
RIGHT HERE IN RIVER CITY!
WITH A CAPITAL "T"
THAT RHYMES WITH "P"
AND THAT STANDS FOR POOL...

Scene 11

(INTERVIEWER 2 *is wrapping up with* ELIZABETH, *pleasant, sweet, dressed in black.)*

INTERVIEWER 2. Well your grades, recommendations all look pretty good.

ELIZABETH. Thank you.

INTERVIEWER 2. Is there anything else you can tell me about yourself? Something that's maybe not on the page.

ELIZABETH. Yeah, let's see...I never played sports in school but I've played in a number of rec leagues. Volleyball, soccer, basketball. I volunteer at a soup kitchen every month, I'm a practicing vampire, and I teach sailing during the summer at a sleep away camp. Is that what you were looking for?

INTERVIEWER 2. Yeah, definitely, um...I'm sorry, can you...elaborate a little on, uh—

ELIZABETH. Soup Kitchen? Well, I actually started because of my parents. They were very big into community service.

INTERVIEWER 2. No, not... I'm sorry, it sounded like you said you were a "practicing vampire."

ELIZABETH. Oh. Yes. Pretty much my whole life.

INTERVIEWER 2. Okay. So...you think you're a vampire?

ELIZABETH. Oh, no, no, no. That would be, no...

INTERVIEWER 2. Oh, okay, I guess I'm a little—

ELIZABETH. I'm a practicing vampire. It's completely different.

INTERVIEWER 2. So is this like a club or...role playing game?

ELIZABETH. Um...no, it's more serious than that. Basically, I live my life in preparation for the day when I will, hopefully, turn into a vampire.

INTERVIEWER 2. Turn into?

ELIZABETH. Right. So, I sleep in a coffin, avoid garlic, eat lots of bloody meat, chew with my fangs...all in the hopes that one day, if I'm diligent enough...I will turn into a vampire.

INTERVIEWER 2. I see, uh...well then, uh, what are you doing here now? I mean, you shouldn't be out during the day, right?

ELIZABETH. That's a common stereotype. Vampires, just like humans, can walk freely in daylight without receiving even the slightest irritation to the skin.

INTERVIEWER 2. I see. So your more like those *Twilight* vampires.

(ELIZABETH gives INTERVIEWER 2 the evil eye.)

ELIZABETH. Is that an attempt at humor?

INTERVIEWER 2. No, I...

ELIZABETH. Because I don't find it funny, at all. In fact, I find it pretty insulting and frankly...pretty vampirist.

INTERVIEWER 2. Vampirist? Elizabeth! You're not going to turn into a vampire. There's no such thing as vampires!

(ELIZABETH stands up, extremely insulted.)

ELIZABETH. Wow. That may be the most offensive thing I've ever heard. I'm going to leave now.

INTERVIEWER 2. Are you...is this some kind of joke? Did Saunders put you up to this?

ELIZABETH. No, this is very serious. And when I get a hold of the NVUA, you're going to have a public relations nightmare on your hands.

INTERVIEWER 2. NVUA?

ELIZABETH. National Vampires Union Ah-ah-ah. All vampires should be respected and given blood.

INTERVIEWER 2. *(At the end of his rope:)* Alright, well, you go and call the NVUA and say hello to Dracula, and Lestat, and all those whiny *Twilight* kids.

ELIZABETH. Sure. I will. Because we're just all the same to you! Honestly, I expected more out of this university.

(ELIZABETH storms out. INTERVIEWER 2 rubs his head. He picks up his phone and dials the front.)

INTERVIEWER 2. *(Blowing off:)* A union for vampires. Pffa.

(INTERVIEWER 2 hangs up the phone. Then looks out the window suspiciously.)

Scene 12

(INTERVIEWER 1 and BEN are in mid laugh.)

BEN. And the entire audience is COMPLETELY drenched!

INTERVIEWER 1. Oh man! Wow!

BEN. Needless to say that was the LAST time I ever went to Sea World.

(The laughter peters out.)

INTERVIEWER 1. Well I've gotta tell you Ben, everything looks great. Solid SATs, GPA high above our school's average, and your essay was... well to be honest, quite moving.

BEN. Well, this is such a great university, I'd be honored to attend.

(They stand up and shake hands.)

INTERVIEWER 1. Hey, we'd be lucky to have you. Are you applying to any other schools?

BEN. Nope. Just here.

INTERVIEWER 1. Oh, okay, great. Great.

(Beat.)

BEN. So...

INTERVIEWER 1. Uh...yes?

BEN. I'm in then?

INTERVIEWER 1. Well, no. I mean not yet. I have to pass this along to my supervisors and...

(BEN releases his hand and sits down. Has a cold, calculating look on his face.)

INTERVIEWER 1. It's a process, you know, I can't officially—

BEN. *(Dead pan and intense:)* Sit down.

INTERVIEWER 1. What?

BEN. Sit down, won't you?

(INTERVIEWER 1 sits down.)

INTERVIEWER 1. Is there a problem?

BEN. That depends on you. You see, for reasons I can't entirely explain to you at this moment, it is vital that I attend this university. I've been meticulously planning for this day, years of SAT prep, AP classes, all in the hopes of being accepted. I was intending to hear an answer today.

INTERVIEWER 1. Well, I'm sorry, I...don't have the authority to just let you in right now.

BEN. There are forces at play here friend, forces that you cannot possibly comprehend. But trust me, it is very vital, and not just for me, but for the entire student body and faculty that I am enrolled for the fall semester. Many lives hang in the balance. You don't want to be held responsible for the loss of life, do you?

INTERVIEWER 1. Of course not...but...how is me letting you in today going to save lives?

BEN. The world is a series of connections and plans, every human being affects another, every decision has a consequence, and this decision... this decision will be the most important one you'll ever make.

INTERVIEWER 1. Ben, you're being incredibly vague and...besides, it's not as simple as "me letting you in."

BEN. An oral agreement is legally binding in this state. So, in fact, it is that simple.

INTERVIEWER 1. Look, what I can tell you is that it's practically a done deal, I'm going to give you a great recommendation, and with your stats—

BEN. THAT'S NOT...what I'm asking for.

(Tense beat.)

INTERVIEWER 1. Ben, let's not ruin what was a great interview by—

BEN. I'm not leaving until I get my answer.

INTERVIEWER 1. Well you're going to have to because I have another prospective coming in at one.

BEN. No you don't. Your four o'clock cancelled this morning. You don't have another appointment until Rebecca Smith at 4:45.

(Beat. INTERVIEWER 1 is now kinda freaked out.)

INTERVIEWER 1. How did you...did you break into my e-mail or something?

(BEN looks straight ahead.)

INTERVIEWER 1. Okay, you know what, I'm not sure what happened here, but I'm going to have to call security.

(INTERVIEWER 1 picks up the phone. He clicks the receiver a couple of times.)

INTERVIEWER 1. Hello I...hello, hello?

BEN. Phone troubles?

(INTERVIEWER 1 slowly puts the phone down. He gets up and backs away.)

BEN. Doors locked. And we're ten stories up so the windows wouldn't be a very...safe option either.

INTERVIEWER 1. Alright, who are you?

BEN. A name is but a label, and I have many labels but that's not important right now. What's important is that you, tell me, right now...exactly what I was hoping to hear.

INTERVIEWER 1. Ben if I could I would, it's just—

(The lights go out. BEN immediately turns a flashlight, under-lighting his face. When INTERVIEWER 1 talks, he points the light on him.)

BEN. It's only an outtage friend. Circuits break all the time.

INTERVIEWER 1. Please, I don't have any real authority. An acceptance from me would be meaningless—

BEN. Then there's no reason not to say it.

INTERVIEWER 1. Why are you doing this?

BEN. I'm not doing this, you're doing this. And it can all go away with three little words—

INTERVIEWER 1. But it won't—

BEN. NO! THOSE AREN'T THE RIGHT WORDS! SAY IT! JUST SAY IT!

INTERVIEWER 1. Okay! I...you've been accepted. You've been accepted. You'll be enrolled in the fall semester upon hearing of your acceptance.

> *(The lights come back on. BEN turns the lights off. A tense moment, then...)*

BEN. *(Switching back:)* Oh man! That's great! I can't even tell you how... I gotta call my mom. It was so nice to meet you.

> *(BEN cheerily leaves the room. INTERVIEWER 1 collapses into his seat.)*

Scene 13

> *(JASON THE AMAZING [though not really]! Cape, top hat, pulls out a card.)*

JASON. So then is THIS your card?

INTERVIEWER 2. No.

JASON. But where there's a diamond, there must be a...Jack of all trades...in clubs.

INTERVIEWER 2. Still not my card.

JASON. Darn it. I was practicing all week.

INTERVIEWER 2. Look, I'm very glad you have hobbies outside of school, but maybe we can get back to—

JASON. Oh, sure, sure, sure. After...you show me the card UNDERNEATH YOUR SEAT.

> *(INTERVIEWER 2 looks under his/her seat and picks up a playing card.)*

INTERVIEWER 2. "Rules on how to Play Texas Hold 'em?"

JASON. And who makes the rules, but a KING.

INTERVIEWER 2. Hey, that's actually my card.

JASON. Really?

INTERVIEWER 2. No.

JASON. Okay, okay...let's try this. Pick a number between one and five thousand. NO, wait, first tell me your favorite color, then pick a number.

Scene 14

(INTERVIEWER 2 *enters* INTERVIEWER 1's *office, defeated.*)

INTERVIEWER 1. Not one?

INTERVIEWER 2. Not a single...one.

INTERVIEWER 1. This is bad.

INTERVIEWER 2. This is...extremely bad.

INTERVIEWER 1. You must have been too critical. I'm sure you saw at least one kid we could recommend.

INTERVIEWER 2. Hey, if you want to look through my files, be my guest.

(INTERVIEWER 1 *looks through* INTERVIEWER 2's *files.*)

INTERVIEWER 2. Well if you're gonna look at mine, then I'm gonna look at yours.

(*They read in silence for a bit.*)

INTERVIEWER 1. What does "practicing vampire" mean?

(INTERVIEWER 2 *closes the file for him/her and shakes his/her head "no." They continue to look.*)

INTERVIEWER 2. Whoa, what about Ben? He got a near perfect SAT score and his GPA—

INTERVIEWER 1. NO!

INTERVIEWER 2. But his SATs—

INTERVIEWER 1. No...just...trust me.

(*A knock on the door.* EMILY *comes in.*)

EMILY. Hi, my name's Emily Court...I have an appointment at 5?

INTERVIEWER 1. Oh my Gosh, right. Sorry, I...got a little side tracked.

EMILY. Oh, no problem, should I wait?

INTERVIEWER 1. No, please, come in, uh...

(INTERVIEWER 1 *looks for her file.* INTERVIEWER 2 *finds it and gives it to* INTERVIEWER 1.)

INTERVIEWER 1. Okay. Thank you. Um...Emily, so...wow, nice record. Valedictorian of your class? They decided that already?

EMILY. Normally they wait until the end of the year but...I guess my GPA was too high for anyone to catch up to me. I mean, there are a lot of really bright students at the school, so...I was just as surprised to find out this early.

INTERVIEWER 2. I'm also really impressed with the variety of after school programs you've amassed. First chair cellist, president of the student council, member of the thespians, and treasurer for something called the "relief club."

EMILY. It was a club formed by me and three friends as a public outreach...we do shelter meals, food drives, build houses...there wasn't really anything like that at our school.

(INTERVIEWER 1 and INTERVIEWER 2 *look at each other in glee. Finally.)*

INTERVIEWER 1. Well, Emily, we should tell you that...

(EMILY's phone rings. EMILY *scrambles to answer it.)*

EMILY. I'm so sorry. I never leave my phone on normally it's just... *(She looks at the number:)* ...this is my mom, I told her not to call unless it was really, really, urgent—

INTERVIEWER 1. No, go ahead. It's fine.

EMILY. I'm so sorry. I'll be quick. *(Answering her phone:)* Hello? Yeah, no it's going fine. Any news? Oh my God! OH MY GOD! I GOT IN! I AM OFFICIALLY AN IVY LEAGUER! AAAAAHHHHH!!!

(EMILY dances around, ecstatic.)

EMILY. And what about the Scholarship...? ...Are you kidding me! ARE YOU...but they hardly give out any money let alone a free ride! OH MY GOD! MOM! I'm gonna cry, I...I know it's all happening...I... *(To the Interviewers:)* I'm sorry, I just have to...thank you, sorry...

(EMILY leaves the room, screaming, jumping, etc.)

(The two INTERVIEWERS sit for a moment, deflated.)

(INTERVIEWER 1 looks through a file sadly.)

INTERVIEWER 1. This guy does magic.

(INTERVIEWER 2 closes the file. They sit.)

End of Play

DARCY'S CINEMATIC LIFE

by Christa Crewdson

Cast of Characters

DARCY, fifteen years old. Smart, sensitive, and strong
LIZA, a very popular girl who dislikes Darcy because she refuses to act like the rest of the "in crowd"
TIFFANY, sidekick to Liza
VICTORIA, sidekick to Liza
CHAD, the love interest, sweet, but not so bright
DARCY'S MOM, kind, means well, but is not real hip
DARCY'S DAD, supportive, loves his daughter
TONY, Darcy's little bratty brother

Ensemble members play the following small roles:

KINDERGARTEN CLASSMATES
DARCY'S CLASSMATES
DARCY'S TEACHERS: MS. NIBBS, MR. FRANK, MR. B.
THE TWINS, from her marriage in a daydream sequence
REPORTERS
JIM
A SOUTHERN LAWYER
BAILIFF
JUDGE
JURY
TWO GAP WORKERS
TWO MALL RAT BOYS
TWO MALL RAT GIRLS
NERD FASHION SHOW RUNWAY MODELS
THE DRAGON
SCREAMING FANS
TOWNSFOLK
MR. D., the chaperone on the bus
BUS DRIVER

Acknowledgments

Darcy's Cinematic Life was originally produced at Boston Latin School, May 2005. It was performed by students in the Connections Program, class of 2009.

For My Husband

DARCY'S CINEMATIC LIFE

(Blank stage. Light up on DARCY *who is Center Stage.)*

DARCY. I'm Darcy. Some people think I'm

(Light up on LIZA.)

LIZA. Weird.

(Light up on MOM.)

MOM. Darling.

(Light up on LITTLE BROTHER.)

BROTHER. Dorky.

(Light up on TEACHER.)

TEACHER. Unique.

DARCY. I like to think of myself as a highly creative citizen of the universe. I am certainly not your typical teen. Teen. I hate that word. I am not a teen, I am a person of above average intelligence. And in addition to my above average intelligence, I have what people call...

MOM. An overactive imagination.

TEACHER. A daydreaming problem.

DARCY. I prefer to think of it as my mind creating little movies in my head. It is not daydreaming. You see, I get to thinking of something and my mind just takes over. Thoughts come to life, right before my eyes. It's...

MOM. An overactive imagination.

DARCY. That's my mom. I also have a...

BROTHER. Dork.

DARCY. Little brother. And a...

DAD. Hi, pumpkin.

DARCY. Dad. I also have a nemesis, and arch enemy...Liza.

(Light up on LIZA.)

LIZA. Liza.

DARCY. Liza. Who pronounces it that way? Liza and I have had...

MOM. Issues.

DARCY. Issues, since kindergarten. She's one of the perfect people. You know the perfect people. I know you do. In other words she's a...

MOM. Nice girl. Why don't you invite her over?

DARCY. Like in any good story, there is also a true love.

(Light up on CHAD.)

CHAD. Chad.

DARCY. Chad. I have been in love with Chad since preschool. But he, well...

(CHAD looks at her.)

CHAD. Hi Katie.

DARCY. It's Darcy. He doesn't really feel the same way. But I'm getting ahead of myself. I should start at the beginning. I've always been different. See in kindergarten...

> *(Music begins—The Jackson Five's "ABC." ENSEMBLE enters as children and creates the preschool. DARCY joins the group.)*

MS. NIBBS. Different people have different things that are important to them. Today we have all brought in things that are important to us. Who would like to share first? Gail?

> *(GAIL stands in front of the class.)*

GAIL. This is Boo.

MS. NIBBS. I can't quite see what Boo is.

GAIL. It's Boo.

MS. NIBBS. Boo seems to be a...uh...a string.

GAIL. Boo!

MS. NIBBS. Well, Boo seems like a...very good...friend. Who's next? Chad?

> *(CHAD rises.)*

CHAD. I have Hoppy.

MS. NIBBS. And who is Hoppy?

CHAD. My frog.

MS. NIBBS. Is Hoppy in the box? Let's see. *(Takes box and opens it.)* Chad, did you poke holes in the box for Hoppy to breathe?

CHAD. No.

MS. NIBBS. Oh dear.

CHILD. I want to see Hoppy!

MS. NIBBS. Well, Hoppy is...sleeping right now.

CHAD. I something wrong with Hoppy?

MS. NIBBS. No, he's just...

> *(CHAD grabs the box.)*

CHAD. Hoppy? Hoppy? What's wrong with Hoppy?

MS. NIBBS. Chad, sometimes pets move on to heaven and...

> *(DARCY jumps up and grabs the box and begins to act like a surgeon in an episode of ER.)*

DARCY. Give me some room people! You *(To teacher:)* compress on his chest while I give him mouth to mouth. Have the crash cart standing by.

MS. NIBBS. What?

DARCY. Just do it!

MS. NIBBS. I don't know...

DARCY. Pull yourself together woman! *(Mouth to mouth ensues.)* 1, 2, 3, 4, 5...1, 2, 3, 4, 5

CHAD. Hoppy's alive!!!! He's alive!!!!

> *(Class cheers and teacher collapses in her chair.* CHAD *looks at* DARCY *in awe until, in all the celebration,* LIZA *smiles at him, and then he is transfixed.)*

MS. NIBBS. Ok, everyone settle down. We have time for one more presentation. Liza?

LIZA. I brought some of my Barbies. I have every single Barbie there is. I have Rollerblading Barbie, Beach Party Barbie, Prom Barbie.

> *(Smiles at* CHAD.*)*

DARCY. *(Steps out of the scene as her older self.)* Barbie—the wonder or obsession of young girls everywhere. Beach Party Barbie? What about a Barbie that could be a role model? How about Neurosurgeon Barbie, or President Barbie?

LIZA. And Cheerleader Barbie.

DARCY. And as she droned on endlessly naming Barbies my mind created one of my movies and all of a sudden Liza was a Barbie.

> *(ENSEMBLE fades away except for LIZA and two girls.)*

And two little girls were playing with her. Then they began fighting over her, pulling and pulling until her arms popped off!

> *(We see this happen. LIZA runs off screaming. DARCY laughs. The classroom scene is recreated and DARCY is back in the scene.)*

MS. NIBBS. Darcy, it's rude to laugh at other people!

> *(ENSEMBLE fades away. DARCY speaks to the audience as her older self.)*

DARCY. Not much has changed since then. It's like that movie *Groundhog Day.* Every school day is the same. Liza is mean to me, Chad ignores me and I try to find ways to amuse myself in this institution of monotony. Anyway, I have to confess that for the first time in my life I am grappling with a problem. A...ugh...teen problem. I am after all only human, as much as I hate to admit it. I'm talking about the impending class trip to the art museum. Now I know you might think a field trip to the museum is no big deal but to a slightly different, semi-outcast like myself, it is a major deal. There are many critical factors *(Uses visual aides—charts and graphs during the following speech:)* 1) Who you sit next to on the bus. It's a long ride, not to mention everyone will be judging who you sit with. 2) Finding a group to hang with for the day. This strategy is a little more difficult. My normal strategy is to stand close enough to an "accepted group" to look like I am with them, but not close enough for them to know I am there. To an outside observer it appears that I am part of the group. *(ENSEMBLE enters and begins to set the classroom scene—present day.)* This requires extreme concentration, extreme planning...

DARCY. Homeroom.

MR. FRANK. Darcy?

DARCY. Here.

MR. FRANK. Chad?

CHAD. Here.

MR. FRANK. Liza?

LIZA. *Liza.* Here.

MR. FRANK. Victoria?

VICTORIA. Here.

MR. FRANK. Tiffany?

TIFFANY. Here.

> (MR. FRANK *continues to call names softly during the following dialogue.)*

LIZA. Is this field trip tomorrow going to be lame or what?

VICTORIA. I know. The Art Institute. Whatever.

TIFFANY. How come we never take a field trip to like go shopping on Michigan Avenue?

LIZA. Really! Who cares about a bunch of paintings by some dead guys?

DARCY. Actually, the Art Institute is one of the most famous museums in the world. It is the cultural gem of our city of Chicago. It houses many famous works including Georges Seurat's *A Sunday on La Grande Latte.*

LIZA. Who? La what?

DARCY. Georges Seurat, with what resembles scientific precision, tackled the issues of color, light, and form. Inspired by research in optical and color theory, he juxtaposed tiny dots of colors that, through optical blending, form a single and, Seurat believed, more brilliantly luminous hue in the viewer's eye. To make the experience of the painting even more intense, he surrounded it with a frame of painted dots, which in turn he enclosed with a pure white, wooden frame, which is how the painting is exhibited today.

LIZA. So?

DARCY. Billions of tiny little dots that all come together to form one painting? You don't think that's amazing?

LIZA. No. The only dots I'm concerned with are the different colored dots they use to mark the sales at Saks Fifth Avenue. A pink dot is 50% off. A brown dot is 40%...

CHAD. Hey, were you guys talking about that painting with the dots?

LIZA. Yes.

CHAD. That painting is awesome. It's pretty tripped out.

DARCY. Ok, I am aware that Chad is not an intellectual, and I am perfectly content with that. I am smart enough for the two of us.

CHAD. Art is cool.

DARCY. The sound of his voice invokes a movie—one I have seen many times before. "The poet's eye, in a fine frenzy rolling, doth glance from heaven to earth, from earth to heaven, and as imagination bodies forth the forms of things unknown, the poet's pen turn them to shapes, and gives to airy nothing a local habitation and a name." That's Shakespeare.

> *(ENSEMBLE changes to a prom scene. MR. FRANK walks around, separates kids. Kids dance, and music plays. LIZA stands alone glaring as CHAD and DARCY dance.)*

DARCY. *(To audience:)* Fast forward to high school. Me and Chad at the prom!

CHAD. Darcy, these past four years have been the best of my life.

DARCY. Mine too!

CHAD. I can't bear the thought of being away from you next year so I want you to promise that you won't so much as look at another guy at college.

DARCY. I won't.

CHAD. I want to give you this. *(Hands her a ring.)*

DARCY. Oh Chad, it's beautiful.

CHAD. It's just a little ring until I can afford to buy you a real engagement ring.

DARCY. Cut to the future—our wedding.

> *(ENSEMBLE creates this scene. MOM and DAD and BROTHER enter. MOM cries at the ceremony.)*

DARCY. Then twins!

> *(Two ENSEMBLE members dressed alike, pop their heads out from behind a baby carriage. MOM cries.)*

DARCY. And we spend our twilight years sipping lemonade on the porch. In our home, home, home.

LIZA. *(Simultaneously with Darcy's line:)* Homeroom is over Darcy.

> *(They exit, CHAD knocks a book off her desk by accident as he exits. Bell rings. Ensemble shifts to a hallway scene, people wander, bumping into each other.)*

DARCY. The hallway.

> *(LIZA bumps into her.)*

LIZA. Sorry. *(Laughs with TIFFANY and VICTORIA.)*

DARCY. Passing in the halls takes skill. The 48.2 feet from homeroom to science class is a treacherous path. I find that studying old football films helps to create a strategy of navigation—find the holes. The 1985 Chicago Bears films are the best.

(The ENSEMBLE *enter and set themselves on opposite sides of the stage. The movement that follows is staged as a slow motion football play. When* DARCY *passes through, the* ENSEMBLE *breaks out of slow motion and creates the science class scene. Kids are at tables with goggles. A mad scientist looking teacher stands before the class.)*

MR. B. Settle, settle.

DARCY. Science class. This is the one place I have a little clout because of my superior knowledge in this particular field. I am always flooded with offers of...

ENSEMBLE. Will you be my lab partner?

DARCY. I know I'm being used, but it might secure me a seat on that bus.

*(*LIZA *crosses to* DARCY.*)*

MR. B. Projects are due today as you know.

LIZA. *(To* DARCY:*)* You did the project, right?

DARCY. Of course.

LIZA. Good.

MR. B. Group 1—your presentation please.

ENSEMBLE MEMBER. We explored the chemical reaction of substance 1, sugar *(Pours into vial.)* and substance 2, salt. *(Pours into vial. Nothing happens.)*

MR. B. So you have proven that there is no reaction?

ENSEMBLE MEMBER. I guess so.

MR. B. Boring. F. Next group.

DARCY. I... I mean we, have reached our limit or have surpassed the boundaries of the typical 8th grade science project. Right Liza?

LIZA. We have?

MR. B. You have?

DARCY. So, I... I mean we, decided to conduct a social experiment. We took a homeless man, we will call him Jim, and gave him the tools he needed to succeed in society. We bathed him, fed him, typed up a resume and found him a job at Home Depot. I...we, proved that humankind can bounce back from the edge of desperation and despair if given the chance. Jim, come on in.

(JIM enters.)

DARCY. Tell us how you are today Jim?

JIM. Great, they made me Assistant Manager today at the Depot!

DARCY. "The way for a young man to rise is to improve himself every way he can, never suspecting that anybody wishes to hinder him." —Abraham Lincoln.

(He winks/flirts with LIZA *who is horrified. The rest of the class is speechless.)*

MR. B. A⁺?

(ENSEMBLE moves in a mechanical/robotic way creating the lunch line.)

DARCY. Lunch. A social jungle. Finding a seat is the equivalent to a pinball game. *(She, as if in a pinball game, bounces from table to table—kids yell "Saved" when she reaches a seat. Finally she sits.)* T-minus 22 hours and counting until the field trip. I try to ignore the maddening noise of the cafeteria. But the sound of adolescent shrieking creates the next movie. The shrieks become those of my adoring fans as I take the stage for my national tour. I am Darcy, international pop star. Diva of all divas! I am the envy of every teen in the world! Ok, I might be a brain but I'm allowed to have typical adolescent girl fantasies ok?

*(*DARCY *and* ENSEMBLE *members create a dance routine complete with screaming fans.* MOM *is there crying again. Bell rings and* ENSEMBLE *recreates hallway scene traffic.)*

DARCY. T-minus 18 hours and counting. As I stand upon the precipice of the school curb I await my next horror: the dreaded clothes shopping with mom, fully equipped with little brother.

*(*DARCY, MOM, *and* BROTHER *form the car, bouncing and swerving in chairs.)*

MOM. How was your day?

DARCY. Fine.

MOM. Tony, sit down. Anything new?

DARCY. No.

MOM. Fine. Tony sit down. Is anything wrong?

DARCY. No.

MOM. Fine. Tony sit down. Here we are!

DARCY. The mall. The most horrific place on earth. *(ENSEMBLE creates the mall scene—people shop, kids gossip, etc.)* Miles and miles of identical stores.

2 ENSEMBLE MEMBERS. Hi, welcome to The Gap.

DARCY. Identical food.

2 ENSEMBLE MEMBERS. Burger? Fries?

DARCY. And identical people.

2 ENSEMBLE GIRLS. Like oh my god!

2 ENSEMBLE BOYS. Dude, no way!

DARCY. I would rather travel 100 miles to Indiana to shop rather than come here where everyone shops. With my luck I always run into...

MOM. Isn't that your friend Liza?

DARCY. Mom, she's not my friend.

MOM. Darcy, she's walking this way, it's rude not to say hello.

DARCY. Rude is what I'm going for mom.

MOM. Hello Liza.

LIZA. Hello. Hi Darcy.

DARCY. Hi.

MOM. Doing a little shopping?

LIZA. Yes we are. Darcy, I didn't know you shopped here.

MOM. Well, we thought we'd splurge. You know, live a little.

LIZA. I think Darcy looks great in anything she wears. No one can pull off girls clothes from Sears like Darcy.

DARCY. Well, we really have to go. Right mom?

MOM. If you want to shop with your friends for a while that's ok with me.

DARCY. *(To audience:)* "There is no better indication of a man's character than the company which he keeps."—Machiavelli.

MOM. What honey?

DARCY. Nothing. Really mom, let's just go!

MOM. Bye girls. Nice to see you.

LIZA. Bye Darcy.

MOM. I don't know what your problem is with her. She seems like such a nice person.

> (ENSEMBLE *members create a clothing store—mannequins, shoppers, customers, clerks.)*

DARCY. I don't bother to try and explain to my mom anymore that encounters like these are fake, not to mention incredibly painful. She only sees what she wants to—that her daughter is friends with nice girls like Liza.

MOM. *(Points to a dress.)* Isn't this darling!

DARCY. Darling is not the word I would choose.

MOM. Oh! Look at this!

DARCY. Mom's idea of fashion is...is...well...even my superior vocabulary can't find the right word, so I'll use my little brother's favorite word— dorky. If she had her way, I'd be all buttoned up and in plaid or some other monstrosity. Cut to the first scene in the next movie—the mom fashion show—mom, a designer having her clothes modeled on the runway...

> (ENSEMBLE *members walk the runway in very nerdy clothes in Paris style fashion show—lots of attitude, others play photographers, a song plays throughout.)*

DARCY. T-minus 18 minutes to the field trip. Dinner. The definition of dinner in Webster's should be "a time where families sit down together to eat and try to make their dull, boring lives sound interesting."

(Family members create the dinner table scene.)

DAD. This squash is delicious honey.

MOM. Thank you.

*(*BROTHER *burps.)*

MOM. Tony!

DAD. So, guess who sold the Thompson house today?

DARCY. My dad sells real estate. He tries to make it sound glamorous, as if he's selling mansions, but he mostly handles split ranches and vacant lots.

MOM. You?!?

DAD. No, actually, Pete Piker did. I was so close to selling that worthless piece of...

MOM. Honey!

DAD. Land. I was going to say land. Pete Piker slides on in and sells it right out from under my nose.

BROTHER. I shot a spit ball at Lydia McDermott today. It hit the back of her head. She didn't even notice, so she walked around with it all day.

DARCY. *(To audience:)* See? I wish my family was one of those loud families in the movies where everyone is animated and emotions fly around the room. Now that would be exciting!

(Family changes into loud, Sopranos-like boisterous family.)

DAD. This pasta is perfect!

MOM. Of course it is. It's Mama's recipe. God rest her soul.

*(*BROTHER *burps.)*

MOM. Antonio!

DAD. What's the matter with you? So, guess who sold the Thompson house today?

MOM. You?!?

DAD. No, that no good Pete Piker did. I was so close to selling that worthless piece of...

MOM. Mario! Watch your language. The children!

BROTHER. I've heard it all before.

DAD. Where? I bet that little weasel friend of yours Benito says stuff like that.

DARCY. Benito is cute.

DAD. Cute? If I ever see you so much as look at that no good...

MOM. Mario!

DARCY. I'll look at who I want!

DAD. Oh no you won't! Not as long as you live under my roof!

MOM. Mario!

DARCY. Well maybe I'll move out!

DAD. You're 13! Where are you going to go?

BROTHER. Can I move out too dad?

MOM. Antonio!

DAD. I am the head of this household and what I say goes! And I say no one is moving out!! Except maybe me!

MOM. Mario!

(Scene escalates to yelling and then transitions back into reality.)

DAD. Pass the yams please.

DARCY. Then after dinner—TV.

(BROTHER and SISTER move to sit in front of a TV.)

BROTHER. It's my night.

DARCY. No, it's not. It's Wednesday, so it's my night.

BROTHER. Aw, we have to watch that stupid *Law & Order.* I hate that show. It's so boring!

DARCY. No, it's not. If you gave it a chance you might learn something.

BROTHER. Yeah? Like what?

DARCY. Like how to tell when someone might be out to do you in.

(Glares at BROTHER who looks scared.)

(To audience:) I can never concentrate on what's on. My mind just takes over.

(Law & Order music. ENSEMBLE creates a courtroom scene. LIZA is on the stand. Other ENSEMBLE members make up the BAILIFF, STENOGRAPHER, JURY, JUDGE, and DARCY'S LAWYER.)

BAILIFF. Case number 261, Darcy versus Liza.

TIFFANY & VICTORIA. *Liza!*

JUDGE. Order!

BAILIFF. Darcy is suing Liza for emotional damages, pain, and suffering.

LAWYER. *(Southern, showy character:)* Your honor, ladies and gentlemen of the jury, I shall prove beyond a shadow of a doubt that Liza...

TIFFANY & VICTORIA. Liza!

JUDGE. Order!

LAWYER. That Liza has caused years of emotional suffering for my client, Darcy. Although Darcy is an extremely successful, well adjusted young woman, she is here today to set an example, to prove a point, to stand up for all highly intelligent, above average, citizens of the universe that are tormented by the perfect people! I call Liza to the stand.

BAILIFF. Do you swear...

LIZA. Whatever.

LAWYER. How do you know Darcy?

LIZA. We go to school together.

LAWYER. I see. And how would you classify your relationship?

LIZA. Relationship? We have no relationship.

LAWYER. Haven't you on occasion been lab partners?

LIZA. Yes.

LAWYER. And didn't you take credit for work she did.

LIZA. I helped!

LAWYER. How? How did you help?

LIZA. I...well...I...

LAWYER. What were the projects you helped with?

LIZA. The one with the thingy.

LAWYER. The thingy?

LIZA. Yeah, the thingy.

LAWYER. Isn't it true that you simply took credit for the work?

LIZA. No.

LAWYER. Isn't it true that you were hanging out with your friends while Darcy did all the work?

LIZA. No.

LAWYER. Isn't it true that you used Darcy to get a good grade?

LIZA. No.

LAWYER. Isn't it true that you have done nothing but torment Darcy since kindergarten?

LIZA. NO.

LAWYER. Isn't it true LIZA, that you take great joy in making others feel bad?

LIZA. No. *(Starting to break down.)*

LAWYER. Isn't it true that you are the most wicked, evil, cruel girl on the face of this earth?

LIZA. No.

LAWYER. Isn't it true that inside you are an empty, insecure person, and that's why you torment others—to make yourself feel better? Isn't it? Isn't it?!!!!!

LIZA. Yes, yes, it's all true!

LAWYER. I rest my case.

(DARCY steps forward. ENSEMBLE fades away. Alarm clock goes off.)

DARCY. T-minus 3 hours until the trip. Morning. Mornings around here are pretty typical. Lots of rushing, complaining, scarfing down food and running out the door.

(Family enters and is rushing around.)

MOM. *(To* DARCY:*)* Honey, go back upstairs and put on that nice outfit we bought yesterday. For heaven's sake you're going to the Art Institute today! You need to dress appropriately!

DARCY. Mom, no one else is going to be dressed up. I'll look ridiculous!

BROTHER. What's new?

MOM. Tony! Young lady, go change. We don't have time to argue!

DARCY. Fine!

MOM. Where's Scruffy?

BROTHER. Where's my hockey stick?

DAD. Hon, where are my car keys?

BROTHER. We're out of Pop-tarts?! What the...

DAD. Tony!

MOM. Scruffy? Here girl!

BROTHER. Scruffy's a girl?

DAD. Hon, car keys?

BROTHER. I thought Scruffy was a boy.

DAD. Hon, car keys?

MOM. Scruffy? No dear, Scruffy's a girl.

BROTHER. Ew. A girl? Why the heck is a girl dog named Scruffy?

MOM. *(To* DAD:*)* Help me out here will ya?

DAD. Son, we didn't want to upset you. When we first got Scruffy home you gave him that name. After the first visit to the vet, your mother and I were informed that Scruffy was a her...a she.

BROTHER. Why didn't you tell me?

MOM. What does it matter?

BROTHER. I hate girls!!

DAD. Has anyone seen my keys?

MOM. This is good. I'm glad you know about Scruffy. Now she can start showing her feminine side.

BROTHER. Ugh!!!! *(Exits.)*

DAD. Keys? Anyone?

MOM. Scruffy? Scruffilina? Muffy Scruffy? *(Exits.)*

DAD. Where's the phone book? I need to call a taxi. *(Exits.)*

DARCY. I've always loved those old movies where there's a scene that takes place in the morning and introduces you to the quaint little town where the movie takes place. I wish that mornings were like that around here. I wish that my walk to school was a cornucopia of hellos and well wishes from neighbors and shopkeepers.

(ENSEMBLE *forms a quaint town scene complete with fruit vendor, children playing, riding bikes, kids having potato sack races, shopkeepers sweeping.)*

KID ON BIKE. Morning Darcy!

SHOPKEEPER SWEEPING. Hiya Darcy!

FLOWER SELLER. Be sure to tell your mother I said hello!

FARMER WITH CHICKENS. You sure do look pretty today Darcy!

WOMAN WITH PACKAGES. *(She drops some,* DARCY *picks them up.)* Why thank you Darcy. You're the sweetest thing!

> *(The idyllic scene continues until the* ENSEMBLE *becomes the present day hustle of kids going to school.)*

DARCY. Then there's reality.

> (KID *zooms by on bike.)*

KID. Out of my way!

> (LIZA, VICTORIA, *and* TIFFANY *walk by and bump into her.)*

LIZA. Sorry, I didn't see you. Oh, did you buy that cute little outfit at the mall yesterday?

DARCY. No, I pulled it out of a dumpster on the way to school today and put it on.

VICTORIA. It looks like it.

DARCY. Well, at least I made an effort to look like I am going to a museum, not a Britney Spears concert.

TIFFANY. Ugh, like no one listens to Britney anymore.

DARCY. You're missing the point.

LIZA. Well excuse us. I guess we don't know what to wear to go stand in front of a painting and look at a bunch of dots!

TIFFANY. Who's going to be looking at the paintings? I'm gonna be looking at the guys from the other schools!

LIZA. And they'll all be looking at us! *(Looks at* DARCY.) "Us" doesn't include you of course.

DARCY. Of course. "It has been said that a pretty face is a passport. But it's not, it's a visa and it runs out fast."

LIZA. Whatever.

> *(They leave laughing.* ENSEMBLE *enters and creates the homeroom again.)*

MR. FRANK. Ok, I think you all know what I expect of you today. Only your best behavior at the museum will suffice.

DARCY. T-minus 13 minutes until the trip. I can't do it. I have to think of some way out! I could pretend to have an allergic reaction to something. No, that's done too much. The last successful fake allergic reaction was two years ago—Terry Anderson in math said he was allergic to Ms.

Vessy's perfume. That bought him a whole extra day to study for the final. I could cut off my leg with a pencil. No, that would take too much time. I could fake a demonic possession. No, too Hollywood. I have to face the music, I'm going to have to get on that bus.

MR. FRANK. Ok, let's head out.

(DARCY and the ENSEMBLE walk in a line following the teacher.)

DARCY. I feel like I'm in a chain gang heading to prison. *(The line takes on the chain gang feel and ominous music plays until we reach the bus.)* Oh yellow nemesis of mine. I have been awaiting your cruel fate. Ok, this is it. Got to get just the right seat. I'll have exactly 8.5 seconds once on the bus to survey the seating choices. *(They enter the bus set up. DARCY stands in the aisle surveying the seats and the kids.)* Choice one—Lenny the loner. Choice two—Renee the mooch. Choice three—Mr. Donovan, Steve Donovan's dad. A chaperone. *(DARCY stands undecided and is pushed down into the seat next to MR. DONOVAN by some passing kids. She looks miserable.)* "I would consent to have a limb amputated to recover my sprits."—Samuel Johnson.

MR. D. Well, that's an odd name for a girl.

DARCY. That's not my name I was...never mind. *(To audience:)* In addition to my extreme motion sickness, I am listening to Mr. Donovan's forty-five minute story of how difficult it is to have automatic sprinklers put in your lawn.

MR. D. So who would have thought that titanium would work. Not me. No siree.

DARCY. Finally the museum. *(ENSEMBLE exits the bus and other members form the museum scene. Some are patrons, paintings, sculptures.)* To distract myself from the failure of good positioning on the bus, I will focus my mind on the museum. I've been here many times so I know exactly where all the exhibits are that I like. I'll try to share some of my knowledge of art with my fellow classmates.

(Three groups of students are spread out in front of paintings. She approaches group one.)

DARCY. Concentrating on outdoor scenes of everyday life, Monet attempted, in such works as *On the Bank of the Seine, Bennecourt,* to capture conditions of light and atmosphere with bright colors and lively, broken brush strokes.

STUDENT 1. I wonder where the snack bar is?

(DARCY approaches group two.)

DARCY. Van Gogh's self-portraits reveal the profound insecurity and frustration of a gifted man, whose odyssey in search of acceptance and peace of mind is powerfully expressed in his work.

STUDENT 2. I think this is the dude that cut off his ear.

STUDENT 3. Sick!

DARCY. I give up.

(ENSEMBLE *fades away and* CHAD *is left by himself to look at a painting.* DARCY *thinks for a minute, starts to exit, then summons her courage and walks over to him.*)

DARCY. Well, Jean-Luc Godard said that art attracts us only by what it reveals of our most secret self.

CHAD. I always knew that Star Trek show was deep.

DARCY. Excuse me?

CHAD. Jean Luc Picard, Captain of the Enterprise on *Star Trek the Next Generation.* He was always saying deep stuff like that.

DARCY. No I meant...never mind. So, you like the painting?

CHAD. Yeah, I do.

DARCY. Me too. No artist has dominated the 20th century in the way Pablo Picasso has. Though Spanish, he spent most of his life in France, and produced a body of work in a variety of styles that influenced nearly every major trend of the first half of this century.

CHAD. I wonder who this is a picture of?

DARCY. His subjects were society's outcasts, lonely figures.

CHAD. I wonder why he's lonely?

DARCY. Maybe no one understands him. Maybe he feels like he was born during the wrong time or place. Maybe he feels good about himself, he's just waiting to find where he belongs.

CHAD. You get all that from just looking at the painting?

DARCY. Kind of. That's just my interpretation though. Why do you think he looks so sad?

CHAD. Maybe he wants to be alone, so he can be himself. I mean, maybe he's sick of everyone always expecting him to be their friend, to be nice, to be funny, to be perfect. Maybe being everything to everyone makes him really lonely.

(LIZA, VICTORIA, *and* TIFFANY *enter.*)

LIZA. We better go rescue Chad.

TIFFANY. Hi Chad.

CHAD. Hey guys. Seeing some good stuff?

LIZA. I am now.

DARCY. Ugh.

LIZA. Did you say something?

DARCY. No, I have a hairball, that's all. Better move, I don't want to cough it up on you!

LIZA. Gross. Let's go.

DARCY. Hey Liza, there's a Picasso around the corner that looks just like you. You should check it out!

LIZA. Really?

DARCY. Yeah, it's uncanny.

LIZA. Let's go. You coming Chad?

CHAD. Yeah.

> *(They exit.)*

DARCY. Cut to a scene from an adventure movie. I play the hero and Chad the helpless lad who has been caught in the clutches of the evil dragon. *(ENSEMBLE enters and forms the dragon's body—LIZA is the head.)* I have to slay the mighty beast in order to save him. But she is the mighty beast. *(Slow motion fight sequence ensues where DARCY frees CHAD from the dragon.)* I slay the dragon and free the lad who is eternally grateful. We ride off into the sunset to...

> *(ENSEMBLE enters and recreates boarding the bus.)*

MR. FRANK. Darcy, the bus is leaving. Darcy?

DARCY. Right, the bus. Just as bad as a dragon. This is one beast I can't conquer. I know my fate. Doomed forever to sit alone or with a chaperone. Hopefully there will be an empty seat and I can close my eyes and pretend to sleep. To pretend that hundreds of eyes aren't staring at me, judging me. At least in forty-five minutes this day will be over and I can move on to the next outing or dance or group project to worry about.

> *(Steps onto the bus. There is a seat open next to CHAD. LIZA is right behind DARCY. A slow motion sequence happens; music is* Chariots of Fire *theme song. CHAD waves to DARCY and she and LIZA wave back and then they struggle to get to the seat. In the end DARCY sits next to CHAD and LIZA is stuck next to MR. D.)*

CHAD. Hey.

DARCY. *(Turns to the audience:)* "There will come a time when you believe everything is finished. That will be the beginning."—Louis L'Amour.

CHAD. Does he play for the Red Sox?

> *(DARCY shrugs and smiles at the audience.)*

> *(Blackout.)*

End of Play

THE WHOLE SHEBANG

by Rich Orloff

Cast of Characters

THE STUDENT, earnest, enthusiastic and anxious

THE DEAN, wise, patient, experienced, balanced

PROFESSOR A, skeptical, critical, cool

PROFESSOR B, instinctual, passionate, warm

A MAN, 40s, average, unexceptional, human

A WOMAN, the man's wife, just as unexceptional

Place

A college classroom.

Time

The present.

Production Notes

The "A" and "B" connotation is for script purposes only. In the program, the professors should be listed in some other manner, such as "The Professor on the Left" and "The Professor on the Right," or "The Tall Professor" and "The Short Professor," or something like that.

Acknowledgments

The Whole Shebang was first performed on December 2, 1988 at the Second Generation Theater Company (Kelly Kane, executive producer) in New York City. It was directed by William Pomerantz. The cast included Donald Emmerich (Student), Judith Granite (Dean), Stephen Bittrich (Professor A), Jerry Rockwood (Professor B), Scott Sowers (Harvey) and Sarah McKenzie (Edna).

The Whole Shebang is part of Rich Orloff's trio of one-act comedies entitled *Ha!,* also published by Playscripts, Inc. The three comedies can be performed by an ensemble cast ranging from six to fifteen (7 m., 3 w., 5 either). For more information, please visit www.playscripts.com.

THE WHOLE SHEBANG

(Before the play begins, we hear the following announcement:)

VOICE. The following is a true story. Some minor changes have been made because the actual event took place in a dimension beyond human comprehension.

(Lights up on a college classroom, arranged for an oral exam. PROFESSOR A, PROFESSOR B, and the DEAN sit behind a large table. On the table are strewn all sorts of papers, photographs, charts and such. Each professor has a legal-sized notepad. Across from where the professors sit is an area where students give their presentations. In this area could be some visual aids, such as the periodic table of the chemical elements, Leonardo da Vinci's diagrams of man and woman, etc. At the side are a few chairs.)

(As the scene begins, the DEAN and both PROFESSORS are chatting amiably.)

DEAN. ...and all in all, it was one of the best presentations I've seen this semester. A-plus work from start to finish. I'm sure that's one student who's going to go far.

PROFESSOR B. I'm glad to hear it.

DEAN. *(Checking his, or her, watch:)* We might as well start.

PROFESSOR A. No reason to make the poor boy more nervous than he already is. *(Or "girl" and "she," if the STUDENT is played by a woman.)*

(The DEAN crosses to the door, opens it and calls out.)

DEAN. Are you ready?

STUDENT. *(Offstage, a bundle of nerves:)* Yeah...I'm...I'm, uh—

DEAN. It's time to start.

STUDENT. *(Offstage:)* I'm coming.

(The STUDENT enters. He carries a globe, a briefcase and some papers, etc. He appears very anxious and pressured.)

STUDENT. *(To the DEAN:)* I'm, uh, there is—there's just one part of my presentation I don't have with me yet.

DEAN. Do you want us to wait?

STUDENT. Oh, no. My roommate is getting it. It should be here any second now... I hope.

DEAN. Please relax. This is just an informal review.

STUDENT. You told me my grade depended on this.

DEAN. *(Comforting:)* Try not to think about it.

PROFESSOR B. We've all read your thesis and supporting material...

(PROFESSOR A places a hand on a tall stack of material.)

PROFESSOR A. *(Wishing there had been less:)* All of it...

DEAN. Actually, I must confess I haven't gotten to all of it. I'm sure you can fill me in on anything I missed.

STUDENT. I'll try my best.

DEAN. Why don't we begin with a brief summary of your project?

STUDENT. All right. For my master's thesis, I elected to devise a self-sustaining and self-evolving, matter-based ecosystem in a universe of three dimensions. And so I created the heavens and the earth.

DEAN. Now that you've devised this planetary ecosystem, how do you feel about it?

STUDENT. Well, to be honest...I think it's good.

PROFESSOR B. Could you be a little more specific?

STUDENT. Certainly. I think the Earth has succeeded in every way I hoped it would. The amount of gravity is sufficient to keep things on the planet and yet light enough to let trees grow tall and animals run and jump. The weather cycle, given its complexity, is quite efficient. Photosynthesis and oxidation balance each other effectively. All in all, the Earth is fundamentally capable of sustaining itself.

PROFESSOR A. Unless, of course, the human being blows it all up.

DEAN. The human being?

PROFESSOR A. Those are the two-legged creatures with the smelly armpits.

DEAN. Oh, yes. We'll get to them later. *(To the* STUDENT:*)* Go on.

STUDENT. In designing the Earth, I considered aesthetics an essential aspect. I'm fully aware I could've simplified the ecological chain; there's no vital need for zebras or kidney beans. But I wanted to create a planetary ecosystem that was not only efficient but also beautiful and wondrous.

PROFESSOR A. Kidney beans are beautiful and wondrous?

STUDENT. Maybe not in themselves, but without them, there'd only be two-bean salad.

DEAN. *(Pointing to the element chart:)* It is very impressive how much diversity you created from so few elements.

STUDENT. Thank you. It was the only way I could create a whole universe and stay within budget.

DEAN. I'm most impressed with your creation of water.

PROFESSOR A. I must admit, so am I. It may be one of the most efficient liquids any student has designed.

PROFESSOR B. I like how when the temperature drops below freezing, you've designed it so that water falls as snowflakes instead of ice cubes.

STUDENT. Thanks. That took a lot of work.

DEAN. *(Reviewing a paper:)* Here's a most impressive statistic: Over 453 zillion snowflakes so far, and only 12 have been alike.

STUDENT. Thanks.

PROFESSOR A. By the way, why did you have an ice age?

STUDENT. I...I... Well, to be honest, I screwed up.

DEAN. Well, that happens. It was early in the term.

PROFESSOR B. I think one of your major aesthetic accomplishments is the fish. I never thought there could be one type of creature with so many colorful variations. Why you even bothered with creatures that slither, crawl and fly, I'm not sure.

STUDENT. Well, you have to understand that—

PROFESSOR B. They're just adorable.

STUDENT. Thank you.

PROFESSOR B. Of course, I could do without catfish.

STUDENT. They're good scavengers.

PROFESSOR B. They're ugly. Couldn't you give them a little silver stripe down their side, or *something?*

PROFESSOR A. Can we begin discussing the human being? It seems to me that everything else is insignificant in compar—

PROFESSOR B. Fish are not insignificant.

PROFESSOR A. Granted. Nevertheless, the human being does seem to be the determining factor in the eventual success or failure of the planet.

DEAN. Good point. Let's examine the human being.

STUDENT. I consider the human being the crowning achievement of my universe.

PROFESSOR B. *(Looking at some photos:)* You know what I like best about human beings?

PROFESSOR A. What?

PROFESSOR B. Their feet. Not only are feet durable and sophisticated in their design, they're— Well, they're very cute.

STUDENT. Thank you.

PROFESSOR B. *(Referring to the photos:)* Can I save these?

STUDENT. Sure.

PROFESSOR A. I have one question regarding the human being.

STUDENT. Yes?

PROFESSOR A. Why did you make them so stupid?

DEAN. That's a biased question.

PROFESSOR A. All right, I'll rephrase it: Why didn't you make them smart?

STUDENT. I think they're smart. They've created great civilizations. They've developed magnificent tools and brilliant works of art. Their awareness of the universe is increasing exponentially.

PROFESSOR A. Stop exaggerating. It took them centuries just to come up with the concept of the sandwich. How smart do you have to be to think of putting a piece of meat between two slices of bread?

STUDENT. But look at what else they've done. Look at what they've done with their languages. Look at English. With only 26 letters, they've built a body of literature with great power, feeling and insight.

PROFESSOR A. So? The creatures on one of the other student's planets created a body of literature that's twice as profound, and with only 17 letters. No inefficient letters like X or Q. Imagine inventing a letter you can only use if it's followed by a U. What was going on in their heads?

STUDENT. Still, any species that has produced William Shakespeare...

PROFESSOR A. Isn't he the one who wrote, "What a piece of work is man! How noble in reason, how infinite in faculty."

STUDENT. Yes.

PROFESSOR A. What a bunch of self-serving rubbish.

DEAN. You don't expect a good grade just because you created one genius, do you?

STUDENT. Of course not. The species has also produced Socrates, Freud, Madame Curie, Gandhi, Darwin—

PROFESSOR A. All of whom were resented, misunderstood, ostracized or killed. This is how human beings treat their geniuses.

PROFESSOR B. And what type of organism would let the Marx Brothers make only 13 movies? They were easily good for another dozen.

DEAN. What I don't understand is, why are human beings so arrogant? They act as if they own the planet just because they're one step up from apes.

STUDENT. The humans do have much to be proud of.

PROFESSOR B. If any creature has a reason to be arrogant, it's the cow.

DEAN. I missed the section on cows.

PROFESSOR B. This one animal spends all day doing nothing but eating grass, and at the end of the day, she secretes a liquid that is not only nutritious, but it can also become cheese and yogurt and butter and over three-dozen flavors of ice cream. Now if cows aren't arrogant, why are humans? Granted some of them secrete milk, too, but you can't even make cottage cheese from it.

STUDENT. May I remind you the human being is the sole creature capable of transforming milk into all those other products. Without the human being, the Earth would have been a mass of raw material with unrealized potential.

PROFESSOR A. Are you saying it's a better planet because of cheese doodles?

STUDENT. There's more to the picture than that.

PROFESSOR A. From what I see, the rest of the planet would be just as well off if the human being didn't exist.

STUDENT. Yes, but—

DEAN. It appears they can barely manage their own lives, let alone the life of the planet.

PROFESSOR A. Most of them, to quote one of their own, live "lives of quiet desperation."

PROFESSOR B. Except for New Yorkers, who seem quite vocal about it.

DEAN. Why did you give these creatures domain over the planet?!

STUDENT. Well, you see...

 (The STUDENT *sighs and checks his watch.)*

DEAN. Yes?

STUDENT. My roommate was supposed to transport a couple of human beings here so I could... It's very hard to understand them unless you meet them up close. They really are wondrous creatures.

PROFESSOR B. Wondrous they may be, but do you honestly think they can run the planet as well as cows? You would never see Holsteins enslaving Guernseys because of "the white cow's burden."

STUDENT. Look, I'll admit it. I did make one major error in designing the human being.

PROFESSOR A. Their capacity for cruelty?

STUDENT. No.

PROFESSOR B. Their proclivity towards prejudice?

STUDENT. No.

DEAN. Their desire to destroy that which they can't control?

STUDENT. No, no, no.

DEAN. What then?

STUDENT. None of them seem to do sex right.

PROFESSOR A. They certainly try hard enough.

STUDENT. When the universe was still in draft form, I realized I had to create some mechanism to compensate for the brutalizing aspects of life, something sweet and inspiring that would ensure a peaceful planet. And so I created the physical intimacy.

PROFESSOR A. *(Wanting more information:)* And?

STUDENT. And I saw it was good.

PROFESSOR B. Are you saying the world would be a safer place if people had more—?

STUDENT. I'm not talking about quantity; I'm talking about quality. It is psychologically impossible to detonate a nuclear device if you've just had a satisfying intimate experience.

DEAN. *(Skeptical:)* Really.

STUDENT. Oh, yes. But I don't mean just sex, even though that's great for procreation and curing acne. But when humans are willing to reveal their souls during an intimate connection, they're reunited with all of the energy flowing through the universe. This spiritual union was designed to cleanse fear from the soul, so that the human's capacity for goodness would rise to the surface and transform into enlightened action. *(Noting* PROFESSOR A *and* B's *disbelief:)* It worked great in test cases.

> *(From the hallway, we hear voices.)*

MAN. *(Offstage:)* What do you mean "Go in there"?! Maybe I don't want to go in there!

WOMAN. *(Offstage to the* MAN:) Don't cause a scene!

MAN. *(Offstage:)* This jerk's causing the scene! Look, buddy, I don't know who you are, but I'll go in there when I'm good and ready!

> *(A* MAN *comes flying into the room, as if thrown in by someone else. A* WOMAN *follows quickly. Both are dressed for bed. They look around, quite bewildered about what's going on.)*

MAN. What the—

STUDENT. Oh, good. Just in time. I'm so glad you're finally here.

MAN. What's going on here?!

> *(The* STUDENT *pulls up a couple of chairs.)*

STUDENT. Make yourselves at home.

WOMAN. *(Frightened:)* Where are we?

STUDENT. Just sit. You're late.

WOMAN. Late for what?

STUDENT. Relax. This won't take long... Please.

> *(The* HUMANS *look at each other and hesitantly sit down.)*

STUDENT. *(To the* PROFESSORS:) I'd like to introduce two typical human beings: John and Mary Doe. They're not extraordinary in any way, which is exactly why I chose them. John and Mary live with their two children in Dayton, Ohio. John works as an urban planner, helping to prepare Dayton for the future. Mary is a doctor, specializing in internal medicine. Although their jobs show their dedication to their fellow humans, it is as parents that John and Mary feel their greatest responsibility. Their two children are sensitive and alive, and also excellent students. John and Mary have many hobbies. Mary plays the dulcimer, and John recycles aluminum. I am proud to put the destiny of Earth in the hands of average people like these: John and Mary Doe.

MAN. We're not them.

STUDENT. You're not John and Mary Doe?

MAN. No, I'm John's brother, Harvey Doe, and this is my wife, Edna Doe.

EDNA. Hi.

STUDENT. But I told my roommate to bring up—

EDNA. They're on vacation. We're house-sitting for them.

STUDENT. Really? *(To the* PROFESSORS:*)* See how caring the human being is?

EDNA. Well, John and Mary have a wide-screen TV. We don't.

HARVEY. Uh, can I ask a question?

STUDENT. Yes?

HARVEY. Who are you, and why are we here?!

STUDENT. Well, since you asked, my roommate teleported through a warp in dimensional barriers to Dayton, Ohio, where he realigned your molecules into a pure energetic code. Then he teleported you here and, having analyzed your cellular structure and DNA, re-atomized you into this dimension.

HARVEY. Yeah, I figured it was something like that.

EDNA. You don't hope to gain information so you can destroy our planet, do you?

STUDENT. Oh, no.

EDNA. 'Cause we don't know a thing. Honest.

PROFESSOR A. *(Whispering to* PROFESSOR B:*)* I believe them.

STUDENT. *(To the* HUMANS:*)* Don't worry. This is just what, in our dimension, is the equivalent of one of your universities. These are professors in my department, and I'm a student. You're just here as part of my project.

HARVEY. Oh, yeah? And what's your project?

STUDENT. I created the heavens and the earth.

(It takes a moment for this to fully sink in on the HUMANS.*)*

HARVEY. Wait a second. Are you telling us that you're—

STUDENT. I am who I am.

EDNA. Sounds like him.

HARVEY. You mean to tell us that, like the entire universe is just like...a science fair project?

STUDENT. More or less.

HARVEY. Suddenly, I feel so cheap.

STUDENT. So if my professors could just ask you some questions, it would really help my grade.

HARVEY. I work my fingers to the bone, and all I am is part of some nerd's science project?!

EDNA. Harvey, please. *(Whispering:)* You'll go to Hell.

STUDENT. Oh, don't worry. Nothing you say here will be held against you.

HARVEY. Eh, I don't care. With my luck, I could give the Pope CPR and I'd still go to hell.

STUDENT. *(Beginning to have intelligent doubts about these folks; to the* PROFESSORS:*)* Maybe this wasn't such a good idea. These aren't the ones I planned—

DEAN. But they are average human beings, aren't they?

STUDENT. I'm not sure they're as common as John and Mary.

EDNA. The other day my hairstylist called me one of the most common people she knew.

DEAN. Well, then.

STUDENT. I really don't think these people are in any condition to be questioned.

PROFESSOR A. That's too bad. I've got so many questions I'd like to ask them.

HARVEY. Go ahead. Waste your time. Ask about my life.

STUDENT. Actually, I think we've bothered them enough—

PROFESSOR B. I think this is a wonderful opportunity to gain some insight into the human condition.

STUDENT. But these aren't the ones I wanted to—

DEAN. Why don't you just sit and be quiet for a while?

STUDENT. But I don't think you'll—

DEAN. *Very* quiet.

STUDENT. But if—

DEAN. *Sit.*

> *(The* STUDENT *sits.)*

DEAN. Now then, Harvey and Edna, why don't you tell us a little about yourselves?

EDNA. Not much to say. We're just people. Ordinary people.

PROFESSOR B. Harvey, what is your occupation?

HARVEY. You mean, what did I used to do, before a bunch of pea-brained numbskulls laid me off?

> *(The* STUDENT *sighs.)*

DEAN. Yes.

HARVEY. For fourteen years, I worked on an assembly line. I got up every morning, drove twenty miles and spent eight hours tightening nuts.

PROFESSOR A. Why were you laid off?

HARVEY. My entire division was replaced by a silicon chip.

PROFESSOR A. I see.

HARVEY. Apparently, sand can do my job better than I can.

PROFESSOR B. Have you tried to get help from your *(Looks at document:)* union?

HARVEY. Not yet. But I do plan to talk to my local union official, as soon as he's paroled.

EDNA. The guy was framed.

HARVEY. It's her brother.

EDNA. He was doing a friend a little favor. So his friend did him a little favor. It was in cash; no one was supposed to know.

PROFESSOR A. Have you considered changing careers, Harvey?

HARVEY. Well, I've thought about becoming a truck driver, but amphetamines give me headaches.

PROFESSOR A. I see.

HARVEY. I do have an interview next week at the toxic waste dump. They tell me garbage is a growth industry.

DEAN. Edna, do you work?

EDNA. Oh, yeah. I'm a supermarket check-out clerk.

DEAN. What's that?

EDNA. Well, after people buy their groceries, I wave their food over a scanner and then put it in a bag while the customers stare at me like I'm not smart enough to do this.

PROFESSOR B. And how often each day do you do this?

EDNA. Oh, I don't know, probably a hundred times.

PROFESSOR B. Are you concerned that this might eventually become boring?

EDNA. Oh, it got boring after the fourth bag.

PROFESSOR A. Then why don't you change jobs?

EDNA. Gee, I don't know. Most of life is boring, isn't it?

STUDENT. If I can just put this into the perspective—

DEAN. Later. You'll get a chance.

STUDENT. But—

DEAN. Sit.

(The STUDENT *sits.)*

PROFESSOR A. Do the two of you have children?

EDNA. Oh, yes. Michael, who's sixteen, and Wendy, who's just about thirteen.

PROFESSOR B. Can you describe them?

EDNA. They're just wonderful.

PROFESSOR A. Harvey?

HARVEY. They're pips.

PROFESSOR B. Are they good students?

(Simultaneously:)

EDNA. They're okay.   **HARVEY.** Hah.

PROFESSOR A. What do they excel at?

(HARVEY and EDNA think about this. Nothing comes to mind.)

PROFESSOR A. Anything?

EDNA. Michael was just made group leader at his drug rehabilitation center.

PROFESSOR B. Does Wendy take drugs?

EDNA. Oh, no. Never. She knows better.

HARVEY. She just spends all day in the bathroom, dyeing her hair unnatural colors.

EDNA. *(Trying to put things in a good light:)* Some of which are *very* creative.

HARVEY. Yeah, like one day her head's going to end up in an art gallery.

EDNA. She's going through a rough time. She still hasn't gotten over the shock of menstruation.

HARVEY. *(To the STUDENT:)* Not to question your ways or nothing, but couldn't you think of anything better than *puberty?*

STUDENT. No, not really. I tried.

EDNA. Harvey, please.

HARVEY. Well, he's supposed to be all-knowing and all-powerful, and he can't even make their teeth grow in straight. *(To the STUDENT:)* Do you know how much that cost me?

EDNA. Harvey, please. We're supposed to be representing the entire human race.

PROFESSOR A. I think you're doing a *splendid* job.

PROFESSOR B. How's your "intimate relations"?

(Simultaneously:)

EDNA. Pardon me?   **HARVEY.** Hey!

DEAN. We really could use the information.

EDNA. *(A bit defensive:)* It's fine.

PROFESSOR B. Harvey?

HARVEY. *(Unconvincingly:)* Yeah, it's fine.

PROFESSOR A. So you're both completely satisfied with your intimate relations?

(Simultaneously:)

EDNA. Completely.   **HARVEY.** More or less.

PROFESSOR B. More or less?

HARVEY. *(Seeing EDNA's look:)* It's fine. It's just fine.

DEAN. Is it?

HARVEY. *(To the* STUDENT*:)* Well, you designed women. You know how it is.

PROFESSOR A. How is it?

HARVEY. They just don't seem to like it as much as men.

EDNA. I like it.

HARVEY. *(A bit surly:)* Yeah, I know you like it.

EDNA. I like it just fine.

HARVEY. You don't always like it.

EDNA. I always fulfill my obligations, don't I?

HARVEY. I can't tell you what a turn-on that attitude is.

EDNA. Maybe it's because I get tired of hearing you yell out Britney Spears[1] name when you get excited.

HARVEY. I did that once, and you've brought it up fifteen million—

EDNA. I swear there isn't a single female celebrity he hasn't slept with. In his mind, that is.

HARVEY. This isn't the place to discuss this.

EDNA. They want to know what we're like!

HARVEY. *(Overlapping with the above; to the* STUDENT*:)* Hey, I've got a question!

STUDENT. Yes?

HARVEY. When you designed women, why did you make it take 'em so long to rev up?

STUDENT. Actually, if their response cycle hasn't been repressed, it shouldn't take long at all.

HARVEY. *(To* EDNA*:)* See! I told you it wasn't his fault.

EDNA. Well, it wasn't mine.

PROFESSOR A. *(Mimicking the* STUDENT*:)* Excuse me. Has either of you ever had a spiritual union where you feel reunited with the energy flowing through the universe, so that all of your goodness rises to the surface and transforms into enlightened action?

HARVEY. Hey, what do you think we are, perverts?

EDNA. We have read many of the manuals. Harvey loves looking up words he doesn't know.

PROFESSOR B. Do you believe that intimacy is important in a relationship?

HARVEY. You mean—?

PROFESSOR B. Intimacy... Being open and vulnerable.

EDNA. I think intimacy is the keystone of a healthy relationship.

---

[1] Or any current female celebrity.

PROFESSOR B. And what makes you say that?

EDNA. I read it in last month's *Cosmo*.

DEAN. Cos—

HARVEY. It's a "woman's" magazine.

EDNA. But I do think it's important. After all, without real intimacy, sex would be nothing but, uh...

HARVEY. Fun.

STUDENT. *(Standing:)* If I can... *(Sensing what the* DEAN *is about to say:)* I know—"Sit."

PROFESSOR A. Harvey and Edna, what would you say has been the best moment of your lives?

EDNA. Oh, that's easy. It was the day Harvey proposed to me. It was the first nice day of spring, and we were having a picnic in the park. I had made chicken salad sandwiches and potato salad and carrot-raisin salad and macaroni salad—

PROFESSOR B. Did Harvey make anything?

HARVEY. I think I picked up a six-pack.

EDNA. No, you were going to, but since I had to go back to the store to pick up more mayonnaise, you decided to let me get it.

DEAN. Why couldn't Harvey purchase the mayonnaise when he went to buy the six-pack?

> *(HARVEY and* EDNA *look at each other. Apparently, this idea never occurred to them.)*

EDNA. Anyway, so we were having this picnic, and when we finished eating, I wiped Harvey's mouth with my napkin, and he wiped my mouth with his—

HARVEY. It's this thing we do.

EDNA. And, and I remember, I remember Harvey looking right in my eyes and saying..."Let's make it legal." And I thought, this man knows what I want.

PROFESSOR A. And was that day the best moment of your life, too, Harvey?

HARVEY. Uh, yeah, yeah, of course, yeah.

EDNA. You don't have to lie to them. You told me what you thought was the best.

HARVEY. Well, the day I proposed was *one* of the best.

PROFESSOR B. What was the best?

HARVEY. Well, okay, um, it was last summer, and well, I was having this really lousy day, I mean, 100 percent sucko lousy.

DEAN. "Sucko"?

PROFESSOR B. A colloquial adjective derived from the verb "suck."

HARVEY. The important thing is, the day stunk. It was like maybe a hundred degrees out, and maybe a hundred percent humidity, and it was even worse in the house because all of our air conditioners had just been repossessed. And then the mail came, and it was all bills, big bills, and I got so upset I didn't know what to do, and so I turned on the TV. But we were behind in our cable bill, so that didn't work either, and I got so mad I threw a shoe at the TV. It didn't break, thank uh— *(Glimpses at the* STUDENT*)* —whatever and then I just left the house and went into the backyard.

PROFESSOR A. And that was the best moment of your life?

HARVEY. I'm getting to it. So on my way to— You know, I hate being interrupted— On my way to the backyard, I stopped in the kitchen and got myself a beer. Now I don't know if any of you guys are beer drinkers... I guess not. Usually, when you drink beer, it's either too cold, or not cold enough, or it's got too much foam, or it's just a lousy brand. And you still drink it, because that's what life's about, accepting the beer you're given, but it's nothing that, nothing you'd ever get *enthused* about. But this beer, it was delicious. Just right. I can still remember sitting in my backyard, thinking, "I'm broke, I'm unemployed, and I've no escape—not even TV. But this moment, *this moment,* is perfect."

STUDENT. I really must interrupt—

DEAN. I told you—

STUDENT. But I don't think it's fair to judge the whole human race based on such a limited sample.

HARVEY. Hey, take a little responsibility for your own actions, why don't you?

EDNA. We're going to Hell, I know it.

HARVEY. He said we could say what we want.

EDNA. *(Whispering to* HARVEY:*)* Yes, but we don't know if he's going to be loving and forgiving or righteous and vindictive.

STUDENT. Why do you insist upon giving me human qualities? It's quite a projection.

HARVEY. Hey, you created us.

STUDENT. But I gave you free will!

HARVEY. That's it. Pass the buck.

STUDENT. I am not passing the buck.

HARVEY. You and your "free will." What good is it, huh? I exert my free will all over the place, and all it does is get me thrown out of bars.

STUDENT. You don't understand the concept. I gave you choices—

HARVEY. Yeah, like being able to vote for a president and then making all the candidates jerks?

STUDENT. There's more to it than that.

HARVEY. Hey, if I really had free will, do you think this is the life I would have free-willed?

STUDENT. Maybe it is!

HARVEY. Yeah, well, let me tell you, if you designed me so that I'd make the free will choice of *this* life, then you're really sick.

EDNA. Harvey!

STUDENT. You could have made better choices.

HARVEY. I can't afford better choices! My credit cards are already up to the limit!

DEAN. Excuse me—

EDNA. Harvey—

HARVEY. It's like everything that's great about life, he's supposed to get credit for, and everything that's lousy is supposed to be our fault. Well, it's not fair!

EDNA. Harvey, please.

HARVEY. It's just not fair!

DEAN. Excuse me! ...I'm sorry, but our time is almost over.

PROFESSOR B. If I may, I have one final question.

DEAN. Go ahead, Professor.

PROFESSOR B. *(To the* HUMANS:*)* Do you think the world is getting better or worse?

HARVEY. Oh, worse.

EDNA. Much worse. Everyone knows that.

PROFESSOR A. Then why do you keep living?

HARVEY. Whaddaya mean?

PROFESSOR A. Your lives vary in quality from boring to dismal. Your future holds no promise. Why do you keep living?

(HARVEY *and* EDNA *think for a moment, look at each other.)*

EDNA. I just dropped ten pounds. I'm not going to die now.

HARVEY. Yeah.

PROFESSOR A. And this is why you keep on living?

EDNA. Well, well, we also have to stick around for our kids.

HARVEY. Yeah!

EDNA. After all, if it weren't for us, who'd be their role models?

(The PROFESSORS *exchange looks with each other.)*

HARVEY. *(To* EDNA:*)* I think you just blew it.

EDNA. They're good kids.

HARVEY. I know, I know, they're great kids. But you can't tell that by looking at 'em.

EDNA. They're going to be fine, eventually. They're just going through a difficult phase.

HARVEY. Yeah, it's called life.

PROFESSOR A. I still don't understand. With your attitudes, why do you two keep living?

HARVEY. Hey, if you're suggesting I drop dead, *forget it.* It'd make too many people happy.

EDNA. There are things in life to look forward to, you know. Special things, things that make life worth living.

PROFESSOR A. Name three.

EDNA. Well...the day after Thanksgiving, there are some great sales... And on days off, sometimes I wear pajamas till noon... Oh, and about every six months, I bag someone's groceries, and they'll say "thank you" like they really mean it.

PROFESSOR A. Don't you think those are rather trivial things?

EDNA. So? I lead a rather trivial life. I know it.

HARVEY. I don't think you guys realize how hard it is being a human being.

PROFESSOR B. Is it difficult?

HARVEY. You bet it is.

EDNA. You never feel like you have enough brains.

HARVEY. And you're always getting these impulses—these urges—that make no sense whatsoever.

EDNA. Your kids look to you for answers, and you can't think of anything. So you end up giving them the same stupid answers your parents gave you.

HARVEY. When I think there are people dumber than I am, I get scared. *(To the* STUDENT:*)* So why'd you do it?

STUDENT. Do what?

HARVEY. Why'd you make us so messed up?

STUDENT. You're missing the point! I didn't create the human being so that each one would work perfectly. I created the human being so that humanity as a whole would work perfectly.

HARVEY. But humanity as a whole doesn't work perfectly!

EDNA. It doesn't work perfectly at all. And we have it better than most people.

DEAN. Do you?

EDNA. Oh, yes. Most people, if they get through childhood without dying of hunger or disease, all they got left is a life of misery, pain and injustice.

STUDENT. But I gave human beings all the resources they need. Why, I've given you the ingredients for paradise.

EDNA. Ohh...you're a real tease, you know that?

STUDENT. What do you mean?

EDNA. You made the world so wonderful, and our lives so difficult. I mean, maybe we're not the best examples of human beings, but, well, we're trying as hard as we can, and, and we want to be decent people and we want our kids to turn out right and we want to have happy lives, and, and we're trying so hard, but... *(Breaks into tears.)* You know what it's like to know you're doing your best and that your life still stinks?

HARVEY. *(To the* STUDENT:*)* Good work, buddy. *(Comforting* EDNA:*)* Hey, come on. Don't cry. You do okay.

EDNA. I do not.

HARVEY. You do, too. You're a good mother, you're a good wife, and you're one of the best supermarket clerks in Dayton.

EDNA. You really think so?

HARVEY. Hey, as far as I'm concerned, anytime someone has *you* bag their groceries, it's their lucky day.

EDNA. Thanks.

HARVEY. And if our kids turn out okay—

EDNA. If?

HARVEY. And *when* our kids turn out okay, it'll be all because of you.

EDNA. Well, you had a lot to do with—

HARVEY. I hope they don't end up like me at all. That's *my* hope for the future.

DEAN. I think we're ready to decide your grade.

STUDENT. But all humans aren't like this. If only you had met John and Mary.

HARVEY. Of course. Show off a couple of bozos you've made life easy for.

STUDENT. I gave them the exact same universe I gave you.

HARVEY. You sound just like my dad sometimes, you know that?

STUDENT. *(To the* PROFESSORS:*)* John and Mary have done so much with their lives.

HARVEY. John's the biggest phony in Dayton.

STUDENT. He is not!

HARVEY. Oh, yes he is. Even when he goes to church, it's not to pray. He just wants to suck up to you.

PROFESSOR A. I see.

HARVEY. And Mary's worse.

PROFESSOR B. Is she, Edna?

EDNA. Do I have to be honest?

DEAN. We'd appreciate it.

EDNA. Well then, Mary—who, for the record, no longer has the nose you gave her—I mean, she may spend all day healing the sick, but have you ever tried to just sit down and have a nice conversation with her? "I helped so many people today, Edna. Of course, not as many as you checked out."

HARVEY. They're great human beings, all right. I'm sure they would have given you all the answers you wanted.

EDNA. And for the rest of our lives, they would have bored us at dinner parties saying, "We helped the Almighty get an A."

STUDENT. Can I just say one thing on my behalf?

DEAN. Go ahead. This is your chance.

HARVEY. Yeah, go ahead.

EDNA. Yeah.

PROFESSOR B. Please.

PROFESSOR A. We're listening.

STUDENT. I...um... *(Sighs, then:)* They looked so good on paper.

DEAN. Thank you. We'll caucus now to decide your final grade.

(The PROFESSORS *gather together and start to whisper. We occasionally hear some arguing tones.)*

EDNA. They decide right on the spot?

STUDENT. Yes.

HARVEY. What degree are you going for, anyway?

STUDENT. My M.U.

HARVEY. M.U.?

STUDENT. Master of the Universe.

(We hear some heated mumbling.)

PROFESSOR B. You have to consider the exquisite beauty of their design.

PROFESSOR A. But they're not practical.

HARVEY. *(To the* STUDENT:*)* Can I ask you a question about the universe that has troubled me since I was a kid?

STUDENT. Sure.

HARVEY. How come there's maple-walnut ice cream and butter-pecan ice cream, instead of maple-pecan and butter-walnut?

STUDENT. I don't think I can answer that one.

HARVEY. Nobody can.

DEAN. Despite all their flaws, they have survived for thousands and thousands of years.

PROFESSOR B. And they have such nice feet.

PROFESSOR A. Their feet are indeed nice. It's from the ankles up that they make me nervous.

PROFESSOR B. Still, their genetic engineering is most advanced.

DEAN. And they're also biodegradable.

HARVEY. *(To* EDNA:*)* This is going to make some story to tell our friends.

STUDENT. Oh, I'm afraid once you're teleported back to Earth, you won't remember a thing.

HARVEY. *(To* EDNA:*)* So much for going on talk shows.

EDNA. And I had already decided what I was going to wear.

HARVEY. Let's face it. We're going to have to spend the rest of our lives as average people.

EDNA. *(Softly:)* Darn it.

DEAN. Yes, yes, yes. There is much wrong with the project. I still don't think it's fair to call the student an underachiever.

PROFESSOR A. I don't know why he created them; they serve no useful purpose.

PROFESSOR B. Maybe they're not perfect, but there is something so beautiful and special about them.

EDNA. *(To the* STUDENT:*)* Is it, is it okay if I take off my slippers?

STUDENT. Go right ahead.

EDNA. Thanks.

> *(*EDNA *takes off her slippers and rubs her feet. Without the* STUDENT *noticing, this gets* PROFESSOR B's *attention.)*

HARVEY. Your bunions acting up again?

EDNA. *(Defensively:)* Yes.

HARVEY. You gotta stop buying those teeny shoes. You don't got teeny feet.

EDNA. I buy shoes the right size.

HARVEY. No, you don't. You keep insisting your feet are smaller than they are. That's why your feet are always in such lousy shape.

> *(*PROFESSOR B *walks over to* EDNA *and examines her foot.)*

PROFESSOR B. I'm changing my grade.

> *(*PROFESSOR B *returns to the other* PROFESSORS.*)*

EDNA. What did I do?

STUDENT. Nothing.

> *(The* PROFESSORS *end their conference.)*

DEAN. We've decided your grade.

> *(The* PROFESSORS *resume their previous positions. The* STUDENT *and the* HUMANS *face them.)*

DEAN. There is much that is commendable about your project, both in Earth's evolutionary ability and its astonishing variety of beauty. The human being is wondrous and fascinating. Nevertheless—

HARVEY. *(To* EDNA:) Uh, oh.

EDNA. Shhh.

DEAN. The three of us agree that the human being's design is tragically flawed. Look at them. They're so scared and confused by their own drives. What good are all their noble qualities when by adulthood, most of them have developed a grudge against life itself? I'm afraid we're going to have to give you a C plus.

STUDENT. C plus?!!!

EDNA / HARVEY. *(Simultaneously:)* C plus?!!!

DEAN. I'm sorry.

HARVEY. Wait a second. We do not live in a C plus universe.

EDNA. It's at least a B.

STUDENT. I created fruits and vegetables and birds that fly and fish that swim and artists and athletes and thinkers and leaders, and all I get is a C plus?! I gave this project everything I had. Everything!

PROFESSOR A. Some of us felt the grade was generous.

HARVEY. *(To the* PROFESSORS:) All I can say is—it's easy to sit back and judge. Real easy. How do you guys know you're not just somebody else's science project? Huh?! I bet right now some higher being is giving your entire dimension a D.

PROFESSOR B. I don't understand. After all your complaints—

HARVEY. So I was in a bad mood! You got us at a bad time.

EDNA. It was just before bedtime.

HARVEY. And on Saturday night, if you get my drift.

EDNA. Those Saturday nights mean a lot to us.

HARVEY. *(To* EDNA, *surprised:)* They do?

EDNA. You know they do.

HARVEY. Well, I sorta hoped, but, uh, I never assumed...

EDNA. Well, of course.

HARVEY. I keep worrying one day they'll come up with a silicon chip—

EDNA. No... Never.

PROFESSOR A. *(Getting ready to go:)* I don't see why they go on living. I really don't.

EDNA. *(Fed up:)* I'll tell you why!

DEAN. Why?

EDNA. *(Straining hard to think of a reply:)* Well...because... *(Suddenly inspired:)* Because things could get better, that's why!

HARVEY. That's right. Things could always get better.

PROFESSOR B. And what makes you think that?

HARVEY. *(To EDNA:)* Tell 'em.

EDNA. I haven't the slightest idea. I guess we were just designed that way. When push comes to shove, I guess we were designed to have...faith.

(Everyone looks at the STUDENT. He smiles and nods.)

HARVEY. *(To the PROFESSORS:)* See? He's not as big a jerk as you think he is.

DEAN. I'm sorry. The grade is final.

PROFESSOR A. *(To the STUDENT:)* You want my advice? Next time, don't design them in your own image. It's very narcissistic.

(PROFESSOR A exits.)

PROFESSOR B. *(To the HUMANS:)* Take care of your feet, and always treat cows with respect.

(PROFESSOR B exits.)

DEAN. *(To the STUDENT:)* Now don't be too hard on yourself. You did your best.

STUDENT. That makes it even more depressing.

DEAN. It's only a universe. It'll pass.

(The DEAN exits. The STUDENT starts to clean up.)

EDNA. Uh...I'm sorry if we blew your grade.

STUDENT. It's my fault. I should've never goofed off on the seventh day.

EDNA. Well, if it means anything, we are glad you created us.

STUDENT. Are you...? Are you, Harvey?

HARVEY. Well, all in all, when I think about it, I mean, life's not that bad, once you get over the disappointment that it stinks.

STUDENT. I'll remember that.

HARVEY. I mean, I think we're completely messed up; but I'm glad we're here.

STUDENT. Thanks.

HARVEY. So you want to grab a brew?

STUDENT. I better have you teleported back to Earth.

HARVEY. Oh, yeah, well, sure.

EDNA. By the way, if there is such a thing as reincarnation—

STUDENT. I really can't discuss such things—

EDNA. You don't have to tell me, but if it does exist, could you bring me back as a bunny rabbit? Everybody likes bunny rabbits.

HARVEY. And could you bring me back as an eagle?

EDNA. An eagle?

HARVEY. Yeah. Just once I'd like to fly real high on my own power, real high, so I could look down and get a clear view of the whole shebang.

STUDENT. That's a very nice desire, Harvey.

HARVEY. Yeah, well, I got my moments.

STUDENT. Shall we go?

HARVEY. Okay.

STUDENT. After you.

> (HARVEY *and* EDNA *exit. The* STUDENT *is about to go, but then he turns around and picks up the globe.)*

STUDENT. *(Shrugs to himself:)* I think it's good.

> *(The* STUDENT *sighs, puts the globe under his arm, and exits. The lights fade.)*

End of Play

A FUNNY THING HAPPENED ON THE WAY TO FIFTH PERIOD

by Jason Pizzarello

For more information about rights and permissions, see page 9.

Cast of Characters

TOMMY, bookworm

BURP, head bully

BUGS, aspiring bully

STEVE, friendly jock

CORA, his girlfriend

VERONICA, a nerd with anger issues, Steve's sister

STEPHANIE, lead actress

CHAD, lead actor, Stephanie's boyfriend

KIA, math dork

SHELLY, the costume shop girl

MUSICAL THEATER ACTRESSES

MATH GEEKS

OTHER STUDENTS

Set Up

—All the action of the play takes place in a school hallway in front of 3 sets of lockers.

—The play is organized by class periods.

—Every time the bell rings, marking the end of class, students start to fill the hallway.

—After first bell, students start to make their way to class.

—By second bell, only a few late students are left. And as soon as they hear the second bell, they run off.

Scenes

—Before school

—After 1st period

—After 2nd period

—After 3rd period

—After 4th period / Before 5th period

Author Notes

Feel free to change the references to "high school" to "middle school" and the "prom" to the "dance" or "school dance." Whatever works for your school or group. Also, any casting decisions that require characters to change gender are fine by me.

Production Notes

Since the play is a farce, the pace of action should be quick and almost frantic. The dialogue should be delivered with snap and without any pauses or moments between lines.

Although the action takes place in a busy hallway, and students can/should be mingling and moving in a natural way, be careful that none of the "stage business" becomes too distracting. For example, the character of Bugs occasionally picks things out of his hair and eats them, or Burp...burps. Although these can be funny bits, they are susceptible to *over hamming.* Just make sure they don't distract from the main action of the scene.

For the PS crew—you rock.

A FUNNY THING HAPPENED
ON THE WAY TO FIFTH PERIOD

Before School

(3 sets of lockers.

On the left is a gaggle of musical theater ACTRESSES. *They are putting on makeup, costumes, wigs, reading Shakespeare...*

On the right is a friendly-looking jock, STEVE, *arguing with his twin sister,* VERONICA, *who won't stop yo-yoing. Finally* STEVE *grabs the yo-yo and throws it down the hall. She looks like she's gonna cry but instead punches him in the stomach or knocks the books out his hands and runs away. After recovering, he follows her.*

In the middle locker, is TOMMY, *a bookish lower-classman. He gets picked on but his underdeveloped confidence is beginning to brew.*

As TOMMY *reorganizes his trapper keeper, a large bull of a kid,* BURP, *comes up behind him and politely taps him on the shoulder.* TOMMY *turns around and the bull lets a burp rip so loud and foul, you can almost smell yesterday's lunch. But this isn't the first time, and* TOMMY *handles it with grace.* BURP *smiles.)*

TOMMY. Lovely.

(Another bully, BUGS, *not quite as menacing as* BURP, *but still with great potential, stands next to him and claps.* BURP *takes a bow.)*

BURP. Too kind too kind.

TOMMY. Let me guess, you had a burrito and a slurpee for breakfast.

BURP. Cherry slurpee. That counts as a fruit. I like to cover the entire food pyramid. Don't you?

TOMMY. Eating a balanced meal is—

*(*BURP *burps.)*

BURP. Well, enough chit chat. Where's my homework for first period?

TOMMY. *Your* homework? I don't know, where did you put it?

BURP. Where did *you* put it? I didn't do it.

TOMMY. If you didn't do it—

BURP. You did.

TOMMY. I did *my* homework.

BURP. You did *my* homework.

TOMMY. No...I didn't.

BURP. You did *both* of our homework? Tommy, you didn't have to do that. You're too much. You only had to do mine and here you went and did both of ours. I feel bad. That must have taken awhile.

TOMMY. I only did my homework.

BURP. Why would you do that? *(To* BUGS:*)* Why would he do that?

(BUGS, who has been picking things out of his hair and tasting them...shrugs)

BURP. Let me see it. I don't believe you.

(TOMMY takes out the homework.)

TOMMY. See.

BURP. *(He snatches it away.)* So you *did* do my homework.

TOMMY. No, that is mine.

BURP. No, this is mine.

TOMMY. C'mon, Burp.

(BURP burps.)

BURP. If it's yours, why am I holding it?

TOMMY. Give it back.

BURP. You want my homework to copy? Don't you think that's a little unathletical?

TOMMY. You mean unethical?

BURP. I know what I mean. Don't tell me what I mean. You don't know anything about mean. I know mean. I am mean.

TOMMY. When you're right, you're right.

BURP. Nice chattin' with you, Tommy. See ya in class.

(As he exits, BURP *burps while holding his fist in the air.)*

(BUGS is about to follow, but TOMMY *stops him.)*

TOMMY. Hey Bugs, can you wait a second?

BUGS. For you? Three.

TOMMY. Next year, right, I was thinking... He's your mentor, everyone knows you're bound to follow in his footsteps. It's called destiny.

BUGS. It's called Burp. Maybe if you learned his name he wouldn't be so hard on you.

TOMMY. Right. What I'm trying to say is, next year, when you take over this hallway as lead bully, and—

BUGS. Schucks, you're making me blush.

TOMMY. —You don't have to be a bully like him. You can be your own bully.

BUGS. Why would I bully myself?

TOMMY. No I mean you can be a nice bully.

BUGS. I don't think you understand the concept of bullying.

TOMMY. This is your chance to revolutionize the field of bullying. You can be a pioneer.

BUGS. Like Davy Crocket?

TOMMY. Well...sure.

BUGS. I *do* like to kill animals. The other night my dad caught a raccoon under our porch and—

TOMMY. —Bugs, Bugs. I'm sure it was a lovely family dinner, but we're getting off topic.

(First Bell rings.)

BUGS. That's first bell. Don't want to be late. If there's one thing I hate, it's tardiness. And pie. I hate pie. Pie makes me so angry—just be cake already!

TOMMY. Okay, okay. Just think about what I'm saying. Let's work together. There's gotta be something I can do for you to break this viscous cycle of bullying.

(BUGS picks something out of TOMMY's hair and eats it.)

(The group of musical theater ACTRESSES walk by, half dancing, singing a little show tune. STEPHANIE is clearly the lead actress as all the other girls almost move around her.)

(STEPHANIE stops as she's passing TOMMY.)

STEPHANIE. Hey Tommy. Great job working the spotlight in last night's performance. You really knew how to keep it right on me.

TOMMY. Sure, of course. You're the lead.

STEPHANIE. Keep the spotlight on me after the third scene tonight, okay? I have a little extra number choreographed.

TOMMY. I thought the choreographer was handling the...choreography.

STEPHANIE. Trust me, it's gonna bring down the house. You're a peach of a techie, Tommy.

(STEPHANIE and her entourage head off.)

(BUGS is enamored with her. TOMMY watches BUGS watching STEPHANIE.)

TOMMY. Bugs, Bugs, you all right?

(TOMMY shakes BUGS out of a trance.)

BUGS. Stephanie Mezaluna. She's quite a fox. She could make a grown man cry. She could make a sheep throw himself to the wolves. She could make a shark swim backwards.

TOMMY. You like her huh? You wanna marry her? You wanna have little bug children?

BUGS. No, I just wanna take her to the prom.

TOMMY. The prom?

BUGS. I know—you're surprised I don't already have a date. Actually I asked Alice the lunch lady. But apparently she doesn't leave the cafeteria.

TOMMY. Too bad you already need your tickets to the prom. Today's the deadline.

BUGS. *When* today?

TOMMY. End of lunch. By fifth period.

BUGS. So that's our deadline.

TOMMY. Our deadline?

BUGS. *(Dramatic beat.)* If you don't get me a date for the prom with Stephanie Mezaluna by fifth period I will make your life next year—the rest of your pathetic high school career—a living nerd hell. You don't even know what a bully is.

TOMMY. Gulp.

BUGS. You don't need to say gulp, Tommy. Just gulp.

TOMMY. That seems fair.

(Second bell rings.)

BUGS. Shoot! I'm late for Home Ec!

(BUGS runs out. TOMMY gulps.)

After 1st Period

(A bell rings. Classes let out and kids flood the hallway. [this can also be accomplished with sound.])

(Some of the kids clear, and TOMMY is back at his locker, switching out some books. BUGS approaches him.)

BUGS. So did ya get me a date yet?

TOMMY. I was just in class with you.

BUGS. But with technology today...thought you woulda texted her by now or something.

TOMMY. No I didn't.

BUGS. Well you better get on it. I heard you need your tickets by fifth period.

TOMMY. You heard that from me.

BUGS. I knew I heard it somewhere.

TOMMY. Here's your problem. You can't date Stephanie Mezaluna.

BUGS. Sure I can.

TOMMY. She only dates actors. *Lead actors.* Are you a *lead* actor?

BUGS. Just make it happen. Your future alive self depends on it.

TOMMY. You mean "my life depends on it"?

(*STEPHANIE and her entourage are at their lockers.*)

BUGS. She's right there.

TOMMY. It will never work. How am I—

BUGS. Simple.

(*BUGS pushes TOMMY into the gaggle of theater ACTRESSES at their lockers. TOMMY bumps into STEPHANIE.*)

TOMMY. Ha...ha... Hi.

(*As TOMMY begins talking to STEPHANIE, we switch over to:*)

(*STEVE and his girlfriend, CORA, back at their lockers.*)

CORA. Is your mom seriously going to make you take Veronica to the prom? I mean, she's like practically your sister.

STEVE. She *is* my sister.

CORA. That's what I mean. Isn't that outlawed?

STEVE. I don't know. Probably should be. But my mom doesn't think it's right for her to miss it.

CORA. Then tell her to take someone.

STEVE. It's not that simple. She'll only go with Chad Glamorville and he'll never take her. But once we're there, we can be together.

CORA. I don't care, you're supposed to take *me*. As your girlfriend, I have certain inalienable rights. One is a date to the prom.

STEVE. What are the others?

CORA. Do I need to write them down again?

STEVE. You better just make me a copy of the whole contract.

(*VERONICA has snuck up behind them, yo-yoing menacingly.*)

VERONICA. Break it up. Break it up. No fraternizing with the help.

STEVE. Uh...okay.

CORA. Was that a joke or an insult or what?

VERONICA. Oh, hello Cora, I didn't see you there. Did you just get here or have you been here the whole time? (*She starts snort laughing.*)

CORA. Why can't you just go to prom with one of these other dorks?

VERONICA. Because I will ONLY go with the love of my life, the dreamiest of all walking dreamings...Chad Glamorville. Lead actor in four out of the five school plays. He would have been lead in all five, but he had to drop out of *Annie* when he got mono. Would you like me to recite the rest of his theatrical resume?

(*CORA stops a MATH GEEK in the hallway. He yelps.*)

CORA. Listen, kid, I want you to go to the prom with Veronica. Okay?

(*VERONICA silently threatens him with her yo-yo.*)

MATH GEEK. She, um...scares me.

(VERONICA yo-yo's at him. He runs away.)

VERONICA. Chad Glamorville or death.

CORA. Ugh. I give up.

(CORA storms off.)

STEVE. *(To VERONICA:)* Thanks. Thanks, alot.

(STEVE follows after CORA.)

(Back to STEPHANIE and TOMMY. BUGS watches, and pretends to busy himself.)

STEPHANIE. You want me to go to the prom with Bugs?

(They look over at BUGS and catch him eating something from his hair.)

STEPHANIE. Why would I do that? Unless you know something I don't, like the world is ending. Or he's a famous actor or something.

TOMMY. That's exactly right. Actually.

ACTRESS 1. Oh my god the world is ending? How do I look?

ACTRESS 2. Totally ready.

ACTRESS 1. Thanks, you're sweet.

TOMMY. No...he's... *(Pulling STEPHANIE aside:)* I shouldn't really be saying this...but he's...a professional actor.

STEPHANIE. Yeah right. How could he be? He's not even in any of the school plays.

TOMMY. He...only acts in New York.

STEPHANIE. What part?

TOMMY. Uh... The city part.

STEPHANIE. Cool.

TOMMY. His agent won't let him act in school plays. It might...hurt his career. He has a reputation to uphold.

STEPHANIE. Yeah, I understand that.

TOMMY. His agent is very strict when it comes to parts.

STEPHANIE. I'm strict about my parts too. Who's his agent?

TOMMY. His agent's name? Uh...Kris...tooff...Baba...balooch. Kristoff Bababalooch.

STEPHANIE. Huh.

TOMMY. You've probably heard of him.

STEPHANIE. Yeah, totally. His supposed to be...really strict.

TOMMY. Yeah, that's him. He's Croatian. That's how they are. From an island there. An international talent and entertainment island.

STEPHANIE. Cool. Think he'd ever come here to the school? Like as a talent scout?

TOMMY. I don't know. Probably not. He's very busy.

STEPHANIE. Oh. That's a shame.

TOMMY. But who knows. It wouldn't hurt to ask.

STEPHANIE. Wow, great. Oh my God I'm so nervous. I hope I don't forget to go to the bathroom. How terrible would that be to have an "accident" on stage.

TOMMY. Does that happen?

STEPHANIE. Sometimes. A few of the girls wear diapers. Right girls?

ACTRESS. It's called being a prepared actress.

(First bell rings.)

(STEPHANIE and ACTRESSES scatter.)

(SHELLY, the costume shop girl, is walking to class. She wears several layers of clothes and has various needles in her hair.)

SHELLY. Tommy, can I ask you something?

TOMMY. Shelly, you're the costume expert—do actresses wear diapers on stage?

SHELLY. The prepared ones do.

TOMMY. Huh. Never heard of that.

(SHELLY is about to ask TOMMY a question when BUGS pulls TOMMY aside. SHELLY wanders away.)

BUGS. So are we set?

TOMMY. Not yet. But I think she's warming to the idea. One thing though ...and this isn't a big deal at all...I kinda told her you were a professional actor.

BUGS. You told her I'm what?

TOMMY. An actor.

BUGS. An actor?! Ugh. I'd rather be anybody else. I'd rather be a jock.

TOMMY. I didn't have a choice. She only dates actors. Lead actors.

BUGS. But I'm not a lead actor.

TOMMY. You are now. So brush up on your Shakespeare.

BUGS. Shakespeare I know. Shakespeare is not a problem. *To not be, or to not be...is the same question.*

TOMMY. Brilliant...she'll never believe this.

BUGS. How dare you insult my training.

(Second Bell rings.)

(The rest of the students go their separate ways.)

After 2nd Period

(Bell rings, students flood the hallway.)

(TOMMY and BUGS enter mid-conversation from the end of class.)

TOMMY. So just be yourself. But be a professional actor from New York.

BUGS. New York? What part?

TOMMY. The city part.

(TOMMY pulls out a fedora hat.)

TOMMY. Here. Wear this.

BUGS. Am I an actor working for the mob?

TOMMY. Just wear it. It'll add a little persona, a little mystique.

(TOMMY approaches STEPHANIE and she pretends not to notice him coming over. Real suave-like, BUGS leans against her locker without saying anything.)

STEPHANIE. Oh. Hi...Bugs.

(BUGS tips his hat up.)

BUGS. Hiya, sweetheart.

STEPHANIE. I like your hat.

BUGS. Oh this. It's from a show I did last fall.

STEPHANIE. I had no idea you were an actor.

BUGS. I'm many things.

STEPHANIE. That's cool. I like many things.

BUGS. Then you like me.

STEPHANIE. Tommy mentioned Kristoff Bababalooch might be able to make it to our school play.

BUGS. Chrissy Baba-who?

STEPHANIE. Kristoff Bababalooch. Your agent.

BUGS. Oh...right, that guy. Outta sight outta mind you know? Oh sure, he'll come. If you want him to. He loves that kinda junk. I mean he loves theater. School theater. Eats it up.

STEPHANIE. Really? Wow. That would be amazing, Bugs.

BUGS. No problem. I could probably get him to come today. I mean the guy is at my beck and call, ya know?

STEPHANIE. Today?

BUGS. Sure why not.

STEPHANIE. I'm not even wearing the right clothes or makeup or anything.

BUGS. Are you kidding me? You look so hot right now...like the sun on fire.

STEPHANIE. Think so? Thanks. Oh great, am I totally blushing?

BUGS. A little. You have a great blush. Your kinda blush works great on film, too.

STEPHANIE. *(Laughs nervously.)* I should go tell the rest of the cast. This is so amazing.

BUGS. Sure, whatever.

> *(STEPHANIE runs over to the other ACTRESSES who proceed to squeal in delight.)*
>
> *(BUGS, as cool as he can, runs over to TOMMY.)*

BUGS. I need an agent!

TOMMY. Shhhh.

BUGS. *(In a desperate whisper:)* I need an agent.

TOMMY. You have one. Kristoff Bababalooch.

BUGS. Right. I need him. To come to school. Today. I told her he could and now she thinks he's coming here and I need him to come here and seal this deal and this is all your fault and I can't believe I just talked to Stephanie Mezaluna for as long as I did and the hat worked perfectly.

TOMMY. Okay—just calm down. Bugs, calm down. We're gonna figure this out.

BUGS. We're running out of time!

TOMMY. I know. Okay, go find me a suit. The nicest suit you can find.

BUGS. A suit. For your funeral?

TOMMY. Maybe. Find Shelly in the costume shop, tell her I sent you. C'mon—go!

> *(BUGS nods and runs off.)*
>
> *(SHELLY enters.)*

TOMMY. Shelly, what are you doing here? I just sent someone down to the costume shop.

> *(SHELLY sighs and exits.)*
>
> *(TOMMY stops STEVE at his locker.)*

TOMMY. Steve, I need a favor.

STEVE. I already told you I can't make you cool. It's just impossible.

TOMMY. Forget about that. This is something else. Here's what I need you to do.

> *(TOMMY whispers in his ear a very elaborate plan. STEVE nods as if he's understanding. TOMMY finishes.)*

TOMMY. Okay?

STEVE. All I heard was whispers.

TOMMY. Ugh. Okay, I need you to pretend like you're a talent agent from New York named Kristoff Bababalooch who represents Bugs the thug who is pretending to be a professional actor so he can get a date for the prom and you're the only person that looks over 20 in our school, so I need you to dress as Kristoff so I can win my freedom from bully tyranny next year. Okay?

STEVE. Yeah, what's in it for me?

TOMMY. And in exchange I will continue to tutor you free of charge.

STEVE. Yeah but you continue to tutor me free of charge now.

TOMMY. Good point.

STEVE. I'll do it under one condition. You get a date for my sister Veronica for the prom. If she doesn't have a date, my mom is making me take her.

TOMMY. I asked her last month and she turned me down.

STEVE. She wants to go with Chad Glamorville. And only Chad Glamorville.

TOMMY. But he's dating Stephanie Mezaluna.

STEVE. That's the deal.

TOMMY. ...Actually this may work out.

(They shake.)

(First bell.)

(CHAD is walking down the hall, holding a script, rehearsing his lines with himself, even acting out the part a little bit.)

STEVE. Here he comes. Good luck.

(STEVE takes off.)

CHAD. *(To himself, in a Southern accent:)* And that is why, Mama, I ain't ever gonna let nothin' happen to our hogs. Nothin'!

TOMMY. Hey, I need to talk to you about something very important.

CHAD. I have rehearsal.

TOMMY. Just a quick something important. You need to take Veronica Jettlebaum to prom.

CHAD. Veronica Jettlebaum? What are you, sick?

TOMMY. No...but she is. It's Veronica's dying wish to go to the prom. But no one will go with her.

CHAD. What do you mean her *dying* wish?

TOMMY. Let's just hope she makes it.

CHAD. Is she really sick?

TOMMY. No she has a rare disease.

CHAD. What kind of disease? It must be fatal.

TOMMY. No no.

CHAD. But you said she's going to die.

TOMMY. Yes well, we all are eventually.

CHAD. True. And depressing. So what is it then?

TOMMY. It's her...her muscles...are turning inside out.

CHAD. I didn't know they could do that.

TOMMY. They're not supposed to. Like I said it's a very rare condition. She only has 3 weeks to live.

CHAD. I thought you said it's not fatal?

TOMMY. It's not.

CHAD. Then why is she going to die?

TOMMY. I'm not sure. But it seems serious.

CHAD. I'd say!

TOMMY. You don't have to. The doctors said everything that could be said.

CHAD. How sad.

TOMMY. Tragic. It's a tragedy. A *Shakespearean* tragedy. You know all about those I'm sure.

CHAD. I have a background in the classics, yes.

TOMMY. Then you're the only one who understands this situation. You're the only one who can play this heroic role. It's only for *lead* actors.

CHAD. Like me.

TOMMY. Every great actor has their great charity. Brad Pitt, Sean Penn, Keanu Reeves... Have you found yours yet?

CHAD. No...I haven't. Shoot! I need a charity.

TOMMY. Make Veronica Jettlebaum your charity. Take her to the prom.

(Second bell rings.)

CHAD. ...Okay, I'll do it. I'm sure Stephanie will understand. It's for our craft.

*(*TOMMY *and* CHAD *shake and head their separate ways.)*

(The hallway clears.)

After 3rd Period

(Bell rings, students flood the hallway.)

*(*TOMMY *is looking for* STEVE.*)*

*(*BUGS *runs up to* TOMMY.*)*

BUGS. Tommy! Where is he?

TOMMY. Where is who?

BUGS. Kristoff Bababalooch! My agent!

TOMMY. I'm working on it.

BUGS. Well work faster. It's almost fifth period!

*(*BUGS *punches a locker.)*

BUGS. Don't forget I'm a bully!

(TOMMY *sees* STEVE.)

TOMMY. Got it.

(*As soon as* TOMMY *leaves to talk to* STEVE, BUGS *drops the tough guy persona and nurses his hand.*)

BUGS. Owsie.

(TOMMY *and* STEVE:)

TOMMY. We're all set. Veronica has a date to go to the prom with Chad Glamorville.

STEVE. Well that was easy.

TOMMY. Not as easy as you think. I still need you to look and act like a believable talent agent from New York. He's from a Croatian island, okay? Now, Shelly is waiting for you in the costume shop. I need you as Kristoff Bababalooch in this hallway by next period. Can you do it?

STEVE. Sure, sure. Chad's really going to take my sister to the prom?

TOMMY. Yes!

STEVE. Why?

TOMMY. I made it a matter of life or death. Now please just go!

(STEVE *hurries off. On his way out, he runs past* CORA. STEVE *stops and kisses her on the cheek.*)

STEVE. We can go to the prom after all.

CORA. What? How?

STEVE. Kristoff Bababalooch.

CORA. What the heck is that?

STEVE. You'll see.

(STEVE *is on his way out again. Now he runs into* VERONICA.)

STEVE. Veronica! Good news. We don't have to go to the prom together.

VERONICA. What? Why?

STEVE. Kristoff Bababalooch.

VERONICA. Who the heck is that?

STEVE. You'll see.

VERONICA. I told you I'd only go with Chad Glamorville.

STEVE. And you are. Will be. Talk to Tommy. I gotta go get agent-ed.

(STEVE *runs out.* VERONICA *approaches* TOMMY.)

TOMMY. I know you're gonna ask how and why and who but don't worry about those pesky questions, the bell is gonna ring any minute.

VERONICA. What bell?

TOMMY. And no "what's" either.

VERONICA. Steve said—

TOMMY. Yes, Chad Glamorville. And you. And the prom. There's only one catch.

VERONICA. Chad is the catch.

TOMMY. No, well yes, he *is* a catch but the other catch is that you're dying.

VERONICA. That's quite a catch.

TOMMY. Not *really* dying. Just *fake* dying. You said he was worth dying for and now you are.

VERONICA. When did I say that?

TOMMY. I'm sure you thought it. At some point.

VERONICA. What am I dying of?

TOMMY. Here I made a list.

(He hands her several sheets of paper. She flips through it.)

VERONICA. And if I'm dying of all these things he agreed to go with me?

TOMMY. He has a very big heart. Now go read through it. You gotta play that part.

VERONICA. Okay, if it's for Chad Glamorville, it's worth it.

(VERONICA heads off.)

(BUGS confronts TOMMY.)

BUGS. What was that all about?

TOMMY. It's all part of the plan.

(STEPHANIE confronts BUGS and TOMMY.)

STEPHANIE. I thought you said your agent was coming.

BUGS. Yeah I did. And he is.

STEPHANIE. So then where is he?

BUGS. I just talked to him. He happened to be in town. He's on his way. I'll go try his cell again.

(BUGS leaves.)

STEPHANIE. Why would he be in town?

TOMMY. He's a talent scout. He's scouting...for talent.

STEPHANIE. I don't believe you.

TOMMY. If he comes here next period, will you go with Bugs to the prom?

STEPHANIE. I'm already going with Chad Glamorville, lead actor, and I'm not going to just break up with him for nothing.

TOMMY. Bugs' agent will be here.

STEPHANIE. If a New York agent walks down this hall next period, I will go to the prom with Bugs.

(They shake.)

TOMMY. Next period. Promise.

STEPHANIE. And if he doesn't, I'll make sure you never get a date in this school again.

TOMMY. I don't get any now, so...I mean...it's a deal.

(They shake again.)

(CHAD *approaches* STEPHANIE.)

CHAD. Hey.

STEPHANIE. Hey.

CHAD. We need to talk.   **STEPHANIE.** We need to talk.

(First bell rings.)

CHAD. After class.   **STEPHANIE.** After class.

(CHAD *and* STEPHANIE *go their separate ways.)*

(BUGS finds TOMMY.)

BUGS. Tommy.

TOMMY. Bugs. Be patient. I've got it all figured out.

BUGS. No I got it figured out.

TOMMY. I really don't think you do.

BUGS. This is Kia.

(KIA comes out from behind BUGS. She's a puny math geek.)

BUGS. She's a math geek.

TOMMY. I can see that.

KIA. Actually, I'm a math dork.

BUGS. She represents a team of dorks.

KIA. A club to be precise.

BUGS. And they've agreed to be my fans. I figure every famous actor has fans, rights? And I'm a famous actor now, right? So where are my fans?

KIA. *(With unbridled enthusiasm:)* We're right here!

BUGS. See watch this... Go ahead, Kia.

KIA. Oh my God it's Bugs Lowery! Bugs can I have your autograph?!

BUGS. *(A little too rehearsed:)* Of course you can, fan. *(Then, normal back to TOMMY:)* See that? Once Stephanie sees I have fans, it should really seal the deal, don't you think?

TOMMY. And what do they get out of it?

BUGS. They win their bully freedom just like you.

TOMMY. Some deal.

BUGS. All right, fan, see you next period.

(BUGS leaves.)

KIA. Also, we want dates for the prom.

TOMMY. Well you should have thought about that earlier.

KIA. No *you* should have thought about that earlier. It's all right, I know how to get us dates.

    (Second bell rings.)

TOMMY. Yeah how's that?

KIA. We want to be famous, too.

    (KIA and the rest of the hallway students clear out.)

    (TOMMY puts his head in his hands.)

After 4th Period / Before 5th Period

    (Bell rings, students flood the hallway.)

    (SHELLY finds TOMMY. She's covered in even more random pieces of clothing, pins, and accessories.)

SHELLY. Okay, you need to stop sending desperate people to me.

TOMMY. Shelly, you're a life saver. Is everything set?

SHELLY. Of course. I'm a professional.

TOMMY. How do they look?

SHELLY. You'll see soon enough. *(TOMMY looks worried.)* They look great. You owe me. I mean you owe me big. You owe me a night on the town.

TOMMY. Next you're gonna say I should take you to the prom.

SHELLY. Maybe you should.

TOMMY. Okay.

SHELLY. Really?

TOMMY. Sure.

SHELLY. Wow, great. I have to figure out what I'm gonna wear.

TOMMY. Wear one of the five outfits you have on. Or go see Shelly in the costume department. She'll fix you right up.

SHELLY. I bet you say that to all the girls.

TOMMY. Actually I do. But this is the first time I meant it.

SHELLY. Aw, Tommy, that's sweet. I'm not sure what it meant, but you're sweet. It's even sweeter of you to offer to buy our tickets.

    (Before TOMMY can protest, CHAD pulls him aside and SHELLY leaves.)

CHAD. Tommy, I was thinking. The gown Veronica wears to the prom isn't going to be like a hospital gown is it? Because I already rented my tux and we have to match.

TOMMY. Of course not. It's not like she wears a hospital gown to school.

(VERONICA enters in a hospital gown. She has a ton of pale make-up on and dark circles under her eyes. She coughs dramatically and does an exaggerated limping walk.)

(CHAD looks to TOMMY.)

TOMMY. You're a swell guy, Chad. Go talk to her.

CHAD. Is it contagious?

TOMMY. Not more than anything else around here.

(CHAD goes over to talk to VERONICA.)

CHAD. Uh...hi...Veronica.

VERONICA. *(Feigning surprise:)* Oh, hi, Chad. What are you doing here?

CHAD. At school?

VERONICA. Yeah...talking to me.

CHAD. Sorry to hear you're sick. Where's your yo-yo?

VERONICA. Oh...I musta left it at the hospital. When I was there...being treated...for sickness...and stuff.

CHAD. Are you going to be okay?

VERONICA. In heaven?

CHAD. No, now.

VERONICA. Ha, ha. You're cute. All I ever wanted was to be treated... *(cough, cough)* ...like a normal teenager.

CHAD. Maybe I can help with that...

(BUGS enters and finds TOMMY.)

BUGS. Where's Stephanie? I got my fans on standby.

TOMMY. She should be here.

(STEPHANIE enters.)

BUGS. Stephanie.

STEPHANIE. So guys, where's Kristoff?

ACTRESS 1. Yeah, where's this hot-shot agent?

ACTRESS 2. Is he even gonna show?

(STEVE enters as Kristoff Bababalooch, the sleazy New York super agent. He wears an expensive-looking suit and a swanky mustache that keeps falling off. His hair is slicked back and he speaks with a slightly ambiguous European accent.)

STEVE. Bugs, baby! Be wit you in a hot minute.

BUGS. *(Aside to TOMMY:)* Who's that?

TOMMY. *(Aside:)* That's your agent, you nitwit.

(STEVE walks by VERONICA.)

STEVE. Who are you? You've got a great look. Sick is very "in" right now. Here's my card.

(STEVE *throws her a card, then approaches* BUGS.)

STEVE. There he is. You bug-eater-you.

BUGS. *(Immediately playing the part:)* Kristoff! So good of you to come.

(STEVE *air kisses* BUGS *on both cheeks.*)

TOMMY. *(To* STEPHANIE:*)* Whatta I tell ya?

BUGS. Kristoff, I'd like you to meet a very talented actress. No, Tommy, I'm not talking about you, ha, ha... Kristoff, this is Stephanie Mezaluna.

STEPHANIE. It's a pleasure to meet you, Mr. Bababalooch.

(STEVE *air kisses her on both cheeks.*)

STEVE. I've heard wonderful things about your work.

STEPHANIE. Wow, really?

STEVE. And these must be the other actresses.

BUGS. Yes, of course. Let me introduce you. Kristoff, these are...the other actresses.

TOMMY. Stephanie and Bugs are going to the prom together, isn't that, right, Stephanie?

STEPHANIE. Oh...right. That's...right.

STEVE. That's great, great. Crazy kids. I remember my prom. It was inside a volcano. Because I'm from an island or something. We used to play futbol with rotten pineapples coated in pig grease.

(TOMMY *is trying to signal him to stop talking.*)

STEVE. Well...I gotta get going.

STEPHANIE. Already?

ACTRESS 1. Don't you want to see our show?

ACTRESS 2. Or at least sit in on a rehearsal or something?

STEVE. No, no, I can't stay. But send me your headshots.

BUGS. *(Feigning disappointment:)* Are you sure you can't stay, Kristoff?

(CORA *enters and approaches* STEVE. *She looks at him strangely.*)

STEVE. Bugs, why is this strange girl staring at me? Please ask her to leave.

TOMMY. Cora, get out of here.

CORA. Steve is that you?

STEVE. I am Kristoff Bababalooch. And you must be another actress looking for attention.

CORA. What?

TOMMY. Haha. Excuse us.

(TOMMY *pulls* CORA *aside.*)

(*Meanwhile,* STEVE *starts handing out fake business cards.*)

TOMMY. Cora, what are you doing? You're gonna ruin the whole thing.

CORA. Is that Steve?

TOMMY. Of course it is.

CORA. Why is he dressed like that?

TOMMY. *(Takes a deep breath.)* He's playing a talent agent, who represents Bugs who's pretending to be a famous actor to impress Stephanie in exchange for my freedom from his bullying, in exchange for me getting a date with Chad Glamorville, for Veronica who's pretending to be sick, so Steve is free to go to the prom with you.

CORA. *(Beat.)* Aw, that's sweet.

> *(STEPHANIE comes over to them.)*

STEPHANIE. Cora, why did you call Kristoff, Steve?

TOMMY. That's his middle name. It's Croatian.

STEPHANIE. The name Steve is Croatian?

TOMMY. Steve is short for Steve-oph-ittle. Steveophittle.

> *(STEPHANIE is still confused.)*

CORA. Who are they?

> *(She points to KIA and the MATH GEEKS who are posed to swarm BUGS.)*

> *(TOMMY waves at BUGS to get the fans to rush over.)*

> *(BUGS gives them the nod and they come rushing over.)*

KIA. Hey Bugs. Are you really Bugs Lowery, the actor? He's, um...you're... amazing.

MATH GEEK 1. We're really big fans of your work. We've followed your career rather closely.

MATH GEEK 2. Do you think we can have your autograph?

MATH GEEK 3. And a picture with you?

KIA. It'd mean so much to us. And the Bugs fanclub we've formed. It's just a local chapter, but hey, it's just great to be a small part of what you do.

BUGS. Well, sure, I suppose I have a little time for that. Excuse me Stephanie, I'll be right back.

STEPHANIE. You have fans? And a fan club?

BUGS. It's just a local chapter.

STEPHANIE. That's...wow. I didn't realize you were that famous.

BUGS. I try not to let it go to my head.

> *(BUGS starts signing autographs and taking pictures with the MATH GEEKS. STEPHANIE stands by his side.)*

> *(Meanwhile TOMMY has ushered STEVE away from STEPHANIE and the other students.)*

ACTRESS 1. To think we were going to school with him this whole time.

ACTRESS 2. It's just a bunch of math geeks. Hey, Tommy where did Kristoff go? I have to give him my reel.

TOMMY. *(Ignoring her question:)* Actually, those aren't your average math geeks. You're looking at future reality TV stars. They're in the biz. That's probably how they know about Bugs.

ACTRESS 1. Reality TV stars of what?

TOMMY. The show is...about this competitive math team. It's called "Calculate This." It's like a thinking man's "Jersey Shore."

ACTRESS 2. That sounds awesome.

TOMMY. Supposed to be huge. When it gets here. It's only airing in Japan right now, but they're practically celebrities over there.

ACTRESS 2. Oh really...

ACTRESS 1. We should go talk to them.

TOMMY. Better yet, take them to the prom. If you date them now that will be so much more...meaningful...down the road. You know, the TV viewers really respond to that sort of thing. Actually there have been some talks to make "Calculate This" into a movie and then naturally into a Broadway musical. That's what happening with all mediocre movies now. You know how Hollywood is...

ACTRESSES. Oh sure...right...Hollywood...of course...totally...

(The ACTRESSES *all go mingle with the* MATH GEEKS. KIA *gives* TOMMY *a thumbs up behind their back.)*

(STEVE secretly sneaks off with CORA.)

(SHELLY enters and approaches TOMMY.)

SHELLY. Well?

TOMMY. It worked. I think. The mustache was a nice touch. Maybe a little more glue next time.

(STEPHANIE and CHAD approach each other.)

STEPHANIE. Chad. I'm sorry we didn't get to talk last period. But alot has happened since then.

CHAD. I know what you mean. It's like the whole earth rotates every class. And I just think it'd be better if we—

STEPHANIE. —If we maybe, for the prom—

CHAD. —Went with other people.

STEPHANIE. Yes! I mean, I think, I understand.

CHAD. Oh, good. Just out of curiosity, who are you going with?

STEPHANIE. Um...well...Bugs.

CHAD. Oh. Bugs. The wanna-be bully who eats things from his hair?

STEPHANIE. That's just a character he plays. And who are you taking?

CHAD. Veronica.

STEPHANIE. The yo-yo-ing nerd with anger management issues?

CHAD. She's dying, so...

STEPHANIE. A charity case, no, that makes sense.

(Everyone is paired off with their respective others: STEPHANIE *and* BUGS, VERONICA *and* CHAD, STEVE *and* CORA, TOMMY *and* SHELLY, *and* MATH GEEKS *and* THEATER GEEKS.*)*

BUGS. So, you did it, Tommy. You're free and clear from my bullying next year.

SHELLY. *And* you have a really hot date for the prom.

TOMMY. Looks like things may finally be looking up for me.

(BURP enters with a vulgar burp.)

BURP. Everyone, if I could have your attention. I have some exciting news for all of you. Due to my extraordinary lack of academic efforts, you will be delighted to know that I will be gracing you with my presence again next year.

TOMMY. You're staying back...again?

BUGS. Looks like things are finally looking up for you.

(TOMMY approaches BURP.)

TOMMY. Burp, maybe we can work something out. I've done wonders for the people around here.

(TOMMY puts his arm around BURP and they walk out in negotiations.)

(The bell rings.)

(Everyone makes their way out of the hallway.)

(From the other side of the now empty hallway, we hear:)

OFF STAGE VOICE. Last chance for prom tickets! Last chance!

(Everyone runs back on and through the hallway to get their tickets.)

End of Play

SMALL WORLD

by Tracey Scott Wilson

For more information about rights and permissions, see page 9.

Cast of Characters

MAN 1

MAN 2

MAN 3

WOMAN 1

WOMAN 2

WOMAN 3

Acknowledgments

Small World was originally commissioned by the Guthrie Theater, (Joe Dowling, Artistic Director) and was performed through the Guthrie's summer conservatory program—A Guthrie Experience for Actors in Training—in 2001.

SMALL WORLD

(Lights up on three couples meeting at separate benches. They have never met before. It is a first, blind date for all. Unless specified, MAN 1 speaks only to WOMAN 1, MAN 2 only speaks to WOMAN 2, and MAN 3 only speaks to WOMAN 3. When it reads MAN 1,2, etc. the specified characters are speaking simultaneously. Also, [...] indicates the characters are finishing the previous sentence.)

MAN 1. Stacy?

WOMAN 1. Bob?

MAN 2. Lucy?

WOMAN 2. Bill?

MAN 3. Alice?

WOMAN 3. Tim?

ALL. Hi!

MAN 1. I've never been on one of these blind...

MAN 2. ...Computer...

MAN 3. Newspaper ad...

MAN 1,2,3. Dates Before.

WOMAN 1,2,3. Neither have I.

(They sit.)

MAN 1,2. It's a beautiful day here in the park.

MAN 3. Maybe we should have gone to the park.

WOMAN 1,2. Yes.

WOMAN 3. No.

MAN 3. Oh.

WOMAN 3. I have allergies. *(Pause.)* But still you...

WOMAN 1,2,3. Couldn't ask for a more...

WOMAN 1. Beautiful...

WOMAN 2. Wonderful...

WOMAN 3. Pretty...

WOMAN 1,2,3. Day today.

MAN 1,2. Would you like to go for a walk around the...

MAN 1. Lake.

MAN 2. Flower garden.

MAN 3. Wanna go to a movie?

WOMAN 1. Maybe in a minute.

WOMAN 2. I'd like to sit here for a few minutes.

WOMAN 3. Can we talk first?

MAN 1,2,3. OK.

ALL. So...

WOMAN 1,2. I understand you work in...

WOMAN 1. ...the health care...

WOMAN 2. ...the music...

WOMAN 1,2. Industry.

WOMAN 3. I am so lonely.

MAN 1. Yes, I am a home health aid for the elderly.

MAN 2. Yes, I'm writing a book on jazz.

MAN 3. I...uh...

WOMAN 1,2. That's...

WOMAN 1. Wonderful.

WOMAN 2. Exciting.

WOMAN 3. Please help me.

MAN 1,2. So...

MAN 3. Uh...

MAN 1,2. What do you do?

MAN 3. How can I help you?

WOMAN 1. Oh, I'm just an office manager for a small office.

WOMAN 2. I'm a computer consultant.

WOMAN 3. Just be real with me.

WOMAN 1,2. But I really want to...

WOMAN 3. Be really, really, really, really, really real with me.

WOMAN 1. ...work in TV.

WOMAN 2. ...own a farm someday.

WOMAN 3. Un-orchestrate your emotion to my song.

MAN 1. Interesting.

MAN 2. Great.

MAN 3. Wait a minute.

MAN 1. I have a friend...

MAN 2. I know someone...

MAN 3. Have you read that book...

MAN 1. ...who works in TV.

MAN 2. ...who owns a farm.

MAN 3. *(Recalling the name of a book:)* Think it...

WOMAN 3. Say It...

MAN 3. Speak It...

MAN 3 / WOMAN 3. Now!!! The Interactive Guide to Kicking Your Inner Child's Ass.

MAN 1. She says TV is...

MAN 2. He says farming is...

MAN 3. I love that book.

MAN 1,2. A lot of work.

MAN 3. It changed my life.

MAN 1. ...but rewarding.

WOMAN 1. Yeah.

WOMAN 2. Yup.

WOMAN 3. It changed my life too. *(Pause.)* Before I read that book I was so polite all the time. I was into...

MAN 3 / WOMAN 3. Pseudo-Ultra-Judo-Fake-Bonding.

WOMAN 3. Like it says in the book! Before I read that book, I would have come here today and just had a...

WOMAN 1,2. So...

WOMAN 3. ...shallow conversation.

WOMAN 1,2. It must be really rewarding to...

WOMAN 3. ...about nothing.

WOMAN 1. ...help the elderly.

WOMAN 2. ...write about jazz.

WOMAN 3. But because of that book I feel strong enough to say to you: HELP ME!!!!

MAN 1,2. It's so rewarding.

MAN 1. I couldn't begin to tell you.

MAN 2. Jazz is my life.

MAN 3. I will help you. What's wrong.

WOMAN 3. You see, I'm not really over my...

      (Lights up on MAN 1.)

...last boyfriend.

MAN 1. Some people get depressed when they look at the elderly.

WOMAN 3. He told me he was a home health aid for the elderly.

MAN 1. But I don't. I feel hopeful.

WOMAN 3. But he only had one patient.

MAN 1. ...to have lived so long and experienced so much.

WOMAN 3. ...his mother.

MAN 1. It's a beautiful thing.

WOMAN 1. Wow.

MAN 3. Ewwwww.

WOMAN 3. Every time I would go over his house he would excuse himself every few minutes, and go into another room. I just thought he had a bladder problem, but then one day I heard someone talking. I asked him. *(To* MAN 1*:)* Who was that?

MAN 1. *(To* WOMAN 3*:)* No one. You're hearing things. I live alone.

WOMAN 3. *(To* MAN 3*:)* But one day, I tiptoed behind him and peeked in the room. There was an old woman in a chair. He was calling her...

MAN 1. Momma.

WOMAN 1. *(To* MAN 3*:)* I was very understanding. *(To* MAN 1*:)* Oh, honey, is this your mother? You take care of her? That's nothing to be ashamed of. It's sweet. Your mother and all those others too. *(To* MAN 3*:)* Then this woman, who is like so wrinkled a prune would stare in awe says...

WOMAN 2. *(As mother:)* Who are you? Who are you? I'm his one and only patient. His one and only. Get out! I'm the only one who gets their feet shaved around here. You're stepping on my toenail clippings. GET OUT! GET OUT!

WOMAN 3. Two days later he was like...

MAN 1. *(To* WOMAN 3*:)* I tried to be a home health worker, but Momma takes up all of my time. I love Momma. I love Momma. I love Momma. I do. Before that she and Grandma took up all of my time. I love Grandma. I love Grandma. I love Grandma. I do. But Grandma is dead now, and soon, Momma will be dead too. Then you can move into my house, and we'll have kids. Two boys and two girls. We'll teach them to be good little home health workers too 'cause, like Momma says, by the time we grow old our Social Security check won't buy us a cup of milk.

WOMAN 1. You are so noble.

MAN 3. Ewwwww.

WOMAN 3. But I still think of him.

MAN 3. I know what you mean, I'm still hung up on my girlfriend too.

　　　　(Lights up on WOMAN 2*.)*

She said she wanted to be a farmer.

WOMAN 2. I know it's a lot of work, but to be out in the fresh country air...

MAN 3. ...a chicken farmer.

WOMAN 2. ...communing with nature every day, feeding the land, feeding the chickens.

MAN 3. But that's not all she wanted to do with those chickens.

　　　　(MAN 3 squirms in his chair.)

WOMAN 2. *(To* MAN 3*:)* What's wrong with you?

MAN 3. *(To* WOMAN 2*:)* I've got hay in my butt. God, that is the last time we go to a farm.

WOMAN 2. *(To* MAN 3*:)* What? No!

MAN 3. *(To* WOMAN 2*:)* Yes, it is.

WOMAN 2. *(To* MAN 3*:)* But farming is my life.

MAN 3. *(To* WOMAN 2*:)* But you don't own a farm. I don't understand why we have to sneak in other people's barns to make love all the time. At first, it was exciting, but now it's just weird.

WOMAN 2. *(To* MAN 3*:)* You're so conventional.

MAN 3. *(To* WOMAN 2*:)* I am not...I...

> *(There is the sound of a chicken.)*

MAN 3. *(To* WOMAN 2*:)* What was that?

> *(Sound of a chicken.)*

WOMAN 2. *(To* MAN 3*:)* Nothing.

MAN 3. It sounded like. *(To* WOMAN 3*:)* I opened the closet door and there were all these chickens. Chickens everywhere. *(To* WOMAN 2*:)* What the...

WOMAN 2. *(To* MAN 3*:)* Don't touch them. I love them. See how soft and gentle.

MAN 3. You can't... We can't keep chickens in the apartment.

WOMAN 2. *(To* MAN 3*:)* Quiet! Don't yell in front of them. *(Pause.)* See they are so sweet and gentle. Like kittens with feathers. But sexy. Very sexy. That clucking drives me wild. Please just touch the chickens baby! Touch the chickens!

MAN 2. I love nature too.

WOMAN 3. Yuuucchhh.

MAN 3. What's wrong with us?

WOMAN 3. For me it has been a pattern. A pattern of unhealthy relationships. The other guy I dated...

> *(Lights up on* MAN 2*.)*

A die-hard jazz lover.

MAN 2. Jazz is truly the only great American art form.

WOMAN 3. So I thought.

MAN 2. In its rhythms we hear America. In its tunes we see ourselves.

WOMAN 3. I studied everything I could about jazz so I could get close to him. I bought thousands of recordings. One day I bought him this Miles Davis recording. It took me six months to find it. I was going to surprise him and slip it into his record collection. I must have hit some secret door because *(To* MAN 2*:)* Honey...

MAN 2. *(To* WOMAN 3*:)* Yeah, baby.

WOMAN 3. Uh...I wanted to give you this.

(Hands him CD.)

MAN 2. *(To* WOMAN 3*:)* Oh, wow. Miles Davis session number 73. Oh, wow, baby, thank you, thank you.

WOMAN 3. *(To* MAN 2*:)* Uh-huh. Um... I was going to put it with your other records, and surprise you.

MAN 2. *(To* WOMAN 3*:)* Uh-huh. This is perfect baby thank you so much...

WOMAN 1. *(To* MAN 2*:)* And I found this.

*(*WOMAN *shows him CD.)*

MAN 2. *(To* WOMAN 3*:)* Oh...uh... Yeah. You know, I was holding that for my mother...my mother.

WOMAN 3. *(To* MAN 3*:)* A Yanni CD. *(To* MAN 2*:)* No you weren't.

(She dumps a whole bunch of CDs at his feet.)

WOMAN 3. *(To* MAN 2*:)* Yanni, John Tesh, Enya, Celine Dion, Phil Collins. What is this about? I though you were cool.

MAN 2. *(To* WOMAN 3*:)* Hey, be careful! You're going to scratch them. *(Pause.)* One night I couldn't sleep alright. So, I turned on the radio. They were playing *Desert Siren* by Yanni.

(He hums tune.)

It was so relaxing.

(He hums.)

So calming.

(He hums.)

Yanni is beautiful.

(He hums tune.)

Someday, he'll be appreciated.

(He hums tune.)

Someday.

(He hums.)

Someday.

WOMAN 2. *(To* MAN 2*:)* I want you to teach me everything you know about music.

MAN 3. John Tesh. Ewwwww.

WOMAN 3. So, you see it must be me.

MAN 3. No, no, no. Don't assume that. I dated this woman.

WOMAN 1. I know TV is supposed to be this vast wasteland.

MAN 3. Who wanted to work in TV.

WOMAN 1. But I think it's a powerful and effective medium...

MAN 3. So, she watched a lot of TV.

WOMAN 1. ...to communicate and express ideas.

MAN 3. But then I noticed she began to only watch one program.

(Theme from The Jeffersons *plays.)*

MAN 3. *(To* WOMAN 1:*)* Honey, do we have to watch...

WOMAN 1. *(To* MAN 3:*)* Shhhhh.

MAN 3. *(To* WOMAN 1:*)* But you've seen this episode a hundred times already.

WOMAN 1. *(To* MAN 3:*)* Shhhhh.

MAN 3. *(To* WOMAN 3:*)* All day and night, *The Jeffersons.* She would tape the show and watch it in fast forward and reverse.

WOMAN 1. *(To* MAN 3; *pointing to TV:)* See! Right there! Right there!

MAN 3. *(To* WOMAN 1:*)* What?

WOMAN 1. *(To* MAN 3:*)* Lionel just said...Pop Taht Tuoba Erus Ton Mi.

MAN 1. *(To* WOMAN 1:*)* What?

WOMAN 1. *(To* MAN 3:*)* He said...Pop Taht Tuoba Erus Ton Mi.

MAN 3. *(To* WOMAN 1:*)* What are you saying?

WOMAN 1. *(To* MAN 3:*)* Oh, I have a little language for Lionel. You see, I believe he's giving me a message. So, I speak his line backwards so I can understand.

MAN 3. *(To* WOMAN 3:*)* Giving you a message?

WOMAN 1. *(To* MAN 3:*)* Yes. Us. Us a message. To the world.

MAN 3. *(To* WOMAN 1:*)* Uh...

WOMAN 1. *(To* MAN 3:*)* Did you know Lionel created the show *Good Times.*

MAN 3. *(To* WOMAN 1:*)* Uh...honey...

WOMAN 1. *(To* MAN 3:*)* And the man that replaced him on the show was his brother. His very own brother.

MAN 3. *(To* WOMAN 1:*)* Honey, I...

WOMAN 1. *(To* MAN 1:*)* But he's gone now. No word of him since 1979. I can't find him. But I will. I know I will. Pop Taht Tuoba Erus Ton Mi. Pop Taht Tuoba Erus Ton Mi. Pop Taht Tuoba Erus Ton Mi.

MAN 1. I've never thought of TV that way before.

WOMAN 3. I'll never watch *The Jeffersons* again. *(Pause.)* In honor of you.

MAN 3. Listen, I have to tell you...

MAN 1,2,3. I really like you.

MAN 1. You're wonderful.

MAN 2. ...terrific...

MAN 3. You've touched my inner song and let me tell you baby, it ain't playing Yanni.

(WOMEN *smile and laugh in unison.*)

WOMAN 1,2,3. Well...

WOMAN 1. I think you're great...

WOMAN 2. Fantastic...

WOMAN 3. You've touched my inner song...

WOMAN 1,2,3. ...too.

MAN 1,2,3. I would love to...

MAN 1. Get to know you.

MAN 2. Spend some more time with you.

MAN 3. Coordinate your soul with mine.

WOMAN 1,2,3. *(They all sigh.)* Great!

MAN 1,2. But first I have to...

MAN 1. Stop at home for a minute.

MAN 2. Stop by the record store.

MAN 3. My afternoon is completely free.

WOMAN 1. Oh, I suppose you have to check on your patients.

WOMAN 2. Are you buying the latest jazz CD?

MAN 1,2. Uh...yeah...yeah...

WOMAN 1,2. Oh, that works out because I have to...

WOMAN 1. Set my VCR to record a program.

WOMAN 2. Stop by this new chicken farm.

WOMAN 3. My afternoon is free too.

WOMAN 1,2. So, I'll see you later then.

MAN 1,2. So, I'll see you later then.

ALL. Great!

WOMAN 1,2,3. But, I tell you, I just can't believe someone like you...

WOMAN 1. ...isn't taken...

WOMAN 2. ...hasn't been snatched up yet...

WOMAN 3. ...is free...

MAN 1,2,3. Well, I can't believe you are...

MAN 1. ...available...

MAN 2. ...not married...

MAN 3. ...unattached.

ALL. There are just too many crazy people there.

(They all laugh.)

WOMAN 1. I'm telling you...

MAN 1. You got that right.

WOMAN 2. Tell me about it.

MAN 2. I could tell you stories.

WOMAN 3. Hell, between the two of us...

MAN 3. I guess we dated every crazy person out there.

WOMAN 1,2. My last boyfriend...

MAN 1,2. ...Girlfriend...
...was a pathological liar!

WOMAN 1,2. ...was a pathological liar!

(They gasp in disbelief.)

WOMAN 1. Really?

MAN 1. No kidding.

WOMAN 2. What are the chances of that?

MAN 1,2,3. It really is a small world.

WOMAN 1,2,3. A small world.

End of Play

THE ABSOLUTE MOST CLICHÉD ELEVATOR PLAY IN THE HISTORY OF THE ENTIRE UNIVERSE

by Werner Trieschmann

For more information about rights and permissions, see page 9.

Cast of Characters

INSTRUCTOR, can be a male or female

PREGNANT WOMAN

BIKER, male

NEW AGE WOMAN

STEPHANIE, captain of the cheerleaders

BETHANY, cheerleader

BRITTNEY, cheerleader

CHEERLEADER #4, female cheerleader

CHEERLEADER #5, can be male/female cheerleader

MISFIT #1, a clown, male or female

MISFIT #2, the goth kid, male

MISFIT #3, the normal girl who can be black, white or purple (OK, maybe not purple) as long as she doesn't appear eccentric or unusual in dress or manner

Place

An elevator.

Time

Now.

Setting

A box of light to represent an elevator.

For my wife Marty, who gave me the time to write this and who is great company in an elevator.

The Absolute Most Clichéd Elevator Play in the History of the Entire Universe

(Lights up on a noticeably PREGNANT WOMAN standing in the elevator. There is a soft ring indicating the elevator door is opening. The PREGNANT WOMAN steps to the side as a BIKER walks on.)

PREGNANT WOMAN. Hi.

(The PREGNANT WOMAN clutches her belly.)

PREGNANT WOMAN. Oh!

(BIKER grunts an answer back.)

(Now the NEW AGE WOMAN, who is holding a flower and wearing a loose-flowing dress and a floppy hat, walks on the elevator.)

NEW AGE WOMAN. Peace.

PREGNANT WOMAN. Hi.

(The PREGNANT WOMAN clutches her belly.)

PREGNANT WOMAN. Oh!

(BIKER grunts something.)

(Now the INSTRUCTOR walks on the elevator.)

INSTRUCTOR. First floor please.

PREGNANT WOMAN. That's where we're all going.

INSTRUCTOR. Oh OK. Thanks.

(The PREGNANT WOMAN clutches her belly.)

PREGNANT WOMAN. Oh!

NEW AGE WOMAN. Peace.

(BIKER grunts something.)

(Now the elevator door closes [indicated by sound like a bell or with a light change]. The INSTRUCTOR takes a moment to notice each of the occupants of the elevator, who are now standing in a straight line.)

INSTRUCTOR. Interesting.

*(There is a noise and the lights go off and quickly come back on. EVERYBODY in the elevator bends at the knees at the same time to indicate the elevator has stopped. **Author's Note:** There is no need to make this look natural. In fact, it would be better if it looks exaggerated and choreographed.)*

ALL. Whoa!

PREGNANT WOMAN. We've stopped.

NEW AGE WOMAN. Stopped?

PREGNANT WOMAN. *(Tries pushing some buttons:)* The elevator isn't moving anymore. This isn't working.

BIKER. Push the buttons.

PREGNANT WOMAN. I am pushing the buttons!

BIKER. Push 'em harder. Like this.

> (BIKER *slams his fist against the imaginary buttons.* **Note:** *If there could be a sound effect, like a crack, great. Otherwise everyone should just react like the* BIKER *has really hit the panel hard.)*

BIKER. Uh. That didn't work.

PREGNANT WOMAN. You think?

INSTRUCTOR. Interesting.

PREGNANT WOMAN. This is fantastic. We're stuck and I'm nine months pregnant!

NEW AGE WOMAN. Wow, that's soooo beautiful.

PREGNANT WOMAN. That we're trapped in an elevator?

NEW AGE WOMAN. No, the miracle of birth. Our mother God is smiling down on your blessed womb.

PREGNANT WOMAN. Yeah, it's great.

NEW AGE WOMAN. All of nature is in harmony. You are one with the pollinated flower and the mother cub in her cave. You are singing with one voice of all creatures who take part in the cycle of life.

BIKER. *(To* NEW AGE WOMAN:*)* Are you for real?

NEW AGE WOMAN. The path to enlightenment has many winding paths and you could say that I am traveling on a holistic detour filled with daily meditation, trail mix and many other wonderful, life-affirming rituals.

BIKER. *(To* NEW AGE WOMAN:*)* Man I don't know you, but I want to hurt you.

INSTRUCTOR. Interesting.

PREGNANT WOMAN. So how are we going to get out of here?

BIKER. We need to get help quick. I don't like closed-in places. It makes me insane. When I get crazy, I get...crazy!

> *(Everybody stares at* BIKER *and gulps.)*

NEW AGE WOMAN. Oh I know. Does anybody have a cell phone?

PREGNANT WOMAN. I left mine at home.

INSTRUCTOR. I don't own one.

> *(Everybody stares at the* INSTRUCTOR.*)*

INSTRUCTOR. I'm afraid I'm a bit of a Luddite.

PREGNANT WOMAN. A what?

INSTRUCTOR. Never mind. I don't have a cell phone.

BIKER. I had one but it was bugging me so I stomped it.

PREGNANT WOMAN. OK.

NEW AGE WOMAN. Wait! I have mine right here.

PREGNANT WOMAN. Why did you ask us if we had one?

NEW AGE WOMAN. It seemed like the thing to do.

PREGNANT WOMAN. Whatever. Would you just call somebody and let them know we're trapped in this elevator and that I am very pregnant!

NEW AGE WOMAN. *(Looking at her phone:)* There's no signal. Oh, bummer.

BIKER. *(Grabbing the phone:)* Let me see it.

(BIKER *drops the phone on the ground and starts to stomp on it.*)

PREGNANT WOMAN. Hey!

NEW AGE WOMAN. Stop it!

(BIKER *stops stomping on the phone.*)

BIKER. Oh. Sorry.

PREGNANT WOMAN. OK, how are we going to get out of here now? Come on, somebody needs to think of something. Did I happen to mention that I am very pregnant?!

INSTRUCTOR. Interesting.

PREGNANT WOMAN. *(Turning on* INSTRUCTOR*:)* Now you are getting on my nerves.

INSTRUCTOR. What?

PREGNANT WOMAN. You keep saying "interesting" like this is all so amusing to you.

BIKER. Yeah man, you keep saying "interesting" like that I am gonna have to do something.

INSTRUCTOR. Like what?

BIKER. *(In the* INSTRUCTOR's *face:)* Something "interesting" with my fists.

INSTRUCTOR. Well, I don't have a cell phone but I think I can help get us out of here.

NEW AGE WOMAN. That would greatly increase your karma.

PREGNANT WOMAN. Fine. How?

INSTRUCTOR. Well, I teach playwriting.

PREGNANT WOMAN. You teach playwriting?

INSTRUCTOR. Yes.

PREGNANT WOMAN. Are you joking?

INSTRUCTOR. No.

PREGNANT WOMAN. *(In the* INSTRUCTOR's *face:)* Listen pal, I don't know if you've ever been pregnant, but it's no walk in the park. My doctors tell me I could be dropping this precious bundle like any minute and my feet are filled with water which, by the way, is just a guess on my part since I haven't seen them in three months and, oh yeah, did I mention that I haven't had a good night's sleep in forever since I have two little legs kicking me in the kidneys all night and I weigh about one thousand pounds so I think it would be in your best interest not to get all cute with the sleep-deprived, thousand pound PREGNANT WOMAN!

INSTRUCTOR. OK, but I've seen this a number of times.

PREGNANT WOMAN. Seen what?

INSTRUCTOR. First time playwrights use the device a lot in order to demonstrate conflict. They put a collection of various characters in an elevator.

BIKER. Hey! You better watch who you're calling a "various character."

INSTRUCTOR. It's their way of coming up with a scene where nobody can leave. The elevator breaks down and the various charac—

(BIKER gives the INSTRUCTOR a menacing look.)

INSTRUCTOR. —the random made-up people trapped in the elevator are often extreme stereotypes.

BIKER. Now I'm an extreme stereotype?!

INSTRUCTOR. You're a big guy who wears black leather. Here's something else. You own a motorcycle.

BIKER. A Harley, dude.

INSTRUCTOR. A Harley. Naturally. You're a biker. That might even be the name of your character. Biker. Yes, like I said, really obvious. You are conservative, with maybe a smidge of racism. Probably more than a smidge. You tend to lean to the violent and compulsive side.

BIKER. You are so wrong it makes me want to pound your face.

INSTRUCTOR. All right, before things get out of hand, let me ask you one question. Where are you going when we get out of this elevator?

BIKER. The rally for the death penalty at the courthouse.

INSTRUCTOR. Oh, see, I'm sorry, but this is real lame. It's going to struggle to get a C.

(INSTRUCTOR points to the NEW AGE WOMAN.)

INSTRUCTOR. What do you want to bet that this woman—who, I must note, is wearing a long, loose-flowing dress and sniffing a flower—is going to the same death penalty rally?

NEW AGE WOMAN. Whoa, he's right, I am.

INSTRUCTOR. And what do you bet that she is going to *protest* the death penalty and you're going to *support* it. Opposite sides. The elevator just happens to get stuck and not one person has a cell phone. Wa-la. Instant —and clichéd—conflict.

BIKER. Ha.

INSTRUCTOR. What?

BIKER. I hate the friggin' death penalty. I *hate* it. It is a scourge upon the United States of America.

NEW AGE WOMAN. That is far out.

BIKER. *(To* INSTRUCTOR:*)* Double ha. She hates it, too.

NEW AGE WOMAN. No, that is like far out, as in I can't believe you don't think we have the right to fry the murdering scumbags.

BIKER. You're for the death penalty?!

INSTRUCTOR. Hold on. You're clearly meant to be some kind of New Age hippy chick. You were going on earlier about the blessed womb and mother God. I was guessing you're a massage therapist.

NEW AGE WOMAN. I'm a yoga instructor.

INSTRUCTOR. Same thing. You're sniffing a flower!

NEW AGE WOMAN. Well I am a peaceful person at heart but I'm all for revenge. I think it's very natural.

BIKER. *(To* NEW AGE WOMAN:*)* You're a bloodthirsty lunatic!

NEW AGE WOMAN. So I guess you would let the scumbag killers have HBO and spend their afternoons on the golf course!

BIKER. You're exaggerating my position!

NEW AGE WOMAN. Your position is indefensible!

BIKER. Now you're hurting my feelings!

> (NEW AGE WOMAN *pulls out a big sign that reads "Let Me Pull the Switch!"* BIKER *pulls out a big sign that reads "An eye for an eye equals a sty!")*

NEW AGE WOMAN. Let me pull the switch!

BIKER. An eye for an eye equals a sty!

> (NEW AGE WOMAN *and* BIKER *continue to shout their slogans as they march in a circle around the* INSTRUCTOR *and* PREGNANT WOMAN. **Note:** *The slogans continue during the first part of the next exchange and then they get softer before they stop—but the two continue marching.)*

PREGNANT WOMAN. *(To* INSTRUCTOR:*)* What are you going to do about this?

INSTRUCTOR. I don't know.

PREGNANT WOMAN. You need to figure something out.

INSTRUCTOR. Why?

PREGNANT WOMAN. I'm having—whoaahh!—contractions.

INSTRUCTOR. I could have predicted that.

PREGNANT WOMAN. You need to shut up with the predicting and get going with the solution.

INSTRUCTOR. Look maybe if we can find out who wrote the play then we can ask them to bring it to a quick conclusion.

PREGNANT WOMAN. Oh that is a great idea! I really like it. We can get right on that as soon *we get out of the elevator!*

INSTRUCTOR. But usually there is a stand-in for the author somewhere in the cast. So if one of us is the playwright, then we can talk to that person and convince them to end it. After that I'd also like to give them some advice about structure and character definition. Maybe reacquaint them with the precepts of Aristotle.

PREGNANT WOMAN. Yeah, I bet you're a real firework in the classroom. We can start with the cheerleaders.

INSTRUCTOR. The cheerleaders?!

PREGNANT WOMAN. What? They're right over there.

(Lights now reveal the five CHEERLEADERS, *dressed in cheerleading uniforms and holding pom-poms.)*

INSTRUCTOR. There's a squad of cheerleaders in this elevator?

PREGNANT WOMAN. It's a really big elevator.

INSTRUCTOR. This is a really bad play!

STEPHANIE. OK, squad, where are our spirit smiles? I see a few downy frownies. We don't like downy frownies, do we?

BRITTNEY. Stephanie?

STEPHANIE. Yes Brittney.

BRITTNEY. Bethany and I are trying to maintain our spirit smiles but it's hard to keep them when we're trapped in an elevator that could at any moment, ya know, plunge to the bottom and kill us all in like a really gruesome way.

BETHANY. *(Enthusiastic:)* Like bloody yogurt bars!

CHEERLEADER #4. Yeah. And I need to go to the bathroom.

CHEERLEADER #5. I'm severely claustrophobic.

STEPHANIE. Squad! Battle stance please!

(The rest of the CHEERLEADERS *stand at attention.)*

STEPHANIE. Please look inside yourself and find the inner cheerleader inside each of you. The cheerleader that is the envy of the entire school. The cheerleader that is a model of courage and strength. The cheerleader that recovered to cheer after the Great Pyramid Tragedy of '06. Ready! OK!

CHEERLEADERS.
We have spirit yes we do!
We have spirit how about you!
Yay! All right! Yay!

PREGNANT WOMAN. OK, listen up. Over here. Which one of you perky little jumping beans wrote this play?

INSTRUCTOR. This clichéd play.

PREGNANT WOMAN. Fess up. Who wrote this stinker?

INSTRUCTOR. I don't think our playwright is in this bunch.

STEPHANIE. You don't think a cheerleader can be a playwright?

INSTRUCTOR. I don't think so, no.

STEPHANIE. I would like to respectfully disagree. We are chronic over-achievers. Bethany has just finished working on a particle accelerator and Brittney is head of a major financial cartel offering micro-loans in Indonesia. I have just created and designed a marketing campaign for my own energy drink, Berry Berry Spirit Blast. We are also on the yearbook staff. If anybody in this elevator has written a play, it would be one of us.

INSTRUCTOR. No. Playwrights are loners. They don't have spirit. They're misanthropes.

PREGNANT WOMAN. What?

STEPHANIE. Misanthrope. It means a dislike of people in general. The word is taken from the title of a play by the French Restoration playwright, Molière.

PREGNANT WOMAN. Great. We're stuck in here with a team of ponytail Einsteins.

INSTRUCTOR. Now I am wondering why there's a cheerleading squad in here in the first place. What purpose do they serve?

PREGNANT WOMAN. Why do they have to serve a purpose? Nothing that's happened so far has made any sense. Like that crazy Biker and that woman.

> (*The* INSTRUCTOR *turns around and sees that the* BIKER *and the* NEW AGE WOMAN *are gone.* **Note:** *Some time after the march, the* BIKER *and* NEW AGE WOMAN *walk off the stage. If you want to take lights down on them that's fine, but they should just leave, drawing as little attention to their exit as possible.*)

INSTRUCTOR. Hey, what happened to them? They're gone.

PREGNANT WOMAN. They could be hiding.

INSTRUCTOR. Hiding?! Where?!

PREGNANT WOMAN. Well, don't look at me because I don't know!

INSTRUCTOR. The playwright has forgotten about them. So they're gone. This play just gets worse and worse. It's just amateur hour.

BRITTNEY. I dunno, like could it be that the playwright that trapped us in this elevator hates cheerleaders?

STEPHANIE. Brittney?!

BRITTNEY. What, Stephanie?

STEPHANIE. I know you've been under a lot of pressure lately with the collapse of the Indonesian monetary system.

BRITTNEY. Like you have no idea.

STEPHANIE. But nobody hates us.

BETHANY. Stephanie, Brittney is, like, right. We are hated because we are popular and attractive and because all the photos in the yearbook were out of focus.

STEPHANIE. Nobody hates us. Besides those photos weren't out of focus —those were activity shots!

INSTRUCTOR. Hold on. She might have something there.

BRITTNEY. And like all this spirit stuff gets like so old.

BETHANY. You know sometimes instead of having spirit I would rather eat two bags of Oreos and watch TV.

STEPHANIE. Bethany!

BRITTNEY. *(To* BETHANY:*)* Have you like ever wondered what we're doing all this cheering for anyway?

INSTRUCTOR. Now that sounds like a playwright!

PREGNANT WOMAN. *(Grabbing* BRITTNEY:*)* Listen here, you little messed up Cheerleader Barbie, you better let me out of this play or you're going to deliver this baby yourself!

BRITTNEY. Like yell at somebody else. I certainly didn't write this play. I think theatre is a dead medium.

STEPHANIE. Squad. Battle stance!

 (The rest of the CHEERLEADERS *don't move.)*

STEPHANIE. Squad? Your captain asked for a battle stance!

CHEERLEADER #4. I still really need to go to the bathroom.

CHEERLEADER #5. I'm about to have a panic attack.

STEPHANIE. I want to see some spirit right now! If we don't have spirit, we are nothing! Spirit is what makes us special! I like being special! If I'm not special, then I might as well be one of those misfits! I am not going to be like that!

INSTRUCTOR. Misfits? What misfits?

STEPHANIE. Those misfits right over there!

 (Lights come up on three MISFITS. *The* GOTH KID, *dressed in black, is sitting on the floor. The* CLOWN *and the* NORMAL GIRL *are standing up, waiting.)*

INSTRUCTOR. More people?! What's wrong with this playwright? Have they never been on an elevator?

NORMAL GIRL. Hi.

STEPHANIE.
I have spirit yes I do!
I have spirit how about you!

(The CLOWN *waves and honks a horn.)*

INSTRUCTOR. This playwright is sick, sick, sick.

PREGNANT WOMAN. What now?

INSTRUCTOR. *(Whispering and pointing:)* The clown!

(The CLOWN *waves again and honks its horn.)*

INSTRUCTOR. Agggh! Here. Stand here.

(The INSTRUCTOR *puts the* PREGNANT WOMAN *next to the* CLOWN.*)*

PREGNANT WOMAN. So it's a clown, so what?

INSTRUCTOR. They're creepy.

(The CLOWN *now honks its horn and pulls out two long balloons. Everybody except the* INSTRUCTOR *watches as the* CLOWN *tries—in a wild, almost violent manner—to twist the balloon into an animal.)*

INSTRUCTOR. What is going on?!

PREGNANT WOMAN. He/she's trying to make something.

(The CLOWN *tries to give the balloon animal, which doesn't look like anything, to the* INSTRUCTOR, *who keeps turning away. Finally the* INSTRUCTOR *turns around and accepts the balloon.)*

INSTRUCTOR. What is it?!

CLOWN. Antelope.

(The CLOWN *smiles and honks its horn again.)*

PREGNANT WOMAN. *(To* INSTRUCTOR:*)* I'm thinking you're the misfit here.

STEPHANIE.
I have spirit yes I do!
I have spirit how about you!

PREGNANT WOMAN. Well, besides her.

NORMAL GIRL. It's quite normal to be afraid of clowns. There's even a name for it. Coulrophobia.

INSTRUCTOR. *(To* PREGNANT WOMAN:*)* See. She's right. It's normal.

PREGNANT WOMAN. I don't care about the clown. I don't care about your stupid phobia. I care about getting out of this elevator and having this baby and getting as far away as possible from all of you lunatics.

INSTRUCTOR. *(Pointing at the* GOTH KID:*)* Alright, alright. What about him?

BETHANY. Oh. That's the Goth Kid. Everybody knows him.

BRITTNEY. Oh yeah. He wears black. He writes poetry and sends them out as text messages.

BETHANY. His poems are very sad and dark.

BRITTNEY. Somebody forwarded one of his poems to my cell during my first period class and I like cried all day long.

BETHANY. Yeah he is like a great poet. Like Billy Joel or something.

BRITTNEY. There was one I got in study hall that was about a puppy with three legs. He walks around in circles. Very tragic.

BETHANY. Very sad.

(The GOTH KID *stands up and reads his poem. He is really into it. Really into it.)*

GOTH KID. The title is "This Wasted Life."

There is a puppy
With three legs.
Trio the puppy.
He walks around in a circle
On a leash
Like we walk around
This life
Whimpering
And this makes me want
To cry
Who will listen to my tears?

*(*BETHANY *and* BRITTNEY *scream as if at a rock concert.)*

INSTRUCTOR. "Who will listen to my tears?"

BRITTNEY. I love him!

BETHANY. Like, no, I love him!

*(*BRITTNEY *and* BETHANY *are on opposite sides of the* GOTH KID, *pulling on him.)*

GOTH KID. Will you please stop?

BETHANY. Where do you come up with your ideas for your poems?

BRITTNEY. Are you depressed right now? That's like so deep!

*(*BETHANY *and* BRITTNEY *scream again and hang on to the* GOTH KID.)*

PREGNANT WOMAN. *(To* INSTRUCTOR:*)* C'mon now, this has to be our playwright.

INSTRUCTOR. I don't know.

PREGNANT WOMAN. He's the biggest misfit, which is your definition of playwright, right?

GOTH KID. I take issue with being labeled a misfit. If anybody is a misfit in this elevator, it's those cheerleaders who try to cram their rah-rah corporate sunshine down the throat of a world that is, as everyone knows, dark and meaningless.

BETHANY. Oh my God! You are so right!

BRITTNEY. We are so stupid!

PREGNANT WOMAN. Well?

INSTRUCTOR. Interesting.

PREGNANT WOMAN. Interesting?! That's all you have to say? Interesting. What kind of playwriting instructor are you?

INSTRUCTOR. It's too obvious. It can't be him.

(During the next part, the INSTRUCTOR walks away from the group as he talks out loud to himself.)

PREGNANT WOMAN. *(Grabbing her stomach:)* Woahhh!

NORMAL GIRL. *(To PREGNANT WOMAN:)* What's going on?

INSTRUCTOR. Though this all started out as a big cliché, I must say there have been some twists I didn't see coming.

NORMAL GIRL. *(To INSTRUCTOR:)* I think she's going to have the baby!

STEPHANIE. *(Raising her hand:)* Excuse me, I have something to say.

PREGNANT WOMAN. *(Grabbing her stomach:)* Woahhh!

INSTRUCTOR. Stupid twists, but twists nevertheless.

STEPHANIE. *(Raising her hand:)* Excuse me.

PREGNANT WOMAN. *(To NORMAL GIRL:)* This is not comfortable!

NORMAL GIRL. This sure is one *interesting* elevator ride.

INSTRUCTOR. The death penalty argument I can kind of understand. The highly agitated and highly annoying pregnant woman makes sense, too. It's all a rather transparent way to stir up conflict. But these vapid cheerleaders and this goth poet, I don't get at all. There's no attempt to tie these things together. I don't see any possible resolution in sight.

STEPHANIE. That's it.

(STEPHANIE pulls out a gun and aims it at everybody in the elevator.)

NORMAL GIRL. She's got a gun!

STEPHANIE. Ready!? OK!? Hands up!

(Everybody puts their hands up but the CLOWN.)

STEPHANIE. You too clowny!

(The CLOWN honks its horn and then puts its hands up.)

STEPHANIE. Vapid!? I will have you know that I have maintained a 3.6 grade average even after pulling all nighters working on the marketing plan for my energy drink. Vapid?! Have you every tried to work out the weight distribution on an eight-person pyramid? It ain't that easy!

INSTRUCTOR. Interesting.

PREGNANT WOMAN. For the love of God, just shoot him and we'll all be happy.

STEPHANIE. Oh, I see some downy frownies. Why am I seeing so many downy frownies?

CHEERLEADER #5. You have a gun pointed at us.

CHEERLEADER #4. I still have to go to the bathroom.

STEPHANIE. I want to see some spirit! You know what I am talking about, right?

EVERYBODY.
We have spirit yes we do!
We have spirit how about you!

STEPHANIE. Now can somebody explain to me what's so great about the goth kid? He's lazy and his writing stinks.

NORMAL GIRL. He's a character.

STEPHANIE. He's lame! Oh there's a puppy with three legs and oh let me text you my latest thoughts about how the world is unfair, the cafeteria is out of Dr. Pepper and how my index finger is cramping and then let me text back to you my yawn and inform you that you are not some kind of junior Faulkner but just another high school kid who probably needs to up his depression medication or maybe just spend some time in the sun!

GOTH KID. That's what I would expect a cheerleader to say.

PREGNANT WOMAN. *(To GOTH KID:)* Yeah but she's a cheerleader with a gun. Woaahhh!

STEPHANIE. I don't know what your problem is anyway. I have like never done anything to you.

GOTH KID. Really? You don't remember me? Harold? You cut me after the first tryout last year. Ever since that day I vowed to stand against everything that cheerleading is for.

STEPHANIE. Please understand that the decision wasn't personal. I only serve at the pleasure of cheerleading.

PREGNANT WOMAN. *(To INSTRUCTOR:)* Woahh! Alright genius, now would be a good time to find the playwright!

CLOWN. Golly willickers, did I forget to mention that I'm a doctor?

(The CLOWN honks its horn.)

PREGNANT WOMAN. Hurry!

INSTRUCTOR. Oh I just thought of something.

NORMAL GIRL. What is it?

INSTRUCTOR. Well, one of the things I stress in my class is that if you introduce a gun in the first act...oh...

NORMAL GIRL. What?!

INSTRUCTOR. It needs to go off in the second act.

(All take a step back away from STEPHANIE.*)*

NORMAL GIRL. Is that a rule you can't break?

INSTRUCTOR. Yes. You introduce a gun, you need to make sure it's used. Otherwise, it's just a sign that the playwright hasn't really thought his or her play through.

NORMAL GIRL. I never heard that.

INSTRUCTOR. Well I'm pretty sure it was part of my first lecture.

NORMAL GIRL. I took notes!

PREGNANT WOMAN. *(To* NORMAL GIRL:*)* You're the playwright?! You?! You're completely normal.

NORMAL GIRL. *(To* INSTRUCTOR:*)* See I was thinking that the gun could be funny. She pulls out the gun and then the elevator starts working.

(The lights flash and everybody bends at the knees to signal that the elevator is moving again.)

EVERYBODY. Woaahh!

STEPHANIE. The elevator is working!

*(*STEPHANIE *hands her gun to the* NORMAL GIRL *and then walks over to the* GOTH KID *and whispers in his ear.)*

INSTRUCTOR. *(To* NORMAL GIRL:*)* Yes, but you are in danger of thwarting the audience expectations.

(The PREGNANT WOMAN *pulls out the stuffing from her belly and hands it to the* INSTRUCTOR.*)*

PREGNANT WOMAN. Do you really know anything about playwriting?

INSTRUCTOR. I've taught the class for many, many years.

STEPHANIE and GOTH KID.
We have spirit yes we do!
We have spirit how about you!

NORMAL GIRL. *(To* STEPHANIE *and* GOTH KID:*)* Shut up! I thought the audience would understand that this was a spoof, you know? I know a squad of cheerleaders can't get trapped in an elevator with like seven other people.

INSTRUCTOR. You need to rise above these pedestrian scenarios. Disparate characters stuck in an elevator, well, there's very few times that won't turn into a cliché.

NORMAL GIRL. Couldn't this be one of those times?

INSTRUCTOR. Unlikely.

(Now everybody stands and waits for the elevator to reach the bottom floor. The bell rings and for a moment everybody stands still. Then...)

CHEERLEADER #4. *(Pushing her way through:)* Gangway! I've got to go to the bathroom NOW!

(Everybody steps aside as CHEERLEADER #4 *runs out. Now the other* CHEERLEADERS *and the* GOTH KID, *excitedly discussing cheerleading moves with* STEPHANIE, *walk out.)*

INSTRUCTOR. One of my maximums—maybe I haven't shared this with you yet—is that the best writing only comes through rigorous and dedicated rewriting.

NORMAL GIRL. No. I remember that.

PREGNANT WOMAN. *(To* NORMAL GIRL:*)* I'd see if it was too late to drop the class.

(The PREGNANT WOMAN *walks out.)*

INSTRUCTOR. Are you upset?

NORMAL GIRL. Am I upset? Of course! I worked really hard on this. I spent a lot of late nights.

INSTRUCTOR. Oh, we're not going to sulk. So how would you like to approach this rewrite?

NORMAL GIRL. Well—

INSTRUCTOR. I would strongly recommend a different setting.

(NORMAL GIRL is now smiling.)

NORMAL GIRL. How about if I kept it in the elevator but reduced the number of characters?

INSTRUCTOR. Hmmm. I'm not crazy about it, but I suppose it could work. But that would depend on who you have in the elevator.

NORMAL GIRL. I have that figured out.

(The BIKER *walks back in and stands beside the* INSTRUCTOR. *The* CLOWN *walks up and stands beside him too.* NORMAL GIRL *steps out of the elevator. A bell rings.)*

INSTRUCTOR. *(Looking at the* BIKER *and then the* CLOWN:*)* Please tell me you're going to keep this a short one-act.

NORMAL GIRL. Sorry. This time it's a full-length.

(The CLOWN *honks its horn.)*

BIKER. *(Glaring at the* INSTRUCTOR:*)* Interesting.

(Lights out.)

End of Play

THE SEUSSIFICATION OF ROMEO AND JULIET

by Peter Bloedel

Playscripts, Inc.
website: www.playscripts.com
email: info@playscripts.com
phone: 1-866-NEW-PLAY (639-7529)

For more information about rights and permissions, see page 9.

Cast of Characters

NARRATOR #1
NARRATOR #2
PROLOGUE
SAMPSON
GREGORY
ABRAM
BALTHASAR
CAPITULATE (LORD)
LADY CAPITULATE
MONOTONE (LORD)
LADY MONOTONE
THE PRINCE
ROMEO
BENVOLIO
PARIS
SERVANT OF CAPITULATE
NURSE
JULIET
MERCUTIO
TYBALT
MONK LARRY

Setting

An empty stage.

Production Notes

See the end of the play for two optional endings.

Acknowledgments

The Seussification of Romeo and Juliet was first produced on September 21, 2001 in Mankato, Minnesota at Bethany Lutheran College. It was directed by Peter Bloedel and Jason Jaspersen.

THE SEUSSIFICATION OF ROMEO AND JULIET

(The two NARRATORS enter the playing area. They dress and behave similarly.)

NARRATOR #1. Dear Ladies and Menfolk!

NARRATOR #2. Women and Gents!

NARRATOR #1. You're people of culture and true common sense.

NARRATOR #2. You know what you know, and you like what you like.

NARRATOR #1. Like singing a song, or riding a bike.

NARRATOR #2. Two hour symphonies!

NARRATOR #1. Ping-pong!

NARRATOR #2. Canoeing!

NARRATOR #1. Poetry!

NARRATOR #2. Football!

NARRATOR #1. Or, yellow snowshoeing!

NARRATOR #2. *(Glancing at NARRATOR #1 with disgust:)* We like that stuff too!

NARRATOR #1. It's the greatest!

NARRATOR #2. You bet!

NARRATOR #1. And topping the list...

BOTH. *Romeo and Juliet.*

NARRATOR #2. It's Shakespeare's great classic.

NARRATOR #1. We can't get enough! But make no mistake...

BOTH. Writing that stuff is tough.

NARRATOR #2. Sublime in its scope, no thing is more artful.

NARRATOR #1. It deserves honors and lauds by the cart-full.

NARRATOR #2. The play is just perfect.

NARRATOR #1. Nothing is wrong.

NARRATOR #2. Except that it's almost two hours...

BOTH. *(Glancing at each other and then to the audience:)* Too Long!

NARRATOR #2. The play is still great, so we need not repeat it.

NARRATOR #1. But, you need to be Albert Einstein just to read it.

NARRATOR #2. Now, don't get us wrong, we love William Shakespeare,

NARRATOR #1. But, in this new century he's not very clear.

NARRATOR #2. Yet, only in reverence to him our great hero,
Do we pull "The Bard" back to our level, zero.

NARRATOR #1. We've shortened the play, changed some names, made
   it rhyme
No more of that blank verse, we don't think he'd mind.

NARRATOR #2. A rhyming tetrameter is thought quite useful,

NARRATOR #1. But, could make the play sound a bit Dr. Seussful.

NARRATOR #2. ...And what's wrong with that, why as sure as we're standin',
Seuss is good too, and most folks understand him.

NARRATOR #1. But don't get the notion that the Seussification
Of Romy and J is our one main intention.

NARRATOR #2. We'd never do that.

NARRATOR #1. No we wouldn't.

BOTH. Oh No!
And that's why we're bothering telling you so.

NARRATOR #2. A prologue is given to the top of the play.

NARRATOR #1. A paragraph giving the whole plot away.

NARRATOR #2. It must be important, there must be a reason
For Shaky to put it there.

NARRATOR #1. 'less he's just teasin'.

NARRATOR #2. Our Prologue's addressed...

   *(From offstage, suspended by a long stick, a dress on a hanger
   appears. Being misunderstood, and annoyed, NARRATOR #2 re-
   iterates:)*

Addressed!

   *(The dress is pulled out of sight and the character of the PROLOGUE
   makes a leaping entrance.)*

Our Prologue's addressed, so let's watch and see...

NARRATOR #1. This lamentable,

NARRATOR #2. Horrible!

NARRATOR #1. Gross, comedy.

   (NARRATOR #2 nudges NARRATOR #1, who then realizes a mistake.)

(Oh!) Tragedy.

   *(The PROLOGUE crosses the playing area and continues his/her
   speech to one side, because there will be action taking place behind him/her.)*

PROLOGUE. Verona's the place from where our play is picked.
Two families lived there, and man were they ticked.

   *(Two distinct groups of players materialize behind the PRO-
   LOGUE, representing the two feuding houses of CAPITULATE and
   MONOTONE. Both groups stand there, perhaps in fighting stance,
   looking "ticked.")*

PROLOGUE. Their ancient grudge match happened before the story,
And rekindled hatred made their feud more gory.

> *(The two families growl at one another, or generally show their
> hatred, still in the frozen fighting stance.)*

Straight from the loins of those mentioned above...

> *(LADY CAPITULATE and LADY MONOTONE, both visibly pregnant,
> walk into their respective family huddles, which conceal them.)*

Popped kid one...

> *(Popping sound.)*

> *(ROMEO pops out of the Monotone huddle, crying and sucking on
> a bottle with a nipple. His mother is now visibly not pregnant.)*

And kid two...

> *(Popping sound.)*

> *(JULIET pops out of the Capitulate huddle, crying and sucking on
> a pacifier. Her mother is now visibly not pregnant.)*

And they fell in love.

> *(ROMEO and JULIET walk to center stage and drop their baby
> props. ROMEO dips JULIET and kisses her.)*

Kid one and kid two, later, each took their life...

> *(ROMEO and JULIET punch each other and both drop dead.)*

As a result of their parental strife.
Their families to fighting and feuding were fettered,
But, somehow the death of their kids made it better.
The families were pals now, they'd all go on hikes...

> *(We see members of each family hiking.)*

...Mud wrestle...

> *(We see dirty members of each family running across the stage
> doing wrestling moves—headlocks, etc.)*

...Play lawn darts...

> *(We see members of each family playing lawn darts, or similar
> lawn game.)*

...And pedal their bikes.

> *(Kids ride Dr. Seuss-looking bikes across the stage. All exit, except
> PROLOGUE.)*

Now we're not saying that taking your life
Is an antidote to family tumult and strife.
That's an idea that sure can make plays sell,
But in real life, it just doesn't work out well.
So, kids— Never try this. Forget what you've heard
We're trained professionals and we're insured.

(PROLOGUE *exits.* NARRATOR #2 *enters carrying an odd musical instrument.)*

NARRATOR #2. Just a reminder— This interpretation
Takes nothing from Dr. Seuss as inspiration.
Our thoughts are our own, as I stand alone,
And I play on this xylophone, eight-belled trombone.

(*Exits.)*

(NARRATOR #1 *enters as a boxing announcer. A microphone drops from the ceiling. He/she speaks into it.)*

NARRATOR #1. In this corner, here are Sampson and Gregory,
From the house of Capitulate, they were born ang-o-ry.
And representing the house of Lord Monotone,
Abram and Balthasar—a tenor...

ABRAM. *(High voice:)* Hi!

NARRATOR #1. ...And baritone.

BALTHASAR. *(Low voice:)* Hi!

(*A bell rings and the match starts.)*

ABRAM. Excuse me do you bite your thumb at us sir?

SAMPSON. I did bite my thumb and it hurts, see the pus there?

ABRAM. I think your pus mocks us!

GREGORY. Do you have a quarrel?

ABRAM. No, I don't yet, only this simple moral.
We serve Lord Monotone, as you must know,
And Monotones have on their bellies an "O."
Nothing's more fashionable, what could be better?

GREGORY. Nothing except that you've picked the wrong letter.

SAMPSON. Capitulates all have an "X" on their tummy,
And if you don't have one you're prob-ly a dummy.

BALTHASAR. Do you mean a dummy with a capital "D"?

SAMPSON. Yes, that's what I meant, that's what I meant indeed.

BALTHASAR. Draw if you be men you "X"-bellied fools.

SAMPSON / GREGORY. Now to our anger you've added the fuel.

(*They fight in slow motion as* NARRATOR #2 *enters and speaks.)*

NARRATOR #2. A giant brawl started, you wouldn't believe it,
Capitulate and Monotone came to see it.

CAPITULATE (LORD). Bring me my longsword, the one that cuts deep.
While I'm waiting, I'll yell—"Monotone, you're a creep!"

MONOTONE (LORD). *(In a monotone voice:)* You villain Capitulate! I'm more the man,
And you are the creepiest, creep in the land.

CAPITULATE. *(To* LADY CAPITULATE:*)* Hmmm. The creepiest creep. Does he have a point there?

LADY CAPITULATE. He's lying my love you must never surrender.

> *(Enter* NARRATOR #1.*)*

NARRATOR #1. Enter the prince, royal and wise,

> *(The* PRINCE *enters. All fighting stops and all eyes are on His Majesty.)*

NARRATOR #1. He's had about all he can take from these guys.
A crusader for peace, he stops the fight,
And everyone listens, 'cuz they know he's right.
He pauses and makes the most eloquent speech.

THE PRINCE. Will you jerks knock it off? I've been trying to sleep.

NARRATOR #1. Upon hearing the prince's great message of virtue,
The crowd all dispersed, it was almost past curfew.
Only Lord and Mrs. Monotone stayed.

MONOTONE. Where's our Romeo? I've not seen him all day.
Why won't he fight in the brawls like the others?

LADY MONOTONE. He spends his time day dreaming, why should he bother?

> *(ROMEO enters. He's pathetic. His parents watch him speak.)*

ROMEO. Show me a mistress that is passing fair,
Where I may read who passed that passing fair.
She is too fair, too wisely too fair.
It must be unfair to be passed at the fair.
'cuz fairs, they don't care whose passing them rarely.
Even the fair will pass rarely but barely.
My love is fair, stripped bare, and cooked rare,
But, fair cupid steals my bliss, so I despair.

> *(Romeo's parents exit shaking their heads as if to say, "Where did we go wrong?" ROMEO exits in the other direction.)*

NARRATOR #1. That was young Romeo, kid number one,
But, as we can see he's not having much fun.

> *(She holds up a bottle labeled "Sneezle Fruit Juice.")*

Perhaps he could use some red Sneezle Fruit Juice.
That's the best juice when your mind's on the loose.
It's guaranteed for ten thousand—six uses,
And it's nothing, no nothing like old Dr. Seuss's.
Nor is our play, which can stand on its own.
...Just thought we'd remind you before you go home.

> *(NARRATOR #1 exits. NARRATOR #2 enters.)*

NARRATOR #2. Meanwhile at the Capitulate pad,
There's a suitor for Julie and he's with her dad.

(Enter CAPITULATE, PARIS, *and* SERVANT OF CAPITULATE. NARRATOR #1 *exits.)*

PARIS. Capitulate! I am the man for your daughter.

CAPITULATE. I don't think you'll do.

PARIS. But who could be hotter?
Besides that I brought you some peppermint candy.

CAPITULATE. *(To the* SERVANT:*)* Does he have a point?

(The SERVANT *nods.)*

CAPITULATE. I think you'll be dandy.
Let's have a banquet.
(To the SERVANT:*)* Young man go and get
All of these people whose names I have writ.

*(*CAPITULATE *hands an invitation list to the* SERVANT *and then exits with his arm around* PARIS.*)*

SERVANT OF CAPITULATE. Before I can find all the people and greet 'em,
I need to find help from someone who can read 'em.

(Enter ROMEO *and* BENVOLIO. ROMEO *is chanting his same pathetic litany.* BENVOLIO *is annoyed by it.)*

ROMEO. ...'cuz fairs, they don't care whose passing them rarely.
Even the fair will pass rarely but barely.
My love is fair, stripped bare, and cooked rare,

BOTH. But, fair cupid steals my bliss, so I despair.

BENVOLIO. Romeo, I know your heart has been broken,
Because on this matter you've endlessly spoken.
And I've tried my best to be philanthropic,
But, cousin, I think you've exhausted the topic.
This tether to sadness I think you must cut,
Or, if you don't will you please just shut up?

ROMEO. Benvolio, it is so rare to forbear...

BENVOLIO. *(Interrupting him:)* Hey buddy! What's up? Can we help you there?

SERVANT OF CAPITULATE. Sure enough, if there is help then I need it,
'cuz I've got this list here, and I just can't read it.
To find a strong reader is what I've been hoping...

ROMEO. *(Taking the list:)* I'll read it to you, it will keep me from moping.
(He reads:) These folks can come to Capitulate's party:
Smarty Martino and his boy named Arty,
Bronco Buck Billy, and Buck Billy Buff,
And Lady McDinky, McDucky, McDuff,
Sonny's son Daily, and his pal Baloo,
John Jimmy Jack Jamerson, from Katmandu,
Mercutio and Winnifred Winnie Waters,
Old Uncle Perk and his ninety-six daughters,

Dave from Topeka, and Lady Von Rybald,
Rosaline, Valentine, Livia, Tybalt,
Anyone named Gordie or Tim or Melissa,
Can come to this bash, if you can't then we'll miss ya.
(Finished reading, he says to SERVANT:*)* This party sound great.

BENVOLIO. Like the best of the best.

SERVANT OF CAPITULATE. If you're not a Monotone, come be our guest.

(The SERVANT *exits.)*

BENVOLIO. Romeo, we've got to go crash this wingding.
There's sure to be beauties to make even you sing.

ROMEO. This party will never cure my broken heart,
But, I'll go along with you to take your part.

*(*ROMEO *and* BENVOLIO *exit. Enter* NARRATOR #1.*)*

NARRATOR #1. Meanwhile, back at the Capitulate place,
We meet Juliet full of splendor and grace.

(Enter JULIET. *She trips and falls.* LADY CAPITULATE *and* NURSE
enter from other side of playing area. NARRATOR #1 *exits.)*

LADY CAPITULATE. Nurse where is Juliet? Now where could she be?
I want my daughter, so lead her to me.

NURSE. Oh, little plum dumplin', oh, sweet puddin' pie.
Where's my fragrant blossom—come out don't be shy.
Oh little love monkey, thou sweet chimpanzeezel,
Answer my call and quit hiding, you weasel!

JULIET. *(From the floor:)* How now? Who calls?

NURSE. *(Helping her up:)* Get up off the floor!
It's your Mother, she's waiting just outside your door.

JULIET. *(A bit bewildered from the fall:)* Mom?

LADY CAPITULATE. Yes! It's I. I'm your own dearest Mother.
I've been called the same by your sisters and brother.
I meant to say just what I said when I meant
That I am your Mother, one-hundred percent.

JULIET. I suppose this is a moment I'll cherish.

LADY CAPITULATE. Juliet, you are to marry young Paris.

JULIET. I'm not yet fourteen. Is there some room for doubt?

LADY CAPITULATE. I married young, and look how I turned out.

*(*LADY CAPITULATE *strikes some sort of cheerleader or beauty
pageant pose.* JULIET *is disgusted.)*

NURSE. He is so handsome. He's a man of wax.

LADY CAPITULATE. Here is his picture. He sent us a FAX.

(Hands JULIET *the fax picture. It isn't flattering.)*

LADY CAPITULATE. We're having a party, and there you can meet him.

NURSE. He's so delicious, you'll just want to eat him.

(They exit. NARRATOR #1 *and* NARRATOR #2 *enter.)*

NARRATOR #2. On their way to the party Benvolio and Romeo,
Meet up with their friend Clifford Deacon First Folio
Carmichael Zanzibar Hoos Foos Petruchio
Zip Zip Shabang, also known as Mercutio.

NARRATOR #1. Now, I think you can see by this point in the play,
That there isn't a singular possible way
That our show could have taken on Seuss attributes,
We'd sooner put bounce berry beans in our boots.

(The NARRATORS *exit, "bouncing off." Enter* ROMEO, BENVOLIO,
and MERCUTIO. *They are dressed for a costume party.* ROMEO
is wearing a visor.)

BENVOLIO. *(To* ROMEO:*)* Forget this girl who won't return your affection,
Dance with some others make a new selection.

MERCUTIO. Yes, gentle Romeo, we must see you dance.

ROMEO. My heart is too heavy. There isn't a chance.

MERCUTIO. You love sick dreamer, your dreams aren't all dreamt.
Each man sees a new day and you're not exempt.

*(*MERCUTIO *pulls a flat black disk from his pants. It's a "hole.")*

Do you want to live your whole life in a hole?

(He throws the hole onto the ground. ROMEO *and* BENVOLIO *look
down into it as if it's bottomless.)*

I know what I know and I'm telling you so,
A life should be filled with adventure and bliss,
And that's why I'm bothering telling you this.

(Suddenly we're at the party and CAPITULATE *greets the three
at the door.)*

CAPITULATE. Good evening Gents—there's plenty to eat,

*(Capitulate's party members enter the playing area dancing to
mellow party music playing softly. The ladies have corn cobs
strapped to their feet.* JULIET *is in the party group.)*

And ladies who'll dance despite corns on their feet.
Corn-footed feet are the best feet for dancing,
If I were a youngster you bet I'd be prancin'
Why I might dance now. Wait! Could that be true?
Do I have a point there? I certainly do.

*(The music abruptly changes to raucous dance music playing
loudly.* CAPITULATE *goes and dances for five seconds and then
greets the three at the door again. Mellow music resumes.)*

*(*CAPITULATE *continues—capitulating:)*

Good evening Gents—there's plenty to eat,
And ladies who'll dance despite corns on their feet.

> *(Raucous music again. CAPITULATE goes and dances again for five seconds and comes back to greet the three at the door for a third time. Mellow music resumes.)*

Welcome young fellows, I recall the day
When I'd wear a visor to such a par-tay,
And whisper sweet tales in the young ladies ears.
Have a good time and enjoy these young years.
Wait! That can't be right! Or is it? Tarnation!
Blast this infernal recapitulation.

> *(Holds his head as if in a daze, smiles and goes back to dancing. JULIET and ROMEO are both downstage but on opposite sides of the stage. ROMEO notices JULIET.)*

ROMEO. Ei-hotchee-mama, Growl, Whoo! Hubba-hubba!
That girl is a babe or my name is dumb bubba.

> *(ROMEO pulls his visor down over his eyes to conceal his identity, he goes to JULIET and commences flirting. An alarm goes off. TYBALT rushes down stage from the party group.)*

TYBALT. My Monotone alarm just gave the alert!
I keep it hidden right here in my shirt.
It detects Monotones. It's never wrong.
And this one is foolin' where he don't belong.
This brazen young trespasser needs to be smitten.

CAPITULATE. Dear nephew Tybalt did you lose this mitten?

> *(TYBALT takes the mitten because he did lose it.)*

TYBALT. *(Points:)* Uncle your house has a Monotone there.

CAPITULATE. Leave him alone.

> *(ROMEO takes his visor off for a second and runs his fingers through his hair.)*

CAPITULATE. Wow! Does he have nice hair!

TYBALT. But uncle, that's Romeo, Monotone's son!

CAPITULATE. Lighten up boy I'm not done having fun.
I know not to kill him must fill you with sorrow,
But, look on the bright side, there's always tomorrow.

> *(CAPITULATE goes back and dances again. TYBALT falls back and watches ROMEO like a hawk. ROMEO grabs JULIET's hand and brings her to the center of the playing area.)*

ROMEO. Please, don't think I'm forward, but I think you're hot!

JULIET. *(Aside:)* I can't see his face is it worth it or not?

> *(ROMEO lifts his visor.)*

ROMEO. I have twelve billion, sixty-two million and sixty,
Hormones and all of them want you to kiss me.

JULIET. Hey, you're kind of cute, okay, here, hold my gum first.
It's raspberry, lima bean, sneezle fruit, bratwurst.

(*They kiss.*)

ROMEO. Wow! Hey, you're right, that is good tasting gum.

NURSE. Your mother would like a few words with you, hon.

(NURSE *grabs* JULIET *by the arm and sends her back to* LADY CAPITULATE *who is standing with* PARIS. ROMEO *pops* JULIET's *gum in his mouth.*)

ROMEO. Who is her Mom, if I may be so bold?
Quickly, please tell me before I get old.

NURSE. Her Dad is the host, who bought that main course dish you ate.
Her Mother's no other than Lady Capitulate.
Juliet is her name and she is the fairest.
But don't get ideas. She's marrying Paris.

ROMEO. She's a Capitulate what rotten luck.

BENVOLIO. (*Emerging from the party:*) Romy, we're outta here, this gig is up!
We mustn't stay here, we have to go home-e-o.

JULIET. (*To the* NURSE:) What is his name?

ROMEO. (*With a dashing pose:*) There are those who call me Romeo!

(*Everybody exits.* NARRATOR #1 *enters.*)

NARRATOR #1. Needless to say Romy's heart-ache was done.
He met a new girl and she had good gum.
All of the guests from the banquet had parted,
But not Romeo, he was just getting started.

(ROMEO *runs on.*)

ROMEO. How can I leave here when she holds my heart,
My importantest, blood-pumping, chest body part.

(ROMEO *dashes to the back of the stage and stands as if to hide. He is still in plain view, so a stagehand walks in with a bush and puts it down in front of him. Enter* BENVOLIO *and* MERCUTIO.)

BENVOLIO. Yo, Romeo yo! Where'd he go Romeo!

MERCUTIO. He went home to bed, that's where I'm gonna go.

BENVOLIO. But, I saw him running back toward the feast.

MERCUTIO. Well that can't be right, 'cuz his bed is due East.

BENVOLIO. I'm telling you he didn't go home to bed.

MERCUTIO. My friend, no offense, but you need a new head.

(*They exit.* JULIET *enters pushing on a ladder and an electric megaphone. She climbs to the top of the ladder.*)

ROMEO. Coming back to this place may seem capricious,
But, I just can't help myself, she's gorge-o-licious.

JULIET. *(Into the bullhorn:)* Testing, one, two, Check! Check! Is this thing on?

ROMEO. *(On one knee below the ladder:)* She speaks to herself through
her self-speaking horn.
No thing is more useful to speak private stuff to,
It makes it all louder so others can know too.

JULIET. *(Into the horn:)* Romeo baby-o, baby-o, buff!
Wherefore art thou, I just can't get enough.
Forsake your name, or else I'll forsake mine,
But, if I forsake mine there's a ten-dollar fine.
My tap dancing lessons will prob-ly get cancelled,
No more T.V., root beer floats, no more Seinfeld.
I might get grounded for three or more hours,
So, if there's a name to dump let's make it yours.

ROMEO. Oh, Juliet, you're a pearl of great price.
You're like two pearls only much, much, more nice.
You might be like three pearls—shiny and rare,
But, four pearls? I think I'd be pushing it there.

JULIET. *(Coming down off of the ladder:)* Who is that? Yo! Romeo, Is that you?

ROMEO. Yes, it is I, Romeo that is true.
I heard your whole self speaking speech, through your horn,
And I love you, my love, just as sure as you're born.

JULIET. Let's find the preacher!

ROMEO. Let's get hitched tomorrow.
Enough of this fighting...

JULIET. ...This feuding...

BOTH. This sorrow.

ROMEO. Kiss me once more and send my lips to heaven!

JULIET. I can't anymore tonight, It's past eleven.

ROMEO. *(Scratching his head:)* Well it couldn't hurt if we kissed through
the horn,
Then we'll elope when the sun lights the morn.

> *(They kiss through the horn and the bullhorn alarm goes off.
> They run away blowing kisses to each other. Enter NARRATOR
> #2. Enter MONK LARRY on the opposite side of the playing area.)*

NARRATOR #2. So Romeo ran to the home of Monk Larry,
Not monkey Larry...he's not quite that hairy,
He's just a monk, he's the monkiest one
That Romeo knew and could get the job done.

> *(Enter ROMEO.)*

ROMEO. Oh good! Monk Larry! I'm glad that you're here.

MONK LARRY. *(In a Bronx accent:)* Where else would I be, I've not left
    here in years
You sure are chipper, last time I saw yous,
You were blubbering, moping, and singing the blues.

ROMEO. That was the old me. I'm new and improved.
I'm a hip-hoppin', happenin', cool, righteous dude!

MONK LARRY. How can I help you, my dude filled with glee?

    (ROMEO grabs MONK LARRY's hand and gets down on one knee.)

ROMEO. I need your consent, Monk, will you marry me?

MONK LARRY. *(Grabbing him by the throat:)* Listen punk! I am a monk,
    don't you get it?
I live all alone and I'm wearing a habit.

ROMEO. *(Choking:)* No, No! There's a girl that I've met as of late,
She is the daughter of Capitulate.
Our love is true.

MONK LARRY. Are you sure?

ROMEO. Yes indeed.
One-hundred and ninety percent guaranteed.

MONK LARRY. *(Aside to the audience:)* If I marry the girl to this Monotone
    dude-ling,
It may end the war, all this troublesome feud-ling.
(To ROMEO:) Okay, my young pup, I'll tie your knot,
But, if you're eloping, then you'll need a plot.

    *(MONK LARRY puts his arm around ROMEO and they exit. Enter
    MERCUTIO and BENVOLIO.)*

MERCUTIO. So, Romeo never came home late last night?

BENVOLIO. He never came home and he's still out of sight.
Now, Tybalt the nephew of Capitulate,
Challenges him to a bumballoon fight.

MERCUTIO. A bumballoon fight? That's the worst!

BENVOLIO. Yeah, I know.

MERCUTIO. That would mean curtains for poor Romeo.
Tybalt's the best bumballoonist around,
I've seen him bumballoon twenty men down.
I can hold my own at true bumballooning,
But, lovesick young Romy's been too busy crooning.

BENVOLIO. Here he comes now! Hey Romy, what gives?
You didn't go back to the place where you live.

    (ROMEO enters.)

ROMEO. There's an optometrist whose name is Cupid,
He's opened my eyes, and made me less stupid.

I met a new girl, she's the best of the best.
She passed the Romeo "hot mama" test.

(*Romeo's friends chime in with masculine banter.*)

MERCUTIO. Heeeey, well okay, well okay hey, I say...

BENVOLIO. Heeeeeey!

ROMEO. Yippy-Yeeeea!

MERCUTIO. Yippy, okay ei-yeeea!

(*Enter* NURSE.)

NURSE. Has anyone seen Romeo Monotone?
I need to see him before I go home.

(*Romeo's friends think that the* NURSE *is Romeo's new girlfriend.*)

MERCUTIO. (*Winking and nudging* ROMEO:) Hey there! Not bad, she's a fine catch old son.

BENVOLIO. I guess I was picturing someone more young.

MERCUTIO. (*Love-stricken by the* NURSE:) Wow! She's a babe alright, look at those curls.

ROMEO. What! Are you mental? That's not the new girl.

(MERCUTIO *is dumbfounded.*)

NURSE. (*To* ROMEO:) Juliet, my mistress inquires about you,
But, I think she's missing a half-dozen screws.
As her nurse, I must ask, what makes you so great?
Why do you deserve Miss Capitulate.

ROMEO. I make a great milkshake, all my friends say so.

NURSE. That's good enough for me, so where should we meet you.

ROMEO. We'll meet at Monk Larry's place later today,
He'll marry us there, and then we'll say "hurray!"

NURSE. I love small weddings. What could be humbler?

(*The* NURSE *exits.*)

MERCUTIO. (*Following the* NURSE:) Excuse me there Miss, could I get your number?

(BENVOLIO *and* ROMEO *exit—looking puzzled by* MERCUTIO. NARRATOR #1 *enters.* ROMEO *reenters with* MONK LARRY.)

NARRATOR #1. So Romeo went back to Monk Larry's house. Not a creature was stirring, not even...

ROMEO. (*Screaming in horror:*) A Mouse!

(MONK LARRY *is holding a stuffed pet rodent.*)

MONK LARRY. It ain't a mouse it's a Shnosel-nosed dodrent,
Amongst the tamest of lint-eating rodents.
He lives in my sleeve, with this lint-eating rabbit.

(MONK LARRY *produces a pet rabbit from his sleeve.*)

MONK LARRY. Both of them eat clean, my stinky, bad habit.

ROMEO. I'm just so nervous my stomach's a wreck,
Where could they be?

MONK LARRY. Just a sec. I'll go check.

(MONK LARRY exits.)

ROMEO. I do not like his stinky clothes,
I do not like his Shnosel nose,
I do not like them near or far,
I do not like them in a car,
I do not like them in a tunnel,
I could not push them through a funnel,
I only love the girl I met,

(JULIET and NURSE enter.)

ROMEO. Here she comes. Hey Juliet!

JULIET. I'm sorry that we are late in getting here,
I had to use eight cans of spray in my hair.

NURSE. So, don't light a match!

ROMEO. No, I won't, I vow.

JULIET. So, where is the monk?

ROMEO. Aw! For crying out loud.

NURSE. I'll go and find him. I think I know where.
He'll be back in a jiffy, so never despair.

(NURSE exits. MONK LARRY returns.)

MONK LARRY. Well I couldn't find Juliet anywhere.
Hey! This girl looks good, how 'bout marry her.

ROMEO. This is Juliet you knucklehead monk!

MONK LARRY. Settle down tiger! I don't need this, Punk!
Okay, kneel down, now lets make this quick,
I gotta floss my cat, so he won't stick.
Both of you, make sure your rings are all switched.
You may now kiss the bride, I pronounce you hitched.

NARRATOR #2. Romy and J were now happily married,
They both yelled "hurray," and then off they scurried.
But not all was happy in this neighborhood,
Mercutio and Tybalt were up to no good.
It happened that both of them came to a place,
Where they stopped and they stood, nose to nose, face to face.

TYBALT. I am an East going Tybalt, I say,
You're blocking my path, you're right in my way.

MERCUTIO. I am Mercutio, I always go west,
So you'd better step aside if you know best.

TYBALT. Didn't you hear the words from my mouth?
I won't budge and inch to the North or the South!

MERCUTIO. I challenge you then, to a bumballoon battle.

TYBALT. You think you can beat me? Ha! fiddle-faddle.

MERCUTIO. You want to bumballoon poor Romeo.

TYBALT. Yeah? So big deal, what's it to yo?

> *(They fight with balloons roughly tied into the shapes of swords.* ROMEO *enters.)*

ROMEO. Hold on there fellas! This isn't the way.
Tybalt we're practically kin, I'll explain.

TYBALT. *(Aside:)* When I finish here, one more victim to go.
(Points at ROMEO:*)* His name starts with "R" and rhymes with Omeo.

ROMEO. Hey guys! Quit fighting, 'cuz that's just as bad,
As putting chameleons on top of plaid.

> *(*TYBALT *deals the fatal blow to* MERCUTIO, *leaving his bumballoon weapon stuck in* MERCUTIO's *chest—or under his arm.)*

MERCUTIO. Ouch! Ay-Carumba! I've been bumballooned!

TYBALT. I am the victor of this lame buffoon.

ROMEO. Mercutio!

MERCUTIO. Romeo!

ROMEO. Friend, are you dying?

MERCUTIO. No, I'm feeling fine...and...I am lying.

> *(*MERCUTIO *lets out a blood-curdling scream.)*

ROMEO. Let me pull this bumballoon from your breast.

MERCUTIO. Please, I'd prefer that you call it my chest.

ROMEO. *(Trying to pull out the balloon:)* Chest, breast, whatever, Yoiks!
This thing won't budge.

TYBALT. Prepare to die Romeo! I hold a grudge!

ROMEO. Sheesh! This stuck bumballoon's really a pain.

> *(*ROMEO *finally pulls* TYBALT's *balloon free. He stumbles backwards from the pull, and kills* TYBALT *with his own balloon weapon.)*

TYBALT. With my own bumballoon, now I am slain!

> *(*ROMEO *is stunned that he just killed* TYBALT.*)*

ROMEO. What in the world? Crap! How did this happen?

> *(*TYBALT *quickly wakes up from death to answer* ROMEO.*)*

TYBALT. You caught me off guard. I was too busy yappin'.

> *(*TYBALT *drops dead again.)*

BENVOLIO. Romeo run! Or you're a sitting duck!

ROMEO. Oh I'm fortune's fool, and the plaything of luck!

(ROMEO exits. The PRINCE, the CAPITULATES, and the MONOTONES enter.)

THE PRINCE. What happened here? I'd like to explore
The reason there's two dead guys here on the floor.

BENVOLIO. Tybalt here bumballooned good friend Mercutio,
and then got his bell rung by poor, sweet, young Romeo.

(LADY CAPITULATE sees TYBALT's dead body and rushes to him trying to administer CPR, while delivering her line.)

LADY CAPITULATE. Oh Tybalt-de-dibalt-de-dibalt-de-doo.
My brother's son's third cousin four times removed.
(To the PRINCE:) My kinsman Tybalt lies dead on the floor.
Romeo must die to even the score.

THE PRINCE. Easy there girly-girl! I call the shots.
I am the prince here believe it or not.
I'll banish young Romeo from fair Verona,
As soon as I finish this slice of bologna.

(Everyone exits. NARRATOR #1 enters. JULIET enters from the other side. She sits on a bed that is rolled into the playing area. This represents her bedroom.)

NARRATOR #1. Romeo has to go skip town or else,
The prince might find out and put him on the shelf.

(She does the slit-throat gesture.)

We see here young Julie as she thinks and sits,

JULIET. I'm wife to a banished guy. Man! That's the pits.

NARRATOR #1. Yeah, that's not all, 'cuz there's more pits in store,
Here come her parents, through her bedroom door.

(Enter LADY CAPITULATE and LORD CAPITULATE.)

LADY CAPITULATE. Since poor Tybalt's death fills all our hearts with sorrow...

CAPITULATE. We're bumping your wedding day up to tomorrow.

(LADY CAPITULATE and LORD CAPITULATE exit. NARRATOR #1 exits.)

JULIET. This is the double most "pits" situation.
I'm victim of my father's capitulation.
I can't marry Paris, 'cuz I've got a husband.
I'm sure that's illegal except in Wisconsin.
I need to get help. If I don't, then I'm sunk.
This is a job for old Larry the Monk.

(MONK LARRY enters.)

JULIET. Monk Larry! You've entered my bedroom, but how?

(MONK LARRY pulls a script out of his habit and shows it to JULIET.)

MONK LARRY. Check the script Julie, it's my bedroom now.

JULIET. Ooooh! Is that because this is the magic of theatre?

MONK LARRY. *(Smiling tersely:)* Yes my child. *(Aside:)* She's got less brains than a sea otter.

JULIET. Gentle Monk Larry, I need some assistance.
My wedding's tomorrow despite my resistance.
To Romeo, you'll recall, I am now wed.
But, they'd have me wed Paris...

MONK LARRY. Not if you're dead.
Listen, I've got a plan, but it takes guts,
And you must eat two of these death faking nuts.

> *(He holds up a jar labeled—"Death Faking Nuts.")*

These death faking nuts, they make you look dead.
Paris can't wed, if the bride's dead in bed.
That you are still living won't be understood,
They'll all think you're dead, 'cuz these nuts work good.
Then after the funeral, in a few days,
You'll wake up with Romeo, far, far, away.

JULIET. How'll Romeo know that I'm not really croaked?

MONK LARRY. I'll send him an email, I'll tell him our joke.
In your tomb, when the last tread has been trod,
Romeo will sneak in and collect your bod.

JULIET. I'll take the nuts when evening has come.

MONK LARRY. And I'll send an email to Romeo dot com.

> *(MONK LARRY exits. We see ROMEO off to the side fiddling with his computer. Enter NARRATORS.)*

NARRATOR #2. The monk sent his email with details attached
But, Romeo missed it, 'cuz his PC crashed.
He never learned Juliet was faking disaster.

ROMEO. Shucks! Now I can't play "Double Sneetch Blaster."

> *(Exits.)*

NARRATOR #1. Surely by now, you can see that it's true,
With Dr. Seuss our play has nothing to do.

NARRATOR #2. We'll say it again, in case you were snoozing,
It never dawned on us to make this a Seuss thing.

NARRATOR #1. Later that night Juliet ate the nuts.

> *(JULIET eats the nuts looking around and chewing obnoxiously. Then, very suddenly, she falls over as if dead in her bed.)*

NARRATOR #2. Then in the morning, she wouldn't wake up.

> *(The NURSE enters and screams. Juliet's parents rush in to see what the matter is.)*

CAPITULATE. What! What's the matter! Is Juliet dead?

LADY CAPITULATE. Is her body cold, is there blood on her head?

CAPITULATE. Did you check her pulse? Did you give CPR?

LADY CAPITULATE. Did you give her the Licking Heim-Heim Lick maneuver?

(NURSE shakes her head.)

CAPITULATE. Then why did you scream? Tell me, what's this about?

NURSE. My leg cramped up, I just got done working out.

(NURSE exits.)

LADY CAPITULATE. I'm so glad to hear Juliet isn't dead.

CAPITULATE. She's just a sound sleeper, she's got a good bed.
A good bed means everything to a sound sleep
Now that she's rested, from her bed she'll leap.

LADY CAPITULATE. Juliet wake up it's your lucky day.

(She nudges JULIET.)

CAPITULATE. Today is the day that we give you away.

(Nudges JULIET harder.)

LADY CAPITULATE. We give you to Paris today, the young lord.

(Nudges really hard.)

CAPITULATE. *(Lifting her out of bed:)* Up! Out of bed! Say, she's stiff as a board.

LADY CAPITULATE. She's awfully cold, maybe she froze in her dream.

CAPITULATE. Or, maybe she's dead.

LADY CAPITULATE. It's our turn to scream!

(CAPITULATE nods. They scream and exit carrying JULIET's seemingly dead body. The bed rolls out of sight.)

NARRATOR #1. Meanwhile back on the beach of Kadid,
We meet up with Romeo, that's where he hid.

NARRATOR #2. Benvolio found him there, sunning himself,
Disguised as an "antelope-sun bathing-elf."

BENVOLIO. Romeo wake up, and hear what I say,
Juliet's dead and her funeral's today.

(ROMEO, waking up, is having a hard time remembering who Juliet is.)

ROMEO. *(Scratching his head:)* Juliet, Juliet that name draws a blank,
Help me out here, does she work at the bank?

BENVOLIO. Juliet! She is your own heart's delight,
You married her yesterday, she is your wife!

ROMEO. Oooooh! That Juliet. Yeah, that name rings a bell,
Now what was the message you wanted to tell?

BENVOLIO. Juliet's dead!

ROMEO. Are you kidding me?

BENVOLIO. No!

ROMEO. How did she die?

BENVOLIO. Nobody knows.

ROMEO. It must have been her broken heart that went "Crack!"
I'll kiss her one last time. I must now go back!
Then I'll consume this authentic death cracker.

(ROMEO *holds up a single soda cracker.)*

It'll take me, quickly, out of the picture.
Don't try and stop me, it must be this way,

(BENVOLIO *is obviously not trying to stop him.)*

Without Juliet, I shan't see one more day.
My ears are deaf to your protestations,

(BENVOLIO *is not protesting.)*

My mind is made up, to have life deprivation.

(BENVOLIO, *annoyed at* ROMEO's *overblown dramatics, exits.*
ROMEO *continues.)*

There's nothing, Benvolio, that you can do,
To keep me from dying, I will follow through.
Don't make a scene now, I've told you my notion,
I am a train and my wheels are in motion.

(He *mimics a "choo-choo" train. Realizing he's alone, he coyly*
glances at the audience and blushes.)

Off to Verona I go with my life,
To lay it before my corpse of a wife.

(ROMEO *exits.* JULIET's *body gets rolled out to center stage. Her*
parents and a host of mourners are around her.)

NARRATOR #1. The mourners took one last look at Julie's body,
Then somebody yelled...

VOICE FROM THE LOBBY. Hey! There's snacks in the lobby.

(All *of the mourners rush off stage. Leaving* JULIET *alone.* ROMEO
enters.)

ROMEO. Juliet, honey, to get here I ran.
I tripped on a grave stone and fell on my can.
I came here to give your lips just one more kiss,
And then, when I'm done, I'm gonna eat this.

(He *holds up the authentic death cracker dramatically.)*

It isn't fair that I live, when you're dead,
So I'm gonna trade my life for death instead.
Here comes the kiss so pucker up sister,

(They *kiss.)*

Yippee, yahoo! You're still a great kisser.
That was phase one, now here comes phase two,
I'll eat this cracker, then I'll be dead too.

> (ROMEO *holds the cracker up and makes a big production out of eating it. Suspenseful music comes on and gets louder as he brings the cracker closer to his mouth.* ROMEO *notices this and plays with the music. He moves the cracker away from his mouth and the music gets softer, closer—louder, etc. Finally he eats the cracker and assumes a safety position as if something is going to happen. It doesn't. He stands up straight and waits. He checks his watch. He whistles. The* NARRATORS *enter.)*

NARRATOR #2. Now, there's a reason that Romeo's life isn't halting,

NARRATOR #1. 'Cuz we switched his death cracker with a plain saltine.

NARRATOR #2. We've read this show, and it don't end pretty,

NARRATOR #1. So we tweaked the plot a bit—made it less gritty.

NARRATOR #2. Juliet woke from her death grip like slumber,

NARRATOR #1. And overjoyed, Romeo did a back flip dance number.

> *(He dances. They hug.* MERCUTIO *and* TYBALT *enter.)*

NARRATOR #2. Mercutio and Tybalt weren't really dead,

TYBALT. We were just teasing,

MERCUTIO. Playin' with your head.
We're both great pals now,

TYBALT. He's such a good listener.

NARRATOR #1. They'll both be attending the swish fishing opener.

MERCUTIO. Since both of us now have been on hiatus,
We bought this machine that a nice fella made us.

> *(A "Seuss looking" machine is revealed. It has two openings: One for people to run into the machine and one for people to run out of the machine.)*

TYBALT. It's guaranteed to make angry folks happy,
He ought to know...

MERCUTIO. He's The Feud Fixing Chappie.

NARRATOR #1. So all of the members of both families,
Went through the machine just as fast as a breeze.
It took those "X"s and "O"s off their tummies.

> *(ROMEO *and* JULIET *come out of the machine last, holding a big valentine with all of the "X"s and "O"s alternated on it, representing "hugs and kisses.")*

CAPITULATE. *(Checking his new letterless tummy:)* What were we thinking?

MONOTONE. *(Checking his tummy:)* Wow! Were we dummies!

NARRATOR #2. Long years of bitterness melted away.

NARRATOR #1. Now they had nothing but nice things to say.

NARRATOR #2. Compliments flew!

CAPITULATE. Say! I like that tie.

> (MONOTONE *wasn't wearing a tie before. Now he is and it's especially gaudy.)*

MONOTONE. I like your trousers and...you're a nice guy.

> (CAPITULATE *wasn't wearing the trousers before. Now he is and they, too, are especially gaudy.)*

NARRATOR #1. There wasn't anyone left who felt bugged,

NARRATOR #2. So, they all partook of a giant group hug.

ALL. Group Hug!

> (Lots of *"oohs" and "ohs" and snuggly-cuddly language. All leave except for the* NARRATORS.)

NARRATOR #1. It was official. The feuding had ended,
The lovers kept loving and the families befriended.

NARRATOR #2. All from both families, sold their bumballoons,
And with all the money they bought a pontoon.

NARRATOR #1. And now every night with the fish and the ducks,
They all eat together at pontoon "potlucks."
Now, you may have noticed that no one here died.

NARRATOR #2. What!? Can we help it if our prologue lied?
But, come on! That's no way to end a good play.

NARRATOR #1. Dr. Seuss wouldn't I'd venture to say.

NARRATOR #2. That's right, he wouldn't, and neither would we,
Even though our play is Dr. Seuss-free.

NARRATOR #1. Well okay, it did have a few small Seuss-isms,
Some overblown rhyming, and minor plot schisms.

NARRATOR #2. This stuff is dangerous.

NARRATOR #1. It shouldn't be tried!

NARRATOR #2. To interpret William Shakespeare, Seussified.

NARRATOR #1. Leave that to the artists, they've had the right schoolin'

> (The CAST *appears behind the* NARRATORS.)

NARRATOR #2. They are the pros,

BOTH. And they know what their doin'.

> (NARRATORS *step back into the line of actors and they all join hands.)*

NARRATOR #1. We hope you've enjoyed this tragic lament.

NARRATOR #2. 'Cus we've all enjoyed it...

ALL. One-hundred percent!

(All bow and blackout.)

End of Play

First Optional Ending

(Lights come back up and CAST *chants "one more time" and a speed through with quick entrances and exits is done. The Seussification of Romeo and Juliet speed recap is as follows:)*

NARRATOR #1. Ladies and Menfolk.

NARRATOR #2. Women and Gents.

BOTH. *Romeo and Juliet!* Our Prologue's addressed!

PROLOGUE. Verona's the place that our play is from,
We just gotta tell you don't try this at home.

("West Side Story" music.)

ABRAM. Did you bite your thumb?

GREGORY. Yeah! See the pus?

ALL. Let's fight.

CAPITULATE. Monotone you're a creep!

MONOTONE. You're a creep!

CAPITULATE. You're a creep!

MONOTONE. You're a creep!

NARRATOR #1. Enter the Prince, the royal sap...

THE PRINCE. Will you jerks knock it off? I'm taking a nap!

MONOTONE. Where's Romeo?

LADY MONOTONE. There!

ROMEO. Oh, I'm cooked rare!

NARRATOR #1. Sneezle Fruit Juice! No Dr. Seuss!

NARRATOR #2. Suitor for Julie—He's with her Dad.

PARIS. Capitulate I'm hot! Here have some candy!

CAPITULATE (LORD). Why thank-you boy, I think you'll be dandy!

SERVANT OF CAPITULATE. I can't read! Woe is me. What is my fate?

ROMEO. I can read! Blah, blah, blah, blah, blah, blah, come to the party!
This party sounds great!

BENVOLIO. Yeah!

SERVANT OF CAPITULATE. Yeah!

NURSE. Sweet chimpanzeezle... Where are you, you weasel?

JULIET. Is this a moment I'll Cherish?

LADY CAPITULATE. Of course it is girly, you're marrying Paris.

NARRATOR #2. Zip-zip sha-bang also known as Mercutio.

MERCUTIO. Do you want to live you're whole life in a hole?

CAPITULATE (LORD). Good evening Gents...watch me dance—I've got soul.

(Dance music.)

ROMEO. Ei-hotchee-mama!

TYBALT. Uncle your house has a Monotone there.

CAPITULATE (LORD). Did you lose this mitten? Wow he has nice hair!

ROMEO. I think you're hot!

JULIET. Here hold my gum!

ROMEO. Wow! That's good gum! Yum ditty yum.

NARRATOR #1. Later that night...

BENVOLIO. Where'd Romeo go?

MERCUTIO. He went home to bed!

BENVOLIO. He's not in his bed!

MERCUTIO. You need a new head!

JULIET. Romeo baby-o

ROMEO. Kiss me through the horny-o

(Bullhorn siren.)

NARRATOR #2. Romeo ran to Larry the monkey!

ROMEO. Monkey Larry, will you marry me?

MONK LARRY. Okay my young pup, I'll tie your knot.

BENVOLIO. Hey Romy, what gives? You didn't go back to the place where you live.

ROMEO. This new girl I found past the hot mama test!

ALL. Yippy, okay ei yeeea!

NURSE. Romeo Monotone, what makes you great?

ROMEO. Everyone knows that I make a great shake!

NURSE. Where should we meet you?

ROMEO. Monk Larry's

NURSE. What's Humbler!

MERCUTIO. Hey baby! Don't leave me. Can I get your numbler?

ROMEO. Hey Juliet.

JULIET. I used eight cans of hairspray!

MONK LARRY. She looks good... Marry her... I now pronounce you hitched.

NARRATOR #2. Mercutio and Tybalt were up to no good.

TYBALT. Move!

MERCUTIO. No!

TYBALT. Die!

MERCUTIO. Eieeee!

ROMEO. Mercutio!

MERCUTIO. Romeo!

ROMEO. Let me pull this bumballoon from your breast.

MERCUTIO. It's my chest not my breast!

TYBALT. I am bumballooned!

ROMEO. Crap!

LADY CAPITULATE. Romeo must die.

THE PRINCE. Bologna!

JULIET. This is the pits... They'd have me wed Paris.

MONK LARRY. Not if you're dead. Eat these nuts!

NARRATOR #2. Romeo's PC Crashed!

ROMEO. Double Sneetch Blaster!

NURSE. *(Scream.)*

CAPITULATE. Is she dead?

NURSE. Yes!

CAPITULATE / LADY CAPITULATE. *(Scream.)*

BENVOLIO. Juliet's dead!

ROMEO. Are you kidding me?

BENVOLIO. No!

ROMEO. Sorry I'm late Jules, I fell on my can!

    (They kiss.)

Now I'm the death cracker consuming man!

NARRATOR #1. Romeo danced! And not even once died.

NARRATOR #2. Nobody's dead! They're all still alive.

BOTH. Group hug!

NARRATOR #1. We hope you've enjoyed this tragic lament.

NARRATOR #2. 'Cuz we've all enjoyed it.

ALL. One hundred percent!...

                             End of Play

Second Optional Ending

(To keep each production of this play fresh, the playwright allows each respective playing company the freedom to construct their own "second optional ending." However, the playwright has two rules: 1) It must be a humorous, and a final recap of the show, and 2) It must take much less time than the first "additional, optional ending.")

(Examples: The second, additional, optional ending could be a recap of the show done backwards in 30 seconds. Or, it could be done in Portuguese. Or, it could be done backwards in 30 seconds and in Portuguese.)

(A possible "backwards" scenario is given:)

(The pace should be a bit frenzied, with actors running into place, delivering their lines and then running to the next place.)

(An example is below.)

ALL. *(Delivering lines as if listening to a tape backwards:)* Faster and Backwards! ...Percent hundred-one.

BOTH NARRATORS. Hug group.

ROMEO. Cracker death eat gotta I!

CAPITULATE / LADY CAPITULATE. *(Scream.)*

NURSE. Yes!

CAPITULATE (LORD). Dead she is?

NURSE. *(Screams.)*

JULIET. Pits the is this.

THE PRINCE. Bologna!

LADY CAPITULATE. Die must Romeo!

TYBALT. Bumballooned am I!

MERCUTIO. Breast my not chest my it's.

ROMEO. Test mama hot. Girl new a found I.

MONK LARRY. Knot your tie I'll pup young my okay.

ROMEO. Me marry you will Larry Monkey?

ROMEO. Horn the through me kiss.

JULIET. Buff o baby Romeo.

MERCUTIO. Head new a need you!

BENVOLIO. Go Romeo where'd

NARRATOR #1. Night that later...

JULIET. Gum my hold here

ROMEO. Hot you're think I. Mama hotchee Ei!

CAPITULATE. Dance to want I.

LADY CAPITULATE. Paris marrying you're!

NURSE. Weasel you, you are where...chimpanzeezle sweet.

ROMEO. Great sounds party this. Blah, blah, blah read can I.

CAPITULATE. Dandy be you'll think I.

PARIS. Hot I'm Capitulate.

NARRATOR #2. Dad her with He's Julie for suitor.

NARRATOR #1. Juice fruit sneezle.

ROMEO. Rare cooked I'm.

THE PRINCE. Off it knocks jerks you will.

MONOTONE. Creep a you're.

CAPITULATE. Creep a you're.

MONOTONE. Creep a you're.

CAPITULATE. Creep a you're Monotone.

SAMPSON / GREGORY / ABRAM / BALTHAZAR. Fight let's.

GREGORY. Pus the see, Yeah!

ABRAM. Thumb your bite you did?

PROLOGUE. Place the Verona's

BOTH NARRATORS. Addressed Prologue's our, *Juliet and Romeo*.

NARRATOR #2. Gents and women.

NARRATOR #1. Menfolk and ladies.

(All characters run onto the stage, take a bow and drop dead on the stage—exhausted.)

(Lights out.)

(Final curtain call.)

End of Play

SHOW AND SPELL

by Julia Brownell

For more information about rights and permissions, see page 9.

Cast of Characters

SUNNY SANDSTONE, the cheerleader

MR. SANDSTONE, her father

GREG SANDSTONE, her brother

DAVID LICHTENSTEINBERGER, the overconfident genius

MRS. LICHTENSTEINBERGER, his mom

MR. LICHTENSTEINBERGER, his dad

IMAGINE PEARSON, the drama queen

STAR PEARSON, her mom

DEBRA, Star's assistant

JEFF MATTHEWS, the jock

GRANDPA MATTHEWS, his grandfather

COACH BRICK, his coach

DESIREE WORTHINGTON, the spoiled rich kid

MRS. WORTHINGTON, her mom

ELOISE, her maid

MR. LANFORD, the announcer

Acknowledgments

Show and Spell was commissioned by The New Players Company of Ridgewood, New Jersey. It received its premiere performance on July 20, 2005.

Dedicated to Tim Brownell and Rachael Daum.

SHOW AND SPELL

Prologue

(Lights up on an empty stage. SUNNY, DAVID, IMAGINE, JEFF, and DESIREE stand in a row, facing the audience. MR. LANFORD stands off to the side.)

MR. LANFORD. And the winner of the thirty-seventh annual Waytown County Spelling Bee is...

(Spotlight on SUNNY.)

SUNNY. S-U-N-N-Y S-A-N-D-S-T-O-N-E. Sunny Standstone. I'm a cheerleader from South Waytown. I love cheerleading, and spelling, and cheerleading and spelling at the same time! I'd like to thank my dad, and my brother, Greg, for being the best family a girl could have!

(MR. SANDSTONE and GREG come onstage from the audience and wave. Lights down on SUNNY. Lights up on DAVID.)

DAVID. D-A-V-I-D L-I-C-H-T-E-N-S-T-E-I-N-B-E-R-G-E-R. David Lichtensteinberger. I'm from East Waytown, and my hobbies include studying, learning, and reading books. In my spare time, I like to do science experiments and solve equations. I really did all the work myself, but I'd like to thank my parents for driving me here since I don't have my driver's license yet.

(MR. L and MRS. L join DAVID onstage from the audience and wave. Lights down on DAVID. Lights up on IMAGINE.)

IMAGINE. I-M-A-G-I-N-E P-E-A-R-S-O-N. Imagine Pearson. I'm an actress from West Waytown. I'm the daughter of the famous actress Star Pearson and I have played several parts in her movies, most recently as Girl #5 in her upcoming summer film. I'd like to thank my mom, Star, and her assistant, Debra.

(STAR and DEBRA join IMAGINE onstage from the audience. Lights down on STAR. Lights up on JEFF.)

JEFF. J-E-F-F M-A-T-T-H-E-W-S. Jeff Matthews. I'm a baseball and soccer and basketball and football and lacrosse and tennis and hockey and pickleball champion from Central Waytown. I'd like to thank my dad and my coach, Coach Brick, for teaching me to always give 150 percent.

(MR. MATTHEWS and COACH BRICK join JEFF onstage from the audience. Lights down on JEFF. Lights up on DESIREE.)

DESIREE. D-E-S-I-R-E-E W-O-R-T-H-I-N-G-T-O-N. Desiree Worthington. I'm from North Waytown and my hobbies include shopping, going on cruises, and watching movies in my own private home theater. I'd like to thank my mom for giving me lots of money and my maid for helping my study.

(MRS. WORTHINGTON and ELOISE join DESIREE onstage from the audience and wave. Lights down on DESIREE. Lights back on MR. LANFORD.)

MR. LANFORD. Once more, congratulations to our 2005 champion speller! Thank you, and see you next year!

(End of Prologue.)

Scene One

(Two bedrooms, one on each side of the stage. SUNNY studies in one room; DAVID in the other. SUNNY's room is full of pom-poms and cheerleading trophies; DAVID's is crowded with books. Lights up on Sunny's room.)

SUNNY. *(With pom-poms:)* Azalea. Hmm... Give me an A, give me a Z, give me an A, give me an L-E-A! What does that spell? Azalea! Fustanella. Give me an F, give me a U, give me an S-T-A! Give me an N-E-L-L-A! What does that spell? Fustanella! Yeah!!

GREG. *(Offstage:)* Be quiet, Sunny! I'm trying to listen to music!

SUNNY. Oops! Sorry, Greg! *(Whispering:)* Aberrant. Give me an A, give me a B, give me an E! Give me an R-R-A-N-T! What does that spell? Abberant! Woo!

GREG. *(Offstage:)* Sunny, shut up! Stop cheering your words!

SUNNY. How am I supposed to spell if I can't cheer?

GREG. The way normal people do!

SUNNY. I can't remember words if I can't cheer them. Cessation. Give me a C, give me an E, give me an S—

(GREG enters and grabs her pom-poms.)

GREG. Give me an S-H-U-T-U-P! What does that spell? Shut UP!!! Yay!

SUNNY. Greg! Give me back my pom-poms!

GREG. Not until you promise to stop cheering words!

SUNNY. How am I supposed to practice? Give me BACK my pom-poms!

(SUNNY and GREG struggle over the pom-poms. MR. SANDSTONE enters.)

MR. SANDSTONE. What's going on here? Stop it! Sunny! Greg!

SUNNY. He won't give me back my pom-poms!

GREG. She won't stop cheering!

MR. SANDSTONE. Okay. Greg, give Sunny back her pom-poms.

(GREG does.)

MR. SANDSTONE. Sunny, I don't know what to do with you. When I tried sending you outside to practice, the neighbors complained. When I sent you to practice at school, the custodians complained. Is there any way you can cheer more quietly?

SUNNY. But Dad! I want to do my absolutely positively most very best that I can do!

MR. SANDSTONE. Okay. The bee's in two days. Greg, is there anyway you could go spend the night at a friend's house tonight?

GREG. I'm getting kicked out of my own house so that she can do stupid spelling cheers? That's ridiculous. I'm the older one!

SUNNY. And I'm the happier one!

GREG. So?

MR. SANDSTONE. All right, I can see that's not going to work. Greg, why don't we go out for pizza and to the movies while Sunny studies?

GREG. Now I'm getting *bribed* to leave my own house while my sister studies?

MR. SANDSTONE. It's a good bribe, Greg. Take it.

GREG. I just want to listen to music in my room!

SUNNY. Give me an L-E-D! Give me a Z-E-P-P-E-L-I-N! What does that spell—

GREG. Stop it! See how annoying this is? That's a band, it's not even a spelling word! She's doing it on purpose to bother me!

MR. SANDSTONE. She's just practicing.

SUNNY. For your information, zeppelin also means—

GREG. Dad, tell her to stop spelling my interests.

MR. SANDSTONE. Sunny, please stop spelling your brother's interests.

SUNNY. But Dad, I have to spell everything if I want to win!

MR. SANDSTONE. Greg, just let her spell for two more days. She'll thank you for it. I'll thank you for it.

SUNNY. Give me a G-R-A-T-I-T-U-D-E! What does that spell?

GREG. *(Exiting:)* Arghhh!

SUNNY. Thanks, dad!

MR. SANDSTONE. You're welcome, honey. I know you're working very hard. Please promise me you won't take this too seriously, though. I don't want you just to spell non-stop for the next two days. Promise?

SUNNY. I promise!

MR. SANDSTONE. That's my girl. Now, what do you want for dinner?

SUNNY. Hmm... Give me an S, give me a P, give me an—

MR. SANDSTONE. *(Exiting:)* Okay, okay. I get it. I'll make some pasta.

> *(Lights down on* SUNNY's *room as she continues cheering. Lights up on* DAVID's *room.)*

DAVID. *(Reading the dictionary and muttering to himself:)* Cephalophod, Cepheid, ceraceous. C-E-P-H—

> *(MRS. L enters with a plate of cookies.)*

MRS. L. David?

DAVID. Can't you see that I'm previously occupied, mother?

MRS. L. I was just wondering if you'd like some cookies. You didn't eat breakfast, and you didn't come down for lunch—

DAVID. I'm not hungry. Fulfilling my hunger for knowledge is what satiates me.

MRS. L. I don't want to hear that excuse again, David, you've been saying that since you were two. At least have a cookie.

DAVID. Do they have fish in them?

MRS. L. They're cookies. Why in the world would they have fish in them?

DAVID. Fish is brain food, mother. Omega-three acids. I told you that I refuse to eat anything without omega-three acids until Saturday.

MRS. L. David, I refuse to put fish in cookies. You know how your father reacted after I tried salmon in a pie.

    (MR. L enters.)

MR. L. How's the studying going, David?

    (Reaches for a cookie.)

Yum, cookies.

    (Pauses; sniffs the cookie.)

Do these have fish in them?

DAVID. Unfortunately, no.

MR. L. *(Eating the cookie:)* Mmm, delicious. Even without the fish.

MRS. L. Thank you. I'm glad someone likes them.

MR. L. So how's the spelling going?

DAVID. I'm making progress.

MR. L. Why don't you take a break? It's a beautiful day out! We could throw a ball around.

DAVID. No, thank you.

MRS. L. Would you at least go for a walk with us? I worry about you. You haven't been outside in two days—

DAVID. A Vitamin A deficiency will not affect my spelling.

MR. L. Well, do you want some help with the studying? We could quiz you on the words—

MRS. L. Yes, let's do that.

DAVID. Mother, father, you can't pronounce these words.

MR. L. I'm sure there's another way we could help you practice.

MRS. L. Besides, the dictionary has a pronounciation key.

DAVID. *(Handing over the dictionary:)* All right, fine. Here.

MR. L. *(Looking at the book:)* Okay. Allrighty. Let's see. This word is cer —or maybe ker—or care— *(Handing the book to* MRS. L:*)* Why don't you try this one?

MRS. L. Okay, umm... Your father's right, it's cer—or care—or it could be ker— Its definition is "an instrument for recording chronologically by pen—"

DAVID. This is not a definition bee, this is a spelling bee! I need to hear the word to spell it!

MR. L. I bet you know the word anyway, David. Don't you? Just by that little bit of definition?

DAVID. Yes, I do. It's ceraunograph.

MR. L. I knew it!

MRS. L. You're so smart, dear!

DAVID. That's not the point!

MRS. L. You've got this competition in the bag!

MR. L. Spelling bee championship, here we come!

DAVID. I didn't even SPELL THE WORD YET!

MRS. L. Oh. You're right. You didn't.

MR. L. But I bet you know how to spell it!

MRS. L. I know you can spell it!

DAVID. *(Quickly:)* C-E-R-A-U-N-O-G-R-A-P-H! Okay? Yes, I do know how to spell it.

MR. L. *(Looking in the dictionary:)* Let me check to see if it's right. You said C-E....C-E—what?

MRS. L. He said C-E-R, I think.

MR. L. Did you say C-E-R?

DAVID. It's right! You don't have to check it, it's right. Okay? This is why I don't like to study with you.

MRS. L. He got it right!

MR. L. That's my boy!

MRS. L. Shall we move on to the next word?

DAVID. *(Sighing:)* Fine.

(Lights down on Scene One as they continue to do words.)

Scene Two

(Two different bedrooms. One side is IMAGINE's; her bedroom is full of movie posters and paraphanelia. The other side is JEFF's; it is cluttered with sports equipment and posters.)

(Lights up on IMAGINE sitting on her bed practicing words with DEBRA.)

DEBRA. Blatherskite.

IMAGINE. Umm...oh, I don't know, Debra. What is it?

DEBRA. Think about it.

IMAGINE. This is too hard! I can't do this! I'm not going to win the contest, I'm not going to do well in my AP classes in high school, then I'm not going to get into a good college, then I'm not going to get a good job and I'm going to be a failure for the rest of my life!

DEBRA. Imagine, do we have to go through this on every word?

IMAGINE. It's just...so hard... I have so much pressure! Having a famous mom, trying to be a regular middle-schooler under the glare of the spotlight, taking a ninth-grade level math class, playing center mid on my soccer team. I'm just so stressed out! It's too much for one thirteen-year-old to endure!

DEBRA. Spell the word, Imagine.

IMAGINE. What's the language of origin?

DEBRA. Stop stalling. Just spell the word.

IMAGINE. You know I *have* to ask for the language of origin!

DEBRA. I don't know.

IMAGINE. Oh, fine. What was it again?

DEBRA. Blatherskite.

IMAGINE. Blatherskite. B-L-A-T-H-E-R-S-K-I-T-E. Blatherskite?

DEBRA. You got it.

IMAGINE. Oh, thank goodness! If I had spelled that word wrong, I don't know what I would have done. I would have felt—

DEBRA. If you had spelled the word wrong, I would have told you how to spell it, and you would have learned it. That's all.

IMAGINE. But the humiliation I would have gone through!

DEBRA. Next word: blasphemously.

(STAR enters, cell phone in hand.)

STAR. Did someone say "famously"? That's my cue!

IMAGINE. No, blasphemously, mom. They're different.

STAR. Imagine, dear, how many times do I have to ask you not to call me "mom"? It makes me feel old.

(Her cell phone rings.)

STAR. Debra, would you answer it for me, please?

(STAR hands DEBRA her cell phone. DEBRA answers it.)

DEBRA. Hello? Star Pearson's phone. Hold on one moment. *(To STAR:)* It's for you.

STAR. Is it someone important?

DEBRA. It's your ex-husband.

STAR. I'll call him back.

DEBRA. *(To the phone:)* She's busy at the moment. She'll call you back.

STAR. So how's the studying going, honey?

IMAGINE. It's a disaster. A complete, utter, disaster. I don't want to go through with it. I can't go through with it.

STAR. Is it *that* bad? I don't want you making me look bad at the spelling bee. If you're out in the first round, it's "Star Pearson's kid is dumb" all over the next day's paper. And then do you know what happens?

IMAGINE. What?

STAR. I don't get movie roles. I don't get movie roles because I'm too old and not even a good mother, so I'm stuck doing cameos on sitcoms as the wacky grandmother. Do I look like a grandmother to you?

DEBRA. There's no such thing as bad publicity.

STAR. Debra, this is none of your business.

DEBRA. I just don't think you should put so much pressure on Imagine. She's stressed out enough as it is.

STAR. I suppose you're right. The last thing I need is for Imagine to have a nervous breakdown and wind up in rehab.

IMAGINE. Mom! Rehab is for people who do drugs!

DEBRA. Star, I don't think you're helping your daughter study. Is there a reason you came up?

STAR. Is it too much to ask to visit my daughter a few times a day? To have a laugh with her? To ask her about her day? To talk about boys? To bake cookies together and eat all the dough? Is that too much to ask, Debra?

DEBRA. You didn't ask her how her day was.

STAR. I was about to.

IMAGINE. Mom, you'd never eat cookies. And I'm diabetic, anyway.

STAR. I know, dear. Ooh! That's a good spelling word. Diabetic! How do you spell diabetic, Imagine?

IMAGINE. What's the language of origin?

DEBRA. That's far too easy for her at this point—

IMAGINE. But what if I get caught on a really easy one? What if I think it's so easy that I just spell it really quickly and make a stupid mistake? That would be *mortifying*. That would be the end of my life, just about. I wouldn't know what to do—

DEBRA. Just spell it, Imagine.

IMAGINE. D-I-A-B-E-T-I-C. Diabetic. But that's not the point! There's no pressure here! On Saturday there will be so much pressure: the hot lights, the other spellers, the announcer...who knows what kind of mistakes I'll make?

STAR. Imagine, you are the daughter of Star Pearson. You are a *performer.*

(Star's phone rings.)

Hold on one second.

(Answering the phone:) Star Pearson.

Yes, right.

I don't know, what was she wearing?

Are you serious?

Wow.

I have to get one. No, two. Maybe a half-dozen.

I'll get Debra to do it.

Right.

Okay. Ta-ta!

(Hangs up the phone.)

Sorry, that was a very important phone call. Now, what was I saying.

DEBRA. She's the daughter of Star Pearson. She's a performer.

STAR. Right. You are a Pearson, and we Pearsons do not crack under pressure. Performing is in our veins and you will perform!

IMAGINE. You're right, Star. It's the most important day of my life, but I'll live up to the challenge.

STAR. Now. You practice some more words with Debra. I have to go downstairs. My masseuse will be here any minute now.

(STAR exits. Lights down on IMAGINE *and* DEBRA *as they practice more words. Lights up on* JEFF *and* COACH BRICK.*)*

JEFF. Gargantuan. G-A-R-G-A-N-T-A-N? Gargantuan?

COACH BRICK. No, no, no!

JEFF. Darn!

(JEFF does ten pushups.)

I can't believe I missed that one!

COACH BRICK. You didn't have your game face on, kid. You weren't thinking like a champion!

JEFF. Maybe I need some fuel.

(JEFF drinks Gatorade.)

COACH BRICK. Remember when you were running the mile at the seventh grade track and field championships? And you were behind going into the last lap? And I yelled, "This is the most important race of your life, Jeff"?

JEFF. Yeah. I beat that kid at the very end.

COACH BRICK. And how did it feel?

JEFF. Great!

COACH BRICK. That's the way you're going to feel on Saturday. You just have to keep your game face on. Okay?

JEFF. Got it!

COACH BRICK. Give me ten.

(JEFF *does ten pushups.* GRANDPA MATTHEWS *enters.)*

GRANDPA. What's all this ruckus up here?

JEFF. Hey, Gramps! Just getting into shape for Saturday!

COACH BRICK. Getting him prepped to follow in his grandfather's footsteps!

GRANDPA. You know, back when I won the spelling bee, we had to walk there. I had to walk from Texas to the spelling bee in Washington. And it was snowing for part of the way. And very, very hot for another part of the way. And the words we spelled, most of them hadn't even been invented yet!

JEFF. I've been working really hard, Grandpa. The other kids are smart, but I'll be ready for them.

COACH BRICK. The best defense is a good offense!

GRANDPA. When I won the spelling bee, we couldn't ask any of your silly "language of origin" questions. And we only had five seconds to answer the question! And we didn't have microphones, of course, so sometimes we couldn't hear the word, but we spelled it anyway!

COACH BRICK. Now, Jeff, there's something I need to discuss with you. Man to man.

JEFF. Can Grandpa stay?

COACH BRICK. Yes.

GRANDPA. Back in my day, men didn't talk. We spelled.

JEFF. I know, Grandpa.

COACH BRICK. Jeff, we need to talk about your victory dance at the last competition. The judges said it was a little over-the-top.

JEFF. Over-the-top? All I did was some cartwheels, some pushups, a lap around the auditorium, and a backflip while shouting "I'm number one!"

COACH BRICK. And you can't give the loser sign to kids who spell their words wrong, either.

JEFF. But I beat them!

GRANDPA. Back in my day, we didn't celebrate. I had to turn around and walk straight back to Texas, carrying my trophy with me. My dad made me work on the farm the next morning. I had to work overtime to make up the hours I missed during the spelling bee. And it was during a hurricane!

COACH BRICK. Jeff, what have we talked about poor sportsmanship? You'll get ejected if you don't watch it.

JEFF. I guess you're right. I'll be more careful.

COACH BRICK. Now, let's get back to studying!

JEFF. Grandpa, do you want to help me?

GRANDPA. All right.

COACH BRICK. *(Handing him a sheet of paper:)* Here's the list.

GRANDPA. All right...hmm..., no, that wasn't a word when I was a kid. No, that one wasn't either. Nope. Nope.

(He scans the rest of the list.)

None of these were words when I was in school. They hadn't been invented yet.

COACH BRICK. *(Taking back the list:)* I'm sure some of them were...let's see. Armadillo? Armaments? Armistice? Arpeggio? These words have been around for hundreds of years!

GRANDPA. I never heard of these words. These words are too fancy. We spelled *real* words when I was in the bee.

JEFF. Well, these are the words on the list, so these are the words I need to know.

GRANDPA. All right, we'll try them. Armadillo? What's armadillo?

JEFF. Grandpa, you know what that is.

GRANDPA. Is that something you have to do on the Internet? I don't use the Internet. I'm too old-fashioned for that kind of thing.

COACH BRICK. It's an animal.

GRANDPA. Never heard of it.

JEFF. Armadillo. A-R-M-A-D-I-L-L-O. Armadillo.

COACH BRICK. 'Atta boy! Get down and give me ten.

JEFF. But I got it right!

COACH BRICK. All right, five.

(JEFF starts to do pushups. Lights down on his room.)

Scene Three

(DESIREE's room. DESIREE sits painting her nails while ELOISE studies.)

DESIREE. Eloise, could you turn those pages a little more quietly? You're bothering me.

ELOISE. I'm sorry, Miss Desiree.

DESIREE. It's all right, Eloise. I'm sure you didn't mean it...

ELOISE. Miss Desiree, you understand that I won't be able to spell these words for you on Saturday, right?

DESIREE. Oh, I know. But studying is so *boring*. Once you study them, you can figure out all the little tricks and the hard words. That will make it so much easier for me.

ELOISE. Of course, Miss Desiree. It's just—

DESIREE. What?

ELOISE. A lot of the trick is just studying the words. I could quiz you. I just think you're wasting your time with me studying.

DESIREE. I suppose so. I don't know why Mom can't just buy me the title. That would be so much less work.

ELOISE. I don't know, Miss Desiree.

DESIREE. My life is so hard. I'm missing a day of shopping to do this bee, you know.

ELOISE. I know, dear.

DESIREE. And then it's Sunday, and most of the good stores aren't open on Sundays. So I'm really missing two days of shopping.

ELOISE. Your poor thing. Why don't we try a few words.

DESIREE. I suppose so. If I *have* to.

ELOISE. Okay. Misanthrope.

DESIREE. Misanthrope. M-I-S-A-N-T-H-R-O-P-E. Misanthrope.

ELOISE. Excellent!

DESIREE. Fabulous. Oh, that was exhausting. Time to take a break.

(*She picks up her nail polish.*)

ELOISE. One more, Miss Desiree. How about pharmaceutical?

(MRS. WORTHINGTON *enters. She has a small dog in her bag.*)

MRS. WORTHINGTON. Oooh, pharmaceutical! Let me try!

DESIREE. Hi, mom.

MRS. WORTHINGTON. Maybe Madame DuBois knows how to spell pharmaceutical. (*To the dog in the bag:*) Do you know how to spell pharmaceutical, DuBois? Do you? You're such a good girl! Such a good girl!

ELOISE. Ma'm, I don't think the dog can help Desiree spell.

MRS. WORTHINGTON. Oh, I know. But she is the smartest dog! The smartest! She's just the smartest dog in the whole world! Eloise, are you helping Desiree study?

ELOISE. Of course, Mrs. Worthington.

MRS. WORTHINGTON. Good. Madame DuBois and I are SO excited for the big event. Madame has a brand-new outfit for Saturday. She's going to be the prettiest girl! The most beautiful girl there!

DESIREE. Mom, have you figured out something about the lighting?

MRS. WORTHINGTON. The lighting? I asked Eloise to call.

ELOISE. They said there's no way to change the stage lighting in time for Saturday, Miss Desiree.

DESIREE. Ughh, that's such a pity. The lighting is *horrible* on that stage. Horrible. It completely washes out my complexion. It makes my skin look green. Isn't there something you can do about it, mother? Call in a favor?

MRS. WORTHINGTON. Eloise, did you mention who I am to the people on the phone?

ELOISE. Yes, Mrs. Worthington, they already know who you are. They know Desiree's in the bee. They also mentioned something else?

DESIREE. Is this about the warm-up rooms? I hope it's about changing the warm-up rooms, because the ones last time were *nasty*. The couches looked like they were from the 1990s. And they certainly weren't designer.

ELOISE. No, it's about Madame DuBois.

MRS. WORTHINGTON. What about my best girl? What about the prettiest girl in the whole world?

ELOISE. They don't want a dog in the auditorium, Mrs. Worthington.

MRS. WORTHINGTON. Madame DuBois is *not* a dog! She is a little girl! The most adorable little girl in the whole world! Aren't you? Aren't you dear?

ELOISE. Well, they don't want the most adorable little girl in the whole world in the auditorium.

MRS. WORTHINGTON. *(Covering the dog's ears:)* Shhh! Don't say that in front of her, Eloise. You'll hurt the poor thing's feelings.

ELOISE. I'm sorry, Mrs. Worthington.

MRS. WORTHINGTON. I'll give them a call. I'm sure once I explain the situation, they'll think otherwise.

DESIREE. Mom, would you stop bothering us? Eloise is trying to study. I don't want her distracted.

MRS. WORTHINGTON. Of course, dear. I'm on my way out. Now say good bye to Madame DuBois.

DESIREE. Bye, Madame DuBois.

MRS. WORTHINGTON. Eloise!

ELOISE. What?

MRS. WORTHINGTON. I *said* say good bye to Madame DuBois! We don't want her feelings hurt!

ELOISE. Bye, Madame DuBois. Have a nice afternoon.

MRS. WORTHINGTON. *(Cooing to the dog as she exits:)* She didn't mean it, Madame. She didn't mean to hurt your feelings. No, she didn't. She didn't.

(ELOISE continues to study as DESIREE paints her nails.)

Scene Four

(The prep room before the spelling bee. SUNNY, DAVID, IMAGINE, JEFF, *and* DESIREE *sit preparing for the bee.* SUNNY, IMAGINE, *and* DAVID *are studying.* JEFF *is bouncing a basketball.* DESIREE *is putting on makeup in the mirror.)*

DAVID. Could you please stop bouncing that infernal ball?

JEFF. What? I can't hear you.

DAVID. I'm trying to study. Stop bouncing that ball!

JEFF. This helps me concentrate.

IMAGINE. Let the boy do what he needs to concentrate! You can't take that away from him! That's wrong, it's more than wrong, it's a travesty! It's a tragedy!

SUNNY. Give me a T, give me an R, give me an A—

DESIREE. Did anyone tell you that cheerleading is so five minutes ago? And that cheerleading skirt is seriously out.

DAVID. Anachronism. A-N-A-C-H-R-O-N-I-S-M. Anachronism.

JEFF. There's no point in studying now. All the prep is done, all the hours are put in. Now's the time to get your game face on and reap the benefits of all the training. Practicing is only going to wear you out at this point.

DAVID. You can go about your warm-up and I'll go about mine. Although my warm-up has already won me the National Geography Bee, the National Math Bee, the Young Poet Laureate contest, the Young Inventor's National Competition, and a national break-dance competition.

SUNNY. You won a break-dance competition?

DESIREE. *(Taking out her cell phone and dialing:)* Eloise, can I leave this area? I'm bored. Well, you come back here then? I don't care if you're not allowed to come back here. Come back anyway. Okay. Okay. Bye.

DAVID. No one is allowed back here, you know. They could be giving you illegal assistance.

DESIREE. How could anyone give illegal assistance at this point?

DAVID. We've already been searched. They could bring microphones, wires—

JEFF. Powerbars.

DAVID. There's plenty of technology out there to cheat in this day and age. I'm sure even *you* realize that.

SUNNY. Why would someone ever cheat on a spelling bee? That wouldn't be fair.

IMAGINE. But wouldn't it be so *thrilling* if someone did. Just imagine. We're all spelling, someone asks for the language of origin, when all of a sudden someone jumps onstage, does a dive and tackles the cheater. The cheater fights back, and tons of Secret Service agents rush the stage. But then, it turns out—

(ELOISE *enters secretly.*)

DESIREE. Ooh, Eloise!

ELOISE. Shh... I'm not supposed to be back here.

DESIREE. Did you bring something for me?

ELOISE. *(Taking some magazines out of her bag:)* Yes. Here.

DAVID. Hey! That is not permitted! New materials are not allowed backstage!

ELOISE. They're just fashion magazines.

DAVID. Doesn't matter. They're not allowed.

SUNNY. Just let her have her magazines.

DAVID. I'm going to have to report you—

DESIREE. Oh, forget it. I don't feel like reading anyway.

DAVID. And your mom isn't allowed backstage, either.

DESIREE. Oh, she's not my mom. She's my personal assistant.

JEFF. You have a personal assistant?

DESIREE. Well, she's my maid.

DAVID. Your maid isn't allowed back here either.

ELOISE. That's okay, I was just leaving.

DESIREE. I suppose that's a good idea. Good bye, Eloise.

ELOISE. Good luck!

(ELOISE *exits.*)

DESIREE. I don't need luck.

DAVID. You're right, luck will not help you at this point.

JEFF. *(Losing control of his basketball:)* Oops, heads up!

(The ball hits SUNNY.)

SUNNY. Ouch! My head!

JEFF. I'm sorry. But that's why you need to be quick on your feet! I have reflexes like a cat!

SUNNY. My brain! What if I lose brain cells over this?

DAVID. Maybe I should report you for having that ball back here.

JEFF. It's allowed. I need to warm up.

SUNNY. I need all the brain cells I can get for tonight!

DAVID. You can say that again.

IMAGINE. Maybe we should study together. We could band together, and pool our knowledge, and we could go down in history as the first group to win the spelling bee together—

DAVID, JEFF, and DESIREE. No!

SUNNY. It might work...

IMAGINE. It would be so thrilling!

JEFF. No way. It's every man for himself out there.

SUNNY. It's going to be hard for me not to cheer for everyone else! I'm used to rooting everyone on.

DESIREE. Could you all be quiet, please? I'm trying to study.

DAVID. You're not trying to study.

JEFF. You don't even have any notes.

IMAGINE. You're polishing your nails.

DESIREE. You're right, I was just tired of listening to you all talk.

SUNNY. I could cheer, instead.

DAVID. Please don't.

JEFF. Well, I think she's right. I need to get my game face on. No more talking up the competition.

IMAGINE. But it's so dramatic—

DESIREE. If you don't stop talking about drama I really will start to study.

DAVID. Wouldn't that be earth-shattering. I'm getting my notes.

(DAVID *goes back to his studying.* JEFF *goes back to bouncing his ball and concentrating.* DESIREE *polishes her nails, and* SUNNY *cheers silently.* IMAGINE *does deep-breathing exercises.*)

Scene Five

(*The spelling bee auditorium.* MR. LICHTENSTEINBERGER *and* MRS. LICHTENSTEINBERGER *sit in the front row;* MR. L *has a camera. He is already recording.*)

MRS. L. I still don't understand why David insists that we get here so early.

MR. L. I don't understand why David insists that we start recording the competition before it even starts.

MRS. L. He likes to study the footage for next year.

MR. L. If he wins, he can't compete next year.

MRS. L. And let's hope he does win. Every national competition he wins is one less thing for him to study for.

(MR. SANDSTONE *enters, with* GREG.)

MR. SANDSTONE. Excuse me...is this where the parents and family of the spellers sit?

MR. L. Yes, it is.

MR. SANDSTONE. *(Taking a seat:)* Thank you. Greg, have a seat.

GREG. Why did we have to get here so early?

MR. SANDSTONE. It was important to Sunny that we got a good seat.

MRS. L. Oh, you're the cheerleader's family?

MR. SANDSTONE. Yes, did you read the article in the paper?

GREG. This is so embarrassing.

MR. L. Yes, we did. *(To* GREG:*)* Are you a competitive speller like your sister?

GREG. No.

MRS. L. Are you a cheerleader like your sister?

GREG. No!

MR. L. *(To* MR. SANDSTONE:*)* Does your daughter participate in other competitive academic events?

MR. SANDSTONE. Um... I don't think so. She does cheerleading.

MRS. L. Yes, we know that.

MR. L. We read the article.

MR. SANDSTONE. What does your child do?

MRS. L. He's won several national and regional academic titles, as well as a national breakdancing championship.

GREG. Wow, breakdancing? I guess that's pretty cool.

MR. L. Yes, he started breakdancing when he was very young.

MRS. L. He was three when he won the competition. It was in the four-and-under age category.

(COACH BRICK enters.)

COACH BRICK. Excuse me, is this where the spelling bee takes place?

MR. SANDSTONE. Yes, it is.

COACH BRICK. Have you folks seen an old man wandering around? He talks about the "old days" a lot?

MR. L. No.

COACH BRICK. Maybe he was here earlier.

MRS. L. That's unlikely. We've been here for seven hours.

COACH BRICK. Darn it. He insisted on walking here.

MR. SANDSTONE. Where do you live?

COACH BRICK. We're from Central Waytown. About twenty miles.

MR. L. Why in the world would he do that?

COACH BRICK. He's very nostalgic.

STAR. *(From offstage:)* Debra! Debra, where are you?

DEBRA. *(From offstage:)* I'm just on the other side of the building, ma'm.

(STAR enters from one side of the stage, talking on her cell phone. DEBRA enters from the other side, talking on her cell phone.)

STAR. I would appreciate it if you didn't leave me stranded in the middle of a strange building! You know how the paparazzi are!

DEBRA. *(Hanging up her cell phone:)* Star, I'm sure there are no paparazzi at—

STAR. *(Still talking on her cell phone:)* Debra! Do not hang up on me in the middle of a conversation! Do you know who I am?

DEBRA. We're in the same room. We're standing two feet apart. I could hear what you were saying.

STAR. Debra, I will not tolerate this rudeness from my personal assistant. If the paparazzi saw you treating me this way—

DEBRA. There are no paparazzi here, I can guarantee that. Why don't we have a seat?

STAR. *(Looking at the chairs:)* Ughh, plastic folding chairs? Isn't there something a little nicer for me? Don't they know who I am?

GREG. *(Quietly:)* I don't.

MR. SANDSTONE. Greg, shhh.

COACH BRICK. *(Whispering to GREG:)* I don't know who she is either, son.

(ELOISE enters, looking worried.)

ELOISE. Has a lady with a dog come in?

MR. L. No, definitely not. Dogs aren't allowed at the spelling bee.

ELOISE. Tell that to my boss. No one has seen her?

MRS. L. No.

ELOISE. Oh, thank goodness.

(ELOISE walks to a row of empty seats. She puts down a doggy bed, a bowl of water, and some chew toys.)

GREG. *(Whispering to MR. SANDSTONE:)* Dad, what is she doing?

MR. SANDSTONE. I wish I knew.

(MRS. WORTHINGTON enters, with her dog in her bag.)

MRS. WORTHINGTON. Eloise, I'm glad you're here. DuBois was worried that her beddy-weddy wouldn't be all set up for her. Weren't you worried, my best girl? Weren't you worried about your bed?

ELOISE. It's all set up, Mrs. Worthington.

MRS. WORTHINGTON. Are we late? DuBois couldn't decide between two outfits. She wanted her pink princess costume, but I told her her Burberry sweater would be much more appropriate for the spelling bee. But of course DuBois wins. I just can't say no to the prettiest little girl in the world!

MR. L. Excuse me, but I think I should tell you that dogs aren't allowed in the spelling bee auditorium.

MRS. WORTHINGTON. And why not?

MRS. L. They're distracting to the spellers.

MRS. WORTHINGTON. Well, DuBois is not a normal dog.

MR. L. I don't think the judges will like it if your dog goes to the bathroom in the middle of the spelling bee.

MRS. WORTHINGTON. If DuBois has to use the facilities, I'll take her to the ladies' room.

GREG. She pees in a toilet?

MRS. WORTHINGTON. Surely you don't expect that a dog this cute would pee on the grass or a newspaper like a normal dog. DuBois is much more refined and civilized than that.

ELOISE. Here's the doggy toilet just in case, Mrs. Worthington.

(ELOISE *produces a miniature toilet.*)

MRS. WORTHINGTON. You know what, DuBois says she doesn't have to go, but I'm going to take her just in case. She always says she's fine and then five minutes later wants to run to the bathroom. Eloise, watch the chew toys and make sure they don't get stolen by another dog.

(MRS. WORTHINGTON *exits, holding her bag.*)

(STAR's *phone rings. She answers it.*)

STAR. Hello? This is Star Pearson's phone.
Oh, hi Clarissa!
I know, we haven't seen each other in *ages.*
I know! Let's get facials together next week!
I love that place!

(MR. L *leans over and taps* STAR *on the shoulder.*)

MR. L. Excuse me?

STAR. *(To the phone:)* Hold on a minute, Clarissa. *(To* DEBRA:) Debra, would you find out what this man wants? (STAR *goes back to talking on the phone.*)

DEBRA. What is it, sir?

MR. L. She's not allowed to talk on a cell phone in here.

MRS. L. Cell phones could give an unfair advantage.

DEBRA. How?

MR. L. She could be calling a spelling bee on the East Coast and finding out what words they asked there.

MRS. L. And then beaming the words by text message to her child backstage.

MR. L. Cheating is strictly forbidden at this competition.

MRS. L. Cell phones give parents an unfair advantage.

DEBRA. I'll ask her to hang up.

(DEBRA *silently motions for* STAR *to hang up.* STAR *doesn't.*)

DEBRA. Star, they say that cell phones aren't allowed in this competition.

STAR. This is an important call. Business. *(Back into her phone:)* I love that new Ben and Jerry's flavor too!

(STAR *continues to talk on the phone.* GRANDPA MATTHEWS *enters. He is bundled up for a snowstorm even though it is warm outside.*)

COACH BRICK. Mr. Matthews! You made it! Come have a seat!

GRANDPA. Back in the old days, we didn't have seats. We sat on the floor. Which was covered with snow. And...nails. Snow and nails.

COACH BRICK. How was the walk?

GRANDPA. It was treacherous. The avalanche about forty miles back made the conditions very difficult.

COACH BRICK. But Mr. Matthews, you only live twenty miles away. And it's July.

GRANDPA. I took the long route. You young people these days are always trying to cut corners, always trying to find a shortcut.

COACH BRICK. You almost missed the spelling bee, though.

GRANDPA. Back in my day, I missed the spelling bee, but I still won. I was so intimidating that all the spellers forfeited when they heard I was in the competition. I won by default.

COACH BRICK. I didn't know that.

GRANDPA. Young people these days never listen to their elders.

(MRS. WORTHINGTON *enters.* ELOISE *motions her over.*)

ELOISE. *(Whispering:)* I think it's about to start!

(MR. LANFORD *enters. Everyone applauds.*)

MR. LANFORD. Good evening, ladies and gentleman, and welcome to the thirty-seventh annual Waytown County spelling bee!

GRANDPA. *(Whispering to* COACH BRICK:*)* I won the first thirty-five Waytown spelling bees.

MR. LANFORD. We've got an exciting evening ahead of us with the five regional champions competing to go onto the state competition! The winner of the state competition goes on to nationals. So, without further ado, I present to you our five regional champions!

(SUNNY, DAVID, IMAGINE, JEFF, *and* DESIREE *enter and form a line across the stage.*)

MR. LANFORD. Please welcome Sunny Sandstone!

(SUNNY *waves and does a cheerleader kick.*)

MR. LANFORD. David Lichten—Lichten—David Lich—

DAVID. *(Interrupting:)* Lichtensteinberger.

MR. LANFORD. Well, isn't that a mouthful! Hope you don't have to spell that one tonight!

MRS. L. *(Whispering to* MR. L*:)* They say that at every spelling bee.

MR. LANFORD. Please welcome Imagine Pearson!

(IMAGINE bows and blows imaginary kisses to the audience.)

STAR. *(Whispering to* DEBRA*:)* Debra, I don't think the lighting is good. She looks washed out!

DEBRA. Just let her spell, Star.

STAR. What if the paparazzi takes a picture of her?

MR. LANFORD. Please welcome Jeff Matthews!

(JEFF shoots an imaginary basketball, then scores an imaginary touchdown, then hits an imaginary home run.)

COACH BRICK. *(Whistling:)* All right, Jeff! Way to go, champ!

MR. LANFORD. And finally, please welcome Desiree Worthington!

(The dog barks.)

MR. LANFORD. Is there a dog in here?

(Silence.)

ELOISE. No...that was me. I was cheering for Desiree. *(ELOISE barks.)* See? That's our...special cheer.

MR. LANFORD. Very well. Now, to kick of the thirty-seven annual Way-town county spelling bee... Round One!

Scene Six

(The spelling bee. The spellers are still lined up across the stage; the audience is still seated.)

MR. LANFORD. Okay, let's begin Round 42.

MR. L. *(Whispering to* MRS. L*:)* The camcorder is out of batteries!

MRS. L. Well, do something about it! We can't miss this after taping 41 rounds!

(MR. L tiptoes to the side wall and plugs the camcorder into an outlet.)

MR. LANFORD. Miss Sandstone, are you ready?

SUNNY. Yes, Mr. Lanford! I sure am!

MR. LANFORD. Your word is abecedarius.

SUNNY. Great! Thanks, Mr. Lanford.

(Pause.)

MR. LANFORD. Are you going to spell it?

SUNNY. Oh, yeah! Can I have a definition, please?

MR. LANFORD. Certainly. A poem in which the lines or stanzas begin with the letters of the alphabet in a regular order.

SUNNY. I know a cheer like that!

MR. LANFORD. Spell the word, please, Miss Sandstone.

SUNNY. Okay. Give me an A, give me a—

MR. LANFORD. Miss Sandstone, this is your final warning. If you begin your spelling with "give me a" one more time, you will be out of the competition.

SUNNY. I'm sorry. Abecedarius. A-B-E-C-E-D-A-R-I-U-S. Abecedarius.

(Pause.)

MR. LANFORD. That's correct.

(Polite applause, MR. SANDSTONE whistles.)

GREG. Yeah, Sunny!

MR. LANFORD. Mr. Lichtensteinberger, are you ready for your next word?

DAVID. Of course.

MR. LANFORD. Your word is pococurante.

DAVID. Surely you can come up with something slightly more difficult than that.

MR. LANFORD. Your commentary is not necessary, David. Please spell the word.

DAVID. *(With an obvious yawn:)* Pococurante. P-O-C-O-C-U-R-A-N-T-E. Pococurante.

MR. LANFORD. That is correct.

(Polite applause.)

MRS. L. *(Whispering to MR. L.:)* Did you get that on tape?

MR. L. I hope so!

MR. LANFORD. Miss Pearson, are you ready for your next word?

IMAGINE. I guess so. I mean, when is anyone really ever ready to have their fate in someone else's hands? To have their fate for the rest of their lives, and their children's and grandchildren's fate, all lying on a single word? I'll never be ready for that.

MR. LANFORD. Your word, Miss Pearson, is kamikaze.

IMAGINE. I can't do it! My life is over! There's no way I can spell that word! I'm doomed!

MR. LANFORD. Do you wish to forfeit?

IMAGINE. Yes. No. I don't know.

MR. LANFORD. Which is it?

IMAGINE. What's the language of origin?

MR. LANFORD. The language of origin is Japanese.

IMAGINE. Japanese! Oh! I'm finished! If it was anything but Japanese I could do it, but it's over! I can't do it!

MR. LANFORD. Please either spell the word or forfeit, Miss Pearson.

IMAGINE. Okay. What's the language of origin again?

MR. LANFORD. Japanese.

IMAGINE. Right, okay. Kamikaze. K-A-M-I-C-A-Z-E. Kamikaze.

MR. LANFORD. I'm sorry, that's incorrect.

> *(The audience gasps. All heads turn to* IMAGINE, *waiting for a reaction.)*

IMAGINE. *(Shrugging:)* Oh, well. Whatever. I didn't care that much anyway.

MR. LANFORD. Miss Pearson, you may take a seat.

> *(*IMAGINE *crosses to sit with* STAR *and* DEBRA.*)*

STAR. Don't you know who I am?

DEBRA. Star, your cell phone is ringing.

STAR. Don't answer it! This is more important!

> *(*STAR *hugs* IMAGINE *as she sits down.)*

MR. LANFORD. Remember, we are still in Round 42 until Mr. Matthews and Miss Worthington spell their words. Mr. Matthews, are you ready?

JEFF. Shoot.

MR. LANFORD. Your word is antediluvian.

JEFF. Got it.

> *(He stretches and jogs in place to "warm up.")*

Pass me the definition.

MR. LANFORD. The definition is "made, evolved, or developed a long time ago."

JEFF. Okay.

> *(Stretches and jumps to warm up more.)*

Can you kick me a sentence?

MR. LANFORD. My grandmother's automobile is antediluvian.

JEFF. Okay. It's game time. Antediluvian. A-N-T-I-D-I-L-U-V-I-A-N. Antediluvian.

MR. LANFORD. I'm sorry, that's incorrect.

> *(Another gasp from the crowd.)*

JEFF. Aww, man. I choked. How about a do-over? A D.O.? A mulligan?

MR. LANFORD. No, I'm sorry, Please take your seat.

> *(*JEFF *takes his seat with* COACH BRICK *and* GRANDPA MATTHEWS. COACH BRICK *pats him on the back.)*

GRANDPA. Back in my day, the words were a lot easier. I better start walking home now if I want to make it home in time for Thanksgiving.

(GRANDPA MATTHEWS *gets up and exits.*)

MR. LANFORD. Miss Worthington, are you ready to spell?

(*Pause.* DESIREE *is not paying attention.*)

MR. LANFORD. Miss Worthington?

(DESIREE *is still not paying attention. She is looking at her nails.* ELOISE *takes Mrs. Worthington's cell phone and dials.* DESIREE's *phone rings. She answers it.*)

DESIREE. Hello?

ELOISE. Desiree!

DESIREE. Oh, it's you, Eloise. What do you want?

ELOISE. Desiree! They're waiting for you to spell your word!

(DESIREE *looks up and sees* MR. LANFORD *glaring at her. She hangs up the phone.*)

DESIREE. Sorry about that. I got bored. What's my word again?

MR. LANFORD. I didn't tell you yet.

DESIREE. My maid just called me and said—

MR. LANFORD. Yes, we all know your maid just called you.

DESIREE. So what's my word?

MR. LANFORD. Prospicience. Your word is prospicience.

DESIREE. Oh. Can I have a different one?

MR. LANFORD. No, you cannot have a different one.

DESIREE. Okay. Well, can you, like, use it in a sentence?

MR. LANFORD. The graduates looked toward their futures with prospicience.

DESIREE. Can you give me a normal sentence? Like about something normal?

MR. LANFORD. I'm sorry, Miss Worthington, that's your sentence.

DESIREE. Okay. Umm, can I call my maid?

MR. LANFORD. Of course not. Are you prepared to spell the word or not?

DESIREE. Okay. Umm, Prospicience. P-R-O-S-P-I-S-C-I-E-N-C-E. Prospicience.

MR. LANFORD. I'm sorry, that's incorrect.

DESIREE. (*Hopping off her stool:*) Finally. I was getting so bored up there. (*Checking her watch:*) Yes! The mall is still open for another half an hour! Eloise! Let's go.

(DESIREE *and* ELOISE *exit.*)

MR. LANFORD. We now begin Round 43, and we are down to two spellers: Sunny Sandstone and David Lichtensteinberger.

GREG. *(Whispering to* MR. SANDSTONE:*)* I can't believe she's made it this far.

MR. SANDSTONE. *(Whispering back:)* Now we just have to hope she doesn't get eliminated for cheering instead of spelling.

MR. LANFORD. We'll start with Miss Sandstone. Your word is fibranne.

SUNNY. Okay. Give me a—

GREG. *(Shouting out:)* No, Sunny!

(Embarrassed as everyone looks at him.)

Uh, never mind.

SUNNY. Give me a definition, please.

MR. LANFORD. A linen-like fabric made of spun-rayon yarn.

SUNNY. And...the language of origin?

MR. LANFORD. French.

SUNNY. Umm...fibranne. F-I-B-R-A-N-N-E. Fibranne?

MR. LANFORD. That is correct.

SUNNY. *(Jumping and kicking a little bit:)* Yes!

(MR. SANDSTONE and GREG cheer.)

MR. LANFORD. Mr. Lichtensteinberger, your word is euonym.

DAVID. I won't waste your time. Euonym. E-U-O-N-Y-M.

(MR. L and MRS. L cheer. The next part of the scene takes place as if in fast-forward. The actors speak quickly and do their motions rapidly.)

MR. LANFORD. Round 44. Miss Sandstone. Succedaneum.

SUNNY. Succedaneum. S-U-C-C-E-D-A-N-E-U-M. Succedaneum.

MR. LANFORD. Correct.

(Applause.)

MR. LANFORD. Mr. Lichtensteinberger. Demarche.

DAVID. Demarche. D-E-M-A-R-C-H-E. Demarche.

MR. LANFORD. Correct.

(Applause.)

MR. LANFORD. Round 45. Miss Sandstone. Vivisepulture.

SUNNY. Vivisepulture. V-I-V-I-S-E-P-U-L-T-U-R-E. Vivisepulture.

MR. LANFORD. Correct.

(Applause.)

MR. LANFORD. Mr. Lichtensteinberger. Xanthosis.

DAVID. Xanthosis. X-A-N-T-H-O-S-I-S. Xanthosis.

MR. LANFORD. Correct.

(Applause.)

MR. LANFORD. Round 46. Miss Sandstone. Spoliator.

SUNNY. Spoliator. S-P-O-L-I-A-T-O-R. Spoliator.

MR. LANFORD. Correct.

(Applause.)

MR. LANFORD. Mr. Lichtensteinberger. Odontalgia.

DAVID. Odontalgia. O-D-A-N-T-A-L-G-I-A.

MR. LANFORD. *(Surprised:)* That is...incorrect?

DAVID. What? Wait a minute!

(The scene rewinds. In slow, exaggerated motions and spoken extremely slowly:)

MR. LANFORD. Mr. Lichtensteinberger. Odontalgia.

DAVID. Odontalgia. O-D-A-N-T-A-L-G-I-A. Odontalgia.

MR. LANFORD. That. Is. Incorrect.

(The scene goes at regular speed again. Applause for SUNNY. SUNNY jumps up and down.)

DAVID. But...but...I never get anything wrong!

MR. LANFORD. Please take a seat, Mr. Lichtensteinberger.

DAVID. But I can't lose to a cheerleader!

MRS. L. *(Whispering to MR. L.:)* Stop the tape recorder! Don't record any of this!

DAVID. I bet she doesn't even know how to spell my last name!

MR. L. *(Whispering to MRS. L.:)* I don't know how to spell our last name.

MR. LANFORD. We officially have a winner of the thirty-seventh annual Waytown County Spelling Bee! Congratulations to Sunny Sandstone, who will represent us in the state competition next week!

(MR. LANFORD hands a trophy to SUNNY.)

SUNNY. Wow! I don't know what to say! I'm so excited!

(Everyone applauds and stands up. MR. SANDSTONE and GREG join SUNNY.)

MR. SANDSTONE. Congratulations, Sunny!

SUNNY. Thanks, Dad!

GREG. Sunny...I didn't know you were smart.

SUNNY. I know!

(The crowd starts filing out. DAVID stays in the same spot.)

DAVID. I will not leave this auditorium until I get another word to spell!

MRS. L. *(To MR. L.:)* Stop taping this!

MR. L. It's good blackmail material for when he's older.

DAVID. I can spell sarcophagus. S-A-R-C-O-P-H-A-G-U-S. Sarcophagus! I can spell milieu. M-I-L-I-E-U! Milieu! I can spell—

MR. LANFORD. David, they're shutting the building down. You're going to have to go home.

MRS. L. Let's go, dear. I baked some cookies for you—

DAVID. Cookie. C-O-O-K-I-E. Cookie!

MR. L. You can always take up break-dancing again.

DAVID. I guess there's always the National Science Bee. When is that?

MRS. L. Next weekend, David.

DAVID. Guess I better start studying. Maybe I should try some of that cheering that the cheerleader does...you know, to study better.

(MR. L *and* MRS. L *exchange glances.*)

MR. L. That sounds like a great idea, David.

(DAVID, MR. L, *and* MRS. L *exit.*)

End of Play

CUT

by Ed Monk

Cast of Characters

Because the characters change names throughout the play, they are identified by letters. Numbers added to a character's letter indicate a character change.

Many of the characters are gender-neutral, and can be played male/female as needed.

A, an actress

B, an actor

C, a director

D, a stage manager

E, another director

F, another other director

G, another actress

H, another actor

TECHIE, a techie

JACK, a workman

NICK, another workman

SHANNON, a girl

JENNIFER, another girl

THE DIRECTOR, the director

Setting

The stage of a theater. Onstage is a set for a play. The set is a living room with badly painted flats for walls. The furniture does not match. The effect should be of someone trying very hard to create a nice set, but not quite succeeding. At center stage is a couch. Two easy chairs are on either side of the couch. A bar (actually a table with material draped over it) with various bottles is upstage center, behind the couch. At stage right is a table with a telephone. An unstable door that sticks is stage left. Other various knickknacks are placed about.

Production Notes

(See the end of the play for a note from the author.)

Acknowledgments

This version of *Cut* was first produced at Chantilly High School in Chantilly, Virginia in January of 1999.

This is for
The Herbolich Family of Anaconda, Montana
They came to this country bringing a great treasure.
Love.

CUT

(At rise: The stage is empty. A and B enter through the door, returning from their evening out. A is dressed in a very attractive evening gown; B wears a suit and tie. A crosses to bar and begins to pour a drink.)

A. That was a charming little restaurant.

B. Carol. When are you going to tell him?

A. I don't want to talk about this now.

B. Well I do. It's been six months now. I'm tired of all the sneaking around and the lying and waiting all week hoping that I'll get to spend a few hours with you.

A. Please Brad, I need some more time.

B. What for? You don't love him, we both know that. All you're doing is delaying the inevitable!

(B crosses to A and grabs her.)

B. Carol, I want you now!

(A pushes B away.)

A. I said I need more time! I'm not ready yet!

B. I'm starting to think you'll never be ready.

(A and B stare at each other for several seconds. The audience should get the sense that something is going wrong on stage. IT IS EXTREMELY IMPORTANT THAT THE ACTORS DO NOT OVERSELL OR MUG THIS MOMENT. It should be played very subtly and look and feel exactly as it would in a "real play" when something goes wrong. At this point the audience should still think that this is a "real" play, and should be experiencing those special emotions of watching a live performance crash and burn. Finally B crosses to the table and picks up the phone.)

B. Hello? Oh hello Jason, how did the Wickerman account go?

(Sound of phone ringing.)

C. *(Sitting in the audience:)* CUT!

(C rises from seat and goes onstage.)

MARK! Where was the freaking sound cue?!

(Enter D from stage right, wearing headset and carrying copy of script.)

D. Hey don't yell at me! Steve changed the line again!

B1. I did not!

D. Yes you did! You do it differently every time!

C. What is the line supposed to be?

D. *(Reading from script:)* "I am starting to believe that you will never be ready."

B1. What did I say?

D. *(Mocking the way B said the line:)* I'm starting to think you'll never be ready.

B1. That's the same thing!

D. No, you said I'm instead of I am, think instead of believe, and you'll instead of you will!

B1. Oh for the love of Mike! I give up! Andy, you deal with him!

D. Hey, I go by the script! If you can't remember your lines, that's not my problem!

A1. Can we get on with this? I have to get out of here on time today!

C. All right Steve, just say the line the way it's written.

B1. I like my way better.

D. Oh yeah, it's soooo much better!

B1. Shut up!

C. Just say the line the way it's written.

B1. My character wouldn't say something like that! It doesn't fit! It ruins the whole scene!

C. Look, just say...

B1. No, damn it! Why should I have to screw up my character that I have spent six weeks working on just because that meathead can't figure out when to push a frigging button!?

D. Up yours pal!

C. Knock it off! *(To B1:)* How do you want to say the line!?

B1. *(Exactly as he said it as B in opening scene:)* I'm starting to think you'll never be ready.

C. Fine! *(To D:)* You write it down that way. *(To B1:)* And you don't change it again!

B1. Fine.

D. Sure! As long as the prima donna is happy!

C. *(To D:)* Did you get those flats finished yet?

D. No.

C. Why not!?

D. Because they won't fit out the door.

C. What do you mean?

D. I mean the flats won't fit out the door.

C. Why not!?

D. Because they're too big.

C. Ah hell! Come on!

(C *begins to exit with* D.)

A1. Andy, I have to leave at four!

C. I know honey.

(C *and* D *exit.*)

B. Well, when are you going to tell him?

A1. I don't know.

B1. Sarah, you can't wait forever. I mean even Andy isn't that stupid. He's going to figure out something is going on between us.

A1. Shut up!

B1. O.K. He's your boyfriend.

A1. That's right! We've been going out for three years. And before I throw that away for someone like you, I'm going to be sure about it!

B1. Just what is that supposed to mean?

A1. Nothing.

B1. Hey baby, just because you're feeling guilty about cheating on your boyfriend, don't start dumping on me. You don't like this situation, you can walk away any time you like.

A1. Oh, is that what you told Ashley?

B1. What?

A1. What? You remember Ashley don't you? She's the girl from the last production you were in. She said you were the most wonderful guy she ever met. Right up to the moment you dumped her. We had a very interesting talk about you yesterday. What's the matter hon? Nothing to say?

B1. (B1 *moves to* A1 *and takes her into his arms:*) O.K., so maybe I wasn't too nice to Ashley. But that doesn't mean that... (B1 *coughs into* A1's *face.*) ...LINE!

(E *rises from audience and moves onto stage as* C *enters.*)

E. Aw hell Richard! Every time we get something started, you forget your lines!

B2. It's not my fault!

E. Then whose fault is it?!

B2. Look, I've got more lines than anyone else in this stupid play and I've had strep throat for the last two weeks! I still can't breathe!

A2. Why don't you grow up?

B2. What's your problem?

A2. My problem?! I'll tell you what my problem is! I'm stuck in this lame production with a bunch of amateurs who don't know how to act and a director who thinks he's God's gift to the theatre! This play is going to be the biggest flop in the world! And this is how I get to end my acting career!

C1. What are you talking about? You're not quitting the play, are you?

A2. No. My parents' business is going bankrupt. There's no money left. I have to drop out of school.

E. Can't you get a loan?

A2. I've already got every loan there is! There just isn't any money.

(A2 sits on the couch and begins to cry. After two beats, F rises from audience and moves to stage.)

F. CUT! O.K. Beth, this time I want you to kneel when you cry instead of sitting.

A3. Like it makes any difference! This thing is so confusing nobody's gonna know what's going on anyway!

E1. She's right Pam, this play sucks.

F. Look, I know this isn't Shakespeare, but it's going to be a great play!

B3. Yeah right.

(A3, E1, and C2 also show little enthusiasm.)

F. Well we have to try! What do you want to do? Quit?

(A3, E1, C2, and B3 all nod yes.)

F. Fine! Go ahead! But you can kiss your Equity cards goodbye! Don't you think I know this play sucks!? But this is my first paying job as a director and I'm going to make it work! And if any of you don't like it, you can go to hell!

(Enter G from stage left.)

G. Mrs. Smith, there's a call for you in the office.

F. What?

(Once again a very subtle, puzzled reaction. Something is not right. G repeats the line exactly as she just said it, using the same gestures.)

G. Mrs. Smith, there's a call for you in the office.

F. My name's not Smith.

(This is another character shift for everyone but F.)

G1. All right, what's going on!?

F. What are you talking about?

G1. Did we change the lines again?

F. What lines?

G1. The lines! The lines! *(Pulls out a script:)* You say "go to hell" and I walk in and say, *(Doing the lines and gestures exactly as before:)* Mrs. Smith, there's a call for you in the office. And then you say "thanks Bambi" and exit left!

F. Who are you?

G1. I'm playing Bambi!

F. What are you talking about!? There's no Bambi in this play!

G1. What are you talking about what am I talking about!? We've done this scene a million times! *(G1 shoves script at F:)* See "if any of you don't like it, you can go to hell!" Enter Bambi. That's me! And then I say, *(Exactly as before:)* "Mrs. Smith, there's a call for you in the office."

F. *(Flipping through the script:)* Something weird is going on here. You say I'm just an actor playing the part of a director?

C3. So am I.

E2. So am I.

F. I could've sworn I was directing this play.

G1. No, you were just playing the part of a director who was directing a play that wasn't really a play.

F. I guess I must have gotten into the part a little too much.

A4. Obviously.

F. Say...this may be a really stupid question, but who is directing this play?

B4. What?

F. Who is the director? I can't seem to remember?

(Everybody looks confused.)

E2. Well I'm directing one of the plays.

B4. No, that's a fake play. Who is directing the real play?

C3. What do you mean the real play?

B4. Not the plays within the plays, but the play with everything in it.

A4. I can't remember who the director is. I mean things got so confused with all the plots and whatnot. *(Shouting out to audience:)* HELLO! IS ANYONE OUT THERE?

(TECHIE enters.)

TECHIE. *(To C3:)* Hey, that stinking Fresnel I've been trying to get you to replace for the last two weeks just burned up the last of the blue gels. Whaddya want me to do?

C3. Why are you talking to me?

TECHIE. You're the director aren't you?

C3. Oh, no. I'm just playing the part of the director in the second fake play.

TECHIE. Second fake play?

C3. Yes.

TECHIE. O.K. So who's the director?

B4. We're not sure.

TECHIE. You're not sure?

A4. Yes, it's all a little confusing.

TECHIE. Yeah, right. Well, when you figure out who the director is, tell him we need a new Fresnel and some blue gels. I'm gonna get a smoke.

(TECHIE exits.)

E2. Oh this is ridiculous! Someone must remember who the director is!

G1. When we got here this evening, who else was here?

A4. Well nobody. *(Slips back into* A *character:)* Brad and I had just got back from dinner...

F. No, no! That's the play you're doing!

A4. *(As A4:)* Oh. Yeah. *(To B:)* Brad, do you remember what happened?

B4. My name isn't Brad. It's Steve.

C3. No it's not. Your name is Bob. Steve is the character you play in the second play.

B4. Oh. Right. I knew that. Thanks Scott.

C3. My name isn't Scott.

B4. Oh. Uh...what is it?

> *(There is a pause while* C3 *thinks it over. Finally he pulls out a script and flips through it.)*

C3. Uuuummm...Carol?

A4. No, I'm Carol. I think.

> *(Everybody thinks for a beat and then they all pull out scripts. All of the scripts are different. They all start flipping through the scripts.)*

F. Wait. I think you're Mark, I'm Tom, and you're Tony.

G1. Isn't Tony the Vietnam vet who dies of a heart attack?

> *(E2 starts to die of a heart attack.)*

A4. No, he's not Tony, he's Terry.

> *(E2 immediately stops dying and pops up.)*

E2. Thanks. This is too strange. I'm going home!

> *(E2 exits. After a few beats* E2 *comes back onstage.)*

E2. Does anyone know where I live?

> *(There is a beat and then everyone begins flipping through the scripts.)*

A4. *(Reading from script:)* You live at 22 East 56th Street with your quad- riplegic wife, your suicidal daughter, and your son who is afraid to reveal his homosexuality.

E2. Anyone else?

C3. *(Reading from script:)* You live at the State Hospital for the Criminally Insane where you were committed after shooting six people at the mall.

B4. *(Reading from script:)* A homeless shelter. Where you are waiting for the results of your AIDS test.

> *(There is a beat and then everyone takes a step away from* E2.*)*

E2. I think I'll stay here.

F. Well we still don't know who the director is!

(Enter H *dressed in a dark suit. He has a vaguely Eastern European accent.)*

H. Perhaps I can help answer some of your questions.

G1. Who are you?

F. Are you the director?

H. You might call me that. I do indeed direct events. However, unlike your pathetic little playacting, my direction takes place in the realm of the real. I deal with lives, not parts.

C3. Are you God?

H. Ha! Hardly. Although, for a short time, I did work for him.

E2. Then you're the devil!

H. Some men call me that. Others call me Satan, Beelzebub, Lucifer, Mephistopheles, the Prince of Darkness. As for myself, I prefer being called...

(Sound of phone ringing. There is a short, awkward beat [played very subtly] that says that this isn't supposed to be happening. After the beat, A *walks to the phone and picks it up.)*

A. Hello? Oh hello Jason, how did the Wickerman account go?

(Enter D.*)*

D. Sorry, my bad.

(D exits.)

H. Some men call me Satan, Lucifer, Beezlebub...

E3. Oh forget it! It was really, really lame!

H. You have all been condemned to hell for your sins!

E3. Oh shut up already!

C3. And lose the cheesy accent while you're at it.

H1. It wasn't cheesy!

G1. If it was any cheesier, they'd put it in a can and people could spray it on crackers!

H1. I thought it was good. Besides, the devil thing was a cool idea.

F2. Yeah, it's not like it hasn't been done eight million times before.

H1. Well, what if I was an angel instead of the devil?

E3. Angel, devil, it doesn't make any difference. You still can't act!

F2. Well what are we gonna do about the play?

(The following speech is delivered absolutely seriously. The intent is to fool the audience into thinking that now this is the start of the "real play.")

G2. There is no play, you fool! Haven't you figured that out yet? There's no play and there's no director! There is no reality here! Existence. Identity.

Home. Those are just meaningless concepts! We're all just figments of someone else's imagination! We get up in the morning, put on our clothes and makeup, walk out the door, and spend all day letting other people write lines for us, choreograph our movements, direct our lives. They tell us what to do and what to think and who to love and who to hate. And then one day you wake up and you're not you anymore. You're just some stinking character in someone else's play.

(There is a pause.)

B5. *(Quietly:)* Now do you understand?

G3. Understand what?

B5. *(Pulling out script:)* No, that's the last line of your monologue. "...stinking character in someone else's play. Now do you understand?"

G4. Oh right! Sorry. *(Back to serious character G3 from monologue:)* Now do you understand? *(As G4:)* Do you think I should pause a little longer and say it softer? *(As G3, softer with a bigger pause:)* Now do you understand?

E2. No, I like it better the first way. It has more emotion to it.

G4. Yeah, I think so too.

(There is a pause while everyone looks around trying to figure out what to do.)

A5. You know, this reminds me of when I was a little girl. One day, I went fishing with my father. I remember it was a bright, sunny day and the seagulls looked like delicate little clouds. My father said we had to buy some bait first so we went to this little shack underneath the boardwalk. There was this old immigrant man with a scar across his face and horrible yellow teeth. My father told him we needed bait and the old man opened up a big can and my father told me to look inside and I did and...there were thousands and thousands of worms and they were squirming and crawling all over each other with their blind faces staring straight at me. I started screaming and screaming and then running down the beach just trying to get away from those blank faces looking at me. Finally my father caught me and took me home. So you see Josh, I can't marry you. I'm sorry.

F. Who's Josh?

C4. Whoops! *(Running to A:)* Damn it Betty! I don't give a darn about worms or old immigrant men or your painful skin condition! I love! I need you! I ain't never gonna leave you!

B6. DAD!

C4. What?

B6. Dad! It's me! Your son Bobby! You thought I was killed in that plane crash in Venezuela 15 years ago, but I'm alive!

A6. Why did you do that!?

B7. Do what?

C4. You ruined our scene! What did you butt in for!?

B7. Well I need something to do.

A6. Use your own script!

B7. I get killed on page 25!

E3. Then use your other script, dummy!

B7. What other script?

E3. In the play, you're an actor in a play. So rather than using the script for the play that you're in, use the script from the play that you're supposed to be in, in the play.

B7. *(After pondering for a beat:)* OOOOHHHHHH! I get it! But should I be the character from the play or the character from the play I'm supposed to be in or one that's both. Or neither?

> *(During the following descriptions, B7 quickly pantomimes the characters.)*

G5. Well, your character in the play is a handsome young man from a wealthy eastern prep school but you get killed on page 24. On the other hand, your character from the play that you're supposed to be in, in the play, is a small, dwarfish, evil-smelling con man who pretends to be blind on the streets of New York. However, he doesn't die in the play, he just gets stepped on by a horse.

F2. So what we're talking about here is a basic philosophical question. Is it better to be rich and handsome and die young or short and smelly and get stepped on by a horse but not die?

B7. Gosh, that's a tough one.

C4. Yeah.

> *(There is a pause.)*

A6. Someone have a line here?

> *(Everyone flips through scripts.)*

F2. Nope.

G5. Uh-uh.

H1. All my lines got cut!

> *(Enter JACK and NICK, two workmen carrying a ladder. The ladder is set downstage, center. They are characters right out of Mamet/Shepard/Pinter. The actors should play the scene very low-key, almost deadpan and totally seriously.)*

JACK. Sorry to interrupt folks, just have to change this light bulb, won't be a minute.

NICK. I was talking to Frank down at the Union Hall the other day.

JACK. Yeah? What did Frank say?

NICK. Said it was all over with. They're shutting down the plant at the end of the month.

JACK. Well, that's it then. So they're really moving it to Mexico?

NICK. Yeah. They're gonna pay 'em 50 cents an hour.

JACK. That's just great! And too bad for us I guess.

NICK. *(Looking at ceiling:)* So...uhh...there's the light we gotta fix.

JACK. Oh. That's a 3349. We don't got none of those.

NICK. That's not a 3349...that's...a...whattyacallit? Uh...that's a...uh...a Z 52 Halogen.

JACK. Nope. They took all the 52s out a couple a months ago. That there's a 3349. And like I said, we ain't got none of those.

NICK. How come they took the 52s out?

JACK. Them 52s had too much leakage there. They was putting out some kinda ozone stuff and the EGA *(sic)* said they hadda take them out and put in the 3349s. We ain't got none of those.

NICK. Say, my kid's brother-in-law had some of that ozone stuff at his work. Now's he got the cancer.

JACK. Damn government don't give a damn about the working man. Whole world is going to stinking hell. Sometimes I almost wish I was back in Nam. Say, we could probably put a 3368 up in there.

NICK. My wife left me six years ago. Now, I don't even know how to talk to a woman. Uh...why don't we try one of those 3368s.

JACK. Oh, wait a minute, I just remembered. Those 3368s are bi-pins, not Edisons. It won't fit.

NICK. Nothing fits anymore! When I was a kid, we used to have these woods in back of my house. We'd play there all the time. I went back there last week. They cut all the trees down and put up a Wal-Mart. It's all gone.

JACK. My oldest kid came home for Christmas. We're like strangers. Oh, we sit and watch the games and talk about the weather. But we really don't say anything. I'd like to tell him about Nam. But I just can't.

NICK. When I was 17, I thought I was so tough. I was gonna rule the world. Now, I just want someone to hold me.

JACK. I used to know what life was about. Then I went to Nam.

NICK. Say Jack, I just thought of something.

JACK. Yeah?

NICK. We never tried the light switch.

JACK. We didn't, did we?

NICK. I guess we don't even know if it works or not.

  (They begin to take down the ladder.)

JACK. I guess it's kinda like life.

NICK. How do you mean?

JACK. You have to try to turn it on.

NICK. But what if you don't know how, Jack? What if you don't know how?

JACK. I don't know, Nick. I don't know.

(JACK and NICK exit.)

A5. You know, this reminds me of when I was a little girl. One day, I went fishing with my father. I remember it was a bright, sunny day and the seagulls looked...

F2. We did that already!

A7. So?

F2. So it was stupid the first time!

(Enter SHANNON, a teenage girl dressed sexily. At her entrance, all of the other characters instantly change to become teenagers at a party. Everyone immediately accepts and plays along with the new situation.)

SHANNON. Hi guys! Sorry I'm late but Bobby and I had to make a stop on the way.

(D2 enters carrying two beers, one of which he tosses to SHANNON.)

D2. Yeah, I know what they were stopping for!

(Everyone laughs.)

D2. Where's Bobby?

SHANNON. He had to drive some of the guys over to Karen's party. He'll be back.

(Enter JENNIFER, a teenage girl dressed in nerd fashion.)

JENNIFER. Shannon! Did you see how Bobby pulled out of here? He almost smashed into the Wilsons' car!

SHANNON. He was just fooling around.

JENNIFER. No he wasn't! He's drunk!

SHANNON. No way! He only had a couple of beers.

(Knock at the door. D2 moves to answer it.)

D2. I'll get it.

JENNIFER. More like a couple of six-packs! How can you let him do that!?

SHANNON. What am I? His mother? Besides, he's fine. Why don't you just take a chill?

JENNIFER. I don't believe you! You *say* you love him, but you let him drink and drive! If he was my boyfriend...

SHANNON. But he's not, is he? Why don't you just accept the fact that he's my boyfriend, not yours!

(Everyone else reacts to the fight.)

SHANNON. Here Jennifer, have a beer. Or does that go against your little S.A.D.D. rules!?

(SHANNON tosses beer to JENNIFER, who catches and holds it. Enter D2, looking very upset. Everyone must play this next sequence totally straight.)

JENNIFER. Tom, what's wrong?

D2. That was a policeman at the door. There's been an accident. It's Bobby. He's dead.

(Everyone reacts with shock and horror.)

SHANNON. Oh no... No! No!

(SHANNON runs off crying, followed by D2 who goes to comfort her.)

JENNIFER. Why didn't I take his keys? I knew he was drunk. But I just stood there. I guess I didn't want to look like a nerd. I guess I really didn't love Bobby either.

(JENNIFER exits, crying softly.)

A8. I can't believe it. He was just here. I just talked to him.

F3. It can't be true. There must be some mistake!

G6. No! The only mistake was this!

(G holds up a bottle of beer.)

B8. There's just one thing I want to know.

E4. What's that?

B8. *(After a beat, and then totally breaking the serious mood by bursting out:)* WHO'S BOBBY!?

(As soon as B8 says the line, everyone drops the teenage characters and the sadness over Bobby's death, and reverts to the characters they were just before Shannon came in. Everyone looks at each other.)

F2. I thought you guys knew him.

A7. I never heard of him.

F2. And what about those two girls?

G5. Yeah! Who were they?

A7. That was weird.

F2. Still, it's a shame about Bobby.

C4. Oh yeah, he was a great guy.

(Enter TECHIE.)

TECHIE. Hey, the sound man just spilled his Coke down the sound board. So now we don't have any sound. Whaddya want me to do?

E5. We don't know who the director is yet.

TECHIE. Great. Well, when he, she, or it shows up, tell 'em we need a new Fresnel, some blue gels, a new sound board and a new sound man. I'm gonna get a smoke.

(TECHIE begins to exit.)

A7. Hey, what's your name?

TECHIE. *(Thinks for a second, pulls out a script and looks at the cover:)* Crew chief.

C4. No, your real name.

TECHIE. *(Looks at script again:)* That's all it says here. I'm gonna get a smoke.

F2. But don't you want to know who you really are?

TECHIE. *(Thinks for a beat:)* I'm gonna get a smoke. Actors!

(TECHIE exits stage right as THE DIRECTOR enters from stage left. THE DIRECTOR is dressed very artsy fartsy and carries a huge shoulder bag. She enters in a great hurry.)

THE DIRECTOR. Sorry I'm late, guys.

G5. Who are you?

THE DIRECTOR. Not today Melissa, I'm not in the mood!

F2. Who's Melissa?

C4. Who are you?

THE DIRECTOR. All right! I know you've been waiting here all afternoon! I know that just yesterday I gave you a big lecture on how irresponsible actors are because they're always late! O.K.! The director is late today! I'm sorry! You've made your point! I've just had one of the worst days of my life! I'm afraid we have something to talk about.

B7. You're the director?

THE DIRECTOR. *(Exploding in a fury and throwing a pen at B7:)* You idiot! Didn't you hear a word of what I just said!? My husband, the man I swore to love forever just six months ago, told me this morning, that he was very sorry but that he had fallen in love with another woman and he was leaving me and going with her to Florida. I don't know what I'm going to do. I'll have to move back to Columbus. Not even a year in New York and I'm running home to Mommy and Daddy! I'm sorry, but there's just no way I can direct this play now. Oh my God, how could he... *(She begins to cry.)*

C4. Wow. That was really good!

G5. Yeah. The way she started out all angry and then got softer and softer and then those little choking sounds she made just before she cried. Incredible.

THE DIRECTOR. *(Confused by their reaction:)* What are you talking about?

A7. I don't know. It wasn't bad. But I think it would have been much more effective if she was more devastated. *(Acting out the emotion:)* Almost out of control with grief! She's too calm.

THE DIRECTOR. WHAT ARE YOU TALKING ABOUT!?

E5. Your scene.

THE DIRECTOR. WHAT SCENE? WHAT'S WRONG WITH YOU PEOPLE?!

A7. See, now that's much better! Much more emotional. It touches the audience more deeply.

B7. Definitely. But I think she needs to change some of the lines. They sound a little cliché to me.

G5. Yeah, especially that one about the waitress from Florida. It's been done a million times.

THE DIRECTOR. Have you all gone insane!? This isn't some play I'm talking about! THIS IS MY LIFE!

(They all stare at her as if they have absolutely no idea what she is talking about. In tears, THE DIRECTOR *picks up her bag and begins to run out. However, the bag spills open and its contents scatter all about.* THE DIRECTOR *begins to pick up the mess but breaks down into sobs.)*

E6. Oh my God. I know what's been going on here. All of us have become so wrapped up in our own lives, in our careers, even our parts in this stupid play, that we can't even see when someone close to us is in pain. We've become unfeeling robots. What happens to us? We all try to be good. We all mean well. But somehow that isn't enough. *(Bending down to* THE DIRECTOR *and taking her in her arms:)* Please forgive me. Please forgive us.

*(*THE DIRECTOR *hugs E back and they embrace for three beats, until E lets go and stands up quickly.)*

E7. All right! Who blew their cue!?

(Everyone responds with various "not me," "it wasn't my line.")

THE DIRECTOR. I must be losing my mind. Why are you doing this to me!? What did I do to deserve this?!

*(*THE DIRECTOR *runs offstage crying.)*

C4. Nice exit.

F2. Oh yeah. Really effective.

(There is a pause while everyone tries to decide what to do.)

B7. Well.

G5. Well.

C4. *(Looking at watch:)* It's getting late.

H1. Anyone have any idea of how we get out of here?

(Everyone flips through scripts.)

F2. Nothing here.

H1. Me neither.

A7. Well we just can't stay here forever. We have to do something!

G6. *(G6 makes the sound of the phone ringing:)* RING...RING... *(She moves over to the phone and picks it up:)* Hello? ...Oh my God! It's Bobby! ...Is he all right? ...I'll be right there!

(G6 hangs up phone and runs offstage.)

B. Carol! If you don't tell him tonight that you're leaving him forever, then I'll handle things my own way!

(B pulls out a gun.)

A. Brad! What are you doing with that gun!?

B. I won't let him have you for another second! And if I have to kill him to do it, so be it!

A. Brad, no! I won't let you !

(A and B struggle over the gun. There is the sound of a shot and A falls dead to the floor.)

B. What have I done!? What have I done!?

(B runs offstage. There is the sound of a gunshot, the sound of a body falling, then the sound of a scream. C walks over and stands above A's body. The next lines should be an exact duplication of A's delivery of the monologue.)

C5. You know, this reminds me of when I was a little girl. One day, I went fishing with my father.

(C5 begins to exit, continuing the monologue until he is offstage.)

I remember it was a bright sunny day...

H. *(As Devil character:)* You have all been condemned to hell for your sins! For all eternity! And now I shall return to... *(Trying to think of what to say:)* ...my...office! In hell!

(H exits, laughing an evil laugh.)

F3. *(To E:)* I've told you before Roger, there can only be one director in a production and I am the director for this show! For your information, you are not Laurence Olivier! You are not even Keanu Reeves! I've had it! You want to be the director?! Go ahead! Because I quit!

(F storms offstage. E mutters something under her breath about F. Then she notices that she is all alone onstage and gets very nervous. She cannot think of what to do, but then sees A's body on the floor.)

E8. She's dead! Oh the pain! The pain! I can't live anymore! I'm going to kill myself!

(E looks around for something to kill herself with, but can only see a fork on the table. She picks it up and with a shrug stabs herself.)

This is the end! I am dying! The face of death approaches!

(E falls dead. However, after several seconds of silence she opens her eyes. Then she stands up.)

E9. Just a flesh wound, I guess.

(Looks around in desperation for a few seconds, and then finally points to the back of the theater.)

LOOK!

(E9 turns and runs as fast as she can offstage. After a few beats, we hear a voice over the PA system.)

THE VOICE. All right people, not bad. Let's do it again. Close the curtain, kill the lights and...ACTION.

End of Play

Some Notes on Production

For the play to work, from the time of the first "cut" the audience should never be sure if they are watching the "real" play. Hopefully, each time a "new" play is added, the audience should be fooled into thinking that at last, this is "it." For this to occur, two things must happen:

The actors must resist the temptation to mug or ham it up. Each character must be true to every scene they are in. That is, they are to act as if they are real actors trying to do their best in a real play. Even though they may be playing 8 different characters, they all must be real characters. A character that is so broad or exaggerated that it clearly could not be a real person destroys the desired effect.

At every "cut" or switch indicated in the story, the actors must change their characters. These character changes must be instantaneous, and do not stop the flow of the action. As in a real rehearsal, when something goes wrong you drop the character you are playing and become yourself to fix the problem. For example, in the first scene, A and B are playing sophisticated lovers. As soon as we hear the first "cut," they immediately drop those characters. A could become a Texan beauty pageant queen and B could become a California hippie. These changes are accomplished with body movements, vocal patterns, and alterations in costumes and props. Someone puts on a pair of sunglasses, takes their hair up or down or changes their clothing, etc. Of course, there are also emotional changes.

There should never be a time when the real actors onstage communicate to the audience that they know what's going on. A nudge-nudge, wink-wink, aren't-we-cute attitude ruins the play.

I hope it is not too confusing. Anyway, it's a fun play to rehearse (wait until people forget their lines).

Good Luck,
Ed Monk

CHECK PLEASE

by Jonathan Rand

Cast of Characters

GIRL
GUY

LOUIS
MELANIE
KEN
MARY
MARK
PEARL
TOD
SOPHIE
BRANDON
LINDA
MANNY
MIMI

Setting

A restaurant. Two dinner tables.

Time

Now.

Production Notes

This play was originally written with the intention of having the same two actors play the roles of Girl and Guy, and having 12 different actors play the rest of the roles. Another fun option would be to cast the play using four total actors, with all 12 characters except Girl and Guy split between two quick-change artists. The other option (which I least prefer) would be to cast every scene with a different pair of actors.

There are two more plays in this series: *Check Please: Take 2* and *Check Please: Take 3*. For more information, please visit www.playscripts.com.

Dedicated to Christy

For your free consulting services,
Breathtaking vocal stylings,
And your friendship

CHECK PLEASE

Scene 1

LOUIS. Hi.

GIRL. Hi there.

LOUIS. It's great to meet you.

GIRL. You, too.

LOUIS. So how long have you lived here?

GIRL. Almost a year. Feels longer, though.

LOUIS. Three years for me. It's a great city.

GIRL. Definitely. What do you like most about it?

LOUIS. What do you like most about living here?

    (Pause, as GIRL *is only slightly noticeably confused.)*

GIRL. Well...I love walking my dog in the park. Especially on a pretty day.

LOUIS. Oh yeah? I'm a little different, I guess. I'm more the kinda guy who likes walking my dog in the park on a pretty day.

    (He chuckles.)

GIRL. No, I like that, too. I just said so.

LOUIS. So do you like TV?

GIRL. No.

LOUIS. Me, too! I love it!

    (Pause.)

GIRL. Are you listening to me at all?

LOUIS. Sometimes I like to curl up with some popcorn and get my Leno on. You like Leno?

GIRL. You really aren't listening.

LOUIS. Me, too! Jay Leno just cracks—me—up.

GIRL. This is ridiculous.

LOUIS. His comedy is a gift from the gods. You know what I'm talking about? Yeah, you know what I'm talking about. I'm straight-up *addicted* to his show. We have the exact same comic timing, me and Jay. And yeah, sure I'm funny, but I've got flaws. Like sometimes I'm *too* funny. That's the worst! But hey, enough about me. Tell me about you.

GIRL.
You're still talking.
My presence here makes no difference at all.
Wow...

267

GIRL. Or I could just leave now, since you're a self-centered tool.

(A pause; we assume he is going to break.)

LOUIS. I'm a Capricorn myself.

(Blackout.)

Scene 2

GUY. Hi.

MELANIE. Hi.

GUY. It's so great to finally meet you.

MELANIE. Same here!

GUY. So where are you fr—

MELANIE. Wait, before you— Sorry. *(Meekly:)* This is so rude, but the Bears game is on right now? You don't mind if I check the score...

GUY. Oh, not at all. Totally.

MELANIE. *(As she pulls out her cell phone to check her web-browser:)* Thanks. I know this is such an awful thing to do on a first date, but it's late in the fourth quarter in a playoff game.

GUY. No worries.

MELANIE. Thanks. *(As she checks:)* I love the Bears. Great defensive line this year. *(Sees score; reacts a little.)* Okay, I'm done. That wasn't so bad, was it?

GUY. What's the score?

MELANIE. Packers by seven.

GUY. Uh-oh.

MELANIE. Nah, it's no big deal. It's just a game, right? So c'mon—enough about football. Let's hear about "Mister Mystery." Harriet's told me tons about you.

GUY. Man... The pressure's on now.

(They laugh together, genuinely. MELANIE's laugh then fades directly into her next line, which is suddenly serious.)

MELANIE. I'm just gonna check one more time.

(She digs into her purse.)

GUY. *(Smiling:)* No worries.

MELANIE. Is it all right with you if I wear this earpiece? I promise it won't be distracting.

GUY. Sure.

MELANIE. *(As she puts the earpiece in her ear:)* I'm making the worst first impression, aren't I...

GUY. Not at all.

MELANIE. It's just because it's the playoffs. I'm usually normal.

GUY. It's really no—

MELANIE. Come on!!

GUY. What?

MELANIE. Oh, nothing—the line only gives Forte[1] this huge running lane, but he fumbles the handoff. Sure, Pace recovered, but come on—this is the playoffs. You don't just cough up the ball like that. Now you're staring at third and long, and the whole season is riding on one play.

GUY. I hope ev—

MELANIE. WHAT?!

GUY. What?

MELANIE. PASS THE BALL!!

GUY. What's wrong?

MELANIE. It's third and long— Who runs it on third and long? Did Cutler suddenly FORGET that he has an ARM?!

(GUY *looks around subtly at the other patrons.*)

Oh my God. I'm being loud, aren't I.

GUY. *(Trying hard to be convincing:)* No...

MELANIE. Oh, I am. I'm so sorry. Look, how about this: I'll make it up to you. After dinner I'll buy you dessert at this tiny little bistro on 11th that nobody knows about. I think you'll just—PASS THE BALL!! Jesus, people! It's FOURTH DOWN! Pass the FRIGGING BALL!

GUY. Listen—we could go to a bar with a TV or something.

MELANIE. Oh please, no. I wouldn't do you that to you. The game's pretty much over anyway. *(She takes a deep breath, and is now very calm.)* Okay. I'm done. I got a little carried away there, didn't I? Let's order.

(*They peruse for a moment, as if nothing has happened.*)

GUY. *(Indicating the menu:)* Oh. Harriet said we should definitely try the—

(MELANIE *suddenly lets out a bloodcurdling shriek and rips the menu in half.*)

GUY. Or we could order something else.

MELANIE. *(Downtrodden:)* They lost...

GUY. Oh. I'm sorry.

MELANIE. *(Starting to tear up:)* They lost. The season's over.

GUY. Well—

---

[1] Throughout this scene, use position-appropriate names currently on the Bears roster.

(MELANIE *breaks down, bawling.* GUY *thinks for a moment, then takes out a handkerchief and offers it to* MELANIE. *She uses it to blow her nose.*)

GUY. I'm so sorry. Is there anything I can do?

MELANIE. *(Still weepy:)* The Bears suck...

GUY. Aww, no. They don't suck.

MELANIE. They do... They suck.

GUY. They're probably just having a bad season—

(MELANIE *grabs his collar, pulls him extremely close, and speaks in a horrifying, monstrous, deep voice.*)

MELANIE. THE BEARS SUCK.

GUY. *(Weakly:)* The Bears suck.

(Blackout.)

Scene 3

GIRL. Hi.

KEN. Hello.

(He kisses her hand, lingering there a second too long.)

GIRL. It's great to meet you.

KEN. The pleasure...is all mine.

GIRL. So...where are you from? I can't place the accent.

KEN. I was raised in the mountains of Guam...and was born...on the shore of New Jersey.

(Beat.)

GIRL. Do you want to order some appetizers?

KEN. Anything...which will ensure happiness for your beautiful lips.

(He looks at menu, unaware of her subtle look of disbelief. She finally looks down at her menu.)

GIRL. Ooh! The shrimp cocktail looks good.

KEN. Shrimp... A creature of the ocean. The ocean...which is not nearly as lovely as the ocean of your eyes.

GIRL. Listen, can I ask you sort of a...blunt question?

KEN. Anything which your heart desires will be—

GIRL. Yeah yeah. Are you going to be like this for the rest of dinner?

KEN. Whatever do you mean?

GIRL. You know, all creepy and nauseating?

(Pause.)

KEN. Yes.

(Blackout.)

Scene 4

GUY. Hi.

MARY. Hi.

GUY. It's so great to finally meet you.

MARY. Same here! Listen: I was wondering if you were free next Friday.

GUY. Uh, I think so. Why?

MARY. Well, if dinner goes well tonight, I wanted to go ahead and schedule a second date.

GUY. Oh. Okay, sure.

MARY. See, 'cause here's the thing: My parents are having a house-warming party at their new place on August 2nd, and if you and I hit it off tonight and end up getting serious, that party would be the perfect opportunity for you to meet them, so I'd like to squeeze in six dates beforehand, because if we don't, my parents might be skeptical of our relationship, which, after you pop the question, could make everyone uncomfortable during the ceremony, which could then carry over during our three-week honeymoon in Cozumel, and more important than anything else, it could really take a toll on little Madison.

(Pause.)

GUY. Wow...

MARY. What? What is it? You don't like the name Madison? We could change it. My second and third picks are Kim and Blanket.

GUY. No, all of those are...great names...

MARY. Something's on your mind. You know you can always tell your little bunny rabbit *anything.*

GUY. The problem is: you seem to have our whole relationship figured out—and we just met thirty seconds ago. *(Chuckling:)* I mean, you've got everything pinned down but the wedding dress.

MARY. Does that make you uncomfortable?

(Beat.)

(As she withdraws several boxes:) Because if it does, we can pick it out now.

(Blackout.)

Scene 5

(Lights up to MARK *dressed in nothing but a burlap sack. He's looking at the menu, as if nothing is out of the ordinary.* GIRL *is looking at him, expressionless. After several moments, he folds the menu, his dinner decision made. He looks up. Pause.)*

MARK. *(Innocent:)* What?

(Blackout.)

Scene 6

GUY. Hi.

PEARL. Hi.

GUY. It's so nice to meet you.

PEARL. Same here. Julia's told me a lot about you.

GUY. She's a great girl.

(The moment GUY *begins speaking the above line,* PEARL *quickly and slickly steals a fork.* GUY *thinks he saw wrong.* PEARL *continues on as if nothing has happened.)*

PEARL. Yeah. So much fun to be around. We've been friends for something like...six years, I think?

GUY. *(As* PEARL *quickly steals the rest of the utensils:)* Where'd you meet? In school?

PEARL. Yeah. We played soccer. Both second-stringers, keeping the bench nice and warm for everyone else.

(They laugh together. During their laugh, PEARL *swipes her napkin.)*

Seriously, Julia is one of my favorites. And she's got great taste, so when she told me about you, I was definitely on board.

(The moment GUY *begins speaking the next line,* PEARL *swiftly and deftly removes the flower from the vase, pours the contents of her glass into the vase, pockets the glass, and replaces the flower in the vase.)*

GUY. That's very—sweet...

PEARL. No, really—I've been looking forward to this for a while.

GUY. *(As* PEARL *takes the flower:)* I'm flattered.

PEARL. So... You hungry? I'm about ready.

*(PEARL *picks up her menu;* GUY *does likewise. The moment* GUY *begins speaking,* PEARL *slides the menu into her jacket.)*

GUY. I'm pretty hungry, too—you know, I can see that you're stealing. You don't have to play it off like you're not.

PEARL. What? What are you talking about?

GUY. *(As PEARL steals a plate:)* I'm sitting right here— See? There. You just stole a plate.

PEARL. Wow...that's a cruel accusation...

GUY. *(As* PEARL *steals sugar holder:)* Accusation?! I'm watching you steal those sugar packets right now? How can you honestly believe I don't notice.

PEARL. *(Starting to leave:)* Look, I don't know what your problem is with me as a person, but this is really insulting. I'd better go.

GUY. Wait. Listen: if you'll stop stealing things, I won't get on your case. Okay?

> *(Pause.)*

PEARL. Okay...

GUY. Yeah?

PEARL. Yeah...

GUY. Great. So where are you from—?

> *(She whips the tablecloth off the table and starts stuffing it down her pants. Or, if possible, in one swift motion she swipes the tablecloth, an article of clothing from* GUY, *and one or both chairs.)*

> *(Blackout.)*

Scene 7

> *(GIRL is sitting across from* TOD, *a little boy—regardless of the age of the actor portraying this role, it should be immediately and abundantly clear that* TOD *is far too young for* GIRL. *A long pause.)*

GIRL. This may sound insensitive, but...how old are you?

TOD. What's yer favorite animal?

GIRL. No, I'm serious. I really want to know your age.

TOD. I like elephants.

GIRL. I think there's been a misunderstanding. See, when your profile said you were still in school, I assumed you meant college—

> *(She is suddenly interrupted by* TOD's *elephant impression. Beat.)*

GIRL. That's very lifelike.

TOD. Do you have a scar? I have a scar! Do you want to see it?

GIRL. No, that's all right.

> *(Before she can finish her thought,* TOD *throws his leg up on the table, rolls up his pant leg, and shows the scar on his knee.)*

TOD. I got it from kickball. Do you see it?

GIRL. Honestly, how old are you?

TOD. *(A quick display on his fingers:)* This many. Will you be my girlfriend?

GIRL. Your girlfriend.

TOD. 'Cause Katie Johnson always brings boring lunch to school and Courtney Shuler smells like horses.

GIRL. You've got a lot of girlfriends.

TOD. Yeah will you be my girlfriend?

GIRL. *(Sarcastically:)* Fine... But only if you pay for dinner.

TOD. You got it!

> *(He quickly produces a huge piggy bank and a hammer, and smashes the piggy bank. Or he opens the bottom and quickly dumps all of the change on the table. Blackout.)*

Scene 8

> *(SOPHIE enters the restaurant. She is a very old woman, edging toward the table in a walker. GUY just stares. Blackout.)*

Scene 9

> *(BRANDON and GIRL are in mid-laugh.)*

BRANDON. I didn't even—

GIRL. —I know, I know—

BRANDON. —I mean, seriously!

GIRL. —I know, right?

> *(They settle down from the laughter.)*

BRANDON. So listen—all joking aside...this is fun! I'm really having a good time.

GIRL. Me, too! This has been great.

BRANDON. Hasn't it?

GIRL. Ugh! There's a fly in my water.

BRANDON. Gross. Here, take mine. *(To offstage:)* Waiter? Can we get another water?

GIRL. You are so sweet.

BRANDON. Ah, c'mon.

GIRL. No really.

BRANDON. Anyone would do that.

GIRL. Actually, you'd be surprised. With the luck I've been having on dates...

BRANDON. Really? But you're so fun. And beautiful.

GIRL. Oh please.

BRANDON. No. I mean it.

GIRL. You are just too good to be true.

BRANDON. C'mon, Robin.

(Pause.)

GIRL. What?

BRANDON. What?

GIRL. Who?

BRANDON. What?

GIRL. Who's Robin?

BRANDON. What do you mean?

GIRL. You just called me Robin. Who's Robin?

(BRANDON fidgets.)

GIRL. Is it your girlfriend?

BRANDON. No.

GIRL. Who is she?

BRANDON. He.

GIRL. He?

BRANDON. He.

GIRL. You're gay?

BRANDON. No! Well, yes. But Robin's my agent. I'm an actor.

GIRL. You're gay.

BRANDON. Yeah.

(Pause.)

GIRL. And why am I on a date with you?

BRANDON. Okay... I'm sorry I didn't tell you this sooner, but it would've totally backfired if I did. Here's the deal: I'll be playing Stanley in a local production of *Streetcar*, and since I'm a method-actor, I won't be able to get the part down until I method-act straight.

GIRL. Method-act.

BRANDON. Yes. I can't be Stanley Kowalski until I truly experience what it feels like to woo a woman.

(Pause.)

GIRL. So let me see if I can follow: you had me get dressed up for dinner, drive all the way downtown, and get my hopes destroyed after thinking

I'd finally met a halfway decent guy—all so you could get a better feel for being straight?

(*Beat.*)

BRANDON. You don't mind, do you?

(*Pause. She takes her glass of water and douses his face. Pause.*)

BRANDON. Oh my god. That was perfect! The ultimate heterosexual dating moment! I've got it! I'm in! I'm straight! STELLAAAAAAAAAAA—

(*She grabs the other glass of water and douses his face again.*)

(*Blackout.*)

(*Note: The character of Brandon should NOT be played as flamboyantly gay—the audience should only be made aware of that fact when he explains it during the date. The actor should play the part completely straight throughout.*)

Scene 10

LINDA. Hi.

GUY. Hi.

LINDA. I've been looking forward to this for a while.

GUY. Me, too. Sorry about all the rescheduling.

LINDA. Pssh, whatever, it's cool. Oh, shoot. Hold on. I forgot to—

(*She starts rummaging through her purse, and after a couple of seconds, dumps it on the table and starts looking through the items.*)

GUY. What's up? What's wrong?

LINDA. Oh, it's this silly thing. I've got this pill I need to take or else I get all weird. (*Back to her purse:*) I know I brought them. They've gotta be— You know, whatever. I'll be fine.

GUY. You sure? We could go to a pharmacy or something.

LINDA. Nah it's no big deal. It's just a precautionary drug, you know? It won't kill me if I don't take it for one night. I just may be a little out of whack. You probably won't even be able to tell. Whatever. So—anyway.

GUY. (*Smiling:*) Anyway.

LINDA. It's nice to finally meet you.

GUY. The feeling's mutual.

LINDA. (*Suddenly sarcastic, morose, in a monotone voice:*) Oh yes. It's so *awesome* to finally put a name with a face.

GUY. Heh. Yeah. Seriously.

LINDA. *(Giggly/bubbly:)* You're funny; you're cute.

(Gruff:) He's not cute. You just haven't been out in a while.

(Snobby:) That is NOT—TRUE. He is GOOD—LOOKING.

(Jittery:) Shhhhhhhh... You're embarrassing yourself...

(Aggressive:) Quit freaking out.

(Easily offended:) Why are you jumping all over me?

(Little girl:) She started it!

(Motherly:) Girls, don't fight. What would your father say.

(Fatherly:) Oh, let 'em fight.

GUY. Are you all right?

LINDA. *(Aggressive, to* GUY:*)* You stay out of this!

(Reasonable:) Hey, leave him alone.

(Gruff:) Oh, he can take care of himself.

(Monkey:) Ooh ooh, ah! ah!

(Snobby:) Who brought the monkey?

(Pushover:) I did. I'm so sorry.

(Aggressive:) A monkey? Come on!

(Motherly:) You are grounded!

(Fatherly:) Get off her case, woman!

(Monkey:) Ooh ooh AAHHH!

(GUY notices a bottle and shows it to LINDA.*)*

GUY. Hey, are these the pills?

LINDA. *(Cheery:)* There they are!

(Gruff:) Took long enough.

(LINDA swallows the pill.)

GUY. Is everything all right?

LINDA. *(Mostly back to normal, but woozy:)* Okay... It kicks in really fast.

GUY. Great.

LINDA. In a couple of seconds, I'll settle into a single personality. But don't worry—nine times out ten it's one of the normal ones.

GUY. But with my luck—

(LINDA suddenly lets out a monkey shriek and lumbers offstage.)

(Pause.)

GUY. She was nice.

(Blackout.)

(Note: Linda's personality switches should be fast. Each personality should be a different level—her voice and demeanor should be changing dramatically throughout.)

Scene 11

GIRL. Hello.

MANNY. Hi.

GIRL. It's nice to meet you.

MANNY. Same.

GIRL. Let's order. I'm starved.

MANNY. Me, too.

GIRL. Wow, this menu's huge!

MANNY. I can never decide when the menu's so big. I can be picky.

GIRL. Ooh! I'm definitely getting the pork chops. What about you?

MANNY. I don't know. Nothing really leaps out.

GIRL. Really? Why don't you tryyyy—the pot roast.

MANNY. Nooo—too dry.

GIRL. Okay. How about...the shrimp scampi.

MANNY. Too moist.

GIRL. Oh.

MANNY. I actually have a tiny bit of hygrophobia.

GIRL. Hygrophobia?

MANNY. It's the fear of dampness or moisture.

GIRL. Oh, okay. How about the eggplant parmesan?

MANNY. Porphyrophobia.

GIRL. What's that?

MANNY. Fear of purple.

GIRL. You could get the cheese plate.

MANNY. Coprastasophobia.

GIRL. Fear of...?

MANNY. Constipation.

GIRL. What about the sushi?

MANNY. Japanophobia. *(Beat.)* It's the fear of—

GIRL. No, I got it. What about this Hawaiian fish? Let's see if I can pronounce it right: Humuhumunukunukuapua'a'.

MANNY. That actually sounds delicious.

GIRL. Great!

MANNY. But I suffer from a rare case of hippopotomonstrosesquippedaliophobia.

GIRL. Which is?

MANNY. Fear of long words.

GIRL. Okay! How about this: peanut butter and jelly.

MANNY. Sorry.

GIRL. What could possibly be wrong with peanut butter and jelly?

MANNY. I recently developed arachibutyrophobia.

GIRL. Fear of sandwiches?

MANNY. Fear of peanut butter sticking to the roof of my mouth.

GIRL. So what *can* you eat?

MANNY. Not much. I do have sitiophobia.

GIRL. Fear of...?

MANNY. Food.

GIRL. Right. So if you have all of these dietary issues, why did you ask me to *dinner?*

MANNY. Good question.

GIRL. Look, how about we just skip this and go to a hockey game or something.

MANNY. Oooh, can't. Pacifist.

GIRL. Mini-golf.

MANNY. Asthma.

GIRL. See a musical.

MANNY. Dependson the musical; I have ailurophobia.

GIRL. Fear of...?

MANNY. Cats.

    (Beat.)

GIRL. Well, what would *you* like to do?

MANNY. Well, I have one or two ideas.

GIRL. Great.

MANNY. But I have decidophobia.

GIRL. Okay, I'll decide for you. How about we call it a night?

MANNY. I can't.

GIRL. Why not?

MANNY. Anuptaphobia?

GIRL. *(Sarcastic:)* What's that? Fear of staying single for the rest of your life?

MANNY. Actually, yes.

GIRL. Oh.

MANNY. On the other hand, it's probably best we end the date now, on account of my deipnophobia.

GIRL. Fear of...?

MANNY. Dinner conversations.

(Beat.)

GIRL. Okay, well in that case, have a good night.

(She extends her hand for a friendly handshake.)

MANNY. You, too! One second.

(He takes out a pair of rubber gloves and starts to put them on.)

(Blackout.)

Scene 12

(GUY is sitting across the table from a fully outfitted mime, MIMI, who, throughout the scene, is extremely over-the-top and exuberant, as stereotypical mimes are. The scene begins with MIMI "leaning" on "something." Mimed actions in this scene will be indicated with brackets. A few moments pass, as we get a feel for the absurdity of the scenario.)

GUY. So what do you do for a living...?

(Beat.)

MIMI. [Pulling something heavy with a rope.]

GUY. You pull rope. *(Pause.)* Look... I respect your profession. I think it's noble what you do... The world needs more people who...climb invisible ladders. But I really don't see how it's appropriate to bring your work to a date.

MIMI. [Battling against harsh winds.]

GUY. Oh yeah, quite a storm in here.

(GUY opens his menu and reads. MIMI mimes picking up an imaginary menu, and peruses it page after page. GUY looks up and watches MIMI do her thing.)

GUY. Okay, I'm gonna go...use the restroom.

(GUY gets up, takes his jacket from the back of the chair.)

MIMI. [You're leaving? Driving away? Far? Bye bye?]

GUY. No, I'm not leaving. I'm taking my jacket with me because...it might get cold in the men's room.

MIMI. [Cold like me in this wild blizzard?]

GUY. Yeah, cold like that.

(GUY starts to leave. MIMI follows close behind, maybe as an airplane pilot, or a bus driver.)

GUY. No, you stay here. You—

MIMI. [Let me feed some chickens. Awww, those chicks are adorable. I love petting these lovely animals.]

GUY. I don't know what that is... Look I have to...

(An idea dawns on GUY has an idea. The following is an extremely loud and animated sequence of events—very frantic for MIMI; sarcastically frantic for GUY.)

GUY. Oh, okay... *(Looking up:)* Oh my God! A BOX!

MIMI. [Where? Where?]

GUY. A huge, glass box, falling from the sky!!

MIMI. [Oh no! Oh no! I can't see it! What in heavens name will I do? Help me!]

GUY. Noooooooo!

(GUY follows "the box" with his finger as it plops directly on the frantic MIMI, who is now very much "trapped" inside the box. Blackout.)

Scene 13

(Lights up to MARK in his burlap sack. He is reading the menu. Long pause.)

GIRL. I give up.

MARK. If you've got a problem with me, why don't you just say it to my face?

GIRL. Okay. You're wearing a burlap sack.

(Beat.)

MARK. It's Versace.

(Beat.)

GIRL. *(As she stands to leave:)* I need to go powder my nose.

(GIRL exits toward GUY's table. The lights on GIRL's table remain up as lights come up on GUY's table. MIMI is still in her box, but she doesn't distract from the main action. GIRL and GUY bump into each other.)

GIRL. Oh, sorry.

GUY. No, no. My fault.

(A short moment of instant chemistry. Then GUY shakes it off, as does GIRL.)

GUY. Well, goodnight.

GIRL. Goodnight.

(They start to go their separate ways.)

GUY. Hold on a second. *(Pause.)* This may seem random, but...do you like football?

GIRL. A little. *(Beat.)* Do you own any burlap?

GUY. No.

> *(Beat.)*

GIRL. Should we go get some ice cream?

GUY. Yes.

> *(They exit together. A few moments pass.* MIMI *finally finds a "key" in her "pocket," unlocks the "door" to the "box" and exits. She moves to* MARK, *"spits" in her hand exuberantly, and extends it to him for a handshake.* MARK *looks up and notices what is going on in front of him.)*

MARK. *(Deadpan:)* Check please.

End of Play

ALIENS VS. CHEERLEADERS

by Qui Nguyen

Cast of Characters

Female Roles:

MARISSA
TINA
MISSY
GABBY
LUCY
MOLLY

Male Roles:

FLINT
YA-WI
LEWIS
PRINCIPAL FORSMAN *(Feel free to rename this character to the name of your own school's principal if you find that sort of thing funny)*

Either:

HURT
BURNOUT
G'BRIL
MIKAH

Character Note

There's also a few one line characters (STUDENT, ANOTHER STUDENT, DIFFERENT STUDENT) and "spacemen" that can be played by any of the available actors.

Setting

Saint Valley High School, and a Spaceship.

Time

The Present.

Acknowledgments

Aliens vs. Cheerleaders received its world premiere on May 28, 2010 in the Fourth Annual Keen Teens One-Act Play Festival, presented by Keen Company (Artistic Director, Carl Forsman; Program Director, Blake Lawrence) and Playscripts, Inc. It was directed by Robert Ross Parker.

About Keen Teens

Keen Teens is a partnership between the Award winning, Off Broadway Keen Company, and the publishing company Playscripts, Inc. Keen Teens strives to enrich the quality of plays being written for high schoolers and give students the opportunity to work with professionals in a full production process. To that end, Keen Teens commissions 30-minute plays written specifically for high school students from some of the most highly regarded playwrights working in theatre today. Keen Teens encourages dynamic, diverse writers to create plays that are fun, theatrical, innovative and which will resonate with young artists and reflect the world in which they live.

Once the plays are written, students in and around the New York City area are cast and participate in a 12 week rehearsal process, giving the students the opportunity to work with professional directors, designers and playwrights on the World Premiere production. Playscripts, Inc. then publishes the plays and makes them available to other theatre groups interested in licensing the plays for future production.

ALIENS VS. CHEERLEADERS

(Lights come up on two teenagers, FLINT *and* MARISSA, *sitting inside a car.* FLINT *is behind the steering wheel. They are on a date.)*

FLINT. You're not going to believe this.

MARISSA. The engine's dead?

FLINT. The engine's dead.

MARISSA. You're right, I don't believe this.

FLINT. I'm serious.

MARISSA. Flint, I'm not some ditz. There's no way I'm gonna fall for this sad attempt at some alone time.
I've seen slicker slickness coming from bucktooth band nerds. I thought more of you than this.

FLINT. Marissa, I'm not lying. The car's dead. Check it yourself if you don't believe me.

(MARISSA tries to start the car. Nothing happens.)

MARISSA. Well, huh.

FLINT. What's that?

MARISSA. I said "huh."

FLINT. As in I'm telling the truth?

MARISSA. As in, yes, you're telling the truth.

FLINT. I told you I'm the upstanding type. There's no way I'd fake a breakdown. What kind of creep do you think I am?

MARISSA. Fine, Flint, I'm sorry.

FLINT. However, since we are broken down now...what do you think we should...do?

MARISSA. Right. And this is why God invented cell phones.

(MARISSA flips out her phone and tries to dial, but nothing happens.)

MARISSA. Huh.

FLINT. What's with the "huh"?

MARISSA. "Huh" as in my phone's dead as well. That's weird.

(Flint's phone is also dead.)

FLINT. Huh.

MARISSA. Yours too?

FLINT. No power.

MARISSA. My watch is also deep-six'd.

FLINT. I'm getting a strange feeling about this.

MARISSA. Likewise.

FLINT. Maybe we should get to walking, Marissa. I think we passed a gas station a couple miles back. It shouldn't take too long to get there.

MARISSA. On foot?

FLINT. What's the worst that can happen?

(*MARISSA and* FLINT *get out of the car.*)

FLINT. Hold up, I got one of those large metal flashlights around here somewhere.

(*Suddenly a bright light appears above them accompanied by a hovering sound.*)

MARISSA. Um, Flint?

FLINT. Here it is!

MARISSA. Flint?

FLINT. This'll help us see our way through the...not so dark?

MARISSA. (*Pointing up:*) What's that?

FLINT. I think running would be a good plan right about now.

(*MARISSA and* FLINT *try to run away, but then suddenly the stage is filled with aliens in spacesuits at all sides.*

They try to rush them, but—

ZAP! FLINT *and* MARISSA *get blasted unconscious by the aliens.*

One of the aliens emerges forward. We do not see his face.)

YA-WI. Yes, this looks to be a good planet to conquer.

(*Cut to...*

Projection: ALIENS

Projection: VERSUS

Projection: CHEERLEADERS

Projection: Saint Valley High School

Lights come up on Saint Valley's Spirit Squad doing a cheerleading sequence.)

SQUAD. (*Cheering:*) Y-E-L-L
EVERYBODY YELL YELL
GET ROUGH, GET TOUGH
WE'RE GETTING FIRED UP
TO HIT THE FIELD, TO BE MEAN
WE'LL SQUASH THE OTHER TEAM
CAUSE WE'RE SMOOTH, WE'RE FLY
WE ARE SAINT VALLEY HIGH!!!

(*Spotlight on* MOLLY, *a hip hipster girl who's been watching them cheer.*)

MOLLY. Cheerleaders: top of the food chain in popularity, bottom feeders when it comes to any sort of actual original coolness. I mean, seriously, with the noted exception of "Hey, Mickey, you're so fine, you're so fine you blow my mind," has anyone with a pom-pom ever substantially contributed anything positive to the overall socio-political landscape? I don't think so.

Anyone with any true sense of style, wit, or intellect would rather suffer daily beatings from the lame and dimwitted than be caught in one of those tacky and utterly whack uniforms.

> *(Lights up on LEWIS, a Harry Potter-esque nerd, getting picked on by two jocks.)*

HURT. Yo, Harry Potter, where you rushing off to?

BURNOUT. Yeah, why you rushin'?

MOLLY. However, this is high school where indeed anyone with any true sense of style, wit, or intellect suffers just that.

LEWIS. My name's not Harry Potter.

HURT. I think it is. I think you're a little wizard. Show us a magic trick, wizard!

LEWIS. Don't touch me.

HURT. Or what?

BURNOUT. Yeah, or what?

> *(MOLLY enters.)*

MOLLY. Or I'll have to show you two little lady-dogs my favorite slight of hand.

HURT. Oh yeah, and what's that?

MOLLY. Tattooing your behinds with my Nike swooshes.

BURNOUT. Um, I don't think that's an actual magic trick.

> *(HURT goes for a sucker punch. MOLLY reverses the move and slams him into the ground. BURNOUT tries to help, but MOLLY easily takes him out too. Both the bullies lie on the ground in pain.)*

LEWIS. Wow. Thanks, Molly.

MOLLY. You okay, Lewis?

LEWIS. Yeah.

MOLLY. Let's get to class.

> *(MOLLY and LEWIS exit. As they do, they pass four cheerleaders [TINA, MISSY, GABBY, and LUCY] who have clearly been watching them the whole time during the fight.)*

MOLLY. Now time for some important intros. The four pom-poms that have been giving Lewis and I the evil-eye are Missy Maguire, Gabby Hendricks, Lucy Christian, and Tina Carpenter. These four make up the heart of Saint Valley High's award-winning cheerleading team.

> *(A cool beat drops. As the following monologue happens, a spotlight hits each of the girls as they are being described.)*

MOLLY. First up is Missy Maguire. A star athlete on Saint Valley High's soccer, field hockey, and softball teams. She acts as the squad's muscle. Whenever they need someone for the base of the pyramid, it's her biceps they use to hold them up. She's a perfect combination of beauty and brawn.

(A shot of MISSY *finishing an energy drink and then crushing it on her forehead [or just her hands depending what's easier].)*

MISSY. I'm in the mood for some danger.

MOLLY. Next is Gabby Hendricks. Along with being able to do perfect round-offs and hitch-kicks, she's also the MVP of the school's mathlete, science, and forensics teams. Nerds have never rocked so much lady-hotness.

(A shot of GABBY *reading Stephen Hawking's "A Brief History of Time." She shakes her head and takes a red pen to correct mistakes.)*

GABBY. This book might as well be written in crayon.

MOLLY. Third is Lucy Christian. She's, well, special.

(A shot of LUCY *trying to eat soup. With a fork. She fails.)*

LUCY. Why is soup always so hard to eat!

MOLLY. And, finally, Tina Carpenter, head cheerleader. Also captain of the Saint Valley High champion debate team, president of the young political leaders of America club, and this year's Homecoming Queen. Athletic, pretty, and popular, she's the epitome of, well, evil. And, right now, she's in my way.

TINA. Hey.

MOLLY. Excuse us.

TINA. What's your name?

MOLLY. What's it to you?

TINA. I'm student council president. I take it as my personal duty to know each and every student here on campus.

MOLLY. Is that right?

TINA. That's right.

MOLLY. Then what's his name?

TINA. Uh...

MOLLY. That's what I thought. You're in our way.

TINA. Let me try this again. Hi! I'm Tina—

LEWIS. I'm Lewis. It's a pleasure to meet—

MOLLY. I know who you are.

TINA. If you know who I am, then you know I'm also the head cheerleader for Saint Valley's Spirit Squad.

MOLLY. Well, that would explain the outfit. Seriously, do you girls ever miss wearing pants?

LEWIS. I think it looks quite lovely.

MOLLY. Shut up, Lewis.

TINA. You're quippy. That's cute.
I saw what you just did with those two bullies.

MOLLY. You saw that, huh?

TINA. Yes, you dispatched them pretty easily.

MOLLY. So what? Are you going to tell on me? Is this part of your duties as my student council president?

TINA. No. Quite the opposite actually.
I'm stopping you right now because I think you'd make a great addition to our squad.

MOLLY and LEWIS. What?

TINA. I'm offering you a spot on the Saint Valley High Cheerleading Team. What do you say?

> *(Projection: Meanwhile...)*

> *(Lights shift to FLINT and MARISSA waking up in a dark room.)*

FLINT. Oh man, I am so out past my curfew.

MARISSA. Will you get a grip?

FLINT. My parents are so going to kill me.

MARISSA. We need to get out of here. Look for a door or—

> *(Suddenly, a light appears on three hooded aliens [YA-WI, MIKAH, and G'BRIL]. We cannot see their faces.)*

YA-WI. *(In an ominous voice:)* Rak tiki tiki tee, romb bomb bomb, kerblam!!!

> *(Pause.)*

MARISSA. Uh...what?

YA-WI. RAK. TIKI. TIKI. TEE! ROMB BOMB BOMB. KERBLAM!

MARISSA and FLINT. ...

YA-WI. Rak tiki tiki...

G'BRIL. *(To YA-WI:)* Um, sir, I think you have your translator set to Marcopian.

YA-WI. Fling flang?

> *(YA-WI touches a button on his wrist. There's a beep. He now can speak English.)*

YA-WI. *(To G'BRIL:)* How's this? Does this sound right? *(To MARISSA and FLINT:)* Do. You. Understand. Me?

> *(MARISSA and FLINT nod yes.)*

YA-WI. Good. Good. Now where was I?
I WOULDN'T SUGGEST OPENING THAT DOOR!

> *(YA-WI drops his hood. The other aliens follow suit.)*

YA-WI. *(To* G'BRIL:*)* We completely lost the moment, didn't we? It's gone. I HATE THIS STUPID UNIVERSAL TRANSLATOR! It always defaults back to Marcopian. Seriously, can I get a new one? How am I supposed to come off as a ruthless and ominous intergalactic tyrant if no one understands the words coming out of my mouth?

G'BRIL. We'll get you a new one, sir.

YA-WI. Thank you, that's all I ask. For people to understand me. And for them to cower. I do appreciate a good cowering.

MARISSA. Um, who are you guys?

FLINT. And what's with the door?

YA-WI. The door. Yes, THE DOOR! I WOULDN'T SUGGEST—

MARISSA. Yes, we shouldn't open the door. We get that. Why?

YA-WI. Show them, Mikah.

MIKAH. *(Deadpan:)* Behold. The immenseness of outer space.

MARISSA. What?

YA-WI. You're on my spaceship.

MARISSA. What?

YA-WI. We're aliens.

MARISSA. What?

MIKAH. *(Still deadpan:)* Seriously, you didn't get that? I mean, he's green. She has fuzzy ears. I have a horn sticking out of my head. We're completely alien-like.

YA-WI. And we're here to take over your planet!

MARISSA. What?

YA-WI. I think my translator's still set on the wrong language. It really sounds like she just keeps saying "what" over and over again.

MARISSA. What?

G'BRIL. That's actually what she's saying, Commander Ya-Wi.

YA-WI. Well okay then. *(To* MARISSA *and* FLINT:*)* So Earthlings. How ya doing? The thing is, I'm an alien and, well, at this moment, I need you to...TAKE ME TO YOUR LEADER!

FLINT and MARISSA. ...

YA-WI. Did you two not understand me?

> *(MARISSA and* FLINT *break out into full-out guffaws.)*

YA-WI. Why are they giggling?
TAKE ME TO YOUR LEADER! NOW!
Seriously, G'bril, why are they laughing? Does their species reflexively laugh when they feel thoroughly frightened?
Take. Me. To. Your. Leader!

> *(More uncontrollable laughter.)*

YA-WI. Okay, fine, we'll do it the old fashioned way. Scan their brains!

(MIKAH grabs FLINT and throws a tech-ish looking hat on his head.)

FLINT. Marissa! Help!

MARISSA. Let him go—

> *(MARISSA runs to help FLINT, but G'BRIL pinches her neck which knocks her out.)*

G'BRIL. Patience. You'll get your turn next.

> *(YA-WI then approaches FLINT and also puts on a high tech-ish cap.)*

YA-WI. Mikah, turn on that brain-meldy machine of yours.

MIKAH. It's called a mental-wave-micro-singularity-transcorresponder? It's just one of the single greatest scientific achievements in all the universe —but, ya know, don't worry about getting the name right, it's no big deal at all...

YA-WI. What's that, Mikah?

MIKAH. Nothing, sir. Okay, stay still. Please don't tap your foot, Commander Ya-Wi. Seriously, Commander, don't tap your foot.

YA-WI. I know, I know. Just do it, Mikah.

MIKAH. But—

YA-WI. Do it.

> *(MIKAH flips on the machine. FLINT's body stiffens.)*

YA-WI. Ah, now with our minds fully connected, I will see and experience all the thoughts, wants, and desires running through this young Earthling male's mind!

> *(YA-WI takes in FLINT's thoughts.)*

YA-WI. Wow, this teenage male is really obsessed with the posterior regions of young female Earthlings. I mean, REALLY obsessed. It's a bit freaky.

G'BRIL. Commander Ya-Wi sir, can you ascertain who is the leader of this planet?

YA-WI. Let me see. Posterior, posterior, posterior. Ah, here it is!

G'BRIL. Who is the leader of this planet, my commander?

YA-WI. Set the ship's course to...Saint Valley High School. According to this young male, his leader is a man named...Principal Forsman.

> *(Cut to...*
>
> *Projection: Saint Valley High School Auditorium.)*

PRINCIPAL FORSMAN. Hello, students, this is your Principal speaking, I'd like to take this moment during our pep rally to remind you—

STUDENT. That you love cheeseburgers!?!

PRINCIPAL FORSMAN. I heard that, Mister Nick Francone. That's detention for you! Now as I was saying, I would like to remind you that at tonight's homecoming game, we expect you to—

ANOTHER STUDENT. Party like it's 1999!

PRINCIPAL FORSMAN. Jessica Shay! You're in detention as well. We expect you to behave like—

STUDENT BODY. Go, Cats, Go! Go, Cats, Go! Go, Cats, Go!

(The chanting continues...)

PRINCIPAL FORSMAN. Okay, that's good spirit, but I'm talking right now. I mean it. Calm down. Shut up. Shut UP. Shut up shut up shut up! I will put you all in detention, I swear. Every single one of you! SHUT UP!

STUDENT. You suck, Forsman!

PRINCIPAL FORSMAN. I will cancel this game, I will.

ANOTHER STUDENT. That would be really keen of ya.

PRINCIPAL FORSMAN. These children are animals. ANIMALS!

(Cut to...)

LEWIS. You have to say yes!

MOLLY. No, Lewis, I'm not joining those bunch of Barbies.

LEWIS. But it's the Saint Valley High Cheerleading Team!

MOLLY. And when did you get all support-y of our cheerleading team?

LEWIS. I've always appreciated the fine art of...cartwheeling.

MOLLY. Oh really?

LEWIS. Really.

MOLLY. It has nothing to do with the overabundance of young ladies that you'd suddenly have access to because your BFF is a new member of the squad?

LEWIS. No.

MOLLY. Lewis?

LEWIS. No! I don't care about access to...young...athletic...tight bodied ...females.

MOLLY. Right.

LEWIS. I don't.

MOLLY. I saw how you were looking at Tina Carpenter. You were totally crushing.

LEWIS. I was not.

MOLLY. You so were!

LEWIS. I wasn't!

MOLLY. No. Then why not? Are you blind? She's gorgeous, smart, and really really smiley. What's not to like?

LEWIS. Well...

MOLLY. Yeah?

LEWIS. Um...the truth is...I sorta have feelings for someone else.

MOLLY. Yeah? And who's that?

LEWIS. Well...um...it's—

(Suddenly a light appears over MOLLY and LEWIS accompanied with a hovering sound.)

MOLLY. What in the bad-word is that?

LEWIS. RUN!

(As LEWIS and MOLLY try to escape, the room is filled with space-men again. They raise their lasers at MOLLY and LEWIS.)

MOLLY. Yeah. That can't be good.

(And right when we think MOLLY and LEWIS are goners, TINA, MISSY, GABBY, and LUCY appear.)

LUCY. Whaddup, icky space people!

GABBY. Aren't you guys a little short to be Storm Troopers?

MISSY. I think it's time for somebody to phone home.

TINA. Attack formation alpha go!

(The CHEERLEADERS attack. The ALIENS fight them back the best they can, but the girls are too skilled and beat them up. The ALIENS retreat.)

TINA. Are you two okay?

MOLLY. What the heck just happened?

TINA. This is what I was trying to tell you before.

MOLLY. Tell me what before?

TINA. About joining the team.

MOLLY. The cheerleading team?

MISSY. Yo, pigtails, clearly we do more than just cheerlead.

GABBY. Tina, I wasn't able to make a clear ID of any of the invaders' uniforms, but it did look like they were traveling in a discontinued light-wave ship from the Tingarian Region outside Gamma Cassiopeiae.

MOLLY. Was that even English?

LUCY. I really like your hair.

TINA. Gabby, hit the boards and see if there's any info on any rogue ships coming from Tingaria.
Missy, you notice anything specific about them?

MISSY. They're well-armored. I hit them hard and yet they kept running. That's not cheap battle gear they're wearing. They came to do some war.

TINA. That's not good.

MISSY. Nope.

MOLLY. TINA!

TINA. What? Oh, sorry. Yes, Molly?

MOLLY. What are you guys?

TINA. Us? Well that's kind of hard to explain.

GABBY. We're a covert military tactical strike force aimed at defending our planet from extraterrestrial invaders.

TINA. Okay, maybe not that hard.

MISSY. We've been trained in over twenty-seven different forms of martial arts including space kung fu, space karate, and space krumping.

GABBY. Our mission is to seek out and monitor all E.T.s living on or visiting planetside.

MISSY. And to keep them in check by any means necessary.

LUCY. We also bake really great cookies.

TINA. As you see, we have a situation. If more are on their way, we need every fighter we can get. You interested?

> *(Cut to...*
>
> *An awesome 80s rock song begins playing.*
>
> *As it does, we see a montage sequence of* MOLLY *being trained by* TINA *to take out and defeat aliens. We see her workout, fight, train, dance, and attempt to connect with the girls on her squad.*
>
> *At first she's horrible at doing all these things. She's weak, clumsy, and doesn't seem to be able to work well as a partner with the other four girls. However, as the music comes to a crescendo, she begins mastering all the techniques shown to her.*
>
> *By the end of the sequence,* MOLLY *is leading the squad in an elaborate kata/dance sequence. The last image is of her standing amongst the other four girls in an impressive fight pose.)*
>
> *(Cut to...*
>
> *Projection: School Hallways.)*
>
> *(Lights up on* MARISSA, FLINT, YA-WI, G'BRIL, *and* MIKAH *[who are dressed in ridiculous human costumes].)*

YA-WI. Now where can we find this Principal Forsman leader of yours?

MARISSA. I like apples and butterflies!

FLINT. Puppies are soft!

YA-WI. I'm not following.

MARISSA. Beans beans are a magical fruit.

FLINT. The more you eat them, the more you toot.

YA-WI. G'bril? Mikah? Can I talk to you two for a moment?

G'BRIL. What is it, Commander?

YA-WI. What did you do to these two Earthlings?

G'BRIL. What do you mean?

YA-WI. What do I mean?
Hey Earthlings, what planet are you on?

MARISSA. Poop!

FLINT. Pee!

YA-WI. Notice anything weird about them?

G'BRIL. Nope—

MIKAH. Not really—

G'BRIL. Isn't that how all Earthlings act—

MIKAH. That's what I assume—

YA-WI. They're stupid! You turned them stupid.

G'BRIL. It wasn't me! It was Mikah's mental-wave-micro-singularity-transcorresponder.

YA-WI. His what?

MIKAH. My brain-meldy machine.
It short-circuited these two Earthlings.

YA-WI. You short-circuited their brains?

MIKAH. Well, actually, you short-circuited their brains, Commander.
Remember when I told you not to tap your foot during the scan?

YA-WI. Yes.

MIKAH. Do you remember how you tapped your foot anyways?
Well, that reversed the polarity of the wave-flow and, well, fried their brains a little.

YA-WI. So now how are we supposed to find this Principal Forsman? Without their help, it will be virtually impossible to traverse this complex and dangerous terrain known as High School. We will surely never find this leader of theirs by simply just standing here.

(PRINCIPAL FORSMAN *enters.*)

PRINCIPAL FORSMAN. What are all you students doing out of class?

YA-WI. Excuse me. I am not a student of any kind. I am Commander Ya-Wi of the Carnaxion region.

PRINCIPAL FORSMAN. Ya-Wi? Carnaxion? What is that? Some kind of new hip-hop rappy rap slang? Well, I don't get it. I don't care.

YA-WI. And who are you, sir?

PRINCIPAL FORSMAN. Me? Who am I? You students get more and more disrespectful each and every year. I'm your Principal, son. Principal C. Forsman.

YA-WI. You're Principal Forsman?

PRINCIPAL FORSMAN. Yes, and you five are now in detention! How do you like that?

(The aliens all pull out laser guns and point them at PRINCIPAL FORSMAN's *head.)*

PRINCIPAL FORSMAN. Or then again maybe I should rethink our school's truancy policy.

(Cut to...

Projection: Drama Classroom.)

*(*MOLLY *is doing her hair. She wears a bathrobe to hide her clothes as* LEWIS *sits talking to her.)*

LEWIS. So let's see what this uniform looks like on you.

MOLLY. I look stupid.

LEWIS. Who cares?

MOLLY. You promise not to laugh?

LEWIS. No. If you look ridiculous, I won't just laugh, I might even guffaw. Chuckle. Chortle. Shoot milk through my nose.

MOLLY. Jerk.

LEWIS. So let's see.

*(*MOLLY *removes her robe, revealing her new uniform.)*

MOLLY. Ta-da!
So what do you think?

LEWIS. ...

MOLLY. Lewis?

LEWIS. It's...um...okay, I guess.

MOLLY. I look dumb, don't I? It's dumb.

LEWIS. No. It's certainly not dumb.

MOLLY. So do you like it?

LEWIS. I certainly—
Wow, is it getting hot in here?

*(*LEWIS *and* MOLLY *catch eyes.)*

LEWIS. Uh, what is it?

MOLLY. Can I do something?

LEWIS. What?

*(*MOLLY *removes* LEWIS's *glasses, tussles his hair, and generally "de-nerds" him. As it turns out, he's quite hunky.)*

MOLLY. Wow. Um. Nice eyes. They're...um...nice.

*(*MOLLY *and* LEWIS *begin to "lean." Suddenly* TINA *and her squad run in.)*

MISSY. Not so fast there, Romeo.

GABBY. We're on a code red.

MOLLY. What?

TINA. The school's been infiltrated.

LUCY. Yucky aliens are everywhere.

MISSY. It's time to put our butt-kicking shoes on.

MOLLY. What? Where?

TINA. School's auditorium. They have the entire school and faculty locked up in there.

MOLLY. Um, I don't think I'm ready for this, guys.

MISSY. Don't be a crybaby.

MOLLY. Seriously, I just joined the team. I can't just go out and fight.

TINA. Molly, the school needs our help.

MOLLY. That doesn't mean I'm ready. I'm not actually a cheerleader.

TINA. Molly, destiny doesn't care if you're ready or not. When destiny calls, it calls. Are you with us?

MOLLY. I'm...I'm sorry.

(MOLLY *runs off.* LEWIS *runs after her.*)

TINA. Well, that's unfortunate. However, we still have aliens to stop. Let's go, team.

(Cut to...

Projection: Auditorium.)

(YA-WI *addressing the student body with* G'BRIL, MIKAH, PRINCIPAL FORSMAN, MARISSA *and* FLINT *standing behind.*)

YA-WI. Ahem...
BING BONG. BING BONGY BONG. BING BING BONG BONG! KERBLAM!!!

G'BRIL. Um, sir, your translator is set to...

YA-WI. Marcopian?

G'BRIL. Yes, sir. Marcopian.

(YA-WI *adjusts his translator.*)

YA-WI. I HATE THIS THING!
Now where was I?
Human Earthling creatures of Earth, I am Commander Ya-Wi. We will all be getting to know each other very well very soon. But first, your leader, Principal Forsman, has very important news to relate to you all.

PRINCIPAL FORSMAN. Hello Saint Valley High School students, thank you for assembling today. I would like to take this opportunity to tell you that—

STUDENT. You wear women's underwear!

PRINCIPAL FORSMAN. Nick Francone! This is important news. Please be quiet.

STUDENT. Please stop wearing women's underwear!

PRINCIPAL FORSMAN. Okay, mister, you have detention for the rest of the year!
Now, as I was saying, I would like to inform you all that—

ANOTHER STUDENT. Your ice cream brings all the boys to the yard!

PRINCIPAL FORSMAN. Jessica Shay, I'm trying to relay important information here.

DIFFERENT STUDENT. Like how much you suck, Forsman?

PRINCIPAL FORSMAN. Please focus.

ALL THE STUDENTS. FORSMAN SUCKS. FORSMAN SUCKS. FORSMAN SUCKS.

(The chanting continues.)

PRINCIPAL FORSMAN. Students? Students, calm down. Students!
FINE! YOU KNOW WHAT? I'm glad these aliens are taking over the school.
You see these three here? They're aliens. And they're here to enslave you. And you know what? I'm glad they are. They can have you! I quit!

YA-WI. Um, thank you? So as your leader Principal Forsman was saying —human Earthling creatures of Earth, you are now hereby under the new rule of—

(LUCY and GABBY enter.)

LUCY. *(Stereotypical cheerleader:)* Oh my God, are we like late? Gabby, I told you you were taking way too long putting on your make-up, now we've missed the entire thing!

GABBY. Shut up. I just wanted to try my new blush.

LUCY. Is the pep rally over already? We didn't even get to do our new cheer.

YA-WI. Um, human Earthling female creatures of Earth, I was in the middle of my speech.

LUCY. Wow, this new mascot looks weird.

GABBY. He doesn't look like a cat at all.

YA-WI. I'm not a cat.

LUCY. Yes, you are. Cause we're all Saint Valley High School Wildcats!

GABBY. Hooray!

(As YA-WI's distracted, TINA and MISSY covertly take out MIKAH and G'BRIL.)

YA-WI. No, I'm an alien.

LUCY. No, we're not aliens, silly! We're Wildcats. Roar!

YA-WI. I'm not a cat.

LUCY. Say it. Say "roar."

YA-WI. No. What kind of planet is this? Can you people not realize you're being taken over. I'm taking you over. Seriously, this planet seems to be populated with nothing but...G'bril? Mikah? Where are you?

(TINA and MISSY dump a tied-up MIKAH and G'BRIL onto the stage.)

MISSY. You're messing with the wrong planet, alien scum.

TINA. No one enslaves Earth.

YA-WI. Is that right?

TINA. That's right.

YA-WI. You know what? You're right. You're absolutely correct.

TINA. We are?

MISSY. Well, that was rather anti-climatic.

YA-WI. I've toyed around long enough. I am Ya-Wi, second son of the Carnaxian tribe of Egress. I have taken over dozens of planets and am known throughout the galaxies as the single most dangerous tyrant ever to sail the black-tides of space. When creatures see me, they cower.

TINA. Cute speech. Now get off our—

YA-WI. No. Let me repeat that. When creatures see me. They. Cower.

(Suddenly, lights and sound, YA-WI transforms into an evil-looking beast. This transformation should be theatrically awesome.)

MISSY. What in the bad-word did he just do?

YA-WI. *(Beast-like:)* Ya-Wi's hungry. Time to eat some Earthlings. Roar.

TINA. Come on, Team. Let's rock!

(TINA, GABBY, MISSY, and LUCY jump into fighting formation. As a team, they attack YA-WI. And like a well-oiled machine, they land strike after strike on him. However, in his new form, YA-WI isn't phased by the girls' attacks at all. He then suddenly unleashes a furious attack of this own which takes them each out.)

(He looks over the fallen girls.)

YA-WI. Now. Which one of you shall I consume first?

(YA-WI begins marching towards the fallen girls, but then MOLLY flies in with an impressive strike of her own. It jolts YA-WI back for a moment.)

MOLLY. Hey guys, sorry I'm late! How are you holding up?

GABBY. Blue screen of death.

LUCY. I don't want to go to school, Mom! Go away!

MISSY. I like rainbows.

MOLLY. Okay, I guess I'm gonna have to finish this solo.

TINA. What are you doing? You can't stop him alone.

(LEWIS enters.)

LEWIS. She's not alone.

(YA-WI stalks over and stares at MOLLY.)

MOLLY. I'm not afraid of you.

(YA-WI signals. G'BRIL and MIKAH break their binds and join YA-WI. They too have now turned very scary looking.)

MOLLY. Okay. Maybe I take that back a little.

YA-WI. Roar!

(YA-WI, G'BRIL, and MIKAH attack. MOLLY and LEWIS go at it martial arts style against the three alien beasts using Kung Fu and Capoiera. It's intense. It's awesome. In the end, MOLLY and LEWIS win.)

(G'BRIL and MIKAH begin exiting.)

YA-WI. Whoa, where are you two going? We're not done yet!

MIKAH. We can't beat them, sir.

G'BRIL. Their Kung Fu is too tight.

YA-WI. No, no. This can't be happening. No!

MOLLY. Get off our planet. NOW.

YA-WI. This is not the last you'll see of me, Cheerleaders. Mark my words. You will pay. You. Will. Pay.

MIKAH. No, they won't—

G'BRIL. We're not coming back here—

MIKAH. No way.

YA-WI. You guys suck.

(YA-WI leaves with the other two aliens.)

LEWIS. Wait, is it over?

MOLLY. I think it is.

SQUAD. YAY!

(The girls start celebrating.)

LEWIS. Wait!
There's just one more thing.

MOLLY. What's that?

(LEWIS grabs MOLLY and kisses her.)

MOLLY. Wow.

LUCY. So now what do we do, guys?

TINA. Well, I don't know about you guys, but I'm ready for a curtain call.

MOLLY. Let's do this!

(Music hits. The whole cast comes onto stage dancing. They bust out some fun dance moves for each of their individual bows. The crowd claps and cheers. The cast bows. Lights down.)

End of Play

THE BROTHERS GRIMM SPECTACULATHON

by Don Zolidis

For more information about rights and permissions, see page 9.

Cast of Characters

NARRATOR 1 *(female)*

NARRATOR 2 *(male)*

ACTOR

GIRL

DIRT MERCHANT

RUMPELSTILTSKIN

ENCHANTRESS

THE DEVIL

PRINCE 1

RAPUNZEL

HANSEL

GRETEL

WITCH

DWARF 1

DWARF 2

SNOW WHITE

WITCH 2

PRINCE 2

THE DEVIL 2

THE DEVIL'S GRANDMOTHER

DOCTOR

GOD *(off-stage voice)*

CINDERELLA

Casting Note

Princes, Witches, and Devils may be played by different actors if the director wishes. They may also be played by the same actor should that be the preference.

Production Notes

Feel free to cut this play as needed to fit into time constraints. The easiest way is to simply eliminate one of the fairy tales and have the narrators connect the story around the hole in the narrative. Ad libbing is encouraged to make the story flow properly.

This play is designed to be as flexible and as quick as possible. There should be no scene changes and any set pieces on the stage need to be brought on by the actors.

Ideally, this play would be performed with five actors, two of which would be the narrators who become many other characters throughout the play. Gender switching is encouraged, and costume changes may take place in full view of the audience. It's up to your group, however, if you wish to have a different actor play all of the 20 roles, then that would be acceptable as well. Any number between 5 and 20 performers will work.

A full-length version of this play also exists. For more information, please visit www.playscripts.com.

THE BROTHERS GRIMM SPECTACULATHON

(A largely bare stage. NARRATOR 1, *a rather proper narrator, enters.)*

NARRATOR 1. *(To the audience:)* Hello and welcome to the Brothers Grimm Spectaculathon!

*(*NARRATOR 2 *explodes on to the stage.)*

NARRATOR 2. *(To the audience:)* Sunday Sunday Sunday! It's EXTREME! See! Monster slaying action as the three-headed pig battles the wolf-o-bot in a bone-crushing cage match of death. They'll huff and they'll puff and they'll kick some iron! Aaaaaaahh!

(Pause. NARRATOR 1 *looks at* NARRATOR 2.*)*

NARRATOR 1. What we are going to do here today—

NARRATOR 2. *(Interrupting:)* And then the battle you've all been waiting for: Snow White vs. Sleeping Beauty in a mud-wrestling death match. Who's the toughest of them all? With dwarf-tossing afterwards.

NARRATOR 1. *(To* NARRATOR 2:*)* Can you stop?

NARRATOR 2. *(To the audience:)* What happens when the princesses stop being kind and start being real? And covered in mud? And choking each other and one of them gets the other in a crab hold and—

NARRATOR 1. Okay, stop. We're not doing that.

NARRATOR 2. Flames! Flames!

NARRATOR 1. Enough, [actor's name]. You're weirding them out.

NARRATOR 2. I'm EXTREME.

NARRATOR 1. No you're not. Can we just do the show?

NARRATOR 2. Fine, but I want you to know something: you are no longer considered extreme in my book. Okay? No longer extreme.

NARRATOR 1. This is the Brothers Grimm Spectaculathon!

NARRATOR 2. That's right. And what we are about to do today is going to blow your mind. We are about to attempt something so spectacular you will never be the same.

NARRATOR 1. If you need to go to the bathroom, go now and we'll wait. We don't want accidents.

*(*NARRATOR 2 *points to someone in the audience.)*

NARRATOR 2. You look a little touch-and-go miss. Are you sure? You okay? All right then. *(To* NARRATOR 1:*)* Keep an eye on that one.

NARRATOR 1. A little background to begin.

NARRATOR 2. The Brothers Grimm were brothers named Grimm. They are dead. But in the period before they died the Brothers Grimm wrote 209 fairy tales that we know today—

NARRATOR 1. They didn't write them—

NARRATOR 2. The Brothers Grimm did not write 209 fairy tales that we know today, they were frauds. We should dig up their bodies and spit on their corpses.

NARRATOR 1. No I'm just saying that they were collectors of stories.

NARRATOR 2. Never mind that last part.

NARRATOR 1. And these stories have become extremely popular: We all know them today:

NARRATOR 2. Such stories as The Wolf and the Seven Young Kids—

NARRATOR 1. The Pack of Ragamuffins—

NARRATOR 2. And Straw, Coal, and Bean.

NARRATOR 1. I forgot about that one.

NARRATOR 2. Oh yeah. Straw, Coal, and Bean? Only the best fairy tale in the entire history of the world. I'm literally like crying buckets by the end of it. Freaking amazing. Changed my life. I can't even look at straw, coal, or beans any more.

NARRATOR 1. What's it about?

NARRATOR 2. No idea.

NARRATOR 1. Those might not be household names, but quite a few of these stories have become immortalized in film and television—

NARRATOR 2. Of course they've all been changed by "the mouse." *(Points to a sign that says DISNEY.)* To feed their enormous octopus-like animation empire which sucks the life out of existence and crushes your soul in a death-grip of happy happy songs and talking objects. I can't even speak their name aloud because they're looking for a way to sue me right now. *(Up to the sky:)* You won't win. My uncle is a lawyer! He defended OJ. That means I can kill anyone I want and no one can get me.

(NARRATOR 1 looks at NARRATOR 2.)

NARRATOR 1. O-kay. What we are going to do for you right now is return these fairy tales to their original glory. We have assembled the greatest troupe of actors the world has ever seen and we—

(ACTOR emerges, halfway in costume, scratching himself.)

ACTOR. I thought there was supposed to be catering back here?

NARRATOR 2. There's like a beef thing somewhere.

ACTOR. Where?

NARRATOR 2. I don't know—in the back somewhere.

ACTOR. Is there anything to drink?

NARRATOR 2. No.

(ACTOR exits, annoyed.)

NARRATOR 1. These actors are so insanely talented that—

ACTOR. *(Off-stage:)* I don't see it!

NARRATOR 2. Do you see the radiator?

ACTOR. *(Off-stage:)* No! Oh wait! No.

NARRATOR 2. There's probably someone sitting on it. Move them.

ACTOR. *(Off-stage:)* Oh here it is.

ANOTHER ACTOR. *(Off-stage:)* Hey!

NARRATOR 1. Anyway, in just the short time we have, our crack team of actors is going to perform all 209 fairy tales of the Brothers Grimm.

NARRATOR 2. That's like three stories per minute.

NARRATOR 1. Or a different number if you actually know math. And we're going to keep the original endings intact.

NARRATOR 2. Blood! Violence! Death! People being cut open with scissors!

NARRATOR 1. And to make things more difficult! We are going to perform them as originally intended, which is...

NARRATOR 2. That it's all one enormous mega superstory. That will rock your world.

NARRATOR 1. Are you ready?

NARRATOR 2. I'm so excited I'm going to throw up. Does anyone have a hat? Nope? Excuse me then.

(NARRATOR 2 *exits.* NARRATOR 1 *stretches and does warmups. Perhaps a few wind sprints.)*

NARRATOR 1. Well I don't know when he's coming back. So... Once upon a time there was a girl who was raised by wolves whose mother died in childbirth and she was abandoned by her father who could spin straw into gold and made a deal with a series of elves if they would help him make shoes. There was also a talking fox in there somewhere.

(NARRATOR 2 *returns.)*

NARRATOR 2. And she was beautiful—

NARRATOR 1. Because no one cares about ugly people.

NARRATOR 2. I care about ugly people.

NARRATOR 1. Well no one cares about you. Anyway, there was a girl.

(GIRL *enters in dramatic fashion.)*

NARRATOR 2. And she was poor.

GIRL. Oh I am poor.

NARRATOR 2. Dirt poor.

NARRATOR 1. She couldn't even afford dirt.

(DIRT MERCHANT *enters.)*

DIRT MERCHANT. Dirt for sale! Dirt for sale! Hey, you! Get off the merchandise!

(He exits.)

GIRL. *(Crying:)* I shall flood the ground with my tears!

(The DIRT MERCHANT *returns.)*

DIRT MERCHANT. You're getting it wet! Stop it!

(He exits.)

GIRL. If only I knew where my father was who could spin straw into gold and talk to wolves and make deals with the elves and who was also acquainted with a talking fox.

(An ENCHANTRESS *[played by* NARRATOR 1*] enters.)*

ENCHANTRESS. Excuse me—but I couldn't help overhearing your tale of misery and woe. Tell you what—I will grant you your heart's desire if you give me one small thing.

GIRL. That sounds like a great bargain. I won't even ask what the small thing is because I'm so innocent and trusting!

ENCHANTRESS. Excellent. *(She makes a magical signal:)* I vanish.

(She does not actually appear to vanish. ENCHANTRESS *looks around and covers* GIRL's *eyes.)*

ENCHANTRESS. I vanish again.

(She quickly hides behind something.)

GIRL. What a nice lady.

*(*THE DEVIL 1 *[played by* NARRATOR 2*] enters.)*

THE DEVIL 1. Hey there hot stuff. Oh wait, that's me. Ha ha ha ha!

GIRL. Are you a prince?

THE DEVIL 1. Of darkness.

(He laughs at his own joke.)

THE DEVIL 1. Oh that's a good one! I've got to tell that to the demons back home. Now, I happened to overhear your tale of misery and woe and I'm here to help.

GIRL. Well actually I just—

THE DEVIL 1. Just sign this one small contract and you shall conceive a daughter so beautiful the very earth will want to kiss her. But in a platonic way. Nothing kinky.

GIRL. That sounds like a great idea.

(She signs the contract.)

THE DEVIL 1. Moo ah ha ha ha ha ha!

(He looks around. Then runs off.)

GIRL. This is a busy street.

*(*RUMPELSTILTSKIN *enters, limping.)*

RUMPELSTILTSKIN. Hello there.

GIRL. You're hideous and deformed!

RUMPELSTILTSKIN. Look, I have a great bargain for you—

GIRL. My stomach recoils in horror as you approach!

RUMPELSTILTSKIN. Yes I know that but—

GIRL. Why has God's creation been so perverted?

RUMPELSTILTSKIN. Do you want to hear my offer or not?

GIRL. Sure. Go ahead. You're probably trustworthy and I'm stupid and don't judge people by their appearances.

RUMPELSTILTSKIN. I shall make you rich, rich, I tell you! Beyond your wildest dreams!

GIRL. Can I have my own jet fighter? With Tom Cruise in it? When he was 23 and not into the strange stuff.?

RUMPELSTILTSKIN. He was still into that stuff, he just wasn't advertising it. Anyway, I will make you very rich, not so rich that you can afford the jet fighter, but rich enough. And I ask only one small thing in return.

GIRL. Sounds good.

RUMPELSTILTSKIN. Don't you want to know what the thing is?

GIRL. No, I trust you.

RUMPELSTILTSKIN. Very well.

(NARRATOR 1 *emerges.*)

NARRATOR 1. It was a good day for the girl. She fell in love with a prince.

(PRINCE 1 *[played by* NARRATOR 2*] enters.*)

PRINCE 1. Hey, you're hot!

GIRL. I am hot.

PRINCE 1. Let's get married!

GIRL. Score!

NARRATOR 2. She grew very rich.

PRINCE 1. Hey look I just tripped over a giant pot of gold! What are the odds!

GIRL. Ha ha! Score!

NARRATOR 2. And she conceived a child.

GIRL. Whoah! How did that happen?

NARRATOR 2. Well you see kids, when a prince and a princess love each other very much—

NARRATOR 1. Through magic. The magic of the devil. And that's where babies come from.

(Goes back to being PRINCE 1.)

GIRL. Ah! The baby's coming!

PRINCE 1. Push! Push! Breathe!

GIRL. *(Screaming in rage:)* I'm breathing! How on earth would I not be breathing! I'd be dead if I wasn't breathing! You need to think before you speak!

NARRATOR 2. The miracle of childbirth.

PRINCE 1. You can do it, honey!

GIRL. *(Continuous:)* I hate you I hate you I hate you I hate you I hate you!

PRINCE 1. *(Continuous:)* Focus your anger! Focus your anger!

(GIRL screams. Nothing happens. She screams again.)

PRINCE 1. I can see her little head!

(GIRL screams again. A baby doll is thrown in from off stage. PRINCE 1 snatches it out of the air like a Frisbee.)

PRINCE 1. Oh it's so beautiful!

NARRATOR 2. Years passed.

(PRINCE 1 throws the baby off-stage like a Frisbee.)

NARRATOR 2. And she grew into a beautiful young teenager, Rapunzel.

PRINCE 1. Seriously? We're going with Rapunzel? I liked Amber.

GIRL. That was the name of your ex-girlfriend!

PRINCE 1. We were just friends!

GIRL. Then why do you save her letters!?

(RAPUNZEL enters with a huge mop of hair on her head.)

PRINCE 1. Are you going to wear your hair like that?

RAPUNZEL. Shut up.

GIRL. Darling, we're going to have dinner so wash your hands.

RAPUNZEL. You can't tell me what to do!

PRINCE 1. Don't talk to your mother that way. She sold her soul to the Devil just to have you—

RAPUNZEL. I don't care! I didn't ask to be born! I'm going out.

GIRL. You are not walking out of this house, young lady!

RAPUNZEL. I do what I want! You don't know me.

GIRL. I'm your mother!

RAPUNZEL. So! I'm gonna go hang with the Frog Prince—

PRINCE 1. He's just using you to get some action!

GIRL. You're going to get warts!

RAPUNZEL. He loves me! I don't care if he's green and slimy—

PRINCE 1. I'm not going to listen to this! I'm going to play golf instead!

(PRINCE 1 leaves.)

RAPUNZEL. We're gonna run away together and have tadpoles and—

NARRATOR 1. And just then.

>(NARRATOR 1 *switches into the* ENCHANTRESS.)

ENCHANTRESS. I have returned.

>(NARRATOR 2 *switches into* THE DEVIL 1 *and enters.*)

THE DEVIL 1. Your time is up.

>(RUMPELSTILTSKIN *enters.*)

RUMPELSTILTSKIN. You know I was just passing through the neighborhood and I was thinking that I forgot something like eighteen years ago, and then I was like, oh yeah, I was supposed to get that thing from that girl. And then here I was, right at your house. I mean, that's pretty cool, huh?

GIRL. Fine. What do you want?

THE DEVIL 1/ENCHANTRESS/RUMPELSTILTSKIN. Your child.

>(They all point, then stop to look at each other. Then all begin to argue at once.)

ENCHANTRESS. (Overlapping:) Um—my deal was first—

THE DEVIL 1. (Overlapping:) I'm the devil, no one gets to—

RUMPELSTILTSKIN. (Overlapping:) Well there wouldn't even be a child if I wasn't there providing mood music on the night that—

RAPUNZEL. STOP!! Mom?

GIRL. What?

RAPUNZEL. How many deals did you make?

GIRL. Just three. And I may have promised your hand in marriage to a talking rabbit, but it was dark and—what? I was young! I needed the money! And the baby! And the prince! But really just the money and the baby.

RAPUNZEL. I can't believe you! I hate you! I am so outta here! Why do you think I'm in counseling, huh? You've so ruined my entire life!

GIRL. Oh come on, stop being so melodramatic—so you go with the Devil—

THE DEVIL 1. Thank you. Told ya I had the prior claim.

GIRL. Or the other witch woman or the freaky ugly dwarf guy—

RUMPELSTILTSKIN. If you can guess my name I will release you from—

THE DEVIL 1. It's Rumpelstiltskin.

GIRL. Rumpelstiltskin?

RUMPELSTILTSKIN. Ah! Dang it!

>(NARRATOR 1 *steps forward for a moment.*)

NARRATOR 1. And the little man stomped his feet so hard they broke through the floor, and when he tried to pull them out, he broke in half. *(To* RUMPELSTILTSKIN:*)* Do it.

RUMPELSTILTSKIN. Aaggg!

(RUMPELSTILTSKIN breaks himself in half. NARRATOR 1 jumps back into being the ENCHANTRESS.)

RAPUNZEL. I'm not cleaning that up.

ENCHANTRESS. Now that that horrid little man is gone, I will take Rapunzel.

(She grabs RAPUNZEL.)

THE DEVIL 1. Um...excuse me? I'm the Devil.

(He grabs RAPUNZEL.)

ENCHANTRESS. So?

THE DEVIL 1. Lord of darkness? All that? I think I've got a little bit more claim to this girl than some stupid little witch.

ENCHANTRESS. Enchantress.

THE DEVIL 1. Whatever. Witch.

(They let go of RAPUNZEL and start circling each other.)

RAPUNZEL. Now's the time, Mom! Let's run!

GIRL. Quiet, honey, I'm watching this. Go Devil!

RAPUNZEL. Mom!

GIRL. I just like him better.

ENCHANTRESS. I curse you!

THE DEVIL 1. I curse you right back! You know what, this is stupid. Tell ya what, if you sign this contract here, I will let you take Rapunzel.

ENCHANTRESS. That sounds like a plan.

(She signs the contract.)

THE DEVIL 1. Moo ah ha ha ha! And I disappear in a cloud of brimstone!

(He runs off the stage making cloudy symbols with his hands and returns momentarily as NARRATOR 2.)

ENCHANTRESS. Well, come along Rapunzel.

RAPUNZEL. Where are we going?

ENCHANTRESS. I built this great tower for you.

GIRL. Run along dear.

RAPUNZEL. But Mom. I don't want to go with the evil Enchantress.

GIRL. Yeah and I didn't want to raise a spoiled brat. But sometimes you don't always get what you want. Unless you make a deal with the Devil and some other weird people. See ya.

NARRATOR 2. So the Enchantress took Rapunzel and locked her in a high tower without stairs or door. As for the girl and her prince—

(PRINCE 1 returns.)

PRINCE 1. I'm back from my golf trip. What did I miss?

GIRL. The forces of darkness battled it out for our daughter's soul.

PRINCE 1. Cool. You want to go to Hawaii?

GIRL. Rock on.

(They exit.)

NARRATOR 2. And the girl lived happily ever after. Rapunzel, meanwhile, grew really long hair cause she was a hippie and lived in a tower and didn't bathe cause she was a hippie and eventually found her own prince.

NARRATOR 1. But...our story is not even remotely finished.

NARRATOR 2. No wait, it is finished. It's not yet begun. We need to find out where Rapunzel's mother came from.

NARRATOR 1. She wasn't always known as Rapunzel's mother. When she was younger she was known as

(GRETEL enters. NARRATOR 2 becomes HANSEL.)

HANSEL. Gretel! What are you doing out?!

GRETEL. Nothing.

HANSEL. You seem moody lately. As if something were bothering you.

GRETEL. It's...our mother. And peer pressure. You see, our mother died before we were born.

HANSEL. I remember.

NARRATOR 1. Our next story: Hansel. And. Gretel. Or: After-School Special meets Horror Movie.

GRETEL. I'm haunted Hansel. Haunted by her memory.

HANSEL. I too am haunted. Perhaps we ought to go into the woods where it's dark and scary.

NARRATOR 1. Can we get some cool lighting effects please?

(A cool lighting effect happens. NARRATOR 1 addresses part of the audience.)

NARRATOR 1. Okay. Now you people over here. Awake? Good. Here's what we're going to do. When I point to you I want you to make a scary horror movie music sound like this. *(Imitating the sound of a well-known horror movie:)* Ch-ch-ch-ch-ch. A-a-a-a-a-a. Ch-ch-ch-ch-ch. A-a-a-a-a-a. Can we try that?

(The audience tries it. NARRATOR 1 ad libs a reaction such as "you suck" "what horror movies have you been watching?" "This guy isn't scary" etc. He may make them try again as needed before moving to another section of the audience.)

NARRATOR 1. Now, you guys. You look a little smarter than those people over there. I'm sorry, it's true. Look at this guy over here. He's a freaking genius. Right? He's a freaking genius. Now—when I point to you, I want you to say, "Don't go in there!" Okay, let's try that. One. Two. Three.

(The audience says, "Don't go in there!" NARRATOR 1 ad libs reaction before moving to a third section.)

NARRATOR 1. Now you guys. No good horror movie is complete without heavy breathing. Like this:

(He does heavy breathing.)

NARRATOR 1. You try it. *(Points to a couple in the audience:)* Um...you need to take it outside, okay? This is a family show. *(He moves to a last group of the audience:)* And finally. Since this is an after-school special. I want you to repeat after me: Peerpressure. Peerpressure. Peerpressure. Can you handle that? You're all a bunch of freaking geniuses. Okay? Say the words. *(He addresses the entire audience:)* All right? Everybody got it?! One last test.

(He points at each group in turn very quickly.)

NARRATOR 1. And back with our story.

GRETEL. Hansel, I'm worried about you.

HANSEL. Why?

GRETEL. I saw you smoking behind the school the other day. Why do you do that?

(NARRATOR 1 points to the audience.)

AUDIENCE. Peerpressure. Peerpressure. Peerpressure. Peerpressure.

(NARRATOR 1 stops them.)

HANSEL. Don't tell me what to do, Gretel. Smoking is cool. It makes me feel like a man. A cool man with dark, sultry lungs and a deep, masculine cough. Let's go out in the woods.

GRETEL. I don't know if I want to.

(NARRATOR 1 points at the audience again.)

AUDIENCE. Peerpressure. Peerpressure. Peerpressure. Peerpressure.

(NARRATOR 1 cuts them off.)

GRETEL. Okay.

HANSEL. Smoke?

(NARRATOR 1 points again.)

AUDIENCE. Peerpressure. Peerpressure.

(He cuts them off much faster this time.)

GRETEL. Okay.

HANSEL. So here we are in the woods.

(NARRATOR 1 points to the first audience section.)

AUDIENCE. Ch-ch-ch-ch-ch. A-a-a-a-a. Ch-ch-ch-ch-ch. A-a-a-a-a.

(NARRATOR 1 stops them.)

GRETEL. Something's not right here.

HANSEL. You're just a chicken.

GRETEL. I feel so strange, Hansel. What's that?!

HANSEL. Nothing.

> (NARRATOR 1 *points to the audience again.*)

AUDIENCE. Ch-ch-ch-ch-ch. A-a-a-a-a-a. Ch-ch-ch-ch-ch. A-a-a-a-a-a.

> (*He stops them.*)

GRETEL. It's a house.

HANSEL. It's made out of candy.

GRETEL. What should we do?

> (GRETEL *approaches the door.*)
>
> (NARRATOR 1 *points.*)

AUDIENCE. DON'T GO IN THERE!

HANSEL. Do you think I should try the door? If only I had some kind of clue about what to do.

AUDIENCE. DON'T GO IN THERE!

HANSEL. Huh. Let's go in there.

> (HANSEL *opens the door.* GRETEL *follows.*)

GRETEL. It's dark in here.

> (NARRATOR 1 *points.*)

AUDIENCE. Ch-ch-ch-ch-ch. A-a-a-a-a-a. Ch-ch-ch-ch-ch. A-a-a-a-a-a.

> (NARRATOR 1 *points to other group.*)

AUDIENCE. (*Heavy breathing.*)

> (NARRATOR 1 *keeps both groups going at the same time, then stops them suddenly.*)

GRETEL. Is that your hand?

> (NARRATOR 1 *points.*)

AUDIENCE. (*Heavy breathing.*)

HANSEL. Is that...your hand?

> (NARRATOR 1 *points.*)

AUDIENCE. (*Heavy breathing.*)

> (NARRATOR 1 *points at three groups at once.*)

AUDIENCE. Ch-ch-ch-ch-ch. A-a-a-a-a-a. Ch-ch-ch-ch-ch. A-a-a-a-a-a.

AUDIENCE. (*Heavy breathing.*)

AUDIENCE. Peerpressure. Peerpressure. Peerpressure.

NARRATOR 1. (*To the peer pressure group:*) Oh wait. Not you.

> (WITCH 1 *enters.*)

HANSEL/GRETEL. Aaaaaaah!

> (NARRATOR 1 *stops all noise from the audience.*)

WITCH 1. Are you eating my house?

HANSEL. No!

(HANSEL *puts something behind his back.* GRETEL *looks at him.*)

GRETEL. Were you eating the house?

HANSEL. What? I'm hungry. You should try the floorboards, they're really tasty.

WITCH 1. I'm so disappointed in today's young people. I'm going to have to teach you a lesson. By eating you.

GRETEL. Eating us?

WITCH 1. But not right now. I'm going to fatten you up first.

(*She exits.*)

NARRATOR 1. So Hansel and Gretel were locked away and force-fed sugar water like mice and they got fatter. And fatter. And then they dieted a little bit. But then they got fatter again. Until one day—

(WITCH 1 *returns.*)

HANSEL. Why does my cologne smell like gravy?

WITCH 1. Well my pretties, except you, the boy, you have more of a rugged masculinity about you.

HANSEL. Thanks.

WITCH 1. Well, I need some help cleaning out my oven. I'll take volunteers.

(*Pause.*)

WITCH 1. Anyone?

HANSEL. Ooh. Me.

WITCH. Excellent. Come along, Hamsel.

HANSEL. It's Hansel.

WITCH 1. Oh. Right. Hansel.

(*She laughs evilly.*)

WITCH 1. Can you put this apple in your mouth please?

HANSEL. No problem.

(*She puts an apple in* HANSEL's *mouth as she leads him to the "oven."*)

WITCH 1. Now if you'll just crawl in here.

(NARRATOR 1 *points to the audience.*)

AUDIENCE. DON'T GO IN THERE!

(GRETEL *escapes from her cage.*)

GRETEL. Oh. Hey. I dropped a quarter. Can you pick it up?

WITCH 1. A quarter?

(*She bends down.*)

GRETEL. Eat this, witch!

(GRETEL *shoves* WITCH 1 *into the "oven."*)

WITCH 1. Aaaaaaaah! I'm melting! Oh wait... I'm burning!

HANSEL. Well I'm glad that's over with. Let's eat her house!

NARRATOR 1. So they made it. But the horror wasn't over.

(Points to part of the audience.)

AUDIENCE. Ch-ch-ch-ch-ch. A-a-a-a-a-a. Ch-ch-ch-ch-ch. A-a-a-a-a-a.

HANSEL. Hey Gretel. I was talking to some bad kids down by the park behind the school.

GRETEL. I don't like those bad kids.

HANSEL. And they were telling me that drugs are cool.

GRETEL. Drugs aren't cool!

HANSEL. Come on, Gretel. All the cool kids are doing it.

(NARRATOR 1 points to part of the audience.)

AUDIENCE. Peerpressure. Peerpressure. Peerpressure. Peerpressure.

GRETEL. I don't know, Hansel.

HANSEL. It's fairy dust. Everyone's doing it. It lets you fly.

GRETEL. I don't want to fly!

(NARRATOR 1 points to part of the audience.)

AUDIENCE. Peerpressure. Peerpressure. Peerpressure. Peerpressure.

GRETEL. No!

HANSEL. Fine. I'll do it myself then.

(He runs to the front of the stage.)

NARRATOR 1. And he jumped off a cliff.

HANSEL. I can fly! Maybe.

NARRATOR 1. It's up to you, audience. If you clap hard enough, Hansel will live. Come on people!

HANSEL. *(Imploring the audience:)* Come on people! Let me live!

NARRATOR 1. Come on! Don't you believe a boy can fly!?! Come on!

(A glowing light appears on HANSEL. It gets brighter as the audience claps.)

HANSEL. *(Desperate:)* Come on out there! Please!

(Audience applause and glowing light crescendo. Then the light suddenly goes out.)

HANSEL. Aaaaaaaah.

(HANSEL makes a "splat!" sound.)

(Pause. NARRATOR 1 looks sad.)

NARRATOR 1. You didn't clap hard enough. He died. You know I've...done this show a lot. And every time the audience clapped hard enough to let

Hansel live. Every time. I just don't know what to say. *(NARRATOR 1 picks someone in the audience:)* I think really it comes down to this guy. This guy right here. He didn't clap hard enough. His heart wasn't really into it. How do you face your children, sir? How do you face your children? *(If the audience member is about to respond:)* Don't talk to me.

GRETEL. Hansel?

NARRATOR 1. I'm sorry Gretel.

GRETEL. Oh no. Fairy dust has claimed another young life. Like candles being blown out before their time. *(She sings, falteringly:)* All we are is dust in the wind.

> *(She exits.)*

NARRATOR 1. *(Suddenly chipper again:)* Anyway, after Hansel's untimely death, thank you very much Mr. *(Describes person in the audience.).* She married a wandering woodcutter. And they had a daughter. Who would grow up to make a deal with several supernatural entities who would eventually imprison her daughter in the tower.

> *(NARRATOR 2 returns.)*

NARRATOR 2. But.

NARRATOR 1. There's always a but.

NARRATOR 2. One question remains:

NARRATOR 1. Where did the witch come from?

NARRATOR 2. Funny you should ask. Once upon a time. There was a dwarf.

> *(DWARF 1 enters.)*

DWARF 1. I prefer little person.

NARRATOR 1. In fact, two dwarves.

> *(DWARF 2 [played by NARRATOR 2] enters.)*

DWARF 2. I prefer dwarf.

NARRATOR 1. And these dwarves worked all day in the mines.

DWARF 1. *(Singing:)* I've been workin' on the railroad—

NARRATOR 1. Mines!

DWARF 2. *(Singing:)* Whistle while you work—

NARRATOR 1. We can't use that song.

DWARF 2. I do what I want.

NARRATOR 1. No it's like copyrighted, we can't use it. The Mouse will sue us. So the dwarves worked in the mines, they sang their little song, and then one day they came home to find—

> *(Enter SNOW WHITE. She falls asleep.)*

DWARF 1. What the heck is that thing?

DWARF 2. She's huge! Get her away from me! She's going to eat me!

(DWARF 2 runs.)

NARRATOR 1. You see, in those days, most people were cannibals. Which explains the witch from before. The first dwarf, though, who we will name Dopey—

(NARRATOR 2 enters, coughs and shakes his head.)

NARRATOR 1. Slappy—wasn't afraid.

DWARF 1. Gar. I like ladies. So...uh...baby, I couldn't help noticing that you're in my bed—

(He sits next to her.)

NARRATOR 1. Stop! This is a children's story.

DWARF 1. So I'm going to chop you up and eat you.

(DWARF 1 takes out a fork and knife.)

NARRATOR 1. Time out. Time out.

DWARF 1. What? I'm just going with what my character wants.

NARRATOR 1. You do not get to eat Snow White. You're not the villain of the story.

DWARF 1. No. Look. I've been doing some character work. Slappy has had a hard life. He's been discriminated against for being a dwarf. He works in the mines all day—he's got like the black lung, you know? And he hates the world. He just hates it—

NARRATOR 1. He does not!

DWARF 1. And he wants revenge against the humans who have wronged him, so when this giant chick comes into his home and sleeps in his bed...dinner time.

NARRATOR 1. No. We are going to do this story as written. Snow White cleans house for the dwarves, then she gets poisoned by an apple, then a prince shows up—

SNOW WHITE. *(Waking up:)* Why do I have to clean the house? Is it because I'm a woman?

DWARF 1. Yes.

NARRATOR 1. No it's because you feel sorry for the little dwarves because they're messy and you have OCD and want to make everything nice.

SNOW WHITE. I don't see why I have to be a maid! I'm the princess here, they should be cleaning up for me.

DWARF 1. All right, she's become too much trouble, let's eat her.

NARRATOR 1. We are doing the story as originally written!

(NARRATOR 2 approaches.)

NARRATOR 2. You know, maybe we should just let them rewrite the story.

NARRATOR 1. I don't think so.

DWARF 1. Okay, I got another one. I've been cursed by a witch and I now have supernatural powers—

NARRATOR 2. Besides, sometimes the originals are...how do you say, bad?

NARRATOR 1. Oh really? These are classic stories. Classics!

DWARF 1. And now I can animate zombies. I've always wanted to animate zombies.

NARRATOR 2. Classics, huh? Let me show you a classic. Here we go— number 191. Lean Lisa.

NARRATOR 1. Never heard of it.

(SNOW WHITE *wakes up.*)

SNOW WHITE. Am I beautiful?

NARRATOR 2. You're lean.

SNOW WHITE. Ooh. Skinny. I've always wanted to be skinny.

DWARF 1. Have you thought about ingesting tape worm eggs? It really cleans you out on the inside.

NARRATOR 2. So once upon a time, Lean Lisa lay in bed with her husband, Long Laurence.

DWARF 1. Do I get to be Long Laurence?

NARRATOR 2. Yes.

DWARF 1. Sweet.

(DWARF 1 *and* SNOW WHITE *rearrange themselves.*)

SNOW WHITE. Dear husband, I was thinking.

DWARF 1. I'm trying to sleep, woman.

SNOW WHITE. I'm tired of being poor and hungry. What if we took the cow in the field and tried to get her to have calves? Then we could raise the calves and sell them and we'd have enough money to buy more animals. And then we wouldn't have to starve any more.

DWARF 1. That sounds like a lot of work.

SNOW WHITE. You're lazy!

DWARF 1. Quiet your wagging tongue woman!

(DWARF 1 *strangles* SNOW WHITE.)

NARRATOR 2. And she died. The end.

(SNOW WHITE *dies. Pause.*)

NARRATOR 1. Seriously? That's what it says?

NARRATOR 2. Right here.

NARRATOR 1. Wow. That story sucks.

SNOW WHITE. Can I tell my version now?

(WITCH 2 *enters.*)

WITCH 2. Are y'all gonna need me any time soon?

SNOW WHITE. Yes. We are starting over right now. Once upon a time there was a beautiful girl.

> *(The actors look around.* SNOW WHITE *gets upset. She points to* DWARF 2.*)*

SNOW WHITE. You're going to be Snow White this time.

> *(Author's note: Whatever the double-casting, it is imperative that* DWARF 2 *be played by a male actor.)*

DWARF 2. Really? I've always wanted to be Snow White. I remember my fifth birthday party; it was a dress-up party and all my friends came as Boba Fett and Teenage Mutant Ninja Turtles and that weird thing from the McDonald's commercials. But I was Snow White. And I was so pretty in my little dress and my wig and tiara—that was the happiest day of my life until my mom told me I was a boy. Of course she's the one who'd been dressing me in those clothes since—

NARRATOR 1. And moving on.

SNOW WHITE. She was the most beautiful girl in the entire kingdom.

DWARF 2. I am! I am the prettiest!

SNOW WHITE. But her stepmother was jealous.

> *(WITCH 2 enters.)*

WITCH 2. Snow White.

DWARF 2. Stepmother.

WITCH 2. Is that a zit I see on your face?

DWARF 2. You'd like that, wouldn't you?

WITCH 2. I do believe you're putting on weight.

DWARF 2. Not on this body, sister. These curves are tight and streamlined like a racing yacht owned by a rich Columbian drug dealer.

WITCH 2. I think you might need to tweeze your eyebrows. They're looking ...puffy.

DWARF 2. My eyebrows are sculpted like a block of clay in the hands of a blind god of sculpting eyebrows.

> *(DWARF 2 looks concerned. He looks over to* SNOW WHITE.*)*

DWARF 2. Who writes this stuff?

SNOW WHITE. Just go with it. And the stepmother went to her room and gazed into her magic mirror.

> *(DWARF 1 forms the magic mirror.)*

WITCH 2. Mirror, mirror, on the wall. Who's the fairest of them all?

DWARF 1. *(As the mirror, a drawn-out ghostly voice:)* Well it's certainly not you.

WITCH 2. Curses!

DWARF 1. *(As the mirror:)* Hey that's a good idea. You should try that.

SNOW WHITE. Meanwhile, Snow White had other plans.

DWARF 2. Mirror, mirror, hanging on black hooks. Why must I be judged by my looks?

DWARF 1. *(As the mirror:)* Fashion magazines.

DWARF 2. But I'm so much more! I've got a brain and martial arts skills! I'm going to one of the Seven Sisters after I graduate from high school where I plan on double-majoring in Social Psychology and Women's Studies!

DWARF 1. *(As the mirror:)* I only respond to rhyming questions. Besides, those aren't real majors.

DWARF 2. Okay. Mirror mirror, hanging over there. How do I make the young people care?

DWARF 1. *(As the mirror:)* Put it in a music video with hot chicks.

DWARF 2. That's not a very good—

SNOW WHITE. And just then.

> (WITCH 2 *enters.*)

SNOW WHITE. It was her stepmother.

WITCH 2. Stepmother.

DWARF 2. Snow White.

> (They look confused. SNOW WHITE *gestures that they have it reversed.*)

WITCH 2. Snow White.

DWARF 2. Stepmother.

WITCH 2. Look at me and know despair, Snow White. For I have a lot of money and have been through a lot of plastic surgery in Hollywood. My bust points north, my skin is as smooth as a lake after a storm and I've had all my tattoos lasered off. I've tucked, sucked, vacuumed and erased every visible trace of life experience in the past twenty-seven years, and now, I am more beautiful than even you.

DWARF 1. *(As the mirror:)* Not quite.

WITCH 2. Dang it! Well, how about an apple as a peace offering?

DWARF 2. When are you going to learn Stepmother, that we women shouldn't be judged by our surface beauty but rather by the contents of our brains?

WITCH 2. Um...that's just stupid.

DWARF 2. Well how bout I use my martial arts skills to take you out then?

WITCH 2. Oh it's on!

> (They assume fighting stances. NARRATOR 1 *becomes* PRINCE 2 *and enters. It is also imperative that* PRINCE 2 *is played by a male actor.*)

PRINCE 2. Hey I was just in the neighborhood looking for a girl in a coma to make out with and—whoah! Chickfight!

(DWARF 2 and WITCH 2 square off.)

SNOW WHITE. And it was a glorious battle.

(WITCH 2 pulls on DWARF 2's wig.)

DWARF 2. Ow! Ow! Ow! Ow!

(DWARF 2 stomps on WITCH 2's foot.)

PRINCE 2. Go Snow White!

(DWARF 2 waves coquettishly to PRINCE 2 as WITCH 2 jumps on her back from behind.)

SNOW WHITE. A titanic struggle of good and evil. Purity versus corruption.

(DWARF 2 pulls on WITCH 2's nose, who pokes DWARF 2 in the eyes.)

SNOW WHITE. Until finally.

WITCH 2. I shall transform myself into a black dragon! Ah ha ha ha!

(Pause.)

SNOW WHITE. No that was in the Sleeping Beauty movie.

WITCH 2. I thought we were doing Sleeping Beauty.

SNOW WHITE. No this is Snow White.

(DWARF 2 grabs PRINCE 2's sword and stabs WITCH 2 in the heart.)

DWARF 2. Take that, witch!

WITCH 2. Ah! I'm melting! Actually I'm...bleeding! Aaaaaah.

(WITCH 2 dies.)

PRINCE 2. That was so hot.

DWARF 2. Like somebody else I know, Prince.

PRINCE 2. You're very forward.

DWARF 2. I'm a modern woman. Come on, let's get married.

(She grabs PRINCE 2 and hoists him over her shoulder.)

SNOW WHITE. And just then.

(DWARF 1 enters.)

DWARF 1. Hi ho. Hi ho.

DWARF 2. What'd you just call me?

DWARF 1. Um. Nothing. Look, I'm living with a bunch of other dwarves—

DWARF 2. I've heard enough! You are lucky enough to become my servants. Come with me.

SNOW WHITE. And they all lived happily ever after and avoided traditional gender roles. And the seven little dwarves cooked for them, cleaned the house, and did all that other junk that Snow White was supposed to do in the story. The end.

(NARRATOR 1 *and* NARRATOR 2 *enter once again.)*

NARRATOR 1. That was enlightened.

SNOW WHITE. Thank you.

(She exits.)

NARRATOR 2. But the witch actually survived the vicious stabbing.

WITCH 2. It's just a flesh wound!

NARRATOR 1. Stop.

WITCH 2. What? It is. It's just a flesh wound. I've had worse.

NARRATOR 1. Can we please get through this play without any Monty Python references?

WITCH 2. You're no fun.

(She exits.)

NARRATOR 2. And she decided to make a house out of candy and eat children.

NARRATOR 1. But where did the dwarf come from?

NARRATOR 2. Exactly. You see the true secret origin here is of dwarf number 2. This is a little story I like to call number 95. The Devil's Grandmother.

NARRATOR 1. The Devil has a grandmother?

NARRATOR 2. Everyone has a grandmother. And you need to call yours. Before she dies.

NARRATOR 1. I have a phone call to make.

(NARRATOR 1 leaves.)

NARRATOR 2. I thought she would never leave. Now before I start this very special story, I'd like us all to think about that special old person in our lives. You know the one. And imagine what it would be like to be old for a day.

(Points to someone in the audience in their 40s:)

You already know sir.

(Steps out into the audience.)

Imagine how it must feel to have your best days behind you and only really be waiting for the welcoming arms of death. To feel your body decay, your mind collapse. Tell us about it sir.

(Waits for response from the person in the audience. If no response...)

NARRATOR 2. This man is so old he can't even speak.

(Finds someone sitting with the first person, preferably a wife or girlfriend.)

NARRATOR 2. You must be his caretaker. I pity you.

(NARRATOR 2 returns to the stage.)

NARRATOR 2. Well...this is a very special story brought to you by the Hallmark Channel. Could we get some warm soft fuzzy lighting please? Maybe a kind of soft warm glow around everyone on-stage?

(The lights do not change. NARRATOR 2 speaks up to the light booth.)

NARRATOR 2. Could you try that again please?

(The lights do not change.)

What is your problem? Yeah I'm talking to you! We're trying to have a very special moment here! You're ruining the special moment! What did you just say to me?! This is a family show you walking pile of putrescence! You don't even know what putrescence means do you? You know why you don't know? Cause you went to public school and they don't teach vocab any more! Hey where did you get that picture of my mom?

(NARRATOR 2 reacts in horror.)

You're dead!

(NARRATOR 2 charges through the audience, scrambling to get up into the light booth. He disappears.)

NARRATOR 1. *(On microphone in soothing, hallmark voice:)* And now for a very special hallmark channel presentation: The Devil's Grandmother.

(Lights change on stage.)

NARRATOR 1. Times were tough on the old farm.

(DEVIL'S GRANDMOTHER enters, carrying seeds.)

DEVIL'S GRANDMOTHER. Now that your grandpa's dead, I'll just plant in this garden. It's all I've got left, really.

NARRATOR 1. A special garden. A garden of love.

(THE DEVIL 2 enters.)

THE DEVIL 2. Grandmama! I heard about Grandpa! Could you use a hug?

DEVIL'S GRANDMOTHER. Boy could I.

(They hug.)

NARRATOR 1. And so began a very special relationship between a grandmother and her grandson, who just happened to be the Devil.

THE DEVIL 2. Can I help you plant those peas, Grandmama?

DEVIL'S GRANDMOTHER. Sure you can, Grandson. Just don't let me catch you using that black magic of yours.

THE DEVIL 2. Oh Grandmama!

(They laugh and hug.)

DEVIL'S GRANDMOTHER. Say are your horns getting bigger?

THE DEVIL 2. I'm growing up.

DEVIL'S GRANDMOTHER. So you are. So you are.

NARRATOR 1. But the garden couldn't stay green forever.

THE DEVIL 2. Grandmama what happened?

DEVIL'S GRANDMOTHER. Do I know you?

THE DEVIL 2. What? I'm your grandson, the Devil.

DEVIL'S GRANDMOTHER. Now where did I put my glasses?

(DOCTOR *enters.*)

DOCTOR. I'm afraid your grandmother has Alzheimer's.

(DOCTOR *leaves.*)

THE DEVIL 2. No! It's not fair! It's not fair Grandmama!

NARRATOR 1. So they decided to go on one last road trip together.

DEVIL'S GRANDMOTHER. I've always wanted to see the Grand Canyon.

THE DEVIL 2. We'll make it there. Even though I can't legally drive.

DEVIL'S GRANDMOTHER. Earthly laws never stopped you before.

THE DEVIL 2. You're right!

(*They laugh and hug.*)

DEVIL'S GRANDMOTHER. Who are you again?

NARRATOR 1. It would be the wackiest road trip of their lives.

DEVIL'S GRANDMOTHER. Did you just burn Albuquerque to the ground by calling on the power of Hades?

THE DEVIL 2. Oh Grandmama!

(*They laugh and hug.*)

THE DEVIL 2. Shhh... You didn't see anything.

NARRATOR 1. But maybe, just maybe, they'd learn a little something about the power of the human heart.

THE DEVIL 2. Grandmama we ran out of gas so I stole a human heart and am using it to power our car!

DEVIL'S GRANDMOTHER. Who are you again?

NARRATOR 1. But the greatest lesson would be when they reached the Grand Canyon.

DEVIL'S GRANDMOTHER. You know, Grandson. Me and your grandpa were simple people. We liked simple things. We were supposed to come out here for our honeymoon. Never made it cause there were chores to be done. Boy he woulda loved this view though.

THE DEVIL 2. I could summon him from the dead and place his soul inside a coyote.

DEVIL'S GRANDMOTHER. Wouldn't be the same. Which coyote?

NARRATOR 1. But even very special Hallmark Channel movies have sad endings.

THE DEVIL 2. Grandmama! Grandmama!

(DOCTOR *enters.*)

DOCTOR. She didn't make it.

(*DOCTOR leaves.*)

THE DEVIL 2. No! No! Why, God, why?

GOD. (*Booming overhead voice on microphone:*) BECAUSE YOU'RE THE DEVIL AND I DON'T LIKE YOU.

THE DEVIL 2. I curse you and your kingdom!

GOD. YEAH. I KNOW THAT. WHAT ARE YOU GONNA DO ABOUT IT?

(*DOCTOR enters.*)

DOCTOR. Um...your grandmother didn't have insurance, so I'm going to have to charge you her medical bills for dying, which amount to about twenty three thousand dollars.

THE DEVIL 2. I curse you!

NARRATOR 1. And he shrank and shrank until he became quite small. In fact, a dwarf.

THE DEVIL 2. Now go work in a mine with the rest of your kind.

(*The DOCTOR exits.*)

THE DEVIL 2. I'm going to Disneyland. To work there. In one of those big costumes where I walk around and pretend to be one of the Disney characters. But you don't know which one. So next time you're in Disneyland and you see Chip and Dale walking toward you—

(*NARRATOR 2 enters.*)

NARRATOR 2. And I'm back to prevent lawsuits.

THE DEVIL 2. Too late! Moo ah ha ha ha ha!

(*THE DEVIL 2 exits as NARRATOR 1 enters.*)

NARRATOR 1. But of course we can't really understand that story until we know where the Devil's Grandmother came from.

NARRATOR 2. Can we just pause for a second?

NARRATOR 1. What.

NARRATOR 2. Is that really how the Brothers Grimm recorded that story?

NARRATOR 1. Well that's more of a modern adaptation... You know, we took a few liberties... Okay, fine, the real story is about a couple of soldiers who sign away their souls but the Devil's grandmother feels sorry for them, blah blah blah blah blah! Nobody gets killed in the end. I just thought the title was funny.

NARRATOR 2. Fine. But now we have to fit that into our storyline.

NARRATOR 1. No problem. Because long before she was the Devil's grandmother, she was a little girl.

(*CINDERELLA enters, overacting.*)

CINDERELLA. Oh I am orphaned! Oh I am sad!

(*An ACTOR enters.*)

ACTOR. Can we pause here for a second?

CINDERELLA. Oh how sad I am!

ACTOR. Just hold on.

NARRATOR 1. What is it?

ACTOR. There was like some really bad beef in the catering—

CINDERELLA. Oh the catering is bad!

NARRATOR 1. Uh-oh. I had the beef.

ACTOR. So like everybody is throwing up back here.

NARRATOR 1. Excuse me.

> *(NARRATOR 1 runs off.)*

ACTOR. We don't have enough actors left to do this one.

> *(CINDERELLA stops acting.)*

CINDERELLA. What?

NARRATOR 2. Well I guess we can skip it then. Too bad about the Frog Prince, Little Red Riding Hood, The Talking Fish, Cinderella.

CINDERELLA. NO WE ARE NOT SKIPPING IT.

NARRATOR 2. How many actors do we have left?

ACTOR. Um...me.

CINDERELLA. Now you listen to me you little reject from Nickelodeon— this is my chance to be a star, got it? We are going to tell my story, I am going to get a full-length feature film out of it, and you are going to make me look good, got it?

ACTOR. Well, I—

CINDERELLA. GOT IT? OR I WILL TEAR OUT YOUR TINY HEART AND USE IT AS A CHEW TOY FOR MY HALF-CHIHAUHAU, HALF-DOBERMAN MIX, GOT IT?

ACTOR. Yes, Ma'am.

CINDERELLA. Thank you.

> *(The* ACTOR *exits.* CINDERELLA *immediately goes back to acting sad.)*

CINDERELLA. Oh how sad. Life. So sad.

NARRATOR 2. Okay, so, her mother died and her father remarried—

CINDERELLA. *(Overlapping:)* Mother? Where are you mother? Are you dead?

NARRATOR 2. And the woman he married was beautiful of face but black of heart. Now, Cinderella's stepmother had two daughters, both equally beautiful—

> *(CINDERELLA raises her hand.)*

CINDERELLA. I'm sorry. I think you've got that wrong. I'm the pretty one. They're quite hideous.

NARRATOR 2. Says here they're beautiful too.

CINDERELLA. I think I know my story, thank you.

(She returns to the floor.)

Oh they are so mean to me. Oh so mean. I can barely stand it. My tears, oh so many tears, shall wash these dusty flagstones.

(She cries. The two WICKED STEPSISTERS *enter [played by the same actor or actress in two different wigs].* ACTOR *switches places, voices, and wigs for each role.)*

WICKED STEPSISTER 1. Look what the cat dragged in.

WICKED STEPSISTER 2. Does it smell in here, or is it just her?

WICKED STEPSISTER 1. Oh that was a good one, Jiselle.

WICKED STEPSISTER 2. Thought you'd like it.

WICKED STEPSISTER 1. Oh Cinderella. I need to get ready for the ball—

CINDERELLA. What ball?

WICKED STEPSISTER 1. The ball being thrown by Prince Charming.

WICKED STEPSISTER 2. He's so charming. When I see him I just want to grab his little tights-wearing bottom and squeeze until his guards spray me with pepper spray.

CINDERELLA. Can I come?

WICKED STEPSISTER 1. Of course you can...NOT come. Balls are for people who bathe.

WICKED STEPSISTER 2. But we do have a treat for you. You are going to get us ready for the ball.

WICKED STEPSISTER 1. Make us pretty.

WICKED STEPSISTER 2. Make me prettier than her. I need Charming. I need him. Please.

CINDERELLA. I suppose. I'm going to need a lot of makeup.

NARRATOR 2. So, being the good girl that she was—

CINDERELLA. I'm so good.

NARRATOR 2. Cinderella dressed both her sisters for the ball.

WICKED STEPSISTER 1. I'm so hot.

WICKED STEPSISTER 2. I'm gorgeous.

(ACTOR runs off as WICKED STEPSISTER 2, *then returns and runs off as* WICKED STEPSISTER 1.)*

CINDERELLA. *(Overacting:)* Life. So unfair. The room is spinning. Why, God, why? Why am I just a servant—a slave! Lower than the dust. Lower than the worms who crawl beneath the dust. So low. So so low. I shall now cry myself to sleep as I do every night.

(She cries.)

NARRATOR 2. *(To the audience:)* I think she thinks the Oscar committee is watching. But just then, her wicked stepmother entered.

(WICKED STEPMOTHER [played by the same actor or actress that played the STEPSISTERS, in a third wig] enters.)

WICKED STEPMOTHER. Why Cinderella, what seems to be the trouble?

CINDERELLA. Life! Life and the misery it entails! If only my mother—my poor, dear, dead mother, were alive, she would take me to the ball.

WICKED STEPMOTHER. Come here and sit on your stepmother's lap.

(CINDERELLA eyes her suspiciously.)

CINDERELLA. That's weird.

WICKED STEPMOTHER. Get over it.

(CINDERELLA gingerly sits on her lap.)

WICKED STEPMOTHER. Now—boy, you've really been hitting the pot roast, haven't you? You'd think that eating dust and sleeping on the hearth would make you skinny—

CINDERELLA. I'm big-boned.

NARRATOR 2. Just then, one of Cinderella's stepsisters, Jiselle, entered.

(The WICKED STEPMOTHER looks angrily at NARRATOR 2, dumps CINDERELLA on the floor, runs to the side of the stage and switches wigs.)

WICKED STEPSISTER 2. Mother, aren't you coming?

(She runs back to the chair, grabs CINDERELLA, plants her on her lap and switches wigs.)

WICKED STEPMOTHER. In a moment dear, run along.

(She dumps CINDERELLA, runs back to the other spot on the stage and switches wigs.)

WICKED STEPSISTER 2. Thank you I will.

NARRATOR 2. But then, from the other side of the room, Cinderella's other wicked stepsister entered.

(The ACTOR gives NARRATOR 2 an evil look and rushes to the other side of the stage, switching wigs as he or she goes.)

WICKED STEPSISTER 1. I really need to be going.

(Runs, switches.)

WICKED STEPSISTER 2. You do that. Witch.

(Runs, switches.)

WICKED STEPSISTER 1. What did you just call me?

(Runs, switches.)

WICKED STEPSISTER 2. You heard what I said. Witch.

(Runs, switches.)

WICKED STEPSISTER 1. Oh no you didn't!

(She runs and turns back into the STEPMOTHER, *dropping* CINDERELLA *onto her lap, completely out of breath.)*

WICKED STEPMOTHER. Girls, please! You're both pretty. You're both going to the ball. You both need to exit right now without saying anything else.

NARRATOR 2. And so...they left.

WICKED STEPMOTHER. Thank you. Now, Cinderella, I am a fair wicked stepmother, so...I am going to empty an entire dish of lentils into the fireplace, and once you have picked them all out, you may go to the ball with us.

NARRATOR 2. And with that, she dumped a dish of lentils into the fireplace like she said she was going to do.

(The WICKED STEPMOTHER *exits.)*

CINDERELLA. What are lentils?

NARRATOR 2. They go in soup. And they're difficult to get out of a fireplace. Apparently.

CINDERELLA. Oh, the humanity! Oh Gods! Why must I always be punished!? But what's that? What could it be?

(She pops up to listen.)

My fairy—

NARRATOR 2. It was a swarm of birds.

(ACTOR returns, raising his or her hand.)

ACTOR. Question: Do I have to play each individual bird or can I be collectively, The Birds?

NARRATOR 2. I guess you can be a collective group of birds.

ACTOR. You have no idea how much that means to me.

(ACTOR becomes THE BIRDS *and begins running around tweeting.)*

THE BIRDS. Tweet! Tweet tweet! Tweet tweet tweet!

CINDERELLA. Oh look, birds! They're so beautiful! Come, my little feathered friends, come and peck these lentils out of the fireplace.

(THE BIRDS descend on the fireplace.)

THE BIRDS. Peck peck peck peck peck! Peck Peck peck!

CINDERELLA. Oh I am truly blessed! Thank you birds! Fly, fly to freedom!

(THE BIRDS fly away and immediately transform into the WICKED STEPMOTHER, *who returns.)*

WICKED STEPMOTHER. We're off to the ball!

(She leaves.)

CINDERELLA. How can life be so cruel! WHY?!!!! What's that? My fairy—

NARRATOR 2. It was another swarm of birds, carrying a dress.

(THE BIRDS *enter, carrying a dress.*)

THE BIRDS. Tweet tweet! Tweet tweet!

CINDERELLA. What a lovely dress. Thank you, swarm of birds.

THE BIRDS. Tweet tweet tweet!

CINDERELLA. So who's going to do my hair? Um...what a surprise, a fairy godmother.

(*Pause.*)

Isn't this where she sorta comes in and does her magic thing?

NARRATOR 2. Nope.

CINDERELLA. What?

NARRATOR 2. We're going by the original. There's no fairy godmother. Just a lot of birds.

THE BIRDS. Tweet tweet tweet tweet—

CINDERELLA. Shut up. Let me see that.

(*She takes the book from the* NARRATOR *and reads.*)

CINDERELLA. There's no fairy godmother in here.

NARRATOR 2. I was about eleven when I figured out I didn't have a fairy godmother.

CINDERELLA. Well I can't do this without a fairy godmother. Who's going to turn the pumpkin into a coach?

NARRATOR 2. You walk there.

CINDERELLA. What?! This is retarded! I'm Cinderella! I have a fairy god-mother, and a coach made out of a pumpkin and a bunch of mice turned into coachmen! Oh so there's no mice either is there! Next thing you know there won't even be a glass slipper—THERE'S NO GLASS SLIPPER!? Well, then I don't even know how this story goes! Maybe I just get be-headed at the end? I JUST GET BEHEADED AT THE END?!!

NARRATOR 2. Maybe. I don't know. I haven't read to the end yet.

CINDERELLA. Ahhhhh! I QUIT!

(*She leaves in tears in the middle of a fit, hyperventilating.*)

THE BIRDS. Tweet tweet. Tweet tweet.

NARRATOR 2. Well, guess somebody's not living happily ever after is she? All right then, let's continue with our story.

ACTOR. Um...we can't continue. There's no Cinderella.

NARRATOR 2. Sure there is.

(NARRATOR 2 *stares at* ACTOR.)

NARRATOR 2. Put on the dress, *[name].*

(ACTOR *stares at* NARRATOR 2, *then slowly, unhappily, puts on the dress. Until noted, every part except for* NARRATOR 2 *is now played by the* ACTOR.)

NARRATOR 2. So Cinderella had her dress. And she felt very pretty.

CINDERELLA. I feel very pretty. Thank you birds.

THE BIRDS. Tweet tweet tweet tweet!

CINDERELLA. Now I shall walk to the ball.

NARRATOR 2. But the ball was guarded by a bouncer, a one-armed eye-patch wearing Scottish pirate named Mac.

(CINDERELLA *runs, rips off her dress, puts one arm behind her back, the other hand over her eye and affects a Scottish accent.*)

MAC. Arrgh, What ye be doin' at this here ball? If it's not Scottish, it's crap!

(*Runs and becomes* CINDERELLA.)

CINDERELLA. Well I would like to come in please.

(*Runs and switches to* MAC.)

MAC. Shut it!

NARRATOR 2. And just then Cinderella's wicked stepmother and two wicked stepsisters arrived.

(ACTOR *runs, grabs three wigs and becomes each character in turn.*)

WICKED STEPMOTHER. Cinderella!

WICKED STEPSISTER 1. What are you doing here?

WICKED STEPSISTER 2. You suck!

(*Switches to* CINDERELLA.)

CINDERELLA. I have a dress and I'm going to the ball because the birds brought it to me!

NARRATOR 2. And then the birds came down.

(ACTOR *grabs a feather and waves it.*)

THE BIRDS. Tweet tweet!

NARRATOR 2. And they pecked out Mac's other eye.

(ACTOR *becomes* MAC *again.*)

MAC. Ack! Birds! Me eye!

(*Switches back to* BIRDS.)

THE BIRDS. Peck peck peck peck!

(*Back to* CINDERELLA.)

CINDERELLA. I'm in! Sweet!

NARRATOR 2. And just then.

(ACTOR *quits dancing, runs and becomes the* HERALD *for a moment.*)

HERALD. *(Blowing imaginary horn:)* Dun de dun dun! His royal highness, the Prince!

> *(Switches, becomes* PRINCE CHARMING, *affects a British accent for no apparent reason.)*

PRINCE CHARMING. 'Ello there. We're having a nice time, are we? Blimey. She's gorgeous. Who's that minx?

> *(Becomes* CINDERELLA.*)*

CINDERELLA. My name's Cinderella.

> *(Switches.)*

PRINCE CHARMING. Right-o. Come here and give us a taste, love.

> *(PRINCE CHARMING and* CINDERELLA *begin to dance.* ACTOR *continually switches sides during this conversation, keeping the beat.)*

CINDERELLA. Oh Prince. Stop. You're embarrassing me.

PRINCE CHARMING. I'll do more'n that later. Blimey. Your skin's as supple as a baby's bottom!

CINDERELLA. Oh really?

PRINCE CHARMING. I'd like to pour hot sauce on you and roast you over an open pit till you're brown and tender like a chicken breast.

CINDERELLA. I'd like that.

NARRATOR 2. All right, this is getting weird. I have to say I'm pretty impressed with this guy. Maybe he should win the Oscar.

> *(CINDERELLA [the real one] darts back on to the stage and grabs* PRINCE CHARMING.*)*

CINDERELLA. Oh Prince. You dance divinely.

PRINCE CHARMING. 'Ello. What's all this, then?

NARRATOR 2. And they danced all night long.

> *(CINDERELLA breaks away from him.)*

CINDERELLA. What are these strange feelings? Could it be...love? Oh my heart is beating so fast. What am I to do? Will he love me back?

> *(Pause.)*

Um... Question: wasn't I supposed to drop a slipper or something?

NARRATOR 2. You drop a slipper on your third trip to the prince's balls. The birds keep bringing you more dresses and then you keep dancing and then finally the prince smears pitch on the steps of the palace, and then your shoe sticks, your golden shoe by the way—

CINDERELLA. Golden shoe?

NARRATOR 2. And he comes looking for the foot that fits the golden shoe.

CINDERELLA. Huh. That does sound more comfortable than glass.

> *(ACTOR raises his hand.)*

ACTOR. Can we skip to that part please? I'm going to die.

NARRATOR 2. You know what, why don't you put a little effort into this, okay? Fine. A little of this, a little of that, the prince stops by with a shoe looking for a girl who fits it.

PRINCE CHARMING. 'Ello then. Any of you darlings lost a shoe?

CINDERELLA. Well, I—

(ACTOR switches into WICKED STEPSISTER 1.)

WICKED STEPSISTER 1. Oh I did. I did! Let me see that!

(She takes the shoe.)

WICKED STEPSISTER 1. Hold on one minute. Do you mind if I try this on in the bathroom? I'm shy.

PRINCE CHARMING. Take all the time you like, luv.

WICKED STEPSISTER 1. Excellent!

NARRATOR 2. And of course her foot was too big, so she chopped off her big toe.

WICKED STEPSISTER 1. *(Blood-curdling scream:)* Aarrrrrrrrr- rrrrrrrrrg- ghghgghghg!

(Runs, becomes PRINCE CHARMING.)

PRINCE CHARMING. Say, you all right in there?

(Runs back into the bathroom, hops around on one foot.)

WICKED STEPSISTER 1. Aarrghghgghghghghghg. *(She limps back out:)* It...fits...fine. I...love...you.

PRINCE CHARMING. Bangers and mash! Let's go get married then. 'Op into me carriage.

(WICKED STEPSISTER 1 limps in.)

WICKED STEPSISTER 1. It's...nice...garrrrrhggh.

PRINCE CHARMING. Say, what's all this then? There's blood everywhere.

WICKED STEPSISTER 1. I popped a zit. On my foot.

PRINCE CHARMING. You chopped off your toe, you did!

WICKED STEPSISTER 1. I've never had toes.

PRINCE CHARMING. Out of my carriage you!

NARRATOR 2. So the wicked stepsister went back home and the prince returned to find Cinderella's other wicked stepsister.

WICKED STEPSISTER 2. May I please try the shoe on in the bathroom so no one can watch what I'm doing?

PRINCE CHARMING. Of course, I'm not all that bright.

NARRATOR 2. And once she was in the bathroom, the shoe didn't fit either. So she did the only sensible thing and chopped off her heel.

(Blood-curdling scream.)

WICKED STEPSISTER 2. Son of a mother-witch! Arrghgghghffhfhgh!

PRINCE CHARMING. All right in there?

WICKED STEPSISTER 2. Arrrgghghgghghgh! I'm...fine! *(She limps out:)* See...it fits.

PRINCE CHARMING. Why you're as pretty as a daisy. All right then, let's get married. Jump in me carriage.

WICKED STEPSISTER 2. Sounds...peachy.

NARRATOR 2. But as they were riding.

PRINCE CHARMING. Say—do you smell blood? I'm not terribly observant either. Blimey! Is that blood on your foot?

WICKED STEPSISTER 2. I cut myself shaving. I have hairy feet. Like a hobbit.

PRINCE CHARMING. You cut off your heel you daft wench!

WICKED STEPSISTER 2. I did it for you!

NARRATOR 2. And so the prince returned to the house for a third time.

PRINCE CHARMING. 'Ello there. I realize several of the ladies in this here house have chopped off body parts to fit in this here shoe, but I was just wondering if anyone else fit in it. You see, I'm not very smart, but I make up for it by being very persistent. It makes me ideal to run the government.

(CINDERELLA runs to him.)

CINDERELLA. I will try the shoe.

PRINCE CHARMING. It fits!

CINDERELLA. My love!

PRINCE CHARMING. It is you!

CINDERELLA. It is I!

NARRATOR 2. And they lived. Happily. Ever. After. As for the wicked stepsisters. The swarm of birds pecked out their eyes. Just for fun.

(ACTOR grabs the feather.)

THE BIRDS. Peck. Peck. Peck.

(NARRATOR 1 returns.)

NARRATOR 1. However.

ACTOR. I don't think so.

(ACTOR falls over, exhausted.)

NARRATOR 1. However. That is not the end of the story.

NARRATOR 2. That's the beginning.

NARRATOR 1. Exactly.

NARRATOR 2. I thought you had the beef?

NARRATOR 1. Oh, we were all fine. We just wanted to see if he could do it.

NARRATOR 2. That's not very nice.

NARRATOR 1. Eh. What can you do? Well, we're out of time—

NARRATOR 2. So it's time for the lightning round re-cap!

NARRATOR 1. It is?

NARRATOR 2. Of course. Otherwise no one would be able to follow the narrative. So what we're going to do to finish off the show is re-perform everything we've already done...in two minutes. Ready?

NARRATOR 1. I was born ready.

NARRATOR 2. All right then. And...GO!

NARRATOR 1. Cinderella got pregnant—

CINDERELLA. Heavens!

NARRATOR 1. After they were married.

CINDERELLA. Joyous day!

NARRATOR 1. But her daughter married a demon.

(ACTOR *becomes* PRINCE CHARMING.)

PRINCE CHARMING. This is your fault!

NARRATOR 1. And Cinderella became old.

(THE DEVIL'S GRANDMOTHER *runs on.*)

THE DEVIL'S GRANDMOTHER. I'm old now!

(She shoves PRINCE CHARMING and CINDERELLA off the stage.)

THE DEVIL'S GRANDMOTHER. Grandson!

(THE DEVIL 2 *runs on.*)

THE DEVIL 2. You're losing your mind cause you're old!

DEVIL'S GRANDMOTHER. You're the Devil!

THE DEVIL 2. I know!

(DOCTOR *runs on.*)

DOCTOR. You're sick!

DEVIL'S GRANDMOTHER. Let's go to the—

DOCTOR. You're dead!

DEVIL'S GRANDMOTHER. Ack!

(She dies.)

THE DEVIL 2. I curse you!

(DWARF 2 *runs and shoves* DOCTOR *out of the way, taking his place.*)

DWARF 2. Now I'm a dwarf! I mean little person!

(DWARF 1 *runs in as* THE DEVIL 2 *and* THE DEVIL'S GRAND-MOTHER *run out.*)

DWARF 1. Let's start our own dwarf village with five of our friends!

DWARF 2. That's a great idea!

(SNOW WHITE runs in.)

DWARF 1. Ah a giant hottie!

SNOW WHITE. Ah a dwarf!

DWARF 2. Little person!

DWARF 1. How 'bout you clean our house and tuck us in at night?

SNOW WHITE. You're not going to oppress me!

(WITCH 2 runs in from the other direction.)

WITCH 2. I'm hotter than you!

SNOW WHITE. I don't judge myself by my looks but I am still hotter than you!

WITCH 2. Want to fight about it?

SNOW WHITE. Yes.

(They fight.)

WITCH 2. Your kung fu is stronger than mine.

(She dies. PRINCE 2 enters.)

PRINCE 2. What's going on here?

SNOW WHITE. I'm an emancipated princess and I'm going to take what I want: you.

(She carries the PRINCE off.)

WITCH 2. I'm not dead yet.

(SNOW WHITE runs back in.)

SNOW WHITE. I said no Monty Python!

(She runs out as HANSEL and GRETEL enter.)

HANSEL. Hey let's eat that lady's house!

GRETEL. That's a great idea!

WITCH 2. How 'bout I eat you instead?

HANSEL. How 'bout I push you in an oven and you die!

WITCH 2. Ah I'm dying in an ironic way!

GRETEL. Hey look I'm having a daughter! Ah I'm dying in childbirth! Darn it.

(GIRL runs on, shoves GRETEL off.)

GIRL. Somehow I'm poor.

(THE DEVIL 1, the ENCHANTRESS, and RUMPELSTILTSKIN run on.)

GIRL. Ah the Devil, and Enchantress and a weird guy!

RUMPELSTILTSKIN. Rumpelstiltskin. *(Realizes he's just said his name:)* Darn it!

(Dies.)

ENCHANTRESS / THE DEVIL 1. Deal?

GIRL. Deal.

(They run off and transform into PRINCE 1 *and* RAPUNZEL.)

PRINCE 1. Hey baby let's get married.

(A baby is thrown at them again just before RAPUNZEL *runs on.)*

RAPUNZEL. I hate you all because I'm a teenager.

GIRL. Tough cause I already sold you to the Devil and the Enchantress and the weird guy!

ENCHANTRESS. Come along Rapunzel I have a nice tower for you.

THE DEVIL 1. You can have her as long as you sign this contract.

ENCHANTRESS. Fine!

GIRL. Bye!

PRINCE 1. Bye!

RAPUNZEL. Bye!

THE DEVIL 1. Bye!

(RAPUNZEL and the ENCHANTRESS *exit. Everyone stops, out of breath.)*

NARRATOR 1. And they lived. Happily ever after.

NARRATOR 2. And.

(The ENCHANTRESS *returns.)*

ENCHANTRESS. I hope that contract I signed with the Devil doesn't have any repercussions.

(THE DEVIL 1 enters.)

THE DEVIL 1. You'll find out.

NARRATOR 2. The. End.

(Lights down.)

End of Play

15 REASONS NOT TO BE IN A PLAY

by Alan Haehnel

For more information about rights and permissions, see page 9.

Cast of Characters

1	MEGAN
2	BILL
3	WEATHERMAN
4	GEEK 1
5	GEEK 2
6	GEEK 3
7	GEEK 4
8	OLD 1
9	OLD 2
10	OLD 3
11	OLD 4
12	OLD 5
13	REED
14	W 1
15	W 2
JAKE	W 3
MISTY	TELEVISION REPORTER
MISS GRISWOLD	CECILY
SHARON	BOY
ALAN	MAVIS
EMILY	ZACH
PETE	CHRIS
JANE	MOM
STEWART	NORA
MANDY	CENSOR
1 T	BECCA
2 T	MOM 2
3 T	BABY
4 T	DIRECTOR
5 T	NORM
6 T	BUTCH
7 T	MINDY
TRAVIS	GINA
ROB	

Director's Note

This play is designed to be versatile. If it is too long for your purposes, feel free to cut out segments and rename it "14 Reasons" or "13 Reasons"—however many work well for you. The size of the cast can vary greatly as well. Through doubling or tripling of parts, you could perform this show with a relatively small cast. On the other hand, you could re-assign lines and perform it with a very large group. Genders, also, can be manipulated by simply changing the names of the characters. Feel free to make these kinds of changes liberally. The intent of the play will not be hurt in the least.

A sequel and a full-length version of this play also exist. For more information, please visit www.playscripts.com.

15 REASONS NOT TO BE IN A PLAY

(The cast gathers together on a bare stage—a group of kids in regular street clothes. The full cast will remain onstage throughout the play. As various characters narrate the action, cast members act it out around them. Cast members can also act as furniture and other set pieces where necessary.)

1. We are not here to put on a play.

2. If you came to see a play, it sucks being you.

3. We believe that putting on a play is a bad idea.

4. A horrible idea.

5. A rotten idea.

6. A putrid, stinking, slimy, greenish-liquid-oozing...

7. ...you'd-rather-kiss-your-brother-full-on-the-mouth-than-have-to-deal-with-this idea.

8. We aren't going to do it. Period.

9. So don't ask.

10. Don't plead.

11. And, whatever you do, don't beg. It makes us sick.

12. But we are out here, and you may wonder why.

13. We're out here with a message.

14. We're out here with a warning.

15. We're out here to teach you...

ALL. 15 Reasons Not To Be in a Play! Reason Number 1...

JAKE. Plays suck!

ALL. Reason Number 2...

MISTY. When you were in second grade, you had a teacher named Miss Griswold. She was older than God and she smelled like stale coffee and gym socks. When she came in every morning she said...

MISS GRISWOLD. Now, students, pay close attention. Focus, focus, focus is the key to success.

MISTY. She invented amazing methods of torture using construction paper and popsicle sticks. She turned perfectly normal questions into sadistic games of chance that you would always lose.

SHARON. Miss Griswold, can I go to the bathroom?

MISS GRISWOLD. I don't know. May you?

SHARON. What?

MISS GRISWOLD. May you go to the bathroom?

SHARON. That's what I'm asking. Can I?

MISS GRISWOLD. I am assuming that you can, but I don't yet know if you may.

SHARON. Miss Griswold, I really have to go.

MISS GRISWOLD. Then you can go.

SHARON. Thank-you.

MISS GRISWOLD. But you may not go until I have given permission.

SHARON. You just did!

MISTY. By that time you had either made a puddle on the floor or had run out in desperation, a crime for which you paid by writing "I will not run out of the room in desperation" on the board seven million times with her breathing on you until you got it done. Miss Griswold.

ALL. *(Sinister intonations:)* Miss Griswold!

MISTY. You had Miss Griswold and she decided to put you in a play.

ALAN. You were only in second grade, still in your formative years.

MISTY. The play was about loving the earth and you spent weeks with your hands in papier-mâché trying to put together the costumes and the props.

ALAN. Only seven years old, and so terribly impressionable.

MISTY. It was a play Miss Griswold wrote and it had lines in it like...

EMILY. If we don't get busy and plant all those seeds,
The earth won't be able to meet all our needs!

MISS GRISWOLD. No, no, Emily. Put more emphasis on the word "needs." I want you to really experience that word fully. I want you to taste it in your mouth, do you understand? Say "needs."

EMILY. Needs.

MISS GRISWOLD. Say it like you mean it.

EMILY. Needs.

MISS GRISWOLD. Say it like the most important thing in the world for you to do is to say the word needs.

EMILY. Needs.

MISS GRISWOLD. Emily, say it as if I'm going to take you home and throw you in a hot oven if you don't say it right!

EMILY. Needs! Needs! Needs!

MISS GRISWOLD. Much better.

MISTY. You were small for your age. Everything was so intimidating to you, especially Miss Griswold.

ALL. Miss Griswold!

MISTY. She made you put on a tree costume. It itched like you had lice all over your body. When you tried to turn your head you faced the inside of the tree and you couldn't see.

PETE. *(From inside the tree:)* Miss Griswold, I can't see.

MISS GRISWOLD. *(To* EMILY:*)* Remember now, how are you going to say "needs"?

EMILY. With feeling! With passion! I don't want to go in your oven!

MISS GRISWOLD. Stop crying. We're about to go on. Now where is my head of broccoli?

PETE. Miss Griswold, I can't...

MISS GRISWOLD. Quiet! We're about to start!

ALAN. You felt tiny and inconsequential in a huge, overwhelming world and she shoved you into a tree from which you couldn't escape!

MISTY. You could barely walk because the tree trunk was so small. You had to take tiny steps just to keep your balance. Only ten minutes into the play, Jesse Givens, who was dressed as a skunk, bumped into you. You fell.

ALAN. At age seven, in second grade, you toppled down, down, down, and your short unhappy life flashed before your eyes!

MISTY. You lay on the floor for the rest of the play because your arms were trapped at your sides. Miss Griswold was whispering frantically from the wings...

MISS GRISWOLD. Keep going! Keep going, you little delinquents! There's an audience out there! Don't you dare stop!

ALAN. No child should have to endure such trauma!

MISTY. No one stopped the play to help you up and by the second act of this five-act epic called "Mother Earth is Your Patient and You Are the Nurse" everyone had forgotten you were inside the papier-mâché tree and they started to sit on you during their scenes.

ALAN. Such stress!

MISTY. The papier-mâché buckled over your face and you were sure your classmates dressed like skunks and chipmunks and flowers were going to come crashing through your costume and suffocate you! Hour after hour you could only lay there and stare at your own bark as your classmates recited their horrible lines!

JANE. Oh, earth, oh, earth, we love you like crazy.
We're sorry we sometimes get sloppy and lazy.

STEWART. The trees all around, like maple, beech and ash
Just shouldn't have to put up with all of our trash.

MISTY. When the play was finally over and everyone had taken their bows and had exited the stage, you were still left there, a fallen and forgotten tree feebly calling for help. By the time your mother found you, you had given up and gone to sleep. And in that sleep, you had your first nightmare where Miss Griswold was a giant tree coming at you with a thousand play scripts hanging from her branches and you couldn't run, you couldn't scream, you couldn't move. That dream came back night after night for weeks and months. Eventually, you had it less and less often but every time you have it, even last week, you wet your bed.

ALAN. A classic case of post-traumatic stress syndrome. You poor, poor child.

MISTY. So anytime you hear someone talk about a play you smell papier-mâché and you see the inside of a tree and you hear Miss Griswold's voice saying...

MISS GRISWOLD. Needs! Needs!

MISTY. And you walk away, very, very quickly.

ALL. Reason Number 3!

MANDY. Plays take passion and devotion and commitment. You can't afford to expend any of those things on a play when Travis Thorburn is alive. Look at him!

(The cast starts to hum a hymn of religious devotion.)

MANDY. All passion, all devotion, all commitment you must direct at him and him alone. Listen, Travis Thorburn is your everything. He is your sun and your moon and your breakfast cereal. He is your waking and your sleeping and your daydreams and your night-dreams. He is the taste of toothpaste. He is the cool breeze in your face. Every breath you take in should be exhaled with a single purpose: to say the name Travis.

ALL. Travis, Travis, Travis.

MANDY. Every thought you form should have but a single intention: to visualize Travis.

1 T. I think I see him!

2 T. He looks like a great silver cloud hanging in the sky, the sun streaming through him.

3 T. He looks like an enormous plate of lasagna, bubbling with cheese.

4 T. Like a Greek statue!

5 T. Like a Roman coliseum!

6 T. Like a ticket to the Super Bowl!

MANDY. Like...like...like Travis Thorburn.

ALL. *(Sighing:)* Travis.

MANDY. Do you know what some people do at the end of a play? They bring flowers to the performers!

7 T. Here you go, Sweetie. Nice job!

MANDY. *(Grabbing the flowers, accosting the flower-bringer:)* That is a crime, a sin, an act of utter blasphemy because all of the flowers grown in this world are grown to be strewn at the feet of one person and one person only: *(Laying the flowers at his feet:)* Travis Thorburn. With Travis

Thorburn in the world, can you take time to think about a play, practice for a play, memorize for a play, be in a play?

ALL. Hell, no!

MANDY. How can you even consider it? Look at him! Behold the great Travis! What more can you do than try not to faint when he walks into the room? And if he should ever say to you...

TRAVIS. Get lost. I have a girlfriend.

MANDY. ...what more can you do than feel your aching heart burst into a billion bloody pieces? What more can you do than just lay down and die?

> *(The cast members lie down as if dead. After a second, they sit up suddenly.)*

ALL. Reason Number 4!

ROB. The play might have a part where you're supposed to hold hands with the person next to you and the person next to you might have these wart-like things on their fingers and you'll feel them as you're holding hands with them and you'll be thinking the whole time you're holding hands with them how their hand feels like a toad and you'll be worrying that the wart-like things might be contagious and you'll start seeing yourself covered with these wart-like things from head to toe, I mean, every body part including your face and your elbows and even your navel and you'll practically puke! So it's definitely not worth the risk.

ALL. Reason Number 5!

MEGAN. Because rehearsals and performances will make you run the risk of not monitoring your cell phone and your e-mail on a regular basis. That's very dangerous. Because, yeah, most of what you get are meaningless bits of gossip and Viagra ads, but you never know! The one cell phone call might come, the one e-mail that has to be replied to within five minutes, the one message that will completely change your life. Okay, so it's never happened to you before and it's never actually happened to anyone you know but that doesn't matter. It could happen!

> *(Her cell phone rings.)*

Hello? No, this isn't Carma's Tattoo Emporium. No, I do not want to get a tattoo there, thank-you.

> *(She hangs up, looks back out at the audience.)*

It could happen!

ALL. Reason Number 6!

BILL. Because meteorologists tell us that the beating of a butterfly's wings in South America can trigger a chain reaction that can eventually cause a hurricane to develop half-way across the world.

WEATHERMAN. We can expect sunny skies for the next three days— absolutely gorgeous weather, with a tanning index of 10. Our weather right now is dominated by a sweet and generous high pressure system that should keep us happy for a good long time.

BILL. Putting on a play, with its lines and movements and all, will generate a significant amount of wind and hot air. By consulting the National Bureau of Weather Predicting Guys, with their numerous large computers and clipboards...

GEEK 1. If we take the barometric pressure and divide it by the average rainfall of the eighth most arid region of the Sahara Desert...

GEEK 2. And we take the inverse proportion of the geometric isometric idiosyncratic quadratic equation...

GEEK 3. And two plus two equaling four...

GEEK 4. I think it's going to be a nice day.

BILL. And by consulting with all of the old people sitting on the park benches gumming tuna fish sandwiches...

OLD 1. Say, you remember back in '54 when we had that big hailstorm that took the roof off the old McGivens place?

OLD 2. That wasn't in '54, you ninny! That was in '58. '54 was the year we had the ice storm that took the tree down next to the turpentine factory.

OLD 3. Well, all I can tell you is we're gonna have good weather for the next couple of days. My bunions ain't aching.

OLD 4. And my scalp ain't itching.

OLD 5. And my arthritis ain't flaring up.

BILL. And by consulting with your step-brother who recently almost passed his tenth year of high school...

REED. Uh... No clouds. Guess I'll go outside today.

BILL. By consulting all of these expert opinions on the weather, you can see the kind of disastrous weather that putting on a play will trigger.

WEATHERMAN. So if you've been planning on getting some vacation time, you should certainly take it... Wait a minute! This just in! A sudden disturbance in the air flow has radically changed the forecast. Forget all that I just said! We've got a massive storm coming our way! Rain, snow, sleet, hail, high winds, all are about to clobber us in less than twenty-four hours! Expect massive power outages! Normally, I would tell you not to panic, but, in this case...panic!

GEEK 1. These numbers can't be right! According the algorithmic confabulation of the tenth power of the 39th parallel...

GEEK 2. ...adding in the square root of pi in which the numerator sub-dissects the denominator...

GEEK 3. ...and putting the hard-drive into overdrive we see that...

GEEK 4. We're gonna get clobbered!

OLD 1. Oh, boy, I'm aching!

OLD 3. Mother McCree, my bunions are about to explode.

OLD 4. Feel that vein on my forehead! Feel it pulsing! It hasn't pulsed like that since the Winter of '02!

OLD 2. Run for your lives, you old coots! Head for the Bingo Hall and crawl under a table if you know what's good for you!

REED. Uh... Getting cloudy. I'll stay inside.

BILL. Mother Nature's fury unleashed...

W 1. Listen to that wind howl!

W 2. Look at the size of that hail!

W 3. We're never going to survive this!

BILL. ...causing massive power outages...

(The lights go out.)

ALL. Who turned out the lights?

(The lights come back up.)

BILL. ...food shortages, fear and trembling, panic in the streets, weather-induced chaos and pandemonium, all because...

TELEVISION REPORTER. Clean-up after the biggest storm of the century has barely begun. The governor estimates damages will be measured in the billions of dollars, not to mention the untold lives disrupted. The nagging question, of course, is what triggered this massive storm? What disturbance in the air could have started it? We have here an expert in the field, Reed Brown, who recently almost passed his tenth year of high school. Reed, to what do you attribute this disaster?

REED. Uh...somebody put on a play.

ALL. Reason Number 7!

JAKE. Plays suck!

ALL. Reason Number 8!

CECILY. Because you're just, you're just, you're just too shy. You...you can barely get two words out of your mouth in front, in front of, of an audience. Whenever you have oral presentations in class, you, you, you, you just take a zero. If somebody tries to force you, you start to cry. A play? Oh, no, no, no. You're painfully shy. That would kill you. You would just die from embarrassment, staring out at those lights, knowing that people are sitting there, judging you—judging what you're wearing, what you're saying, the way you're standing. You'd be mortified! I mean, it's a completely unreasonable request, to ask you to be in a play. They might as well tell you to stand against the wall so they can assemble a firing squad and have you shot, right? You're shy, remember? Hands-freezing, armpits-dripping, knees-knocking, head-pounding shy! Is that a problem? Is it? Just because you're shy, can't you be allowed to just stay in a corner and be that way, or does this society absolutely require that, no matter how traumatic it might be, you have to get up on stage and do whatever some script requires? You're shy, darn it! Shy, shy, shy! So what, if the script says sing the ABC's like an opera star, do you have to go ahead and start singing away? *(Singing like an opera star:)* A-B-C-D-E-F-G! That's way too much to ask of a shy person, I'm telling you! If the script should require that you grab some strange guy *(She grabs a boy and interacts with him through this next segment.)* and hold him close to you like he's your favorite teddy bear; if it commands that you stroke his hair and grab his shirt as if you can't live without him...are you supposed to just go ahead and do that? No! You're too shy! If the script calls for you to kiss him passionately...

(She moves as if she is going to do that. The boy breaks away.)

BOY. No, no, no. I'm saving myself.

CECILY. You see! He's too shy for that and so are you! You can't be in a play and you can't sing opera and you can't grope some guy and you just can't possibly make a fool of yourself in front of a crowd full of people because *(Screaming, emphasizing every word with huge energy:)* YOU ARE JUST WAY TOO AMAZINGLY, INCREDIBLY, PITIFULLY... *(Suddenly pausing, realizing the irony, and backing off to a whisper:)* ...shy.

ALL. Reason Number 9!

MAVIS. Your mother wrote you a note that said, "Mavis is allergic to plays. If she is in one, she will break out in hives. Her legs will swell to five times their normal size and she will begin to sneeze uncontrollably. Please excuse her."

ALL. Reason Number 10!

ZACH. Because you'll get all done with the play. You'll be in it and you'll think you did a good job. You'll be feeling okay about the whole thing, thinking "Hey, that wasn't too bad." You'll go out with the cast to get some pizza and you'll hang around with them for a little while talking about how it went and everybody will pretty much agree that the whole thing was a kick. Then you'll go home. You'll walk in the door and you'll have this conversation with your mother:

CHRIS. Hi.

MOM. Well, you're home.

CHRIS. I'm home.

MOM. You're a bit later than I thought you would be.

CHRIS. The pizza took a long time.

MOM. You had pizza.

CHRIS. Yeah.

MOM. I hope you didn't have any pepperoni.

CHRIS. Yeah.

MOM. Yeah, what? Did you have pepperoni?

CHRIS. I don't remember.

MOM. You did.

CHRIS. I don't remember.

MOM. If you're telling me you don't remember then you went ahead and had the pepperoni which always gives you the gas.

CHRIS. Okay, so I had pepperoni. I'll try not to get the gas.

MOM. It doesn't make any difference if you try or not; you'll get it. You won't be able to help it in your sleep.

CHRIS. Okay, okay, I'll close the door.

MOM. Like that will help. You'll just bottle it up all night and when I open the door in the morning, I'll be killed.

CHRIS. It's not that bad.

MOM. You should not eat the pepperoni. Promise me you'll never eat the pepperoni. It's not good for your system.

CHRIS. I promise, I promise. So...how did you like the play?

MOM. Oh, it was good.

CHRIS. How did I do?

MOM. You did just fine.

CHRIS. And?

MOM. And what?

CHRIS. You might as well go ahead and say it.

MOM. Say what?

CHRIS. Say what you didn't like about it, what you didn't like about my performance.

MOM. I didn't say I didn't like anything about it. I said it was good. I said you were fine. What's wrong with being good and fine?

CHRIS. Your good and fine always has a "but" attached to it. So go ahead and tell me.

MOM. What? I don't have a but, except the one I'm sitting on.

CHRIS. Very funny. Tell me, Ma.

MOM. I don't have anything to tell you. The play was good. You were good. You were good in the good play.

CHRIS. But...

MOM. Why does there have to be a "but"?

CHRIS. I don't know why there has to be a "but," but there always is a "but" and you can't stand not to tell me about it so if you don't tell me now you'll probably come in at 1:00 in the morning and wake me up to tell me or you'll decide you'll have to tell me just as I'm heading out the door to go someplace important so go ahead and tell me now.

MOM. Well, maybe, just maybe, Mr. Smart Aleck, I don't have any "but" this time.

CHRIS. Oh, now I know you do. If you try to deny it, it's big.

MOM. Oh, really.

CHRIS. Yes, really. A majorly huge "but" is now hanging in the air above us.

MOM. Well, it will just have to hang because...I don't have one.

CHRIS. Uh-huh.

MOM. That's right.

CHRIS. The play was good.

MOM. It was.

CHRIS. I was good.

MOM. You were.

CHRIS. Great. I feel good about myself, then. I'm glad you enjoyed it. Thanks for coming, Ma. I'm going to bed.

MOM. There was one thing.

CHRIS. I knew it!

MOM. I didn't say "but"!

CHRIS. "There was one thing" is the same as a "but"!

MOM. It is not!

CHRIS. It is so!

MOM. All right, fine, it is! What do you want, perfection? I'm your mother, a thinking human being, believe it or not, so when I go to a play or any other function, I just might have a criticism or two. Is that a crime?

CHRIS. I am so tired.

MOM. So go to bed. I'll tell you about my "but" in the morning.

CHRIS. No, no, go ahead now.

MOM. You're tired.

CHRIS. I'm fine! I am fine! Just like I was in the play—fine! Except, there was at least one little problem, wasn't there? Wasn't there?

MOM. Well...no, you go to bed.

CHRIS. Let me help you, Mother. Repeat after me: I liked the play.

MOM. I liked the play.

CHRIS. I liked your performance.

MOM. I liked your performance.

CHRIS. But...

MOM. But...

CHRIS. Now fill in the blank. I'm listening.

MOM. Well, there are a few things, actually.

CHRIS. Oh, goody.

ZACH. And then you will be up until two thirty in the morning listening to the woman take that good feeling you had and twist it and twist it like a dirty Kleenex until you never want to hear the word play again.

ALL. Reason Number 11!

JAKE. Plays suck!

NORA. Jake, that was reason number one and seven. Can't you tell us anything more?

JAKE. Yeah. Plays suck a lot!

NORA. Could you be more specific?

JAKE. You want me to be more specific? All right, I'll be more specific. Plays suck because they're full of...

> *(Someone claps a hand over* JAKE's *mouth as he goes off, screaming obscenities.)*

CENSOR. This monologue has been reviewed by the National Script Board and found unfit for adolescent consumption.

JAKE. *(Breaking free for a moment:)* You can take all of your plays and you can shove them...

> *(Hand back over his mouth.)*

CENSOR. If you wish to read an unedited version of Jake's monologue, you can find it on the Net at www.playssuck.edu.

JAKE. *(Free again:)* And that's why plays suck!

ALL. Reason Number 12!

BECCA. Because you've got a little sister, three years old. You watched her last night when your mom was trying to get her to eat her peas.

MOM 2. Come on, Sweetie; eat the little green things. They're good for you.

BABY. No.

MOM 2. You like peas. You ate them all up last time. They'll make you grow big and strong. Here come the peas, Honey. Open up, now.

BABY. No! No, no, no!

MOM 2. What's the matter? Why don't you want the peas?

BABY. I don't want yucky peas!

MOM 2. They're not yucky. You like peas. Why won't you eat them?

BABY. Don't wanna! Don't wanna!

MOM 2. You have to eat the peas if you want some dessert.

BABY. Don't wanna! *(Throwing a tantrum:)* I don't want yucky peas! No, no!

BECCA. You watched your little sister throw a fit over the peas and you thought, "That's a beautiful thing." No reasoning, no logic, just pure reaction.

MOM 2. Honey, why are you doing this!?

BABY. I hate peas! I hate them! Waaaa!

BECCA. You think, "Wow, wouldn't that be nice, to go back to that way of thinking?" Somebody comes to you and asks you to do something and your first thought, for no reason at all, is, "No. I don't wanna." And you go with it.

DIRECTOR. You should be in a play.

NORM. No.

DIRECTOR. Why not?

NORM. Don't wanna.

DIRECTOR. But it'll be good for you. You used to like being in plays. It'll help you grow big and strong.

NORM. No, no, no!

DIRECTOR. Why not?

NORM. Because I don't wanna! I don't wanna because I don't wanna.

DIRECTOR. That's no reason.

NORM. Don't wanna, don't wanna, don't wanna!

DIRECTOR. Everyone, Norm is being completely unreasonable. Come on, let's be in a play.

ALL. *(Falling down into a mass tantrum:)* Waaa! No play! Stinky play! Yucky play! Waaa!

(Suddenly, it all stops.)

BECCA. Wasn't that beautiful?

ALL. Reason Number 13!

BUTCH. Because when you're in a play the makeup people sometimes tell you, a guy, you have to wear lipstick and blush. *(Beat.)* And they never have the colors that set off your natural skin tones.

ALL. Reason Number 14!

MINDY. Though you cannot prove it, you suspect you are the most important person in the world. Though you don't know why, you suspect that you are surrounded by spies and assassins whose only mission in life is to eliminate you. Everywhere you go, you catch glimpses of them scurrying around, watching you, observing you every moment of every day. Though you cannot prove it, you heavily suspect that, if you should let down your guard for just a second; if this silent, stealthy army of enemy infiltrators should catch you unawares and take you down, the consequences will be dire. Not only will your family suffer, but so will your community, your state, your nation...your elimination will create a massive domino effect that will lead to the demise of the entire world economy! People will live on the streets and beg for scraps of food the world over if you are not absolutely and completely careful. Though you cannot prove it, you are almost certain that these insidious watchers are just waiting for you to be in a play. They are holding their breaths—fingers poised on triggers, eyes trained on sights—anticipating that one moment at the climax of the play when you will forget that you are the world's most important person and then...poof! In an instant, it will be over. The devastation will begin. Though you cannot prove it, you're certain it will happen if you make the fatal mistake of being in a play.

ALL. Reason Number 15!

    (Long pause.)

1. Go. Go!

2. I don't have Number 15. She has it!

3. I do not. You said you did!

4. You're insane! I never said I had Number 15. Who said I had 15?

5. Wait, wait—I've got it!

6. Great. All right, then.

ALL. Reason Number 15!

7. The play might have a part where you're supposed to hold hands with the person next to you...

8. No, no, we already had that one! You can't do repeats!

7. Oh, we did? That's right, we did, didn't we? Oops. Sorry.

9. This is terrible!

10. What happened to it?

11. Somebody's got to have Number 15. Everybody, look around. Reason Number 15 has got to be here someplace.

12. Wait a minute, wait a minute. Why do we have to have 15? What's the big deal about 15? We already gave the 14 good ones. Hell, 10 would have done the trick! Or two, for that matter! Let's just leave it at that.

13. We can't just leave it at that! We told them we had 15. We gotta come up with 15.

14. Says who?

15. Says your mother.

14. What are you saying about my mother, you...

1. All right, all right, back off. Look, we don't have to panic. We just have to come up with a 15th reason. She's right. We promised it; we should deliver. Now, who saw it last?

JAKE. Plays suck!

2. No, no, no...you can't do that one again, either!

JAKE. Why not? I did it before. And they still suck.

3. It was cheating before; it's worse cheating now.

JAKE. Whatever.

4. All right, look—we obviously lost it, but we can come up with something. Come on, think! Reason Number 15 why not to be in a play!

5. Because...

6. Because...

7. The piranhas!

8. What about the piranhas?

7. They have...teeth! Lots of them.

9. And?

7. And they...they...they're biting little fishies.

10. And?

7. And...the piranhas will...

11. Go on!

7. Will...forget it. I lost it.

12. All right, keep trying! Reason 15!

13. Because...

14. Because...

15. Because...

1. *(Singing from "The Wizard of Oz":)* Because, because, because, because, because! Because of the wonderful things he does! We're off to see the wiz...Sorry. I love that movie.

2. Could we please concentrate?

    (Long pause as they think.)

3. Because being in a play is ordinary.

4. That sounds like Reason 15 to me. Go on.

3. I mean, practically everybody does it, at one time or another.

5. I hear you.

3. Whether it's kindergarten or second grade or high school or whenever it is, somebody gets you to try it, right?

6. That's right!

7. It happens to us all!

3. So, if everybody's doing it, why should you?

8. Oh, yeah!

9. Now you're cooking!

3. You're an individual!

10. Sing it out, now!

3. You're not a sheep for the herding!

11. Oh, no; that's right!

3. You make your own choices in the world, don't you?

12. You better believe it!

13. You've got that right!

3. So when somebody says, "Hey, be in this play," you just say no!

ALL. No!

3. That's right! No, no, no! And why? I'll tell you why.

1. Yes, ma'am!

3. Because plays are ordinary. Story, character, setting, lights, makeup ...all of that is old!

2. Old as the hills, baby!

3. All of that is dead!

15. Deader than my uncle's canary! He died last year.

3. You want new? You want exciting? You try this: You try getting up in front of an audience and telling them, "We're not putting on a play. In fact, we're just going to spend the next half hour telling you why we're not putting on a play. And you, my friends, are just going to have to love it."

14. Did they?

3. Did they what?

14. Love it?

3. I don't know. Should we ask?

12. No...let's just...let's just bow. If they clap, we'll figure they loved it.

GINA. Wait! Wait!

12. What?

GINA. After we bow, and after they clap...what then?

3. Well, we leave.

GINA. Oh.

1. What's the matter?

GINA. Well, I guess I just thought of another reason.

3. Too late!

4. Let her talk.

GINA. *(Starting tentatively:)* Because if you're in a play, you'll go through the whole thing and you'll get near the end. You'll be in, like, the last scene and you'll realize, Hey, I like this. With the lights on bright and with the audience sitting out there and all the actors up on stage with you, you'll realize this isn't so bad. It isn't bad at all. In fact, you'll realize that, for the whole time you've been in the play, you've felt a kind of...a sort of...aliveness that you just haven't ever felt before. You'll tell yourself you're out of your mind. You'll fight it. When you look at the bulletin board and you see the next audition notice, you'll think, "Nah. Uh-uh. No way!" But it'll eat at you and the next thing you know, you'll be in another play. And another. And another. One will barely get over before you'll feel the itch to be in the next. You'll be addicted! And everybody knows that addiction is definitely not good. So...don't do it!

12. Okay. So...now are we done?

3. I think so.

13. Umm...

6. Now what's the trouble?

13. Well, before, we only had 14 reasons, and that was a problem. But now, since Gina added in her bit, we have 16.

7. That's fine! Better too many than too few, I say!

13. It's not fine! Our program says 15 Reasons Not To Be in a Play! Not 14 Reasons, not 16 Reasons...15! 15! 15 Reasons!

8. Okay, okay, don't blow a gasket! We'll figure it out. Somehow.

5. How?

8. Somehow.

9. For not being in a play, we have spent an awful lot of time out here and I, frankly, am sick of it.

8. Then solve the problem!

13. 15 Reasons! Not 16! 15! We can't reprint the programs! 15!

9. All right, all right, already. Sheesh.

6. According to my calculations, the last two reasons were only half reasons.

7. What?

6. They were half reasons.

9. How do you figure that?

8. Because if they were not half reasons, we may be out here for the next three hours trying to figure out how to subtract a reason or start the whole thing over or make everybody tear up their programs and hand-write new ones or turn back time! And since you yourself just said you're sick of being out here, I calculate that the last two reasons were actually half reasons. Got me?

9. Yeah, I can buy that. Everybody, the last two reasons were half reasons. All those in favor?

ALL. Aye!

9. Opposed?

     (Silence.)

8. And since two halves make one, ladies and gentlemen, and since we were at 14 Reasons before this whole problem arose, and since 14 plus one does, indeed equal 15, you have just witnessed...

ALL. 15 Reasons Not To Be in a Play!

End of Play

Author Biographies

Peter Bloedel is a guitar-picking, chainsaw-juggling professor of theater at Bethany Lutheran College in Mankato, Minnesota. He has authored a number of plays available through Playscripts, Inc. including: *The Seussification of Romeo and Juliet, The Rules of Comedy,* and *Jam Jar Sonnets* (www.jamjarsonnets.com). Mr. Bloedel is a member of the eclectic acoustic folk band The Divers (www.thedivers.com), and he is a freelance vaudeville (juggling, music, magic) performer in his spare time (www.heypete.biz). Originally hailing from Minneapolis, he enjoys the smaller-town living of Mankato, Minnesota where he and his wife enjoy raising their children.

Julia Brownell's play *Smart Cookie* won the 2008 Kendeda Graduate Playwriting Award and received its world premiere at the Alliance Theatre in Atlanta, Georgia in January 2009. *Smart Cookie* was workshopped/read by the Minneapolis Playwrights' Center, The Public Theater and Babel Theatre Project. Her short play *Good Girl* was produced by the Actors Theatre of Louisville in January, 2009. She is the recipient of multiple commissions from the McCarter Theatre First Stage Company in Princeton, New Jersey. In addition to her work as a writer, Ms. Brownell has performed in numerous professional improv and sketch comedy groups throughout the Northeast. MFA in Dramatic Writing, NYU-Tisch School of the Arts. BA, Amherst College.

Christa Crewdson is the theatre teacher and director at Buckingham Browne and Nichols Middle School in Cambridge. She also directs the Young Adult Company at Un-Common Theatre in Mansfield where she also runs the company's teen improv troupe, Improv Soup. Ms. Crewdson has directed over 60 productions with children and young adults. She has worked for Looking Glass Theatre, NewGate Theatre, Trinity Rep, and All Children's Theatre, and has taught theatre at Qualters Middle School and Boston Latin School. In addition, Ms. Crewdson is a founding and company member of Improv Jones, a professional improv troupe based in Providence and Boston. Ms. Crewdson received her Master's degree in Theatre from Brown University.

Alan Haehnel teaches high school English and Theater at Hanover High School in Hanover, New Hampshire. He has been involved in theater since college as an actor, director, and writer. His credits include numerous published plays and monologues that have been performed worldwide, the Vermont Playwright's Award in 1993, and several Vermont State Championships for his original one-acts entered in the Vermont One-Act Play Festivals. He lives in Hartford Village with his wife and three children.

Ian McWethy's plays include *Moral Values: A Grand Farce or Me No Likey The Homo Touch-Touch* (The Village Gate Theatre, Jeff Glaser Dir.), *Actor's are F*$@ing Stupid* (The Wild Project, Michael Kimmel dir.), and most recently *12 Incompetent Men (And Women!) (full-length version)* (SoHo Playhouse, Jeff Glaser dir.). Six of his one-act plays have been published by Playscripts, Inc. and have been performed in 45 states as well as Canada, Cambodia, Australia, England, and the United Arab Emirates. Films include *Ostrander* (produced by KiMcWefee Productions 2010), *Brick Henry Is Your Country* (Way Finder Films), and *Spilt Milke* (Zero Point productions). He lives with his lovely and more talented wife in the very tip of Manhattan.

Ed Monk teaches theatre at Chantilly High School in Chantilly, Virginia. He is also an alumnus of Chantilly, where he studied theatre under Elaine Wilson. He is the author of eighteen plays that have been published by Playscripts, Inc. He has been married to his perfect wife Grace for 24 years. Together they have produced 4 perfect children, Marley, Eddie, Maggie and Kelsey. His mother likes everything he writes.

Qui Nguyen. Originally from Arkansas, Qui Nguyen is a Brooklyn-based writer, fight choreographer, and co-artistic director of the OBIE award-winning Vampire Cowboys Theatre Company. His scripts include *Krunk Fu Battle Battle* (East West Players); *Bike Wreck* (produced at Youngblood and Metropolitan Playhouse); *Trial By Water* (produced at Ma-Yi Theater/Queens Theatre in the Park); *Aliens Vs. Cheerleaders* (Keen Teens); and the critically acclaimed Vampire Cowboys productions of *The Inexplicable Redemption of Agent G, Alice in Slasherland, Fight Girl Battle World, Men of Steel, Living Dead in Denmark, Stained Glass Ugly, A Beginner's Guide to Deicide, Vampire Cowboy Trilogy,* and *Soul Samurai.* Additionally, he is a resident playwright of New Dramatists, a member of Ensemble Studio Theatre, co-director of the Ma-Yi Writers Lab, an alumnus of Youngblood, and an advanced actor/combatant with the Society of American Fight Directors. He has an MFA in Playwriting from Ohio University.

Rich Orloff is the author of ten full-length comedies, three comic revues, oodles of short plays (60 of which have been published by Playscripts, Inc. in eight collections), and the play *Vietnam 101: The War on Campus*, which has been produced at colleges and small theaters throughout the country. His most recent comedy, *Funny as a Crutch,* was a *New York Times* Critic's Pick, a *Back Stage* Critic's Pick, and nytheatre.com's Pick of the Week.

Mr. Orloff's short plays have received over 600 productions on six of the seven continents (and a staged reading in Antarctica). His short comedies have been published in *The Art of the One-Act Play, Best Ten-Minute Plays 2007, Take Ten II, An Anthology of American Short Plays* (published in China), *The Bedford Introduction to Literature,* and four times in the annual *Best American Short Plays* anthology series.

Mr. Orloff's full-length plays been presented at such theaters as Arizona Theatre Company, Arkansas Repertory Theatre, Charlotte Rep., Dayton Playhouse, Florida Studio Theatre, New Jersey Rep, West Coast Ensemble, and three times at the Key West Theatre Festival. His plays have won such awards and contests as the Festival of Emerging American Theatre, the Playwrights First Award, the InterPlay International Play Festival, the Theatre Conspiracy New Play Contest, the Pickering Award for Playwriting Excellence and the Abeles Foundation Playwrights Award.

Mr. Orloff has given lectures and workshops on playwriting (especially the art of the short play) at Oberlin College, Central Washington University, Western Michigan University and Miami's City Theatre. He lives in New York City but loves getting out of town. For more about Rich Orloff, visit www.richorloff.com.

Jason Pizzarello most recently developed his farce *When I Had Three Sisters* in The Soho Rep Writer/Director Lab. Some of his other full-length plays include: *Once There Was a Boy,* (produced by the Fordham Alumni Theatre Company; Semi-finalist, Princess Grace Award 2008; Semi-finalist, O'Neill Playwrights Conference 2010); *InsideOut,* (produced at HERE Arts Center, NYC; nominated for an Innovative Theatre Award); *Saving the Greeks: One Tragedy at a Time,* (produced by Push Productions, NYC); and *Give Me Give You.*

His short comedy *Up For Review* was selected by the Actors Theatre of Louisville as a Heideman Award finalist in the 2010 National Ten-Minute Play Contest. Eleven of his plays are published with Playscripts, Inc. and have been produced in over 40 states as well as in Australia, Austria, Brazil, Canada, Germany, Japan, Syria, Thailand, and the UK.

He is also the editor of *Actor's Choice: Scenes for Teens* published by Playscripts, Inc.

Read more at www.jasonpizzarello.com

Jonathan Rand has written five of the top ten most-produced plays in North American high schools, according to the annual survey conducted by the Educational Theatre Association. In the 2009-2010 season, *How to Succeed in High School Without Really Trying* was the 8th most produced; *Hard Candy* ranked 6th; *Check Please: Take 2* ranked 5th; *Check Please: Take 3* ranked 2nd; and *Check Please* topped the list as the #1 most-produced short play for the sixth consecutive season. Since writing his first play in 1997, Mr. Rand's work has been produced by over 5,400 theaters in all 50 states and in 40 countries, including Kenya, China, Egypt, Cambodia, India, Singapore, Botswana, Korea, Indonesia, Kuwait, Malta, Brazil, Malaysia, Jordan, Croatia, and Madagascar.

Mr. Rand's writing is featured in *The Best Stage Scenes 2004, The Best Men's Stage Monologues 2005, The Best Women's Stage Monologues 2006, The Best Stage Scenes 2007, The Best Men's Stage Monologues and Scenes 2009* (Smith & Kraus), *Dramatics* magazine, and *Laugh Lines: Short Comic Plays* (Random House). His comedy *Drugs Are Bad* was selected by the Actors Theatre of Louisville as a Heideman Award finalist in the 2003 National Ten-Minute Play Contest.

Mr. Rand is a graduate of the University of Pennsylvania, and lives in New York City.

Official website: www.jonathanrand.com

Werner Trieschmann's numerous plays—including *Dog Star, Wrought Iron,* and *Killers*—have been staged by Moving Arts in Los Angeles, Ensemble Studio Theatre in New York City, The New Theatre in Boston, Mobtown Players in Baltimore, and Red Octopus Productions in Little Rock, Arkansas. Mr. Trieschmann was a resident at the Mount Sequoyah New Play Retreat in Fayetteville, Arkansas. His play *Lawn Dart* won first prize in the Contemporary Arts Center of New Orleans New Play Competition. He was the first playwright to receive the Porter Prize, an Arkansas literary award recognizing outstanding achievement by an Arkansas writer.

His full-length comedy *You Have to Serve Somebody* is published by the Dramatic Publishing Company; several of his short plays are published by Playscripts, Inc.; his dark one-act comedy *Killers* is published through Original Works Publishing; and a monologue from *Killers* is included in the *The Best Women's Stage Monologues 1999,* published by Smith & Kraus. Mr. Trieschmann has an MFA in Playwriting from Boston University. He currently lives in Little Rock with his wife and two very wild but beloved sons.His website is www.wernertplays.com

Tracey Scott Wilson's current work includes *The Story,* which was first produced at The Joseph Papp Public Theater/NYSF, and transferred to the Long Wharf Theatre. *The Story* has since been produced at thirty theatres nationwide. Additional productions include *Order My Steps* for Cornerstone Theater's Black Faith/AIDS project in Los Angeles; and *Exhibit #9*, produced in New York City by New Perspectives Theatre and Theatre Outrageous; *Leader of the People* produced at New Georges Theatre; two ten-minute plays produced at the Guthrie Theatre in Minneapolis; and a ten-minute play produced at Actors Theatre of Louisville. Ms. Wilson has had readings at the New York Theatre Workshop, New Georges Theatre, The Joseph Papp Public Theater and Soho Theatre Writers Centre in London. She earned two Van Lier Fellowships from the New York Theatre Workshop, a residency at Sundance Ucross, and is the winner of the 2001 Helen Merrill Emerging Playwright Award, the 2003 AT&T Onstage Award, the 2004 Whiting Award and as well as the 2004 Kesserling Prize. Ms. Wilson holds a Master's degree in English Literature from Temple University.

Don Zolidis is a former high school and middle school theatre teacher and is currently a professor of creative writing at Ursinus College. Originally hailing from Wisconsin, Mr. Zolidis received his B.A. in English from Carleton College and an MFA in Playwriting from the Actor's Studio Program at the New School. He has received numerous honors, including the 2004 Princess Grace Award for Playwriting for *White Buffalo,* now published by Samuel French. His plays have appeared or been workshopped professionally at the Ensemble Studio Theatre, Stage West, Purple Rose Theatre, The Victory Theatre, Bloomington Playwright's Project, Chattyboo Productions, Mirror Stage Company, Impetuous Theatre Group, and New Dramatists.

His plays have had amateur productions in all 50 states and 16 countries and have won numerous state championships.

His screenplays have received numerous prizes, including the 2009 PAGE gold medal for drama, 1st prize in the family division for both the 2008 Screenwriting Expo and 2008 StoryPros Contest, and several others. He has one screenplay under option with Will Ferrell's Gary Sanchez Productions and a second in development with an independent producer.

He lives with his wife and his two adorable boys.

Also from Playscripts

Actor's Choice: Monologues for Teens
Actor's Choice: Monologues for Women
Actor's Choice: Monologues for Men

Edited by Erin Detrick
Foreword by Broadway casting director Kate Schwabe

Discover a monologue book like no other. The *Actor's Choice* series was carefully designed to help the savvy actor shine at auditions and get the part. Not only does each book give you an extraordinary array of cutting-edge new monologues, but unlike other monologue books, the source of every monologue is easily accessible—each play is available through one website, where you can read nearly the entire published script online for free. Explore the work of today's most celebrated theatrical voices, including Pulitzer Prize winner David Lindsay-Abaire, Naomi Iizuka, Jane Martin, Jeffrey Hatcher, Lynn Nottage, Tony Award® winner David Henry Hwang, and many more!

"Actor's Choice: Monologues for Teens *is an excellent monologue book for middle and high school students with applications for competition as well as use in drama, speech, or English classes.*"

—The Midwest Book Review

Order online at: **www.playscripts.com**